JAPANESE
NAVAL VESSELS
of World War Two

JAPANESE NAVAL VESSELS
of World War Two
as seen by U.S. Naval Intelligence

Introduction by A. D. Baker III

NAVAL INSTITUTE PRESS

Published and distributed in the United States
of America by the Naval Institute Press, Annapolis,
Maryland 21402

Library of Congress Catalog Card No. 86-63361

ISBN 0-87021-314-8

This edition is authorized for sale only in the
United States and its territories and possessions.

First published in 1987.
Originally published 1942–1944 by
the U.S. Division of Naval Intelligence as
ONI 41-421, Index to All Japanese Naval Vessels;
ONI 41-42, Japanese Naval Vessels; ONI 220J, Japanese
Submarines; and *ONI 225J, Japanese Landing*
Operations and Equipment.

Printed and bound in Great Britain by The Bath Press.

INTRODUCTION

For their third reprint of a Second World War era U.S. Division of Naval Intelligence handbook, Arms & Armour Press and the Naval Institute Press have chosen the warship sections which dealt with the U.S. Navy's Pacific Ocean opponent, Japan. Four separate publications have been bound together: *ONI 41-421, Index to All Japanese Naval Vessels; ONI 41-42, Japanese Naval Vessels; ONI 220J, Japanese Submarines;* and *ONI 225J, Japanese Landing Operations and Equipment.*

The major portion of the reprint, *Japanese Naval Vessels*, first appeared as a loose-leaf compilation in November 1942. Major page changes were distributed in the spring and fall of 1943, but by early 1944, the tide of war was obviously flowing in the United States Navy's favor, and further changes were not issued. The copy from which this reprint was made was removed from the submarine U.S.S. *Pilotfish* (SS-386; six war patrols from May 1944; one 4,000-ton cargo ship sunk) in August 1946 when she was decommissioned for service as a target; the latest update bound with *ONI 41-42* was the *Index*, dated December 1944. *Pilotfish*'s intelligence officers had been diligent in making page-change updates, and those sheets dealing with ships sunk earlier in the war were duly discarded. Ships lost *very* early in the conflict, such as the four carriers destroyed at Midway, were never the subject of ONI's attention for this publication. Conversely, a number of classes whose characteristics and appearances were only dimly known – like the battleships of the *Yamato* class, the *Unryu* class carriers, the command cruiser *Oyodo*, and the light cruisers of the *Agano* class – never received full-scale treatment, appearing only in the *ONI 41-421 Index*. Appended after the auxiliary pages on the Imperial Japanese Navy were short sections dealing with former Allied warships thought to be serving with the IJN (including the Vichy French light cruiser *Lamotte-Picquet*) and the naval forces of Japanese allies Siam and Manchukuo.

The principal function of *ONI 41-42* was to serve as an all-purpose recognition manual. Illustrations filled its pages. Air-brushed plan and elevation tone-drawings, multi-angle photography of carefully-constructed 1:600 scale waterline models and actual photography were used, along with small line-drawings to highlight armament locations and protection schemes and silhouettes to point out unique features differentiating one class from another. Technical information was brief and, more often than not, inaccurate – especially as to wartime armament – but the propulsion section did provide endurance figures at various speeds. A separate column was provided for turns-per-knot data for the benefit of submariners, but scant data was actually available, most entries being entirely blank. A short section on general recognition techniques and memory aids, along with gun armament range tables, preceded the ship entries.

ONI 41-42, then, is of value today primarily for its extraordinary graphics, rather than for its data or thoroughness. Readers needing a more complete guide to the entire wartime Imperial Japanese Navy are directed to Hansgeorg Jentschura, Dieter Jung and Peter Mickel's *Warships of the Imperial Japanese Navy, 1869–1945* [Arms & Armour Press/ Naval Institute Press, 1977], which remains the best one-volume treatment of the subject.

The two shorter ONI studies appended are undated, but appear to have been prepared in 1942–3, from the style of presentation. *ONI 220J, Japanese Submarines*, covers the same ground as the pages in *ONI 41-42*, but in far greater detail and with more extensive illustrations. *ONI 225J, Japanese Landing Operations and Equipment*, is a detailed study of the amphibious tactics, craft, and equipment used by Japanese forces in their rapid series of invasions of Pacific beachheads. The treatment is unique and authoritative.

This reprint is a potpourri – but a fascinating and ultimately valuable one. U.S. Navy scientific and technical intelligence lagged behind operational intelligence capabilities during the Second World War. Signals analyses and code-breaking often gave great detail on Japanese force compositions, locations and plans, but ONI had little opportunity until after the war to discover the characteristics and capabilities of the majority of Japanese ships, weapons and sensors. Ultimately, because of the overwhelming naval power available to the Allies, it was unimportant whether *Yamato*, say, had 16in or 18.1in guns. In fact, the United States Navy knew far less about its principal maritime enemy than any reader today can learn about the supposedly secretive Soviet Navy in the pages of one of the open-source naval references like *Combat Fleets of the World*. Post-war investigations of Japanese ships and equipment revealed details undreamed of during the conflict, and the results were published in the multi-volume *Naval Technical Mission to Japan* series.

ONI 41-42, Japanese Naval Vessels, was, none the less, the best that could be accomplished during the rapid expansion of the U.S. Navy's intelligence arm under wartime conditions, and it remains one of the best collections of photographs and drawings of IJN ships available.

The publishers wish to thank Captain Howard Portnoy, USN [Ret'd], for locating the mint-condition copies of the ONI volumes from which this reprint was made.

A. D. Baker III, November 1986

Issued 12/44

ONI 41-42 I

INDEX TO ALL JAPANESE NAVAL VESSELS

ONI 41–42 Series—*A condensed summary of the appearance and characteristics of Japanese Warships.*

The complete 41-42 Series will include the following booklets:

I — *Index to all Japanese Naval Vessels*
BC — *Japanese Battleships and Cruisers*
CV — *Japanese Aircraft Carriers*
D — *Japanese Destroyers*
MC— *Japanese Minor Combatant Craft*
A — *Japanese Fleet Auxiliaries and District Craft*

NOTE—*In view of the uncertainties as to positive identification of enemy losses, and to prevent possible omissions, this Index lists **all** known Japanese Naval Vessels—regardless of whether these have been reported as "sunk" or "probably sunk." The only vessels not included are the acknowledged losses: BB FUSO Class, CV AKAGI, CV KAGA, CV SORYU, CV HIRYU, CVL CHITOSE Class, CA MIKUMA.*

Prepared by the Division of Naval Intelligence.

BATTLESHIPS

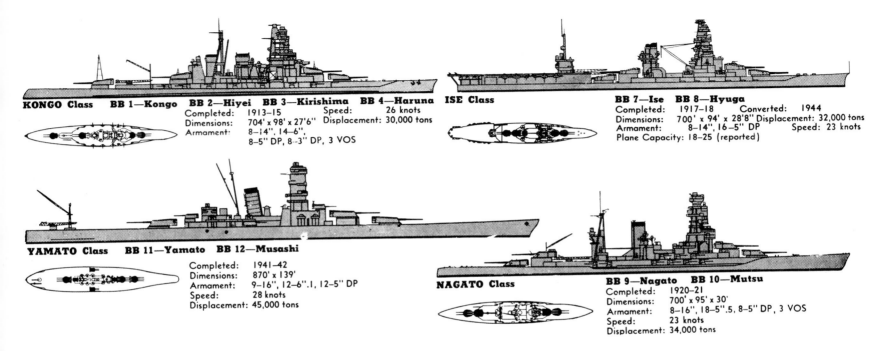

KONGO Class   BB 1—Kongo   BB 2—Hiyei   BB 3—Kirishima   BB 4—Haruna

Completed: 1913–15   Speed: 26 knots
Dimensions: 704' x 98' x 27'6"   Displacement: 30,000 tons
Armament: 8–14", 14–6",
               8–5" DP, 8–3" DP, 3 VOS

ISE Class   BB 7—Ise   BB 8—Hyuga

Completed: 1917–18   Converted: 1944
Dimensions: 700' x 94' x 28'8" Displacement: 32,000 tons
Armament: 8–14", 16–5" DP   Speed: 23 knots
Plane Capacity: 18–25 (reported)

YAMATO Class   BB 11—Yamato   BB 12—Musashi

Completed: 1941–42
Dimensions: 870' x 139'
Armament: 9–16", 12–6".1, 12–5" DP
Speed: 28 knots
Displacement: 45,000 tons

NAGATO Class   BB 9—Nagato   BB 10—Mutsu

Completed: 1920–21
Dimensions: 700' x 95' x 30'
Armament: 8–16", 18–5".5, 8–5" DP, 3 VOS
Speed: 23 knots
Displacement: 34,000 tons

Explanatory Notes

LISTS — Ships built to the same design are presented by classes; otherwise, by individual units.

DRAWINGS — Warship profiles have been shown in several scales in order to separate ships of primary recognition value from those of lesser importance.

STATISTICS — The statistical data are to be interpreted as follows:
  Dimensions: Length (oa) x Beam (extreme) x Draft (mean).
  Displacement: 1142/1470 tons indicates surface/submerged displacement for submarines.

FP—Float Plane.
Displacement: Standard. Speed: Designed.
Armament: Heavy caliber pieces only are listed.
Only confirmed revisions have been included.

CLASSIFI-CATION — The RESTRICTED classification of this booklet necessarily prevents the inclusion of a few vessels and certain data still classified CONFIDENTIAL.

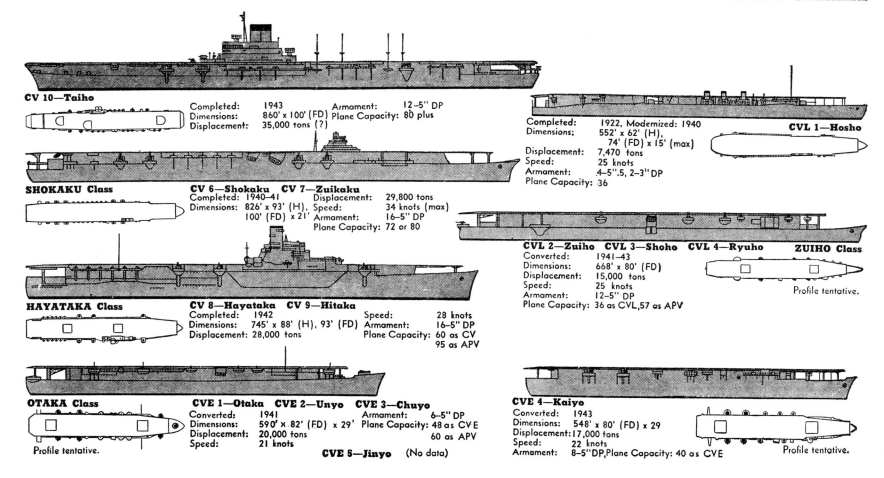

CV 10—Taiho

Completed:	1943	Armament:	12–5" DP
Dimensions:	860' x 100' (FD)	Plane Capacity:	80 plus
Displacement:	35,000 tons (?)		

SHOKAKU Class

CV 6—Shokaku   CV 7—Zuikaku

Completed:	1940–41	Displacement:	29,800 tons
Dimensions:	826' x 93' (H),	Speed:	34 knots (max)
	100' (FD) x 21'	Armament:	16–5" DP
		Plane Capacity:	72 or 80

HAYATAKA Class

CV 8—Hayataka   CV 9—Hitaka

Completed:	1942	Speed:	28 knots
Dimensions:	745' x 88' (H), 93' (FD)	Armament:	16–5" DP
Displacement:	28,000 tons	Plane Capacity:	60 as CV
			95 as APV

OTAKA Class

Profile tentative.

CVE 1—Otaka   CVE 2—Unyo   CVE 3—Chuyo

Converted:	1941	Armament:	6–5" DP
Dimensions:	590' x 82' (FD) x 29'	Plane Capacity:	48 as CVE
Displacement:	20,000 tons		60 as APV
Speed:	21 knots		

CVE 5—Jinyo   (No data)

CVL 1—Hosho

Completed:	1922, Modernized: 1940
Dimensions:	552' x 62' (H),
	74' (FD) x 15' (max)
Displacement:	7,470 tons
Speed:	25 knots
Armament:	4–5".5, 2–3" DP
Plane Capacity:	36

CVL 2—Zuiho   CVL 3—Shoho   CVL 4—Ryuho   **ZUIHO Class**

Converted:	1941–43
Dimensions:	668' x 80' (FD)
Displacement:	15,000 tons
Speed:	25 knots
Armament:	12–5" DP
Plane Capacity:	36 as CVL, 57 as APV

Profile tentative.

CVE 4—Kaiyo

Converted:	1943
Dimensions:	548' x 80' (FD) x 29
Displacement:	17,000 tons
Speed:	22 knots
Armament:	8–5" DP, Plane Capacity: 40 as CVE

Profile tentative.

HEAVY CRUISERS

FURUTAKA Class

CA 1—Furutaka	CA 2—Kako
Completed:	1926
Dimensions:	595' x 50'9" x 16'
Displacement:	9,000 tons
Speed:	33 knots
Armament:	6–8", 4–4".7 DP, 8–24" TT
	2–VOS

AOBA Class

CA 3—Aoba	CA 4—Kinugasa
Completed:	1927
Dimensions:	598' x 50'9" x 16'
Displacement:	9,000 tons
Speed:	33 knots
Armament:	6–8", 4–4".7 DP, 8–24" TT
	2–VOS

NACHI Class

CA 5—Nachi	CA 7—Myoko
CA 6—Haguro	CA 8—Ashigara
Completed:	1928–29
Dimensions:	656' x 62'4" x 18'
Displacement:	11,500 tons Speed: 33 knots
Armament:	10–8", 8–4".7 DP, 16–24" TT ; 4–VOS

Mainmast variation in CA 11, 12.

ATAGO Class

CA 9—Atago	CA 11—Chokai
CA 10—Takao	CA 12—Maya
Completed:	1932
Dimensions:	657' x 64' x 18'
Displacement:	12,500 tons
Speed:	33 knots
Armament:	10–8", 4–4.".7 DP, 16–24" TT
	(quads); 4–VOS

MOGAMI Class

CA 13—Mogami	CA 16—Kumano
CA 15—Suzuya	
Completed:	1935–37
Dimensions:	660' x 65' x 19'
Displacement:	14,000 tons
Speed:	33 knots
Armament:	10–8", 8–4".7 DP, 16–24" TT
	(quads); 4–VOS

TONE Class

CA 17—Tone	CA 18—Chikuma
Completed:	1938–39
Dimensions:	658' x 65' x 18'
Displacement:	14,500 tons
Speed:	33 knots
Armament:	8–8", 8–4".7 DP, 16–24" TT
	(quads); 6–VOS

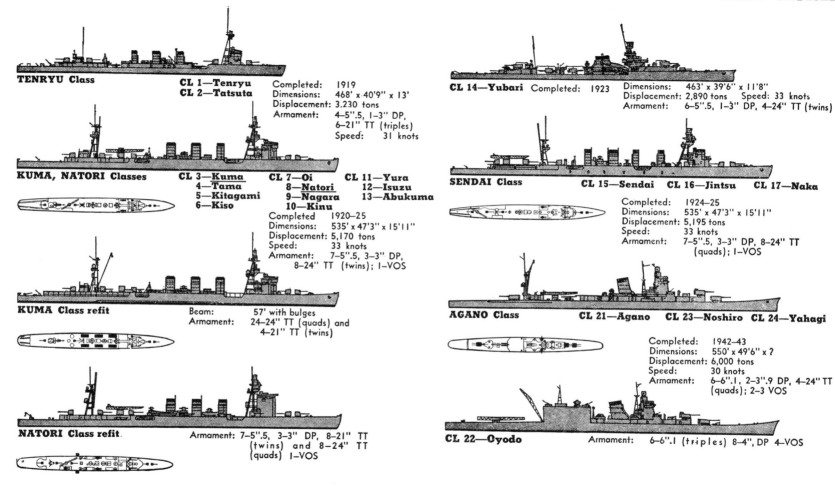

TENRYU Class

CL 1—Tenryu
CL 2—Tatsuta

Completed: 1919
Dimensions: 468' x 40'9" x 13'
Displacement: 3,230 tons
Armament: 4–5".5, 1–3" DP,
6–21" TT (triples)
Speed: 31 knots

KUMA, NATORI Classes

CL 3—Kuma
4—Tama
5—Kitagami
6—Kiso

CL 7—Oi
8—Natori
9—Nagara
10—Kinu

CL 11—Yura
12—Isuzu
13—Abukuma

Completed 1920–25
Dimensions: 535' x 47'3" x 15'11"
Displacement: 5,170 tons
Speed: 33 knots
Armament: 7–5".5, 3–3" DP,
8–24" TT (twins); 1–VOS

KUMA Class refit

Beam: 57' with bulges
Armament: 24–24" TT (quads) and
4–21" TT (twins)

NATORI Class refit

Armament: 7–5".5, 3–3" DP, 8–21" TT
(twins) and 8–24" TT
(quads) 1–VOS

CL 14—Yubari Completed: 1923

Dimensions: 463' x 39'6" x 11'8"
Displacement: 2,890 tons   Speed: 33 knots
Armament: 6–5".5, 1–3" DP, 4–24" TT (twins)

SENDAI Class   CL 15—Sendai   CL 16—Jintsu   CL 17—Naka

Completed: 1924–25
Dimensions: 535' x 47'3" x 15'11"
Displacement: 5,195 tons
Speed: 33 knots
Armament: 7–5".5, 3–3" DP, 8–24" TT
(quads); 1–VOS

AGANO Class   CL 21—Agano   CL 23—Noshiro CL 24—Yahagi

Completed: 1942–43
Dimensions: 550' x 49'6" x ?
Displacement: 6,000 tons
Speed: 30 knots
Armament: 6–6".1, 2–3".9 DP, 4–24" TT
(quads); 2–3 VOS

CL 22—Oyodo   Armament: 6–6".1 (triples) 8–4", DP 4–VOS

DESTROYERS

FLEET DESTROYERS

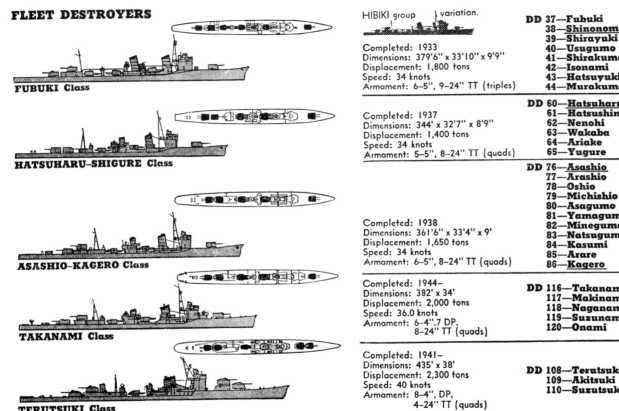

FUBUKI Class

HATSUHARU–SHIGURE Class

ASASHIO–KAGERO Class

TAKANAMI Class

TERUTSUKI Class

HIBIKI group variation.

Completed: 1933
Dimensions: 379'6" x 33'10" x 9'9"
Displacement: 1,800 tons
Speed: 34 knots
Armament: 6–5", 9–24" TT (triples)

DD 37—Fubuki	DD 45—Amagiri	DD 53—Oboro
38—Shinonome	46—Shikinami	54—Akebono
39—Shirayuki	47—Ayanami*	55—Sazanami
40—Usugumo	48—Asagiri	56—Hibiki
41—Shirakumo	49—Uranami	57—Ikazuchi
42—Isonami	50—Yugiri	58—Inazuma
43—Hatsuyuki	51—Sagiri	59—Akatsuki
44—Murakumo	52—Ushio	

Completed: 1937
Dimensions: 344' x 32'7" x 8'9"
Displacement: 1,400 tons
Speed: 34 knots
Armament: 5–5", 8–24" TT (quads)

DD 60—Hatsuharu	DD 66—Shigure	DD 71—Samidare
61—Hatsushimo	67—Shiratsuyu	72—Yamakaze
62—Nenohi	68—Murasame	73—Suzukaze
63—Wakaba	69—Yudachi	74—Kawakaze
64—Ariake	70—Harusame	75—Umikaze
65—Yugure		

Completed: 1938
Dimensions: 361'6" x 33'4" x 9'
Displacement: 1,650 tons
Speed: 34 knots
Armament: 6–5", 8–24" TT (quads)

DD 76—Asashio	DD 87—Shiranuhi	DD 98—Arashi
77—Arashio	88—Kuroshio	99—Hagikaze
78—Oshio	89—Oyashio	100—Nowaki
79—Michishio	90—Hatsukaze	101—Hamakaze
80—Asagumo	91—Natsushio	102—Tanikaze
81—Yamagumo	92—Yukikaze	103—Maikaze
82—Minegumo	93—Hayashio	104—Yugumo
83—Natsugumo	94—Isokaze	105—Akigumo
84—Kasumi	95—Amatsukaze	106—Makigumo
85—Arare	96—Tokitsukaze	107—Kazegumo
86—Kagero	97—Urakaze	

Completed: 1944–
Dimensions: 382' x 34'
Displacement: 2,000 tons
Speed: 36.0 knots
Armament: 6–4".7 DP,
8–24" TT (quads)

DD 116—Takanami	DD 121—Fujinami	DD 126—Okinami
117—Makinami	122—Kiyonami	127—Kishinami
118—Naganami	123—Tamanami	128—Shiranami
119—Suzunami	124—Hayanami	
120—Onami	125—Hamanami	

Completed: 1941–
Dimensions: 435' x 38'
Displacement: 2,300 tons
Speed: 40 knots
Armament: 8–4", DP,
4–24" TT (quads)

DD 108—Terutsuki	DD 111—Shimotsuki	DD 114—Niitsuki
109—Akitsuki	112—Hatsutsuki	115—Fuyutsuki
110—Suzutsuki	113—Wakatsuki	

ESCORT DESTROYERS

MINEKAZE Class

Completed: 1922
Dimensions: 336'6" x 29'3" x 9'6"
Displacement: 1,215 tons
Speed: 34 knots
Armament: 4–4".7, 6–21" TT (twins)

DD 1—Minekaze	DD 6—Yakaze	DD 11—Tachikaze
2—Okikaze	7—Akikaze	12—Nadakaze
3—Shimakaze	8—Yukaze	13—Namikaze
4—Sawakaze	9—Hokaze	14—Numakaze
5—Hakaze	10—Shiokaze	15—Nokaze

MINEKAZE refit

Armament: 2–4".7, 2–21" TT (twin)

KAMIKAZE Class

Completed: 1925
Dimensions: 336'6" x 30' x 9'7"
Displacement: 1,270 tons
Speed: 34 knots
Armament: 4–4".7, 6–21" TT (twins)

DD 16—Kamikaze	DD 19—Matsukaze	DD 22—Oite
17—Asakaze	20—Asanagi	23—Hayate
18—Harukaze	21—Hatakaze	24—Yunagi

MUTSUKI Class

Completed: 1927
Dimensions: 336'6" x 30' x 9'9"
Displacement: 1,315 tons
Speed: 34 knots
Armament: 4–4".7, 6–24" TT (triples)

DD 25—Mutsuki	DD 29—Uzuki	DD 33—Nagatsuki
26—Satsuki	30—Fumitsuki	34—Mikatsuki
27—Kisaragi	31—Kikutsuki	35—Mochitsuki
28—Yayoi	32—Minatsuki	36—Yuzuki

SECOND LINE DESTROYERS

MOMO Class

Completed: 1919
Dimensions: 287' x 25'4" x 7'9"
Displacement: 755 tons
Speed: 31.5 knots
Armament: 3–4".7, 6–21" TT (triples)

ODD 1—Momo	ODD 2—Hinoki	ODD 3—Yanagi

KURI-WAKATAKE Class *A minelaying conversion is shown under minor combatant craft DM.

Completed: 1923
Dimensions: 287' x 26'6" x 8'3"
Displacement: 820 tons
Speed: 31.5 knots
Armament: 3–4".7, 4–21" TT (twins)

ODD 4—Nashi	ODD 13—Hagi	ODD 22—Sumire
5—Take	14—Suzuki	23—Wakatake
6—Kaya	15—Fuji	24—Kuretake
7—Kuri	16—Ashi	25—Sanaye
8—Nire	17—Tsuta	26—Asagao
9—Aoi	18—Hasu	27—Fuyo
10—Kiku	19—Hishi	28—Karukaya
11—Kaki	20—Tade	29—Yugao
12—Tsuga	21—Yomogi	

SUBMARINES

CRUISERS

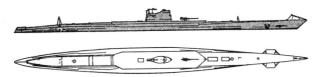

I 1 Class   I 1–4

Completed: 1926
Dimensions: 320' x 29'7" x 15'9"
Displacement: 1,955/2,480 tons

Speed: 18.8/8.1 knots
Armament: 1–5", 6–21" TT
1 FP or several LC carried

I 5 Class   I 5–8

Completed: 1932–38
Dimensions: 320–359' x 30' x 14'5"
Displacement: 1,900–2,230/2,600 tons
Speed: 18–23/8–9 knots
Armament: 1–2 – 5".5, 6–21" TT
1 FP or several LC carried

I 9 Class   I 9–14   Similar.

Completed: 1940–43
Dimensions: 373' x 31' x 14'5"
Displacement: 2,200–2,400/2,600 tons
Speed: 23/8 knots
Armament: 1–5".5, 6–8 – 21" TT
1 FP or LC carried

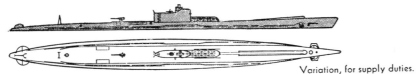

Variation, for supply duties.

I 15 Class   I 15–49

Completed: 1940–
Dimensions: 357–359' x 30'6" x 16'
Displacement: 1,950–2,190/? tons
Speed: 22/7 knots
Armament: 1–5".5, 6–8 – 21" TT
1 FP or LC carried

FLEET

I-351 Class, I-361 Class, I-400 Class, (No data)

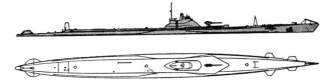

I 153 Class   I 153–160

Completed: 1924–30
Dimensions: 331' x 26' x 16'1"
Displacement: 1,635/2,100 tons

Speed: 20/8 knots
Armament: 1–4".7, 8–21" TT

I 161 Class   I 161–166

Completed: 1926–32
Dimensions: 321' x 26–27' x 16'
Displacement: 1,635/2,100 tons

Speed: 20/8.5 knots
Armament: 1–4".7, 6–21" TT

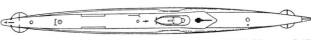

I 168 Class   I 168–175

Completed: 1933–38
Dimensions: 343' x 26'11" x 13'
Displacement: 1,400/2,100 tons
Speed: 23.9/8.8 knots
Armament: 1–4".7, 6–21" TT

I 176 Class   I 176–   Similar.

Completed: 1941–43
Dimensions: 335' x 27' x 13'
Displacement: 1,609/? tons
Speed: 23.5/8 knots
Armament: 1–5".5, 6–21" TT
1 FP or LC carried

COASTAL SUBMARINES

RO 57 Class   RO 57–59

Completed:	1923	Speed:	17/9 knots
Dimensions:	238' x 23'7" x 13'	Armament:	1–3" DP, 4–21" TT
Displacement: 889/1082 tons			

RO 60 Class   RO 60–68

Completed:	1927	Speed:	15.1/7.8 knots
Dimensions:	250' x 24'3" x 12'4"	Armament:	1–3" DP, 6–21" TT
Displacement: 988/1,300 tons			

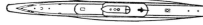

RO 33 Class   RO 33–34

Completed:	1937	Speed:	18.8/8.3 knots
Dimensions:	248' x 22' x 10'9"	Armament:	1–3" DP, 4–21" TT
Displacement: 700/? tons			mines carried (?)

RO 35 Class   RO 35–

Completed:	1943	Speed:	20/8 knots
Dimensions:	.255' x 24' x 12–13'	Armament:	1–25 mm or 40 mm twin, or
Displacement: 950/? tons			3" DP, 4–21" TT

RO 500 Class (No data)

RO 100 Class   RO 100–

Completed:	1944	Speed:	14.2/8 knots
Dimensions:	180' x 20' x ?	Armament:	1–25 mm twin, 4–21" TT
Displacement: 500/? tons			mines carried (?)

MINELAYING SUBMARINES

RO 29 Class   RO 29–32

Completed:	1927	Speed:	12.5/7.3 knots
Dimensions:	243'7" x 20'9" x 12'3"	Armament:	1–4".7, 4–21" TT
Displacement: 655–746/1,000 tons			42 mines carried

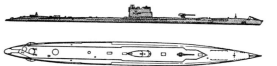

I 121 Class   I 121–124

Completed:	1928	Speed:	14/6.5 knots
Dimensions:	279'6" x 24'6" x 14'1"	Armament:	1–5".5, 4–21" TT
Displacement: 1,142/1,470 tons			42 mines carried

TRANSPORT SUBMARINES

I 52,54 Classes   I 52–58

Completed:	1943	Speed:	16/7.5 knots
Dimensions:	360' x 29'10" x 14'5"	Armament:	1–5".5, 2–21" TT
Displacement: 2,800/? tons			

MINOR COMBATANT CRAFT

TRAINING CRUISERS

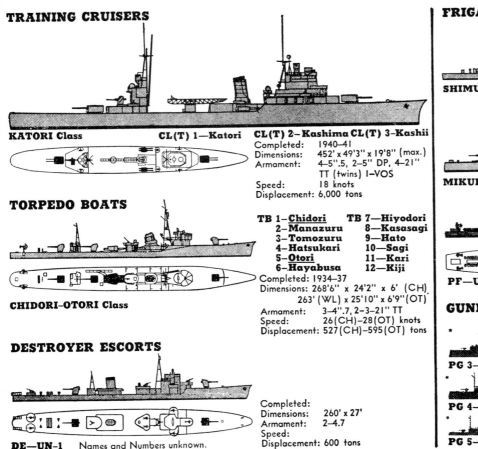

KATORI Class   CL(T) 1—Katori

CL(T) 2—Kashima CL(T) 3—Kashii
Completed: 1940–41
Dimensions: 452' x 49'3" x 19'8" (max.)
Armament: 4–5".5, 2–5" DP, 4–21"
              TT (twins) I–VOS
Speed: 18 knots
Displacement: 6,000 tons

TORPEDO BOATS

CHIDORI—OTORI Class

TB 1—Chidori   TB 7—Hiyodori
   2—Manazuru   8—Kasasagi
   3—Tomozuru   9—Hato
   4—Hatsukari   10—Sagi
   5—Otori   11—Kari
   6—Hayabusa   12—Kiji
Completed: 1934–37
Dimensions: 268'6" x 24'2" x 6' (CH)
            263' (WL) x 25'10" x 6'9"(OT)
Armament: 3–4".7, 2–3–21" TT
Speed: 26(CH)–28(OT) knots
Displacement: 527(CH)–595(OT) tons

DESTROYER ESCORTS

DE—UN-1   Names and Numbers unknown.

Completed:
Dimensions: 260' x 27'
Armament: 2–4.7
Speed:
Displacement: 600 tons

*Next to profile indicates reduced scale.

FRIGATES

SHIMUSHU Class

PF 1-Shimushu PF 9—Mutsure
   2-Kunajiri   10-Wakamiya
   3-Hachijo   11-Fukue
   4-Ishigaki   12-Manju
   5-Etorofu   13-Kanju
   6-Matsuwa   14-Tsushima
   7-Sado   15-Iki
   8-Oki   16-Hirado
Dimensions: 255' x 30'   Armament: 3–4".7 Speed: 16 knots
Completed: 1939   Displacement: 1,000 tons

PF 17-Mikura   PF 21-Chiburi
   18-Miyake   22-Awaji
   19-Amakusa   23-Kasado
   20-Kurahashi   24-Kusakaki
Completed: 1944
Dimensions: 275' x 35'
Armament: 4–4".7
Speed: 16 knots
Displacement: 1,500 tons

MIKURA Class

Completed:
Dimensions: 265' x 33'
Armament: 1–4".7 DP, 1–3" AA,
              14 DC throwers
Speed:
Displacement:

PF—UN-1   Names and Numbers unknown.

GUNBOATS

* PG 3—Asuga
Compl 1915
Length: 215'6"
Displ: 860 tons

* PG 4—Ataka
Compl 1922
Length: 222'0"
Displacement: 725 tons

* PG 5—Hitonose
Completed: 1931
Length: 210'0"
Displacement: 464 tons

HASHIDATE Class   PG 6—Hashidate
                      PG 7—Uji

Completed: 1941
Dimensions: 264' x 35' x 8'6"
Armament: 3–4".7 DP
Speed: 16 knots
Displacement: 1,200 tons

MINELAYERS

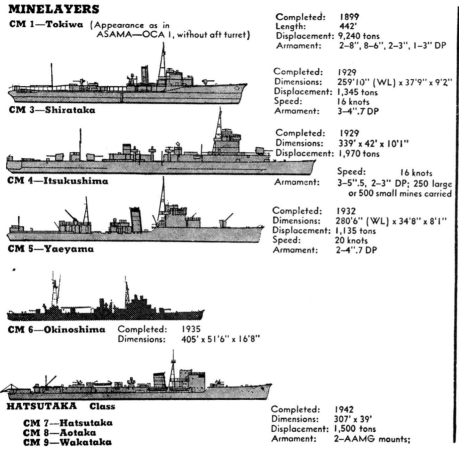

CM 1—Tokiwa (Appearance as in ASAMA—OCA 1, without aft turret)

Completed: 1899
Length: 442'
Displacement: 9,240 tons
Armament: 2–8", 8–6", 2–3", 1–3" DP

CM 3—Shirataka

Completed: 1929
Dimensions: 259'10" (WL) x 37'9" x 9'2"
Displacement: 1,345 tons
Speed: 16 knots
Armament: 3–4".7 DP

CM 4—Itsukushima

Completed: 1929
Dimensions: 339' x 42' x 10'1"
Displacement: 1,970 tons
Speed: 16 knots
Armament: 3–5".5, 2–3" DP; 250 large or 500 small mines carried

CM 5—Yaeyama

Completed: 1932
Dimensions: 280'6" (WL) x 34'8" x 8'1"
Displacement: 1,135 tons
Speed: 20 knots
Armament: 2–4".7 DP

CM 6—Okinoshima
Completed: 1935
Dimensions: 405' x 51'6" x 16'8"

HATSUTAKA Class

CM 7—Hatsutaka
CM 8—Aotaka
CM 9—Wakataka

Completed: 1942
Dimensions: 307' x 39'
Displacement: 1,500 tons
Armament: 2–AAMG mounts;

DESTROYER MINELAYERS

DM-WAKATAKE conversion

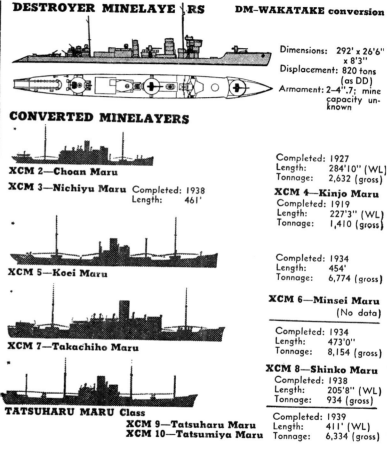

Dimensions: 292' x 26'6" x 8'3"
Displacement: 820 tons (as DD)
Armament: 2–4".7; mine capacity unknown

CONVERTED MINELAYERS

XCM 2—Choan Maru
XCM 3—Nichiyu Maru Completed: 1938 Length: 461'

Completed: 1927
Length: 284'10" (WL)
Tonnage: 2,632 (gross)

XCM 4—Kinjo Maru
Completed: 1919
Length: 227'3" (WL)
Tonnage: 1,410 (gross)

XCM 5—Koei Maru

Completed: 1934
Length: 454'
Tonnage: 6,774 (gross)

XCM 6—Minsei Maru (No data)

Completed: 1934
Length: 473'0"
Tonnage: 8,154 (gross)

XCM 7—Takachiho Maru

XCM 8—Shinko Maru
Completed: 1938
Length: 205'8" (WL)
Tonnage: 934 (gross)

TATSUHARU MARU Class
XCM 9—Tatsuharu Maru
XCM 10—Tatsumiya Maru

Completed: 1939
Length: 411' (WL)
Tonnage: 6,334 (gross)

MINOR COMBATANT CRAFT

MINESWEEPERS

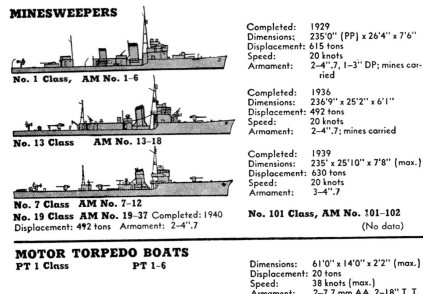

No. 1 Class, AM No. 1-6

Completed: 1929
Dimensions: 235'0'' (PP) x 26'4'' x 7'6''
Displacement: 615 tons
Speed: 20 knots
Armament: 2–4''.7, 1–3'' DP; mines carried

No. 13 Class   AM No. 13-18

Completed: 1936
Dimensions: 236'9'' x 25'2'' x 6'1''
Displacement: 492 tons
Speed: 20 knots
Armament: 2–4''.7; mines carried

No. 7 Class   AM No. 7-12

Completed: 1939
Dimensions: 235' x 25'10'' x 7'8'' (max.)
Displacement: 630 tons
Speed: 20 knots
Armament: 3–4''.7

No. 19 Class AM No. 19-37 Completed: 1940
Displacement: 492 tons   Armament: 2–4''.7

No. 101 Class, AM No. 101-102

(No data)

MOTOR TORPEDO BOATS

PT 1 Class   PT 1-6

Dimensions: 61'0'' x 14'0'' x 2'2'' (max.)
Displacement: 20 tons
Speed: 38 knots (max.)
Armament: 2–7.7 mm AA, 2–18'' T. T.

PT 10 Class

Dimensions: 60'0'' x 16'6'' x 2'6'' (max.)
Displacement: 80 tons
Speed: 29 knots (max.)
Armament: 3–13 mm AA, 2–18'' T. T.

PT 101 Class   (15 units)

Dimensions: 61'0'' x 12'9'' x 4'0''
Displacement: 20 tons
Speed: 38 knots (max.)
Armament: 2–13 mm AA, 1–7.7 mm AA, 2–18'' T. T.

PT 201 Class   (units unknown)

Dimensions: 59'0'' x 14'0''
Displacement: 20 tons
Speed: 24 knots (max.)
Armament: 1–13 mm AA, 2–18'' T. T.

*Next to profile indicates reduced scale.

SUBMARINE CHASERS—LARGE

PC 1 Class   PC 1-3

Completed: 1934
Dimensions: 213' x 19' x 4'11''
Displacement: 300 tons   (max.)
Speed: 24 knots

PC 4 Class   PC 4-12

Completed: 1939
Dimensions: 178' x 18'2'' x 6'6''
Displacement: 270 tons   (max.)
Speed: 20 knots

PC 13 Class   PC 13-49

Completed: 1943
Dimensions: 200' x 24'
Displacement: 300 tons
Speed: 20 knots (max.)
Armament: 1–3'' DP

PC 50 Class   PC 50-60   Completed: 1944   (No data)

SUBMARINE CHASERS—SMALL

SCS 1 Class   SCS 1-50

Completed: 1943
Dimensions: 97' x 19' x 6'6''
Displacement: 100 tons
Speed: 10 knots (max.)
Armament: 2–25 mm AA

SCS 51 Class   SCS 51-100

Completed: 1944
Dimensions: 146' x 15'3'' x 5'6'' (max.)
Displacement: 170 tons
Speed: 20 knots (full)

SCS 101 Class   SCS 101-117   Completed: 1943   (No data)

SCS 151 Class   SCS 151-165   Completed: (No data)

AUXILIARY CRUISERS

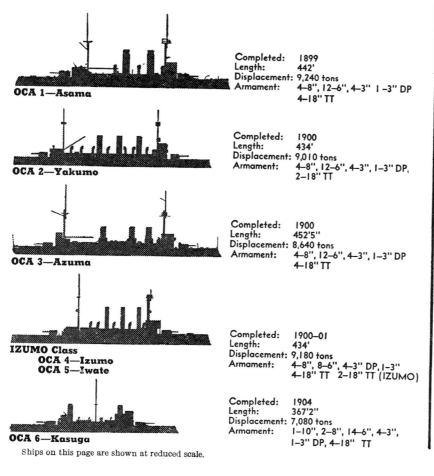

OCA 1—Asama

Completed:	1899
Length:	442'
Displacement:	9,240 tons
Armament:	4–8", 12–6", 4–3" 1 –3" DP
	4–18" TT

OCA 2—Yakumo

Completed:	1900
Length:	434'
Displacement:	9,010 tons
Armament:	4–8", 12–6", 4–3", 1–3" DP,
	2–18" TT

OCA 3—Azuma

Completed:	1900
Length:	452'5"
Displacement:	8,640 tons
Armament:	4–8", 12–6", 4–3", 1–3" DP
	4–18" TT

IZUMO Class
OCA 4—Izumo
OCA 5—Iwate

Completed:	1900–01
Length:	434'
Displacement:	9,180 tons
Armament:	4–8", 8–6", 4–3" DP,1–3"
	4–18" TT 2–18" TT (IZUMO)

OCA 6—Kasuga

Completed:	1904
Length:	367'2"
Displacement:	7,080 tons
Armament:	1–10", 2–8", 14–6", 4–3",
	1–3" DP, 4–18" TT

Ships on this page are shown at reduced scale.

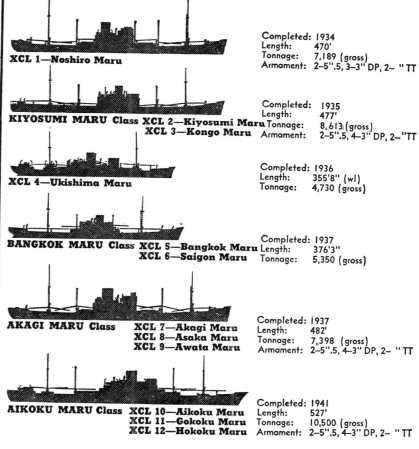

XCL 1—Noshiro Maru

Completed:	1934
Length:	470'
Tonnage:	7,189 (gross)
Armament:	2–5".5, 3–3" DP, 2– " TT

KIYOSUMI MARU Class XCL 2—Kiyosumi Maru
XCL 3—Kongo Maru

Completed:	1935
Length:	477'
Tonnage:	8,613 (gross)
Armament:	2–5".5, 4–3" DP, 2–TT

XCL 4—Ukishima Maru

Completed:	1936
Length:	355'8" (wl)
Tonnage:	4,730 (gross)

BANGKOK MARU Class XCL 5—Bangkok Maru
XCL 6—Saigon Maru

Completed:	1937
Length:	376'3"
Tonnage:	5,350 (gross)

AKAGI MARU Class   XCL 7—Akagi Maru
XCL 8—Asaka Maru
XCL 9—Awata Maru

Completed:	1937
Length:	482'
Tonnage:	7,398 (gross)
Armament:	2–5".5, 4–3" DP, 2– " TT

AIKOKU MARU Class XCL 10—Aikoku Maru
XCL 11—Gokoku Maru
XCL 12—Hokoku Maru

Completed:	1941
Length:	527'
Tonnage:	10,500 (gross)
Armament:	2–5".5, 4–3" DP, 2– " TT

FLEET AUXILIARIES

SEAPLANE CARRIERS

Completed: 1922
Dimensions: 496' x 67' x 27'8"
Displacement: 17,000 tons
Speed: 15 knots
Armament: 2–5".5, 2–3" DP
Plane Capacity: 16

CVS 2—Kamoi

CVS 7—Akitsushima

Completed: 1942
Displacement: 9,000 tons
Speed: 20 knots (full)
Armament: 4–5" DP
Plane Capacity: 14

SEAPLANE TENDERS

AV 1—Takachiho

Completed: 1942
Dimensions: 392'0" x 53'0"
Displacement: 4,500 tons
Armament: 2–4".7 DP

CONVERTED TORPEDO-BOAT TENDERS

XAGP 1—Shuri Maru

Completed: 1928
Tonnage: 1,875 (gross)

XAGP 2—Shinsho Maru

Tonnage: 4,836 (gross)

XAGP 3—Kamikaze Maru

Completed: 1937
Tonnage: 4,916 (gross)

CONVERTED MINESWEEPER TENDER EIKO MARU : 1937

*Next to profile indicates reduced scale.

CONVERTED SEAPLANE TENDERS

Plane Capacity: 13

KAMIKAWA MARU Class
XAV 1—Kamikawa Maru
XAV 2—Kunikawa Maru
XAV 3—Kimikawa Maru
XAV 4—Kiyokawa Maru

Completed: 1940
Dimensions: 508' x 62' x 12' (light)
Tonnage: 6,863 (gross)
Speed: 19 knots
Armament: 2–5" DP

XAV 5—Sanyo Maru

Completed: 1930
Length: 465'
Tonnage: 8,360 (gross)

XAV 6—Yasukawa Maru

Completed: 1930
Length: 455' (PP)
Tonnage: 6,710 (gross)

XAV 7—Okitsu Maru

Completed: 1939
Length: 461'
Tonnage: 6,666 (gross)

SANUKI MARU Class
XAV 8—Sanuki Maru
XAV 9—Sagara Maru

Completed: 1941
Length: 509'0"
Tonnage: 7,100 (gross)

AIRCRAFT TRANSPORTS

XAPV 1—Goshu Maru

Completed: 1940
Dimensions: 460' x 60' x 10'
Tonnage: 8,592 (gross)
Speed: 17 knots
Armament: 2–6"
Plane Capacity: 13 (reported)

FUJIKAWA MARU Class
XAPV 2—Fujikawa Maru
XAPV 3—Mogamigawa Maru

Completed: 1937
Length: 436' (PP)
Tonnage: 6,938 (gross)

KAMOGAWA MARU Class
XAPV 4—Kamogawa Maru
XAPV 5—Keiyo Maru

Completed: 1938
Length: 456'
Tonnage: 6,442 (gross)

XAPV 6—Lyons Maru

Completed: 1920
Length: 462'
Tonnage: 7,018 (gross)

XAPV 8—Nagoya Maru

Completed: 1932
Length: 406'8" (PP)
Tonnage: 6,072 (gross)

XAPV 10—Takasaki Maru

Completed: 1943
Tonnage: 7,000 (gross)

Ships on this page are shown at reduced scale.

CONVERTED SUBMARINE TENDERS

XAS 1—Manju Maru

Completed: 1926
Length: 449'
Tonnage: 7,267 (gross)

XAS 2—Yasukuni Maru

Completed: 1930
Length: 531'
Tonnage: 11,933 (gross)

HIE MARU Class
XAS 3—Hie Maru
XAS 4—Heian Maru

Completed: 1930
Length: 535'
Tonnage: 11,600 (gross)

XAS 6—Aratama Maru

Completed: 1938
Length: 475'
Tonnage: 6,784 (gross)

XAS 9—Soyo Maru

XAS 7—Urakami Maru
Completed: 1941
Tonnage: 4,250 (gross)

XAS 8—Nisso Maru

Completed: 1943
Tonnage: 7,000 (gross)

Completed: 1931
Length: 415' (PP)
Tonnage: 6,081 (gross)

FLEET AUXILIARIES

REPAIR SHIPS

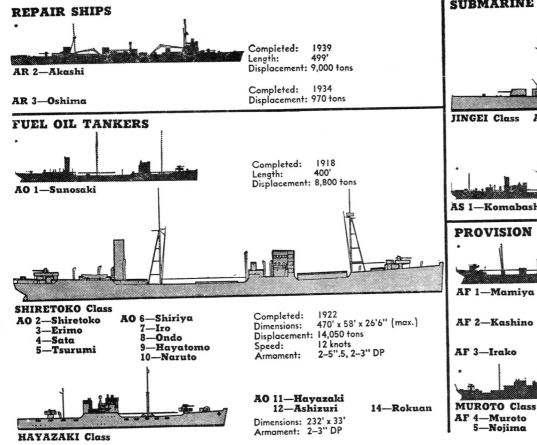

*

AR 2—Akashi
Completed: 1939
Length: 499'
Displacement: 9,000 tons

AR 3—Oshima
Completed: 1934
Displacement: 970 tons

FUEL OIL TANKERS

*

AO 1—Sunosaki
Completed: 1918
Length: 400'
Displacement: 8,800 tons

SHIRETOKO Class
AO 2—Shiretoko AO 6—Shiriya
3—Erimo   7—Iro
4—Sata   8—Ondo
5—Tsurumi   9—Hayatomo
             10—Naruto
Completed: 1922
Dimensions: 470' x 58' x 26'6" (max.)
Displacement: 14,050 tons
Speed: 12 knots
Armament: 2–5".5, 2–3" DP

AO 11—Hayazaki
12—Ashizuri   14—Rokuan
Dimensions: 232' x 33'
Armament: 2–3" DP

HAYAZAKI Class

*Next to profile indicates reduced scale.

SUBMARINE TENDERS

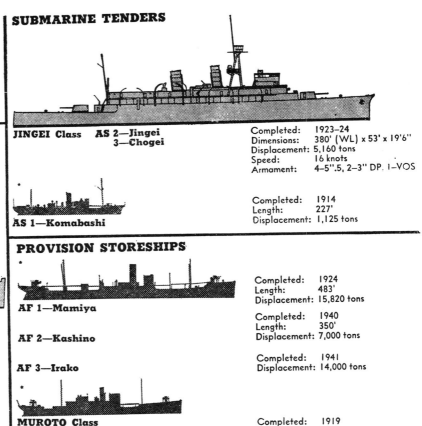

JINGEI Class   AS 2—Jingei
                3—Chogei
Completed: 1923–24
Dimensions: 380' (WL) x 53' x 19'6"
Displacement: 5,160 tons
Speed: 16 knots
Armament: 4–5".5, 2–3" DP. 1–VOS

*

AS 1—Komabashi
Completed: 1914
Length: 227'
Displacement: 1,125 tons

PROVISION STORESHIPS

*

AF 1—Mamiya
Completed: 1924
Length: 483'
Displacement: 15,820 tons

AF 2—Kashino
Completed: 1940
Length: 350'
Displacement: 7,000 tons

AF 3—Irako
Completed: 1941
Displacement: 14,000 tons

*

MUROTO Class
AF 4—Muroto
5—Nojima
Completed: 1919
Length: 345'
Displacement: 8,215 tons

MISCELLANEOUS AUXILIARIES

MLC CARRIERS

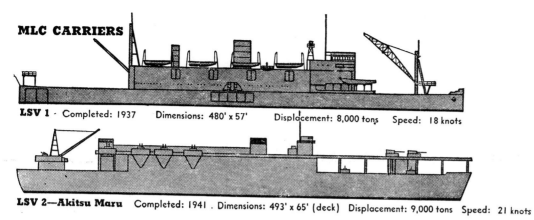

LSV 1 - Completed: 1937   Dimensions: 480' x 57'   Displacement: 8,000 tons   Speed: 18 knots

LSV 2—Akitsu Maru   Completed: 1941 . Dimensions: 493' x 65' (deck)   Displacement: 9,000 tons   Speed: 21 knots

★

APD Numbers unknown. Dimensions: 342' x 36'; mines or LC carried

MISCELLANEOUS AUXILIARIES

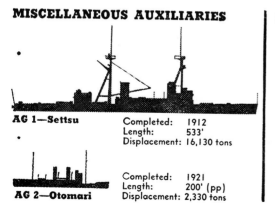

AG 1—Settsu
- Completed: 1912
- Length: 533'
- Displacement: 16,130 tons

AG 2—Otomari
- Completed: 1921
- Length: 200' (pp)
- Displacement: 2,330 tons

SURVEYING SHIPS

AGS 1—Yodo
- Completed: 1908
- Length: 300'
- Displacement: 1,320 tons

AGS 2—Koshu
- Completed: 1904
- Length: 264'
- Displacement: 2,000 tons

AGS 3—Tsukushi
(No data)

AGS 4—Soya
- Completed: 1942
- Displacement: 2,000 tons

CABLE LAYERS

HASHIMA Class   Completed: 1942   Displacement: 2,000 tons
ARC 1—Hashima 2—Tsurushima 3—Tateishi 4—Odate

★

ARC 5—Toyo Maru   Completed: 1937
Tonnage: 3,719 (gross)   Length: 335' (pp)

ARC 6—Yamabato Maru
- Completed: 1937
- Length: 298' (pp)
- Tonnage: 2,557 (gross)

COASTAL MINELAYERS

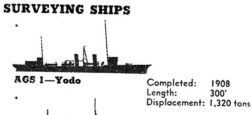

★

TOSHIMA Class
- Completed: 1922
- Length: 162' (pp)   Displacement: 430 tons

CMc 1—Toshima   CMc 6—Ento
  2—Kuroshima   7—Katashima
  3—Katoku   8—Kurokami
  4—Ashizaki   9—Enoshima
  5—Washizaki   10—Kurozaki
                    11—Ninoshima

TSUBAME Class   CMc 12—Tsubame   CMc 13—Kamome
Completed: 1929   Length: 206'8"   Displacement: 450 tons

NATSUSHIMA Class   CMc 14—Natsushima   CMc 15—Nasami
- Completed: 1934   CMc 16—Sarushima
- Dimensions: 225'2" (pp) x 24'6" x 5'8"   Speed: 19 knots
- Displacement: 443 tons   Armament: 2-3" DP

SOKUTEN Class
- Completed: 1940
- Length: 240'7"
- Displacement: 720 tons

CMc 17—Sokuten
  18—Shirakami
  19—Kyosai
  20—Nariu
  21—Ukishima

YURISHIMA Class
Completed: 1943

CMc 22—Yurishima
  23—Nuwashima
  24—Maeshima
  25—Moroshima
  26—Hirashima
  27—Takashima
  28—Araizaki

  29—Ishizaki
  30—Boko
  31—Saishu

No. 1 Class
Completed: 1943

CMc 32—No. 1
  33—No. 2
  34—No. 3
  35—No. 4

HOSPITAL SHIPS

AH 1—America Maru

Completed: 1898
Length: 423' (PP)
Tonnage: 6,070 (gross)

AH 2—Yoshino Maru

Completed: 1906
Length: 464' (PP
Tonnage: 8,990 (gross)

AH 3—Fuso Maru

Completed: 1908
Length: 475' (PP)
Tonnage: 8,196 (gross)

AH 4—Seattle Maru

Completed: 1909
Length: 420' (PP)
Tonnage: 5,774 (gross)

AH 5—Siberia Maru

Completed: 1909
Length: 351' (PP)
Tonnage: 3,461 (gross)

Ship profiles above are at reduced scale.

AH 6—Chicago Maru

Completed: 1910
Length: 410' (PP)
Tonnage: 5,866 (gross)

AH 7—Mizuho Maru

Completed: 1912
Length: 460' (PP)
Tonnage: 8,506 (gross)

AH 8—Asahi Maru

Completed: 1914
Length: 483' (PP)
Tonnage: 9,326 (gross)

AH 9—Kohoku Maru

Completed: 1915
Length: 285' (PP)
Tonnage: 2,574 (gross)

AH 10—Manila Maru AH 11—Arabia Maru

Completed: 1915
Length: 475' (PP)
Tonnage: 9,480 (gross)

AH 12—Hokushin Maru

Completed: 1920
Length: 407' (PP)
Tonnage: 5,820 (gross)

AH 13—Baikal Maru

Completed: 1921
Length: 400' (pp)
Tonnage: 5,266 (gross)

AH 14—Muro Maru

Completed: 1926
Length: 230' (pp)
Tonnage: 1,607 (gross)

AH 15—Teno Maru (ex. Op Ten Noort)

Completed: 1927
Length: 425' (pp)
Tonnage: 6,076 (gross)

AH 16—Mikasa Maru

Completed: 1928
Length: 325' (pp)
Tonnage: 3,143 (gross)

AH 17—Buenos Aires Maru

Completed: 1929
Length: 461' (pp)
Tonnage: 9,626 (gross)

Ship profiles above are at reduced scale.

AH 18—Ural Maru

Completed: 1929
Length: 405' (pp)
Tonnage: 6,374 (gross)

AH 19—Hikawa Maru

Completed: 1930
Length: 535'
Tonnage: 11,622 (gross)

AH 20—Ryuko Maru

Completed: 1935
Length: 298' (pp)
Tonnage: 2,962 (gross)

AH 21—Tachibana Maru

Completed: 1935
Length: 249' (pp)
Tonnage: 1,772 (gross)

AH 22—Takasago Maru

Completed: 1936
Length: 463' (pp)
Tonnage: 9,347 (gross)

DISTRICT CRAFT

SALVAGE VESSELS

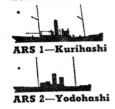

ARS 1—Kurihashi

Completed: 1905
Length: 182' (PP)
Displacement: 1,000 tons

ARS 2—Yodohashi

Completed:
Length: 159' (PP)
Displacement: 800 tons

ARS 3—Saruhashi

Completed:
Length: 140' (PP)
Displacement: 590 tons

ARS 4—Shiragane

Completed:
Length: 133' (PP)
Displacement: 400 tons

CONVERTED SALVAGE VESSELS

XARS 1—Matsuei Maru (No data)

XARS 2—Kasagi Maru

Completed: 1928
Length: 325' (pp)
Tonnage: 3,140 (gross)

XARS 3—Yamabiko Maru

Completed: 1937
Length: 460'
Tonnage: 6,798 (gross)

XARS 4—Hakkai Maru

Completed: 1940
Length: 309' (PP)
Tonnage: 2,921 (gross)

XARS 5—Esa Maru (No data)

XARS 6—Haruta Maru

Completed: 1925
Length: 262' (PP)
Tonnage: 1,515 (gross)

XARS 7—Yushio Maru

Completed: 1927
Length: 185'4" (PP)
Tonnage: 807 (gross)

RIVER GUNBOATS

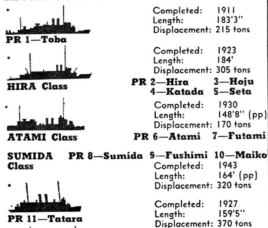

PR 1—Toba

Completed: 1911
Length: 183'3"
Displacement: 215 tons

HIRA Class

Completed: 1923
Length: 184'
Displacement: 305 tons

PR 2—Hira   3—Hoju
4—Katada   5—Seta

ATAMI Class

Completed: 1930
Length: 148'8" (PP)
Displacement: 170 tons

PR 6—Atami   7—Futami

SUMIDA Class   PR 8—Sumida   9—Fushimi   10—Maiko

Completed: 1943
Length: 164' (PP)
Displacement: 320 tons

PR 11—Tatara

Completed: 1927
Length: 159'5"
Displacement: 370 tons

PR 12—Karatsu

Completed: 1928
Length: 210'9"
Displacement: 560 tons

PR 13—Suma

Completed: 1916
Length: 237'6"
Displacement: 625 tons

CONVERTED GUNBOATS

XPG –80 miscellaneous converted merchantmen.
Tonnage: 756–3,300 (gross)

CONVERTED PATROL CRAFT

XPC–130 miscellaneous trawlers, whale-killers, coasters, etc.

CONVERTED MINESWEEPERS

XAM –116 miscellaneous coasters, etc., averaging 300 gross tons.

CONVERTED NET TENDERS

XYN—50 or more miscellaneous converted merchantmen.
Tonnage: 300–6,700 (gross)

COASTAL MINESWEEPERS

No. 1 Class   No. 3 Class AMc 3-25—No. 3-25
AMc 1-2—No. 1-2   Completed: 1943 Displacement: 300 tons

LANDING CRAFT TYPES
VEHICLES AND PERSONNEL

LST Dimensions: 264' x 32'
Armament: 1–3"

Type A—49'4" (Army and Navy designs); 65' (Army)

PERSONNEL AND SUPPLY

Type B—33'   Type H—51'
Type D—38'6"   Type I—47' (dumb barge)
Type E—63'2" (air-screw propelled)
Type F—21'   Collapsible Pontoon—13'7"
Type G—52'-75' (lugger)   Rigid Pontoon—24'6"

SUPPORT

Type C—49' and 60'

FUEL OIL BARGES

Type X—199' (dumb barge)
Type Y—104' (dumb barge)
Type V
Type W

LIGHT CRUISERS

NING HAI Class (China)

Ning Hai
Ping Hai

Completed: 1932–36
Dimensions: 360' x 39'2" x 11'
Displacement: 2,000 tons
Speed: 22 knots
Armament: 6–5".5, 6–3" DP, 4–21" TT (twins)

TORPEDO BOATS

TRAD Class (Siam)

Trad
Puket
Surasdra
Pattani
Rayong
Chandaraburi
Jumbara

Completed: 1937
Dimensions: 223'1" x 21' x 6'4"
Displacement: 385 to 470 tons
Speed: 31 knots
Armament: 3–3" DP, 6–18" TT

COAST DEFENSE SHIPS

DHAMBURI Class (Siam)

Dhamburi **Sri Ayudhya**
Completed: 1938
Dimensions: 246'1" x 42'8"
Displacement: 2,015 tons
Speed: 12.5 knots
Armament: 4–8", 4–3" DP

RATANAKOSINDRA Class
Ratanakosindra (Siam)
Sukhodaya

Completed: 1925–30
Length: 175'
Displacement: 886 tons

GUNBOATS

TAHCHIN Class (Siam)

Tahchin **Maeklong**
Completed: 1937
Dimensions: 269'3" (WL) x 34'5" x 10'3"
Displacement: 1,400 tons
Speed: 17 knots
Armament: 4–4".7, 4–21" TT (twins)

Yat Sen (China)

Completed: 1930
Length: 265'
Displacement: 1,600 tons

Amiral Charner (France)

Completed: 1933
Length: 340'3"
Displacement: 1,969 tons

DESTROYERS

Phra Ruang (Siam)

Completed: 1917
Length: 274'
Displacement: 718 tons

Thracian (Britain)
Hai Wei (Manchukuo) (See ODD MOMO)

Completed: 1922
Length: 276'2"
Displacement: 905 tons

VAN GHENT Class (Netherlands)
Banckert, W. De With

Completed: 1930
Length: 321'10"
Displacement: 1,316 tons

YACHT

Angthong (Siam)

Completed: 1919
Length: 335'3"
Displacement: 2,700 tons

MINESWEEPER

Chao Phya (Siam)

Completed: 1919
Length: 231'
Displacement: 699 tons

SUBMARINES

VIRUN Class (Siam)
Virun
Machanu
Sinsamudar
Blai Jumbol

Completed: 1938
Length: 164'1"
Displacement: 325 tons

FUEL OIL TANKERS

Samui (Siam)

Completed: 1936
Length: 249'4"
Displacement: 1,800 tons

A simplified appearance break-down of the Japanese Navy, introduced in JAN No. 3, is included in this book to serve as a guide in recognizing the warships shown on the preceding pages. This system, called Japanese Warship Recognition, was developed as an aid in reporting Japanese warships under operational conditions. It is now being widely used by the Allied forces in the Pacific theatres.

The system is a simple procedure of progressive observation in three steps:

First —A general DIVISION fitting the ship's appearance is determined.

Second—The ship is keyed into a GROUP within the Division (usually by turrets).

Third —The ship is recognized as one of a CLASS within the group.

The time available for observation and the conditions prevailing at the time of sighting will determine how complete the report of a certain warship can be. A partial report will be of considerable intelligence value.

For example —The observer's report might run as follows in the reporting of an unknown warship:

If unable to determine the division, report—1 WARSHIP.

If division can be determined, report—1 CA.

If division and class are partially determined, report—1 CA, NACHI-ATAGO.

If division and class can be fully determined, report—1 CA, NACHI.

Full presentation of this system, known as JWR (Japanese Warship Recognition), is available in two forms—ONI 229 (for surface vessels and submarines) and JAN No. 3 (for use in the air). A parallel system for recognizing and reporting Japanese merchant ships (JMST—Japanese Merchant Shipping Tonnage) is included in the same publications. These publications were prepared by DNI and A–2 in collaboration with representatives of Allied Air Forces, Naval Intelligence, and C. I. U. in S. W. P. A.

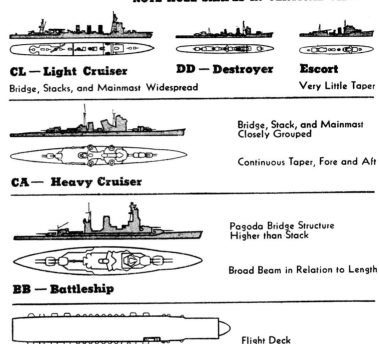

JWR JAPANESE WARSHIP RECOGNITION

NOTE HULL SHAPES IN VERTICAL VIEW

CL — Light Cruiser
Bridge, Stacks, and Mainmast Widespread

DD — Destroyer

Escort
Very Little Taper

CA — Heavy Cruiser
Bridge, Stack, and Mainmast Closely Grouped

Continuous Taper, Fore and Aft

BB — Battleship
Pagoda Bridge Structure Higher than Stack

Broad Beam in Relation to Length

CV — Aircraft Carrier
Flight Deck

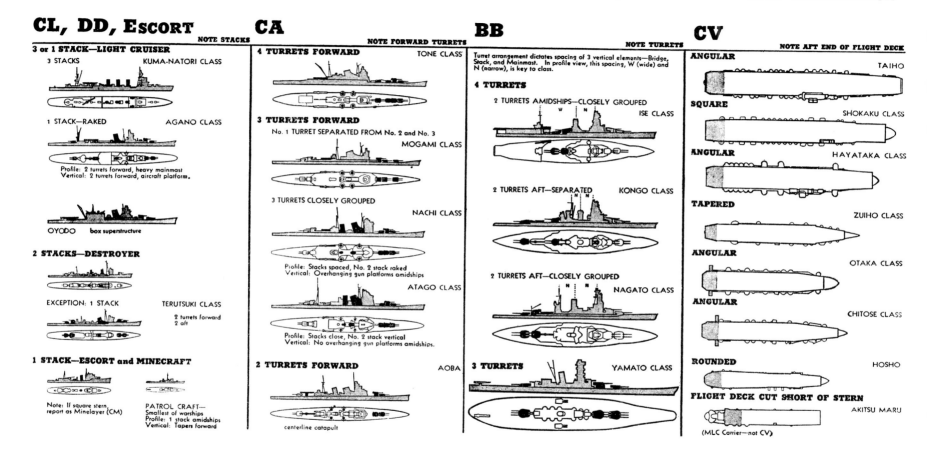

CL, DD, ESCORT
NOTE STACKS

3 or 1 STACK—LIGHT CRUISER

3 STACKS   KUMA-NATORI CLASS

1 STACK—RAKED   AGANO CLASS

Profile: 2 turrets forward, heavy mainmast
Vertical: 2 turrets forward, aircraft platform.

OYODO   box superstructure

2 STACKS—DESTROYER

EXCEPTION: 1 STACK   TERUTSUKI CLASS
         2 turrets forward
         2 aft

1 STACK—ESCORT and MINECRAFT

Note: If square stern
report as Minelayer (CM)

PATROL CRAFT—
Smallest of warships
Profile: 1 stack amidships
Vertical: Tapers forward

CA
NOTE FORWARD TURRETS

4 TURRETS FORWARD
         TONE CLASS

3 TURRETS FORWARD

No. 1 TURRET SEPARATED FROM No. 2 and No. 3
         MOGAMI CLASS

3 TURRETS CLOSELY GROUPED
         NACHI CLASS

Profile: Stacks spaced, No. 2 stack raked
Vertical: Overhanging gun platforms amidships
         ATAGO CLASS

Profile: Stacks close, No. 2 stack vertical
Vertical: No overhanging gun platforms amidships.

2 TURRETS FORWARD
         AOBA

centerline catapult

BB
NOTE TURRETS

Turret arrangement dictates spacing of 3 vertical elements—Bridge, Stack, and Mainmast. In profile view, this spacing, W (wide) and N (narrow), is key to class.

4 TURRETS

2 TURRETS AMIDSHIPS—CLOSELY GROUPED
         ISE CLASS

2 TURRETS AFT—SEPARATED   KONGO CLASS

2 TURRETS AFT—CLOSELY GROUPED
         NAGATO CLASS

3 TURRETS   YAMATO CLASS

CV
NOTE AFT END OF FLIGHT DECK

ANGULAR   TAIHO

SQUARE   SHOKAKU CLASS

ANGULAR   HAYATAKA CLASS

TAPERED   ZUIHO CLASS

ANGULAR   OTAKA CLASS

ANGULAR   CHITOSE CLASS

ROUNDED   HOSHO

FLIGHT DECK CUT SHORT OF STERN
         AKITSU MARU

(MLC Carrier—not CV)

TYPE DESIGNATIONS OF JAPANESE WARSHIPS

Major Combatant Types

BB	Battleship	DD	Destroyer
CV	Aircraft Carrier	ODD	Destroyer, Second Line
CVL	Small Aircraft Carrier	TB	Torpedo Boat
CVE	Escort Aircraft Carrier	SS	Submarine, Cruiser, Fleet
CVS	Seaplane Carrier	OSS	Submarine, Coastal
CA	Heavy Cruiser	SM	Submarine Minelayer
CL	Light Cruiser	APS	Submarine Transport

Minor Combatant Types

DE	Destroyer Escort	OCA	Cruiser, Second Line
PF	Frigate	CL(T)	Training Cruiser
PG	Gunboat	XCL	Auxiliary Cruiser
PC	Submarine Chaser, Large	CM	Minelayer
SCS	Submarine Chaser, Small	XCM	Converted Minelayer
PT	Motor Torpedo Boat	AM	Minesweeper

Auxiliary Types

AV	Seaplane Tender	AR	Repair Ship
XAV	Converted Seaplane Tender	AO	Fuel Oil Tanker
		AF	Provision Storeship
XAPV	Aircraft Transport	LSV	Landing Craft Carrier
AS	Submarine Tender	AG	Miscellaneous Auxiliary
XAS	Converted Submarine Tender	AGS	Surveying Ship
		ARC	Cable Layer

District Craft

CMc	Minelayer, Coastal	XPC	Converted Subchaser
AMc	Minesweeper, Coastal	XYN	Converted Net Tender
XPG	Converted Gunboat	YP	Patrol Vessel
ARS	Salvage Vessel	PR	River Gunboat
XARS	Converted Salvage Vessel		

SYSTEM OF NAMING JAPANESE WARSHIPS

Like the U. S. Navy, the Japanese have a fairly rigid system for assigning warship names. In most instances, a knowledge of the meaning of the name of a Japanese warship will reveal her type classification. Some notable exceptions occur where ships are reclassified as to type but retain their original names, as in the cases of the KONGO Class battleships (ex-battle cruisers) and MOGAMI Class of heavy cruisers (ex-light cruisers). In general, the naming system is as follows:

TYPE	NAMED FOR
Battleships	Provinces of Japan
Aircraft Carriers	Dragons and "Great Birds"
Battle Cruisers	
Large Cruisers	Mountains
Heavy Cruisers	
Cruisers, Second Line	
Light Cruisers	Rivers
Fleet Destroyers ("First Class" DD)	Meteorological names in poetic style
Escort Destroyers ("Second Class" DD)	Trees, flowers, fruits, and islands
Torpedo Boats (*not* PT)	Birds
Large Submarines	"I" and number
Coastal Submarines	"RO" and number
Small Submarines	"HA" and number
Minelayers	Islands, straits, and channels
Minesweepers	Straight numbers
Submarine Tenders (Regular)	Whales
Fuel Oil Tankers Storeships	Headlands and capes
Motor Torpedo Boats Submarine Chasers	Straight numbers

The two accepted methods for transliteration of Japanese words into English spelling are the Hepburn System and the Kokutai (official Japanese) System. The Hepburn System represents the more nearly phonetic approach to spoken Japanese and is followed in this publication.

The following list of equivalents is provided to enable the user of ONI–41–42–I to easily reconcile any Kokutai version of a Japanese ship name with the more familiar or Hepburn spelling.

HEPBURN	KOKUTAI
FU	HU
SHI	SI
SH	SY
CHI	TI
TSU	TU
CH	TY
JI	ZI
JU	ZYU
JO	ZYO

Typical examples are:

Fuso	Huso
Shokaku	Syokaku
Ashigara	Asigara
Mutsu	Mutu

Name	Class	Symbol
A		
Abukuma	Natori	CL 13
Agano	Agano	CL 21
Agata Maru		XYN
Aikoku Maru	Aikoku Maru	XCL 10
Akagi Maru	Akagi Maru	XCL 7
Akashi		AR 2
Akatsuki	Fubuki	DD 59
Akebono	Fubuki	DD 54
Akigumo	Asashio-Kagero	DD 105
Akikaze	Minekaze	DD 7
Akitsu Maru		LSV 2
Akitsu Maru		XPC
Akitsushima		CVS 7
Akitsuki	Terutsuki	DD 109
AM No. 1–6	No. 1	AM
AM No. 7–12	No. 7	AM
AM No. 13–18	No. 13	AM
AM No. 19–37	No. 19	AM
AM No. 101, 102	No. 101	AM
Amagiri	Fubuki	DD45
Amakusa	Mikura	PF 19
Amatsukaze	Asashio-Kagero	DD 95
AMc No. 1, 2	No. 1	AMc
AMc No. 3–25	No. 3	AMc
America Maru		AH 1
Amiral Charner	Bougainville	PG
Amoy Maru No. 1–4		XAM
Angthong		PY
Anshu Maru		XPG
Aoba	Aoba	CA 3
Aoi	Kuri-Wakatake	ODD 9
Aoi Maru		XAM
Aotaka	Hatsutaka	CM 8
Arabia Maru		AH 11
Araizaki	Yurishima	CMc 28
Arare	Asashio-Kagero	DD 85
Arashi	Asashio-Kagero	DD 98

Name	Class	Symbol
Arashio	Asashio-Kagero	DD 77
Arashiyama Maru		XAM
Aratama Maru		XAS 6
Ariake	Hatsuharu-Shigure	DD 64
Asagao	Kuri-Wakatake	ODD 26
Asagiri	Fubuki	DD 48
Asagumo	Asashio-Kagero	DD 80
Asahi	Asama	AR 1
Asahi Maru		AH 8
Asahi Maru No. 2		XAM
Asaka Maru	Akagi Maru	XCL 8
Asakaze	Kamikaze	DD 17
Asama		OCA 1
Asamame Maru		XPC
Asanagi	Kamikaze	DD 20
Asashio	Asashio-Kagero	DD 76
Ashi	Kuri-Wakatake	ODD 16
Ashigara	Nachi	CA 8
Ashizaki	Toshima	CMc 4
Ashizuri		AO 12
Asuga		PG 3
Atago	Atago	CA 9
Ataka		PG 4
Ataka Maru		XAM
Atami	Atami	PR 6
Awaji	Mikura	PF 22
Awata Maru	Akagi Maru	XCL 9
Ayanami	Fubuki	DD 47
Ayukawa Maru		XPC
Azuma		OCA 3
B		
Baikal Maru		AH 13
Banckert	Van Ghent	DD
Bangkok Maru	Bangkok Maru	XCL 5
Banshu Maru No. 18, 51, 56		XAM
Banshu Maru No. 53		XPC
Bisan Maru		XAM

ALPHABETICAL INDEX

Name	Class	Symbol
Blai Jumbol	Virun	SS
Boko	Yurishima	CMc 30
Buenos Aires Ma-ru.		AH 17
Bunzan Maru		XPC
Busho Maru		XPG
Byoritsu Maru		XPC
C		
Chandaraburi	Trad	TB
Chao Phya	"Improved Hunt"	AM
Chiburi	Mikura	PF 21
Chicago Maru		AH 6
Chidori	Chidori	TB 1
Chikuma	Tone	CA 18
Chikushi Maru		XAM
Chikuto Maru		XPC
Chikyu Maru		XPC
Chitose Maru		XPG
Chitose Maru No. (?).		XAM
Choan Maru		XCM 2
Choan Maru No. 2		XPG
Chogei	Jingei	AS 3
Chohakusan Maru		XPG
Chojusan Maru		XPG
Chokai	Atago	CA 11
Choko Maru		XYN
Choko Maru No. 2		XPG
Chosa Maru		XPG
Choun Maru		XPG
Choun Maru No. 15, 16.		XPC
Choun Maru No. 18, 21.		XAM
Choyo Maru No. 2		XAM

Name	Class	Symbol
Chuyo	Otaka	CVE 3
CMc No. 32–35	No. 1	CMc
D		
Daian Maru		XPC
Daido Maru		XPG
Daigen Maru No. 7		XPG
Daigokuten Maru		XYN
Daisei Maru		XAM
Daito Maru		XAM
Daito Maru No. 1		XPC
Daiton Maru		XPC
Derii Maru		XPG
DE-UN-1		DE
Dhamburi	Dhamburi	
E		
Edo Maru		XPG
Eifuku Maru		XPG
Eijo Maru		XPC
Eiko Maru	Converted Mine-sweeper Tender	XPG
Eiryu Maru		XYN
Enoshima	Toshima	CMc 9
Ensui Maru		XPC
Ento	Toshima	CMc 6
Erimo	Shiretoko	AO 3
Esa Maru		XARS 5
Etorofu	Shimushu	PF 5
F		
Fubuki	Fubuki	DD 37
Fuji	Kuri-Wakatake	ODD 15
Fuji Maru		XAM
Fujikawa Maru	Fujikawa Maru	XAPV 2
Fujinami	Takanami	DD 121
Fukue	Shimushu	PF 11

Name	Class	Symbol
Fukuei Maru No. 7		XAM
Fukuei Maru No. 10		XPG
Fukuei Maru No. 15		XYN
Fukushima Maru		XPC
Fumi Maru		XPC
Fumi Maru No. 2		XAM
Fumi Maru No. 3		XPC
Fumi Maru No. 5		XPG
Fumitsuki	Mutsuki	DD 30
Furutaka	Furutaka	CA 1
Fushimi	Sumida	PR 9
Fuso Maru		AH 3
Futami	Atami	PR 7
Fuyo	Kuri-Wakatake	ODD 27
Fuyutsuki	Terutsuki	DD 115
G		
Ganjitsu Maru		XPC
Geiyo Maru		XPC
Gokoku Maru	Aikoku Maru	XCL 11
Goshu Maru		XAPV 1
H		
Hachijo	Shimushu	PF 3
Hagi	Kuri-Wakatake	ODD 13
Hagikaze	Asashio-Kagero	DD 99
Hagoromo Maru		XAM
Haguro	Nachi	CA 6
Hai Wei	Momo	DD
Hakata Maru No. 6		XAM
Hakata Maru No. 7		XAM
Hakaze	Minekaze	DD 5
Hakkai Maru		XARS 4

Name	Class	Symbol
Hakkai Maru		XPG
Hakkaisan Maru		XPG
Hakubi Maru		XPC
Hakusa Maru		XAG
Hakusa Maru		XPC
Hamakaze	Asashio-Kagero	DD 101
Hamanami	Takanami	DD 125
Harukawa Maru		XYN
Harukaze	Kamikaze	DD 18
Haruna	Kongo	BB 4
Harusame	Hatsuharu-Shigure	DD 70
Haruta Maru		XARS 6
Hashidate	Hashidate	PG 6
Hashima	Hashima	ARC 1
Hassen Maru		XPC
Hasu	Kuri-Wakatake	ODD 18
Hatakaze	Kamikaze	DD 21
Hato	Otori	TB 9
Hatsuharu	Hatsuharu-Shigure	DD 60
Hatsukari	Chidori	TB 4
Hatsukaze	Asashio-Kagero	DD 90
Hatsushimo	Hatsuharu-Shigure	DD 61
Hatsutsuki	Terutsuki	DD 112
Hatsutaka	Hatsutaka	CM 7
Hatsuyuki	Fubuki	DD 43
Havant	(see Chao Phya)	AM
Hayabusa	Otori	TB 6
Hayakufuku Maru		XPG
Hayanami	Takanami	DD 124
Hayashio	Asashio-Kagero	DD 93
Hayataka	Hayataka	CV 8
Hayate	Kamikaze	DD 23
Hayatomo	Shiretoko	AO 9
Hayazaki	Hayazaki	AO 11
Heian Maru	Hie Maru	XAS 4
Heijo Maru		XPG
Heiko Maru		XPG
Hibiki	Fubuki	DD 56
Hie Maru	Hie Maru	XAS 3
Hikawa Maru		AH 19
Himeshima Maru		XAM

Name	Class	Symbol
Hinan Maru		XPC
Hino Maru No. 2		XPG
Hinode Maru No. 3		XPC
Hinode Maru No. 5		XPC
Hinode Maru No. 17, 18, 20		XAM
Hinoki	Momo	ODD 2
Hinoki Maru		XYN
Hira	Hira	PR 2
Hirado	Shimushu	PF 16
Hirashima	Yurishima	CMc 26
Hiroshi Maru		XYN
Hirotama Maru		XPG
Hishi	Kuri-Wakatake	ODD 19
Hitaka	Hayataka	CV 9
Hitonose		PG 5
Hiyei	Kongo	BB 2
Hiyodori	Otori	TB 7
Hiyoshi Maru No. 2		XPG
Hoei Maru		XAM
Hoju	Hira	PR 3
Hokaze	Minekaze	DD 9
Hokoku Maru		XPG
Hokoku Maru	Aikoku Maru	XCL 12
Hokoku Maru No. 3		XPC
Hokushin Maru		AH 12
Hokuto Maru		XPC
Hongkong Maru		XPG
Hosho		CVL 1
Hyuga	Ise	BB 8

I

Name	Class	Symbol
I–1–4	I–1	SS
I–5–8	I–5	SS
I–9–14	I–9	SS
I–15–49	I–15	SS
I–52–58	I–52, 54	SS
I–121–124	I–121	SM

Name	Class	Symbol
I–153–160	I–153	SS
I–161–166	I–161	SS
I–168–175	I–168	SS
I–176–	I–176	SS
I–351	I–351	SS
I–361	I–361	SS
I–400	I–400	SS
Iki	Shimushu	PF 15
Ikazuchi	Fubuki	DD 57
Ikuta Maru		XPG
Inazuma	Fubuki	DD 58
Inzan Maru		XPC
Irako		AF 3
Iro	Shiretoko	AO 7
Ise	Ise	BB 7
Ishigaki	Shimushu	PF 4
Ishizaki	Yurishima	CMc 29
Isokaze	Asashio-Kagero	DD 94
Isonami	Fubuki	DD 42
Isshin Maru (?)		XPC
Isuzu	Natori	CL 12
Itsukushima		CM 4
Iwata Maru		XYN
Iwate	Izumo	OCA 5
Iwato Maru		XYN
Izan Maru		XPC
Izumo	Izumo	OCA 4
Izumo Maru	Hayataka	CV 8

J

Name	Class	Symbol
Jikyu Maru		XPC
Jingei	Jingei	AS 2
Jintsu	Sendai	CL 16
Jinyo		CVE 5
Jumbara	Trad	TB
Junzan Maru		XPG

K

Name	Class	Symbol
Kagero	Asashio-Kagero	DD 86
Kahoku Maru		XPG
Kaiyo		CVE 4

ALPHABETICAL INDEX

Name	Class	Symbol
Kaiyo Maru No. 1, 3		XAM
Kaki	Kuri-Wakatake	ODD 11
Kako	Furutaka	CA 2
Kamikaze	Kamikaze	DD 16
Kamikaze Maru		XAPG 3
Kamikawa Maru	Kamikawa Maru	XAV 1
Kamitsu Maru		XPG
Kamogawa Maru	Kamogawa Maru	XAPV 4
Kamoi		CVS 2
Kamome	Tsubame	CMc 13
Kan Maru		XAM
Kan Maru No. 2, 3		XAM
Kanan Maru		XPC
Kanju	Shimushu	PF 13
Kanko Maru		XPG
Karatsu		PR 12
Kari	Otori	TB 11
Karukaya	Kuri-Wakatake	ODD 28
Kasado	Mikura	PF 23
Kasagi Maru		XARS 2
Kasasagi	Otori	TB 8
Kashi	(see Hai Wei)	DD
Kashii	Katori	CL(T) 3
Kashima	Katori	CL(T) 2
Kashi Maru		XYN
Kashin Maru		XPC
Kashino		AF 2
Kashiwa Maru		XYN
Kashiwara Maru	Hayataka	CV 9
Kasuga		OCA 6
Kasuga Maru	Otaka	CVE 1
Kasumi	Asashio-Kagero	DD 84
Katada	Hira	PR 4
Katashima	Toshima	CMc 7
Katoku	Toshima	CMc 3
Katori	Katori	CL(T) 1
Katori Maru		XPG

Name	Class	Symbol
Katsura Maru No. 2		XPG
Katsura Maru		XYN
Katsura Maru		XPC
Katsuragi Maru		XAPV 7
Katsuriki		CM 2
Kawakaze	Hatsuharu-Shigure	DD 74
Kaya	Kuri-Wakatake	ODD 6
Kazegumo	Asashio-Kagero	DD 107
Keiko Maru		XPG
Keinin Maru		XAM
Keishin Maru		XPG
Keiyo Maru	Kamogawa Maru	XAPV 5
Keizan Maru		XPC
Kenkai Maru		XPC
Kensan Maru		XPG
Kiji	Otori	TB 12
Kiku	Kuri-Wakatake	ODD 10
Kiku Maru		XYN
Kikutsuki	Mutsuki	DD 31
Kimikawa Maru	Kamikawa Maru	XAV 3
Kinjo Maru		XCM 4
Kinryu Maru		XCL 13
Kinsui Maru		XPC
Kintoku Maru No. 13		XPC
Kinu	Natori	CL 10
Kinugasa	Aoba	CA 4
Kiri Maru No. 1		XYN
Kiri Maru No. 5		XAM
Kirishima	Kongo	BB 3
Kisaragi	Mutsuki	DD 27
Kishin Maru		XYN
Kishinami	Takanami	DD 127
Kiso	Kuma	CL 6
Kiso Maru		XPG
Kitagami	Kuma	CL 5
Kiyokawa Maru	Kamikawa Maru	XAV 4
Kiyonami	Takanami	DD 122

Name	Class	Symbol
Kiyosumi Maru	Kiyosumi Maru	XCL 2
Koa Maru		XYN
Koa Maru No. 2		XYN
Koai Maru		XYN
Kobi Maru		XCM 5
Koei Maru		XYN
Koei Maru		XYN
Koga Maru		XYM
Kogi Maru		XAM
Koho Maru No. 1-3		AH 9
Kohoku Maru		XYN
Kokai Maru		XYN
Kokko Maru		XPC
Kokuto Maru		AS 1
Komabashi		BB 1
Kongo	Kongo	XAM
Kongo Maru		
Kongo Maru	Kiyosumi Maru	XCL 3
Kongosan Maru		XPG
Korei Maru		XYN
Koshin Maru		XPC
Kosho Maru		XPG
Koshun Maru		XPC
Koshu		AGS 2
Koto Maru		XPG
Kotobuki Maru No. 3		XYN
Kotobuki Maru No. 5		XYN
Kowa Maru		XPG
Kozan Maru		XAM
Kubi Maru		XPC
Kuma	Kuma	CL 3
Kumano	Mogami	CA 16
Kumano Maru		XYN
Kunajiri	Shimushu	PF 2
Kunikawa Maru	Kamikawa Maru	XAV 2
Kurahashi	Mikura	PF 20

Name	Class	Symbol
Kuretake	Kuri-Wakatake	ODD 24
Kuri	Kuri-Wakatake	ODD 7
Kurihashi		ARS 1
Kurokami	Toshima	CMc 8
Kuroshima	Toshima	CMc 2
Kuroshio	Asashio-Kagero	DD 88
Kurozaki	Toshima	CMc 10
Kusakaki	Mikura	PF 24
Kyo Maru No. 1, 3		XAM
Kyo Maru No. 2, 6–8, 10, 13		XPC
Kyodo Maru		XAG
Kyonin Maru No. 1, 2, 3, 5		XAM
Kyosai	Sokuten	CMc 19
Kyuryu Maru		XPC

L

Name	Class	Symbol
LSV 1		LSV
Luzon	(see Karatsu)	PR 12
Lyons Maru		XAPV 6

M

Name	Class	Symbol
Machanu	Virun	SS
Maeklong	Tahchin	PG
Maeshima	Yurishima	CMc 24
Magane Maru		XPG
Maikaze	Asashio-Kagero	DD 103
Makigumo	Asashio-Kagero	DD 106
Makinami	Takanami	DD 117
Maiko	Sumida	PR 10
Mamiya		AF 1
Manazuru	Chidori	TB 2
Manila Maru		AH 10
Manju	Shimushu	PF 12
Manju Maru		XAS 1
Manyo Maru		XPG
Matsu Maru		XYN
Matsuei Maru		XARS 1
Matsukaze	Kamikaze	DD 19

Name	Class	Symbol
Matsuwa	Shimushu	PF 6
Maya	Atago	CA 12
Meigen Maru No. 16, 17		XPC
Meiji Maru No. 1		XPG
Mejima Maru		XAM
Michishio	Asashio-Kagero	DD 79
Mikasa Maru		AH 16
Mikatsuki	Mutsuki	DD 34
Mikura	Mikura	PF 17
Minamiura Maru		XPG
Minatsuki	Mutsuki	DD 32
Minegumo	Asashio-Kagero	DD 82
Minekaze	Minekaze	DD 1
Minsei Maru		XCM 6
Misago Maru No. 1, 3, 8, 11		XAM
Miyake	Mikura	PF 18
Miyo Maru		XAM
Miyuki	Fubuki	DD?
Mizuho Maru		AH 7
Mochitsuki	Mutsuki	DD 35
Mogami	Mogami	CA 13
Mogamigawa Maru	Fujikawa Maru	XAPV 3
Mokuto Maru		XPC
Momo	Momo	ODD 1
Moroshima	Yurishima	CMc 25
Moth (see Suma)		PR 13
Mung Chi (see Asuga)		PG 3
Murakumo	Fubuki	DD 44
Murasame	Hatsuharu-Shigure	DD 68
Muro Maru		AH 14
Muroto	Muroto	AF 4
Musashi	Yamato	BB 12
Musashi Maru		XAM
Musha Maru		XPC
Mutsu	Nagato	BB 10
Mutsuki	Mutsuki	DD 25
Mutsure	Shimushu	PF 9
Myoko	Nachi	CA 7

N

Name	Class	Symbol
Nachi	Nachi	CA 5
Nadakaze	Minekaze	DD 12
Nagae Maru		XYN
Naganami	Takanami	DD 118
Nagara	Natori	CL 9
Nagara Maru		XYN
Nagata Maru		XPG
Nagato	Nagato	BB 9
Nagato Maru		XPC
Nagatsuki	Mutsuki	DD 33
Nagaura		ARS 5
Nagoya Maru		XAPV 8
Naka	Sendai	CL 17
Nakkai Maru		XPG
Namikaze	Minekaze	DD 13
Nampo Maru		XPG
Nanko Maru		XPC
Nariu	Sokuten	CMc 20
Naruo Maru		XAM
Naruto	Shiretoko	AO 10
Naruto Maru		XAPV 9
Nasami	Natsushima	CMc 15
Nashi	Kuri-Wakatake	ODD 4
Natori	Natori	CL 8
Natsugumo	Asashio-Kagero	DD 83
Natsushima	Natsushima	CMc 14
Natsushio	Asashio-Kagero	DD 91
Nenohi	Hatsuharu-Shigure	DD 62
Nichiyu Maru		XCM 3
Nihonkai Maru		XPG
Niitsuki	Terutsuki	DD 114
Ning Hai	Ning Hai	CL
Ninoshima	Toshima	CMc 11
Nippon Maru No. 2		XPC
Nire	Kuri-Wakatake	ODD 8
Niro Maru		XYN
Nissho Maru No. 2, 12, 16		XPG

ALPHABETICAL INDEX

Name	Class	Symbol
Nissho Maru No. 3, 5		XYN
Nissho Maru No. 6		XPC
Nisso Maru		XAS 8
Nisui Maru		XPC
Nitta Maru (see Chuyo)		
Nitto Maru No. 3, 5, 8–12, 15–22		XPC
Niura Maru		XAM
Nohi Maru		XPC
Nojima	Muroto	AF 5
Nokaze	Minekaze	DD 15
Noni Maru		XPC
Noshiro	Agano	CL 23
Noshiro Maru		XCL 1
Noshiro Maru No. 2		XAM
Notoro		CVS 1
Notto Maru No. 3		XPC
Nowaki	Asashio-Kagero	DD 100
Noyagi Maru		XPC
Numakaze	Minekaze	DD 14
Nuwashima	Yurishima	CMc 23

O

Name	Class	Symbol
Oboro	Fubuki	DD 53
Odate	Hashima	ARC 4
Oi	Kuma	CL 7
Oi Maru		XAM
Oite	Kamikaze	DD 22
Oki	Shimushu	PF 8
Okikaze	Minekaze	DD 2
Okinami	Takanami	DD 126
Okinoshima		CM 6
Okitsu Maru		XAV 7
Okuyo Maru		XPG
Onami	Takanami	DD 120
Ondo	Shiretoko	AO 8
Op Ten Noort (see Teno Maru)		AH 15

Name	Class	Symbol
Ose		AO
Osei Maru		XYN
Oshima		AR 3
Oshio	Asashio-Kagero	DD 78
Otaka	Otaka	CVE 1
Otomari		AG 2
Otori	Otori	TB 5
Otowa Maru		XAM
Owari		BB?
Oyashio	Asashio-Kagero	DD 89
Oyo Maru		XPC
Oyodo		CL 22

P

Name	Class	Symbol
Pattani	Trad	TB
PC 1–3	PC 1	PC
PC 4–12	PC 4	PC
PC 13–49	PC 13	PC
PC 50–60	PC 50	PC
Peking Maru		XPG
Phra Ruang	"Thornycroft"	DD
Ping Hai	Ning Hai	CL
PT 1–6	PT–1	PT
PT 101–113	PT–101	PT
Puket	Trad	TB
PT10–	PT–10	PT
PT201–	PT–201	PT

R

Name	Class	Symbol
Ransan Maru		XAM
Ranyo Maru		XPC
Ratanakosindra	Ratanakosindra	
Rayong	Trad	TB
Reisui Maru		XAM
Rikoku Maru		XPC
Rikuzen Maru		XAM
Rio De Janeiro Maru		XAS 5
RO 29–32	RO–29	SM

Name	Class	Symbol
RO 33–34	RO–33	OSS
RO 35	RO–35	OSS
RO 57–59	RO–57	OSS
RO 60–68	RO–60	OSS
RO 100	RO–100	OSS
RO 500	RO–500	SS
Rokko Maru		XAM
Rokuan	Hayazaki	AO 14
Royo Maru		XPC
Rumoi Maru		XAM
Ruyi Maru		XPC
Ryo Maru		XPC
Ryosui Maru		XPC
Ryuho	Zuiho	CVL 4
Ryui Maru		XPC
Ryuko Maru		AH 20

S

Name	Class	Symbol
Sado	Shimushu	PF 7
Saga		PG 2
Sagara Maru	Sanuki Maru	XAV 9
Sagi	Otori	TB 10
Sagiri	Fubuki	DD 51
Sagishu Maru		XPC
Saigon Maru	Bangkok Maru	XCL 6
Saikyo Maru		XPG
Saishu	Yurishima	CMc 31
Saishu Maru No. 1, 2, 6, 7		XAM
Samidare	Hatsuharu-Shigure	DD 71
Samui		AO
Sanaye	Kuri-Wakatake	ODD 25
Sankyo Maru		XPC
Sansui Maru		XYN
Santo Maru		XPG
Santos Maru (see Manju Maru)		XAS
Sanuki Maru	Sanuki Maru	XAV 8
Sanyo Maru		XAV 5

Name	Class	Symbol	Name	Class	Symbol	Name	Class	Symbol
Saruhashi		ARS 3	Shiragane		ARS 4	Soyo Maru		XAS 9
Sarushima	Natsushima	CMc 16	Shirakami	Sokuten	CMc 18	Sozan Maru		XPC
Sata	Shiretoko	AO 4	Shirakumo	Fubuki	DD 41	Sri Ayudhya	Dhamburi	
Satsuki	Mutsuki	DD 26	Shiranami	Takanami	DD 128	Suijo Maru		XPC
Sawakaze	Minekaze	DD 4	Shiranuhi	Asashio-Kagero	DD 87	Sukhodaya	Ratanakosindra	
Sawarabi	Kuri-Wakatake	ODD (?)	Shirataka		CM 3	Suma		PR 13
Sazanami	Fubuki	DD 55	Shiratsuyu	Hatsuharu-Shigure	DD 67	Sumida	Sumida	PR 8
SCS 1–50	SCS 1	SCS	Shirayuki	Fubuki	DD 39	Sumire	Kuri-Wakatake	ODD 22
SCS 51–100	SCS 51	SCS	Shiretoko	Shiretoko	AO 2	Sunosaki		AO 1
SCS 101–117	SCS 101	SCS	Shiriya	Shiretoko	AO 6	Surasdra	Trad	TB
SCS 151–165	SCS 151		Shitamatsu Maru		XYN	Suzukaze	Hatsuharu-Shigure	DD 73
Seattle Maru		AH 4	Shoei Maru		XPG	Suzuki	Kuri-Wakatake	ODD 14
Seian Maru		XYN	Shoei Maru		XYN	Suzunami	Takanami	DD 119
Seikai Maru		XPG	Shoei Maru No. 2		XPG	Suzutsuki	Terutsuki	DD 110
Seiko Maru		XYN	Shofuku Maru		XPC	Suzuya	Mogami	CA 15
Seikyo Maru		XPG	Shofuku Maru		XYN			
Sendai	Sendai	CL 15	Shoho	Zuiho	CVL 3	**T**		
Senyo Maru		XPG	Shokaku	Shokaku	CV 6			
Senyu Maru No. 2		XAM	Shoko Maru		XPG	Tachibana Maru		AH 21
Senyu Maru No. 3		XAM	Shonan Maru No.		XPC	Tachikaze	Minekaze	DD 11
Seta	Hira	PR 5	1–8, 11, 12, 15,			Tade	Kuri-Wakatake	ODD 20
Settsu		AG 1	17			Tahchin	Tahchin	PG
Shigure	Hatsuharu-Shigure	DD 66	Shonan Maru No.		XAM	Taian Maru		XAM
Shikinami	Fubuki	DD 46	16			Taigei	(see Ryuho)	
Shimakaze	Minekaze	DD 3	Shosei Maru		XPG	Taihei Maru		XAM
Shimotsuki	Terutsuki	DD 111	Shosei Maru		XYN	Taiho		CV 10
Shimpei Maru No.		XPC	Shotoku Maru		XPG	Taiko Maru		XAM
1			Showa Maru		XPC	Taishu Maru		XYN
Shimushu	Shimushu	PF 1	Showa Maru No.		XPC	Takachiho		AV 1
Shinfuku Maru		XPG	2, 3, 5, 6			Takachiho Maru		XCM 7
Shinko Maru		XCM 8	Showa Maru No.		XAM	Takanami	Takanami	DD 116
Shinko Maru		XPC	7, 8			Takao	Atago	CA 10
Shinko Maru No. 1		XPG	Shuri Maru		XAGP 1	Takasago Maru		XAM
Shinko Maru No. 2		XPG	Siberia Maru		AH 5	Takasago Maru		AH 22
Shinkyo Maru		XPG	Silvercypress (see		XAV 6	Takasaki	Zuiho	CVL 2
Shinonome	Fubuki	DD 38	Yasukawa Maru)			Takasaki Maru		XAPV10
Shinran Maru		XPC	Sinsamudar	Virun	SS	Takashima	Yurishima	CMc 27
Shinsho Maru		XAGP 2	Sobun Maru		XPC	Takashima Maru		XAM
Shinto Maru No.		XYN	Sokuten	Sokuten	CMc 17	No. 2, 3		
2			Sonobe Maru		XAM	Take	Kuri-Wakatake	ODD 5
Shintohoku Maru		XAM	Sosui Maru		XPC	Takunan Maru		XAM
Shiokaze	Minekaze	DD 10	Soya		AGS 4	No. 1, 3, 8		

ALPHABETICAL INDEX

Name	Class	Symbol
Takunan Maru No. 2, 5–7, 10		XPC
Tama	Kuma	CL 4
Tama Maru		XAM
Tama Maru No. 3, 5–7		XAM
Tama Maru No. 8		XPC
Tamae Maru		XYN
Tamanami	Takanami	DD 123
Tamasono Maru No. 1–3		XAM
Tamura Maru		XAM
Tanikaze	Asashio-Kagero	DD 102
Tatara		PR 11
Tateishi	Hashima	ARC 3
Tatsu Maru		XYN
Tatsuharu Maru	Tatsuharu Maru	XCM 9
Tatsumiya Maru	Tatsuharu Maru	XCM 10
Tatsuta	Tenryu	CL 2
Teiun Maru		XPG
Teno Maru		AH 15
Tenryu	Tenryu	CL 1
Tenyo Maru		XCM 1
Tenzan Maru No. 2		XPC
Terushima Maru		XPG
Terutsuki	Terutsuki	DD 108
Thracian	Admiralty "S"	
Toba		PR 1
Toga Maru		XAM
Tokitsukaze	Asashio-Kagero	DD 96
Tokiwa		CM 1
Tokiwa Maru		XPG
Toko Maru No. 1		XYN
Tokoho Maru No. 5, 10		XAM
Tokunan Maru No. 5		XPC
Tomitsu Maru		XPG
Tomozuru	Chidori	TB 3
Tone	Tone	CA 17
Torijima Maru		XAM
Tosan Maru		XPG
Toseki Maru		XPC
Toshi Maru		XAM
Toshi Maru No. 2, 5, 7, 8		XAM
Toshi Maru No. 3		XPC
Toshima	Toshima	CMc 1
Tosho Maru		XPG
Toyo Maru		ARC 5
Toyo Maru No. 3		XYN
Toyokuni Maru		XPG
Trad	Trad	TB
Tsubame	Tsubame	CMc 12
Tsuga	Kuri-Wakatake	ODD 12
Tsurugisaki (see Shoho)		
Tsukai Maru		XPC
Tsukushi		AGS 3
Tsurumi	Shiretoko	AO 5
Tsuran Maru		XPC
Tsurushima	Hashima	ARC 2
Tsushima	Shimushu	PF 14
Tsuta	Kuri-Wakatake	ODD 17

U

Name	Class	Symbol
Uji	Hashidate	PG 7
Uji Maru		XYN
Unkai Maru		XPG
Ukishima	Sokuten	CMc 21
Ukishima Maru		XCL 4
Umikaze	Hatsuharu-Shigure	DD 75
Unyo	Otaka	CVE 2
Unyo Maru		XPG
Urai Maru		XPC
Urakami Maru		XAS 7
Urakaze	Asashio-Kagero	DD 97
Ural Maru		AH 18
Uranami	Fubuki	DD 49
Ushio	Fubuki	DD 52
Usugumo	Fubuki	DD 40
Uzuki	Mutsuki	DD 29

V

Name	Class	Symbol
"V" Type, Fuel Oil Barge		
Virun	Virun	SS

W

Name	Class	Symbol
"W" Type, Fuel Oil Barge		
Wabi Maru		XPC
Wakaba	Hatsuharu-Shigure	DD 63
Wakamiya	Shimushu	PF 10
Wakamiya Maru		XYN
Wakataka	Hatsutaka	CM 9
Wakatake	Kuri-Wakatake	ODD 23
Wakatsuki	Terutsuki	DD 113
Wake (see Tatara)		PR 11
Washizaki	Toshima	CMc 5
Witte De With	Van Ghent	DD

X

Name	Class	Symbol
"X" Type, Fuel Oil Barge		

Y

Name	Class	Symbol
"Y" Type, Fuel Oil Barge		
Yachiyo Maru		XAM
Yaeyama		CM 5
Yahagi	Agano	CL 24
Yakaze	Minekaze	DD 6
Yakumo		OCA 2
Yamabato Maru		ARC 6
Yamabiko Maru		XARS 3
Yamagumo	Asashio-Kagero	DD 81
Yamakaze	Hatsuharu-Shigure	DD 72

Name	Class	Symbol	Name	Class	Symbol	Name	Class	Symbol
Yamato	Yamato	BB 11	Yomogi	Kuri-Wakatake	ODD 21	Yura	Natori	CL 11
Yanagi	Momo	ODD 3	Yoshida Maru		XPG	Yurishima	Yurishima	CMc 22
Yasukawa Maru		XAV 6	Yoshido Maru		XAM	Yushio Maru		XARS 7
Yasukuni Maru		XAS 2	Yoshino Maru		AH 2	Yuzuki	Mutsuki	DD 36
Yat Sen		PG	Yubari		CL 14			
Yawata Maru (see Unyo)			Yudachi	Hatsuharu-Shigure	DD 69	**Z**		
Yayoi	Mutsuki	DD 28	Yugao	Kuri-Wakatake	ODD 29			
Yobai Maru		XPC	Yugiri	Fubuki	DD 50	Zuiho	Zuiho	CVL 2
Yodo		AGS 1	Yugumo	Asashio-Kagero	DD 104	Zuikaku	Shokaku	CV 7
Yodohashi		ARS 2	Yugure	Hatsuharu-Shigure	DD 65	Zuiko Maru		XPC
Yoko Maru		XPC	Yukaze	Minekaze	DD 8	Zuiko Maru		XPG
			Yukikaze	Asashio-Kagero	DD 92	Zuisho Maru		XYN
			Yunagi	Kamikaze	DD 24			

16—42452–1   U. S. GOVERNMENT PRINTING OFFICE

LIST OF STANDARD IDENTIFICATION PUBLICATIONS

WARSHIP MANUALS

*ONI 41–42 Series	—Japanese Naval Vessels (includes booklets on each category)
*ONI 54 Series	—U. S. Naval Vessels (includes booklets on each category)
*ONI 201 Series	—Warships of the British Commonwealth (includes booklets on each category)
ONI 202	—Italian Naval Vessels
ONI 203	—French Naval Vessels
ONI 204	—German Naval Vessels
ONI 205–235	—Russian Naval Vessels and Aircraft
ONI 206	—Warships of the Minor European Navies
ONI 222	—Statistical Data on Navies
FM 30–50	—Recognition Pictorial Manual on Naval Vessels

*Replacing ONI 41–42, ONI 54–R, and ONI 201, respectively.

SUBMARINE MANUALS

ONI 220–J	—Japanese Submarines
ONI 220–G	—German Submarines

LANDING CRAFT MANUAL

ONI 225–J	—Japanese Landing Operations and Equipment

MERCHANT SHIP MANUALS

ONI 208–C	—Caribbean Small Craft
ONI 208–J	—Japanese Merchant Vessels
ONI 208–J (Suppl. 2)	—Far Eastern Small Craft
ONI 208–R	—Russian Merchant Vessels

AIRCRAFT MANUALS

ONI 232	—Japanese Military Aircraft
ONI 233	—Italian Military Aircraft
ONI 234	—German Military Aircraft
FM 30–30	—Aircraft Recognition Pictorial Manual

RECOGNITION PUBLICATIONS

ONI 223	—Ship Shapes—A Warship Primer
ONI 223–M	—Merchant Ship Shapes—A Merchant Ship Primer
ONI 229, JAN No. 3	{ —Japanese Merchant Shipping Tonnage and Identification / —Japanese Warship Recognition

UNIFORMS

JAN No. 1	—Uniforms and Insignia

CHARTS

GN Series	—German Naval Vessels
*JN Series	—Japanese Naval Vessels
UN Series	—U. S. Naval Vessels
*BN Series	—British Naval Vessels
*U. S. Naval Aircraft	
*U. S. Army Aircraft	
*British Aircraft	
*Japanese Aircraft	
German Aircraft	
Italian Aircraft	
*Standard Merchant Vessel Types	

*Undergoing revision.

AIRCARDS and BULLETINS—8″ x 8″ for CARDEX file

Published in this size are complete series on U. S., Japanese, German, and British Naval Vessels and Aircraft, as well as individual "spot bulletins" on new types of warships, merchantmen, and combat aircraft. A complete list is available upon request.

STANDARD PUBLICATIONS (CONFIDENTIAL) EXIST ON THESE SUBJECTS—

Statistical Summary of Japanese Naval Vessels
German and Japanese Submarine Equipment
Allied Landing Craft and Ships
Manual of Merchant Ships
Various identification and technical studies

ONI 41-42

JAPANESE NAVAL VESSELS

DIVISION OF NAVAL INTELLIGENCE—IDENTIFICATION AND CHARACTERISTICS SECTION

ONI 41-42—JAPANESE NAVAL VESSELS

1. ONI 41-42, Japanese Naval Vessels, is now issued for the first time in the standard loose-leaf form so as to provide greater flexibility and to permit it being incorporated, in whole or part, in the standard U. S. Navy Task Binder. For greater compactness the earlier separate editions of ONI 41 (Surface Views) and ONI 42 (Aerial Views) are now combined for the first time in one manual.

2. As presently issued, ONI 41-42 does not provide complete coverage for the Japanese Navy, and the older editions should be retained until all extant ships described therein have been issued in the new edition. Thereafter the older manuals can be retained or disposed of as the Commanding Officer may elect. A Table of Contents, to be included in an early shipment, will serve as a guide in determining the coverage of this new manual at all times. Under the ever-changing conditions of war it is not now possible, and it never will be possible, to provide complete and definitive coverage for any of the world's navies. While old ships are being lost and new ships are being completed, the vessels in service are constantly being altered in appearance.

3. While the first purpose of all these ONI manuals on the men-of-war of the principal naval powers is for timely and un-mistakable identification and the early estimation of target angle, it is believed that they can be of great tactical value. This and future editions, therefore, will include not only photographs and other illustrations but will contain data regarding the military characteristics of enemy men-of-war. Through these publications and similar media the Division of Naval Intelligence for several months has been trying to provide the fighting forces with all possible information that will assist them in determining whether the stranger is friend or foe and, if the latter, to provide the data for striking under favorable conditions or otherwise reaching a sound decision.

4. ONI 41-42 is being prepared from the best information available to the Navy Department. In the main it is based upon published material and reconnaissance photographs. Except for fragmentary addenda which may be uncovered, the first source has been exhausted. It is expected that future editions will derive largely from reconnaissance photographs and contributions (sketches and descriptions) from combat personnel. Thus, since the proper means are at hand for analyzing, processing, publishing and promptly distributing these manuals, their value will be almost entirely dependent upon the quantity and quality of material received from the Front.

/S/ H. C. TRAIN
CAPTAIN, U. S. NAVY
DIRECTOR OF NAVAL INTELLIGENCE

ONI 41-42

TABLE OF CONTENTS

DIVISION OF NAVAL INTELLIGENCE—IDENTIFICATION AND CHARACTERISTICS SECTION—DECEMBER, 1942

CHARTS

1. PANORAMA OF THE JAPANESE NAVY
2. PRINCIPAL COMBATANT TYPES
3. CHARACTERISTICS OF JAPANESE NAVAL VESSELS
4. NIP NOTES
5. MISTAKEN IDENTITY
6. JAPANESE NAVAL ORDNANCE
7. JAPANESE NAVAL AIRCRAFT
8. JAPANESE RAIDERS
9. JAPANESE NAVAL CAMOUFLAGE
10. JAPANESE RECOGNITION MARKINGS AND SIGNALS
11. JAPANESE LANDING CRAFT

TABLES

1. STRATEGICAL AND TACTICAL DATA OF THE JAPANESE NAVY
2. LIST OF NAVAL VESSELS BY DESIGN CLASSES

HISTORY OF JAPANESE NAVY

SHIP JACKETS

BB 1–4	KONGO CLASS
BB 5	FUSO
BB 6	YAMASHIRO
BB 7, 8	ISE CLASS
BB 9–10	NAGATO CLASS
BB 11	YAMATO
BB 12	MUSASHI
CV 1	HOSHO
CV 4	RYUJO
CV 7, 8	SHOKAKU CLASS
CV 9	ZUIHO
CV 11, 12	HITAKA CLASS
CVS 1	NOTORO
CVS 2	KAMOI
CVS 3, 4	CHITOSE CLASS
CVS 6, 7	MIZUHO CLASS

CA 1, 2	FURUTAKA CLASS
CA 3, 4	AOBA CLASS
CA 5–8	NACHI CLASS
CA 9, 10	ATAGO CLASS A
CA 11, 12	ATAGO CLASS B
CA 13–16	MOGAMI CLASS
CA 17, 18	TONE CLASS
CA 19	AGANO
CL 1, 2	TENRYU CLASS
CL 3–7	KUMA CLASS
CL 8–13	NATORI CLASS
CL 14	YUBARI
CL 15–17	SENDAI CLASS
CL 18–20	KATORI CLASS
DD 1–15	MINEKAZE CLASS
DD 16–24	KAMIKAZE CLASS
DD 25–36	MUTSUKI CLASS
DD 37–44	FUBUKI CLASS (SHINONOME GROUP)
DD 45–55	FUBUKI CLASS (AMAGIRI GROUP)
DD 56–59	FUBUKI CLASS (HIBIKI GROUP)
DD 60–65	HATSUHARU CLASS
DD 66–75	SHIGURE CLASS
DD 76–85	ASASHIO CLASS
DD 86–117	KAGERO CLASS
DD 118–	UNKNOWN CLASS NO. 1
ODD 4–22	MOMI CLASS
ODD 23–29	WAKATAKE CLASS
SS 1	I 151
SS 2	I 152
SS 3–14	I 153 CLASS
SS 15–18	I-1 CLASS
SS 19–21	I 165 CLASS
SS 22	I 5
SS 23	I 6
SS 24–31	I 168 CLASS
SS 32–33	I 7 CLASS
SS 34–69	I 9 CLASS
SS 70–79	I 76 CLASS
SS 80–86	I 101 CLASS
SS 87–94	I 176 CLASS
OSS 10–12	RO 51 CLASS
OSS 13–21	RO 60 CLASS
OSS 22–26	RO 33 CLASS
OSS 27–34	RO 100 CLASS
SM 2–4	RO 29 CLASS
SM 5–8	I 121 CLASS

OCA 1	ASAMA
OCA 2	YAKUMO
OCA 3	AZUMA
OCA 4, 5	IWATE CLASS
OCA 6	KASUGA
CM 1	TOKIWA
CM 2	KATSURIKI
CM 3	SHIRATAKA
CM 4	ITSUKUSHIMA
CM 5	YAEYAMA
CM 7–10	HATSUTAKA CLASS
CM 11–15	SHIMUSHU CLASS
AM 1–6	NO. 1 CLASS
AM 7–12	NO. 13 CLASS
AM 13–18	NO. 7 CLASS
AM 19–24	NO. 19 CLASS
TB 1–4	CHIDORI CLASS
TB 5–12	OTORI CLASS
PG 1	YODO
PG 2	SAGA
PG 3	ASUGA
PG 4	ATAKA
PG 5	HITONOSE
PG 6, 7	HASHIDATE CLASS
PG	SEIZURES
PR 1–12	
PC 1–	
PT 1–	
PY 1–	TRAWLERS
	MISCELLANEOUS MINOR COMBATANT TYPES
ACV 1, 2	OTAKA CLASS
AV 1, 2	KAMIKAWA MARU CLASS
AV 3, 4	KINUGASA MARU
AV 5–15	

MISCELLANEOUS AIRCRAFT AUXILIARIES
TENDERS
FUEL—STORE—CARGO SHIPS
TRANSPORTS AND LANDING CRAFT
BASE CRAFT
MISCELLANEOUS AUXILIARIES
UNCLASSIFIED TYPES
DISTRICTS CRAFT

AERIAL VIEWS

MISCELLANEOUS PHOTOGRAPHS
NEW SHIPS HITHERTO UNKNOWN

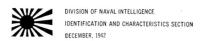

DIVISION OF NAVAL INTELLIGENCE
IDENTIFICATION AND CHARACTERISTICS SECTION
DECEMBER, 1942

NIP NOTES

BATTLESHIPS

when JAP BBs

sail off to glory

they almost always

add a story

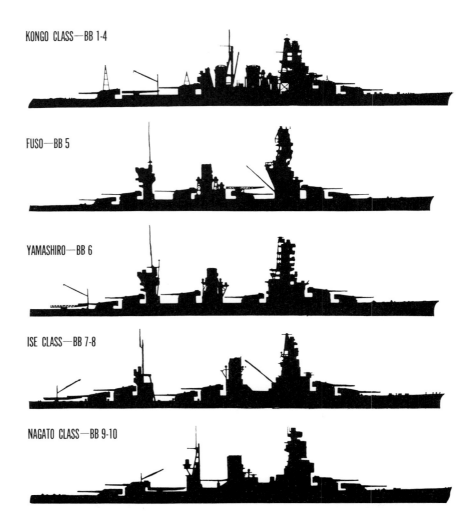

KONGO CLASS—BB 1-4

FUSO—BB 5

YAMASHIRO—BB 6

ISE CLASS—BB 7-8

NAGATO CLASS—BB 9-10

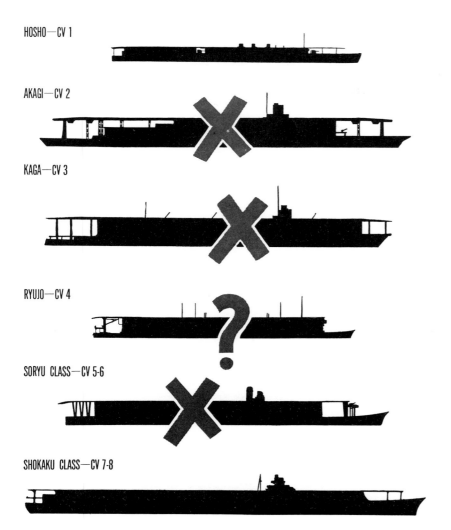

HOSHO—CV 1

AKAGI—CV 2

KAGA—CV 3

RYUJO—CV 4

SORYU CLASS—CV 5-6

SHOKAKU CLASS—CV 7-8

if they have upper works at all

the JAP'S CV'S are very small

and bow or stern

approach to some

suggests a

nagasaki slum

HEAVY CRUISERS

the **NIPS** big cruisers'

forward stack

is always fat

and falling back

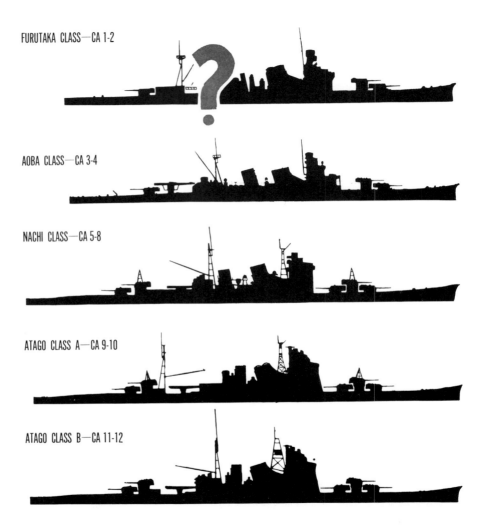

FURUTAKA CLASS—CA 1-2

AOBA CLASS—CA 3-4

NACHI CLASS—CA 5-8

ATAGO CLASS A—CA 9-10

ATAGO CLASS B—CA 11-12

MOGAMI CLASS—CA 13-16

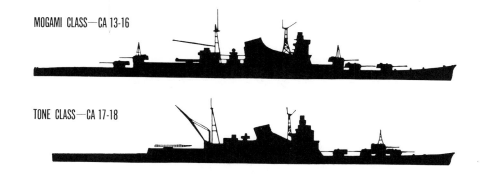

TONE CLASS—CA 17-18

CHIKUMA is a TONE(Y) craft

four turrets fore, a ski-slide aft

it's well with these

in mind to carry

the "hornpipe" of

CL YUBARI

YUBARI—CL 14

LIGHT CRUISERS

NATORI CLASS—CL 8-13

SENDAI CLASS—CL 15-17

all the NATORI cruisers show

three stocky nippos in a row

and SENDAI with her sisters bore,

when last observed, a row of four

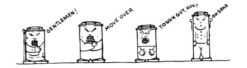

KUMA CLASS—CL 3-7

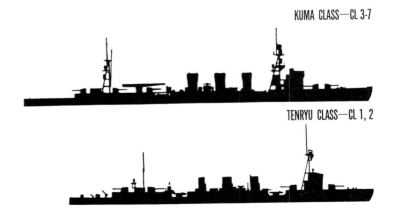

TENRYU CLASS—CL 1, 2

the KUMA class

has for its share

three stacks wide-flared

for anti-flare

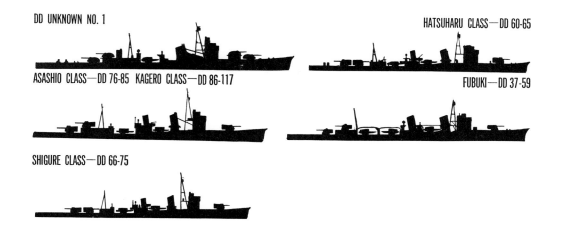

DD UNKNOWN NO. 1

HATSUHARU CLASS—DD 60-65

ASASHIO CLASS—DD 76-85 KAGERO CLASS—DD 86-117

FUBUKI—DD 37-59

SHIGURE CLASS—DD 66-75

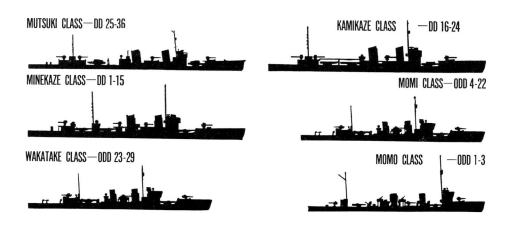

MUTSUKI CLASS—DD 25-36

KAMIKAZE CLASS —DD 16-24

MINEKAZE CLASS—DD 1-15

MOMI CLASS—ODD 4-22

WAKATAKE CLASS—ODD 23-29

MOMO CLASS —ODD 1-3

the newer N ip DD combines

sharp raking stacks and wavy lines

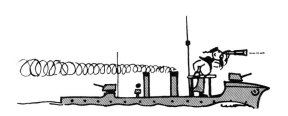

the older ships have upright stacks

and all their bows have turtle-backs

NIP

NOTES

ONI 41-42

RANGE TABLE

DIVISION OF NAVAL INTELLIGENCE—IDENTIFICATION AND CHARACTERISTICS SECTION—OCTOBER, 1942

ESTIMATION OF RANGE BY OBSERVING THE AMOUNT OF SHIP SEEN ABOVE OR BELOW THE HORIZON.

EXPLANATION—TABLE OF DISTANCES OF SEA HORIZON.

THE DISTANCE CORRESPONDING TO THE POSITION AT WHICH THE HORIZON LINE CUTS THE SHIP PROFILE SHOULD BE FILLED IN FROM THE TABLE FOR THE OBSERVER AS FOLLOWS:

THE COLUMN "SHIP BEYOND THE HORIZON" SHOULD SHOW THE SUM OF THE DISTANCES OF THE SEA HORIZON (a) FOR HEIGHT OF EYE, (b) FOR HEIGHTS OF THE RESPECTIVE HORIZON LINES BEHIND THE PROFILE.

THE COLUMN "HORIZON BEYOND THE SHIP" SHOULD SHOW THE DIFFERENCE OF THESE TWO DISTANCES.

EXAMPLE—THE OBSERVER'S HEIGHT OF EYE IS 79 FEET. A SHIP IS SIGHTED BEYOND THE HORIZON WITH THE HORIZON LINE CUTTING ITS PROFILE AT A POINT 15 FEET ABOVE THE WATERLINE.

DISTANCE OF SEA HORIZON FOR 79′=20,610 YDS.
DISTANCE OF SEA HORIZON FOR 15′= 8,980 YDS.
SUM=RANGE OF SHIP   =29,590 YDS.

HEIGHT IN FEET	DISTANCE OF SEA HORIZON	HEIGHT IN FEET	DISTANCE OF SEA HORIZON	HEIGHT IN FEET	DISTANCE OF SEA HORIZON	HEIGHT IN FEET	DISTANCE OF SEA HORIZON	HEIGHT IN FEET	DISTANCE OF SEA HORIZON	HEIGHT IN FEET	DISTANCE OF SEA HORIZON
1	2,320	21	10,630	41	14,840	61	18,110	81	20,870	101	23,300
2	3,280	22	10,880	42	15,020	62	18,260	82	20,990	102	23,420
3	4,020	23	11,120	43	15,200	63	18,400	83	21,120	103	23,530
4	4,640	24	11,360	44	15,380	64	18,550	84	21,250	104	23,640
5	5,190	25	11,590	45	15,550	65	18,690	85	21,380	105	23,760
6	5,680	26	11,820	46	15,720	66	18,840	86	21,500	106	23,870
7	6,140	27	12,050	47	15,890	67	18,980	87	21,630	107	23,980
8	6,560	28	12,270	48	16,060	68	19,120	88	21,750	108	24,090
9	6,960	29	12,490	49	16,230	69	19,260	89	21,870	109	24,200
10	7,330	30	12,700	50	16,400	70	19,400	90	21,990	110	24,320
11	7,690	31	12,910	51	16,560	71	19,540	91	22,120	111	24,430
12	8,030	32	13,120	52	16,720	72	19,670	92	22,240	112	24,540
13	8,360	33	13,320	53	16,880	73	19,810	93	22,360	113	24,650
14	8,680	34	13,520	54	17,040	74	19,940	94	22,480	114	24,750
15	8,980	35	13,720	55	17,200	75	20,080	95	22,600	115	24,860
16	9,280	36	13,910	56	17,350	76	20,210	96	22,720	116	24,970
17	9,560	37	14,100	57	17,500	77	20,340	97	22,830	117	25,080
18	9,840	38	14,290	58	17,660	78	20,480	98	22,950	118	25,180
19	10,110	39	14,480	59	17,810	79	20,610	99	23,070	119	25,290
20	10,370	40	14,670	60	17,960	80	20,740	100	23,180	120	25,400

RANGE AT 20° YDS.	RANGE AT 25° YDS.	RANGE AT 30° YDS.	RANGE AT 35° YDS.	MAXIMUM SURFACE RANGE YDS.	MAXIMUM AA CEILING FT.	RATE OF FIRE PER MIN.	A. P. PENETRATION IN INCHES AT 90°					
							5,000 YDS.	10,000 YDS.	15,000 YDS.	20,000 YDS.	25,000 YDS.	30,000 YDS.
26,900	30,500	33,600	36,000	36,000					17.9	14.4	11.9	10.1
24,300	27,500	30,000	31,950	31,950				16.6	12.8	9.8	7.8	6.5
23,400	26,100	28,400	30,300	32,600				8.7	6.2	4.6	3.5	2.8
16,000	17,800	19,300	20,640	20,640		1.2	8.6	4.8	3.3	2.5		
17,300	19,300	20,900	22,100	23,550		6	6.9	3.8	2.6	1.9		
14,200				14,200		8	5.0	3.0	2.2			
17,300	19,100	20,700	21,900	23,500		12	6.6	3.7	2.5	1.8		
16,200	17,900	19,350	20,350	21,030	33,000		5.3	2.8	1.8	1.5		
13,820	15,200	16,300	17,200	17,900	25,000				1.4			
14,800	16,300	17,500	18,450	19,400			4.2	2.0	1.2			
13,390	14,790	15,900	16,679	17,580			3.6	1.7				
10,800						8	2.5	1.5				
9,000	10,000	10,700	11,250	11,600	20,000		1.1	.6				
			8,000									

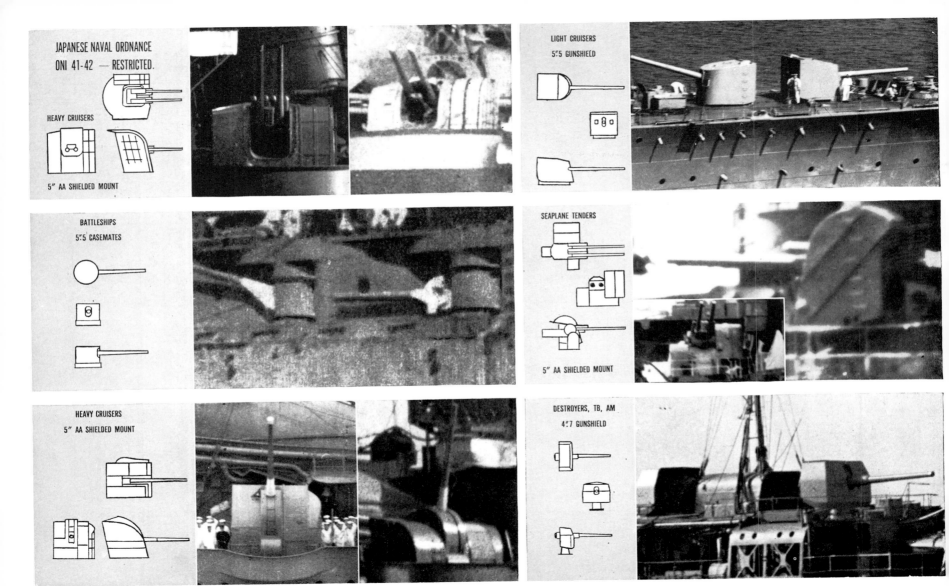

JAPANESE NAVAL ORDNANCE
ONI 41-42 — RESTRICTED.

HEAVY CRUISERS

5" AA SHIELDED MOUNT

BATTLESHIPS
5".5 CASEMATES

HEAVY CRUISERS
5" AA SHIELDED MOUNT

LIGHT CRUISERS
5".5 GUNSHIELD

SEAPLANE TENDERS

5" AA SHIELDED MOUNT

DESTROYERS, TB, AM
4".7 GUNSHIELD

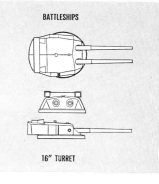

BATTLESHIPS

16" TURRET

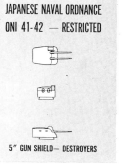

5" GUN SHIELD— DESTROYERS

BATTLESHIPS
14" TURRET

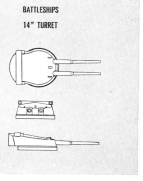

CL YUBARI
5".5 GUN SHIELD

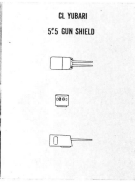

HEAVY CRUISERS
8" TURRET

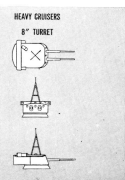

DESTROYERS
5" GUN SHIELD

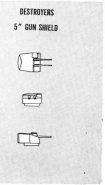

JAPANESE NAVAL ORDNANCE

DIVISION OF NAVAL INTELLIGENCE—IDENTIFICATION AND CHARACTERISTICS SECTION—JULY, 1943

SHIPS AND NUMBER OF ARMAMENT	NOMINAL BORE	CALIBER	ACTUAL BORE	WEIGHT PROJ. POUNDS	MUZZLE VELOCITY FT./SEC.	MAXIMUM ELEVATION
BB—TOSA, MUSASHI, OWARI, YAMATO—9	16″		16″ ?			
BB—NAGATO CLASS—8	16″	45	16″	2,205	2,592	35°
BB—ISE, FUSO CLASSES—12, KONGO CLASS—8	14″	45	14″	1,400	2,592	35°
CA—AOBA CLASS—6, TONE CLASS—8, NACHI, ATAGO, MOGAMI—10	8″	50	7.87″	254	2,789	45°
OCA—IWATE CLASS, YAKUMO—4	8″	40	7.87″	100	2,580	35°
BB—KONGO CLASS—14, FUSO CLASS—16	6″	50	5.9″	100	2,789	45°
OCA—IWATE CLASS, YAKUMO—8	6″	40	5.9″	84	2,296	20°
BB—ISE CLASS—16, NAGATO CLASS—18, CV—HOSHO—4, CVS—KAMOI—2 CL—TENRYU, KATORI CLASSES—4, KUMA, NATORI, SENDAI CLASSES—7 CL—YUBARI—6, SS—I 1-4, I 7, 8—2, I 9-41, I 121-124—1	5.5″	50	5.5″	63	2,789	45°
BB—KONGO, FUSO, ISE, NAGATO CLASSES—8 CV—SHOKAKU, HITAKA CLASSES—16, CVS—CHITOSE, MIZUHO CLASSES—4 CA—NACHI, MOGAMI, TONE CLASSES—8, CL—KATORI CLASS—2 DD—TERATSUKI CLASS—8, ASASHIO, FUBUKI CLASSES—6, HATSUHARU, SHIGURE CLASSES—5 SS—I 5, 6—1	5″	50	5.12″	45	2,900	AA—85°
CVS—NOTORO—2, CA—FURUTAKA, AOBA, ATAGO CLASSES—4, NACHI CLASS—8	4.7″	50	4.72″	45	3,018	85°
DD—KAMIKAZE, MUTSUKI CLASSES—4	4.7″	50	4.72″	45	2,998	45°
DD—MINEKAZE CLASS—4, WAKATAKE, MOMI CLASSES—3	4.7″	45	4.72″	45	2,772	45°
SS—I 51-64, I 101, 104, I 171-175, I 179-185, RO 30-32—1	4.7″	40	4.72″		2,165	20°
SS—I 56, 66, I 78-82, I 168-170—1	4″	40	3.9″	12.5		
CV—HOSHO—2, CVS—CHITOSE CLASS—4, KAMOI, NOTORO—2 CA—TONE CLASS—8, MOGAMI CLASS—4, OCA—IWATE CLASS, YAKUMO—1 CL—TENRYU CLASS, YUBARI—1, KUMA, SENDAI CLASSES—2 NATORI CLASS—3 SS—RO 33-37, RO 57-59—1	3.15″	40	3.15″		2,231	AA—85°
OCA—IWATE CLASS, YAKUMO—4, SS-RO 60-68, RO 100-103—1	3″	25	2.97″			

SIMPLIFIED SILHOUETTES

BATTLESHIPS-BB

KONGO CLASS

FUSO CLASS

ISE CLASS

NAGATO CLASS

SCALE

0	100	200	300	400	500

HEAVY CRUISERS-CA

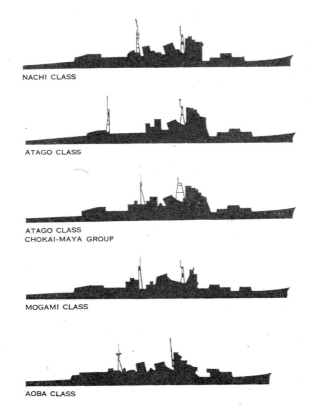

NACHI CLASS

ATAGO CLASS

ATAGO CLASS
CHOKAI-MAYA GROUP

MOGAMI CLASS

AOBA CLASS

TONE CLASS

LIGHT CRUISERS-CL

KATORI CLASS

KUMA-NATORI CLASSES

TENRYU CLASS

SENDAI CLASS

AIRCRAFT CARRIERS—CV

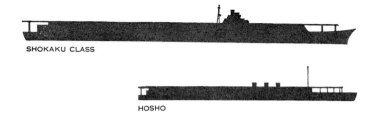

SHOKAKU CLASS

HOSHO

SEAPLANE CARRIERS—CVS

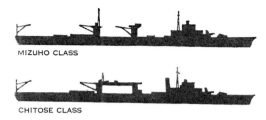

MIZUHO CLASS

CHITOSE CLASS

DESTROYERS—DD

MUTSUKI-KAMIKAZE CLASSES

MINEKAZE-WAKATAKE-MOMI
CLASSES

SHIGURE CLASS

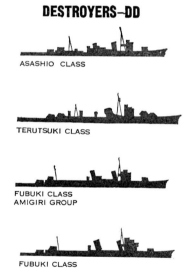

ASASHIO CLASS

TERUTSUKI CLASS

FUBUKI CLASS
AMIGIRI GROUP

FUBUKI CLASS
SHINONOME-HIBIKI GROUPS

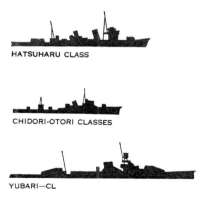

HATSUHARU CLASS

CHIDORI-OTORI CLASSES

YUBARI—CL

SCALE

0   100   200   300   400   500

JAPANESE NAVAL VESSELS — LIST BY DESIGN CLASSES

NOTE—WHERE TWO OR MORE VESSELS ARE KNOWN TO BE BUILT TO A COMMON DESIGN, THEY ARE GROUPED UNDER THE NAME SHIP OF THE CLASS.

—VESSELS NOT SO GROUPED ARE INDICATED AS HAVING SEPARATE APPEARANCE BY BOLDER TYPE

—THE SPELLING OF SHIP NAMES IS THE MOST PHONETIC VERSION, ADOPTED BY THE U. S. NAVY. NAMES IN PARENTHESES ARE A NEWER SPELLING, NOT PHONETIC; THIS SPELLING IS SHOWN TO AVOID CONFUSION.

—NO NOTATION INDICATES AVAILABLE VESSELS; OTHER NOTATIONS ARE SELF-EXPLANATORY.

PRINCIPAL COMBATANT TYPES

BATTLESHIPS

KONGO CLASS:

BB1	KONGO		
BB2	HIYEI		
BB3	KIRISHIMA	(KIRISIMA)	
BB4	HARUNA		

FUSO CLASS:

BB5	FUSO	(HUSO)	
BB6	YAMASHIRO	(YAMASIRO)	

ISE CLASS:

BB7	ISE
BB8	HYUGA

NAGATO CLASS:

BB9	NAGATO		
BB10	MUTSU	(MUTU)	
BB11	**YAMATO**		
BB12	**MUSASHI**		
BB13	**TOSA (?)**		—REPORTED BUILDING
BB14	**OWARI (?)**		—REPORTED BUILDING

AIRCRAFT CARRIERS

CV1	**HOSHO**	(HOSYO)	
CV2	**AKAGI**		—CONVERTED FROM CC; WAR LOSS
CV3	**KAGA**		—CONVERTED FROM BB; WAR LOSS
CV4	**RYUJO**	(RYUZYO)	—REPORTED WAR LOSS

SORYU CLASS:

CV5	SORYU		—WAR LOSS
CV6	HIRYU		—WAR LOSS

SHOKAKU CLASS

CV7	SHOKAKU	(SYOKAKU)
CV8	ZUIKAKU	

ZUIHO CLASS

CV9	ZUIHO	(EX TAKASAKI: EX-AS, EX-AO)
CV10	SHOHO	(EX TSURUGIZAKI; EX-AS, EX-AO)—WAR LOSS

HITAKA CLASS

CV11	HITAKA	(EX IZUMO MARU, CONVERTED WHILE BUILDING)
CV12	HAYATAKA	(EX KASHIWARA MARU, CONVERTED WHILE BUILDING)

NOTE—AT LEAST TWO REGULAR AIRCRAFT CARRIERS ARE BELIEVED BUILDING.

SEAPLANE CARRIERS

CVS1	**NOTORO**	(EX-AO)
CVS2	**KAMOI**	(EX-AO)

CHITOSE CLASS

CVS3	CHITOSE	(TITOSE)
CVS4	CHIYODA	(TIYODA)

MIZUHO CLASS

CVS5	MIZUHO	(MIDUHO)	—REPORTED WAR LOSS
CVS6	NISSHIN	(NISSIN)	
CVS7	AKITSUSHIMA	(AKITUSIMA)	

NOTE—AT LEAST TWO SEAPLANE CARRIERS ARE BELIEVED BUILDING.

HEAVY CRUISERS

FURUTAKA CLASS

CA1	FURUTAKA	(HURUTAKA)	—REPORTED WAR LOSS
CA2	KAKO		—WAR LOSS

AOBA CLASS

CA3	AOBA
CA4	KINUGASA

ONI 41-42

HEAVY CRUISERS (Continued)

NACHI CLASS

CA5	NACHI	(NATI)
CA6	HAGURO	
CA7	MYOKO	
CA8	ASHIGARA	(ASIGARA)

ATAGO CLASS

CA9	ATAGO	
CA10	TAKAO	
CA11	CHOKAI	(TYOKAI)
CA12	MAYA	

MOGAMI CLASS

CA13	MOGAMI	
CA14	MIKUMA	—REPORTED WAR LOSS
CA15	SUZUYA	
CA16	KUMANO	

TONE CLASS

CA17	TONE	
CA18	CHIKUMA	(TIKUMA)
CA19	**AGANO**	
CA20	**OYODO (?)**	—REPORTED BUILDING
CA21		—REPORTED BUILDING
CA22		—REPORTED BUILDING

NOTE—TWO ADDITIONAL UNIDENTIFIED HEAVY CRUISERS ARE CONSIDERED LOST.

LIGHT CRUISERS

TENRYU CLASS

CL1	TENRYU	
CL12	TATSUTA	(TATUTA)

KUMA CLASS

CL3	KUMA
CL4	TAMA
CL5	KITAGAMI
CL6	KISO
CL7	OI

NATORI CLASS

CL8	NATORI
CL9	NAGARA
CL10	KINU
CL11	YURA

CL12	ISUZU
CL13	ABUKUMA
CL14	**YUBARI**

SENDAI CLASS

CL15	SENDAI	
CL16	JINTSU	(ZINTU)
CL17	NAKA	

KATORI CLASS

CL18	KATORI	
CL19	KASHIMA	(KASIMA)
CL20	KASHII	(KASII)

CL21 TO 26 —REPORTED BUILDING

NOTE—EIGHT UNIDENTIFIED LIGHT CRUISERS ARE CONSIDERED LOST INCLUDING A UNIT OF THE SENDAI AND NATORI CLASSES.

DESTROYERS

MINEKAZE CLASS

DD1	MINEKAZE		
DD2	OKIKAZE		
DD3	SHIMAKAZE	(SIMAKAZE)	—REPORTED WAR LOSS
DD4	SAWAKAZE		
DD5	HAKAZE		
DD6	YAKAZE		
DD7	AKIKAZE		
DD8	YUKAZE		
DD9	HOKAZE		
DD10	SHIOKAZE	(SIOKAZE)	
DD11	TACHIKAZE	(TATIKAZE)	
DD12	NADAKAZE		—REPORTED WAR LOSS
DD13	NAMIKAZE		
DD14	NUMAKAZE		
DD15	NOKAZE		

KAMIKAZE CLASS

DD16	KAMIKAZE		(EX NO. 1)
DD17	ASAKAZE		(EX NO. 3)
DD18	HARUKAZE		(EX NO. 5)
DD19	MATSUKAZE	(MATUKASE)	(EX NO. 7)
DD20	ASANAGI		(EX NO. 15)
DD21	HATAKAZE		(EX NO. 9)
DD22	OITE		(EX NO. 11)
DD23	HAYATE		(EX NO. 13) —REPORTED WAR LOSS
DD24	YUNAGI		(EX NO. 17)

DESTROYERS (Continued)

MUTSUKI CLASS

DD25	MUTSUKI	(MUTUKI)	(EX NO. 19)	—REPORTED WAR LOSS
DD26	SATSUKI	(SATUKI)	(EX NO. 27)	
DD27	KISARAGI		(EX NO. 21)	
DD28	YAYOI		(EX NO. 23)	—REPORTED WAR LOSS
DD29	UZUKI	(UDUKI)	(EX NO. 25)	
DD30	FUMITSUKI	(HUMITUKI)	(EX NO. 29)	
DD31	KIKUTSUKI	(KIKUTUKI)	(EX NO. 31)	
DD32	MINATSUKI	(MINATUKI)	(EX NO. 32)	
DD33	NAGATSUKI	(NAGATUKI)	·(EX NO. 30)	
DD34	MIKATSUKI	(MIKATUKI)	(EX NO. 32)	
DD35	MOCHITSUKI	(MOTIDUKI)	(EX NO. 33)	
DD36	YUZUKI	(YUDUKI)	(EX NO. 34)	

FUBUKI CLASS (SHINONOME Group)

DD37	FUBUKI	(HUBUKI)
DD38	SHINONOME	(SINONOME)
DD39	SHIRAYUKI	(SIRAYUKI)
DD40	USUGUMO	
DD41	SHIRAKUMO	(SIRAKUMO)
DD42	ISONAMI	
DD43	HATSUYUKI	(HATUYUKI)
DD44	MURAKUMO	

FUBUKI CLASS (AMAGIRI Group)

DD45	AMAGIRI		
DD46	SHIKINAMI	(SIKINAMI)	
DD47	AYANAMI		
DD48	ASAGIRI		
DD49	URANAMI		
DD50	YUGIRi		
DD51	SAGIRI		—REPORTED WAR LOSS
DD52	USHIO	(USIO)	
DD53	OBORO		
DD54	AKEBONO		
DD55	SAZANAMI		
DD—	MIYUKI		—SUNK BY COLLISION, 1934

FUBUKI CLASS (HIBIKI Group)

DD56	HIBIKI	
DD57	IKAZUCHI	(IKADUTI)
DD58	INAZUMA	(INADUMA)
DD59	AKATSUKI	(AKATUKI)

HATSUHARU CLASS

DD60	HATSUHARU	(HATUHARU)	
DD61	HATSUSHIMO	(HATUSIMO)	—REPORTED WAR LOSS
DD62	NENOHI		—REPORTED WAR LOSS
DD63	WAKABA		
DD64	ARIAKE		
DD65	YUGURE		

SHIGURE CLASS

DD66	SHIGURE	(SIGURE)	
DD67	SHIRATSUYU	(SIRATUYU)	
DD68	MURASAME		
DD69	YUDACHI	(YUDATI)	
DD70	HARUSAME		—REPORTED WAR LOSS
DD71	SAMIDARE		—REPORTED WAR LOSS
DD72	YAMAKAZE		
DD73	SUZUKAZE		
DD74	KAWAKAZE		
DD75	UMIKAZE		

ASASHIO CLASS

DD76	ASASHIO	(ASASIO)	
DD77	ARASHIO	(ARASIO)	
DD78	OSHIO	(OSIO)	
DD79	MICHISHIO	(MITISIO)	
DD80	ASAGUMO		—REPORTED WAR LOSS
DD81	YAMAGUMO		
DD82	MINEGUMO		—REPORTED WAR LOSS
DD83	NATSUGUMO	(NATUGUMO)	
DD84	KASUMI		
DD85	ARARE		

KAGERO CLASS

DD86	KAGERO		
DD87	SHIRANUHI	(SIRANUI)	
DD88	KUROSHIO	(KUROSIO)	—REPORTED WAR LOSS
DD89	OYASHIO	(OYASIO)	
DD90	HATSUKAZE	(HATUKAZE)	
DD91	NATSUSHIO	(NATUSIO)	—REPORTED WAR LOSS
DD92	YUKIKAZE		
DD93	HAYASHIO	(HAYASIO)	
DD94	ISOKAZE		
DD95	AMATSUKAZE	(AMATUKAZE)	

DESTROYERS (Continued)

DD96	TOKITSUKAZE	(TOKITUKAZE)
DD97	URAKAZE	
DD98	ARASHI	(ARASI)
DD99	HAGIKAZE	
DD100	NOWAKI	
DD101	HAMAKAZE	
DD102	TANIKAZE	
DD103	MAIKAZE	
DD104	YUGUMO	
DD105	AKIGUMO	
DD106	MAKIGUMO	
DD107	SHIMAKAZE	(SIMAKAZE)
DD108	KAZEGUMO	
DD109	AKITSUKI	(AKITUKI)
DD110	SUZUTSUKI	(SUZUTUKI)
DD111	TERATSUKI	(TERATUKI)
DD112	HATSUTSUKI	(HATUTUKI)
DD113	WAKATSUKI	(WAKATUKI)
DD114	ARAZUKI	
DD115	NAGANAMI	
DD116	MAKINAMI	
DD117	TAKANAMI	
DD	—UNKNOWN No. 1—NAMES & NUMBERS UNKNOWN	

MOMO CLASS

ODD1	MOMO	—REMOVED FROM LIST
ODD2	HINOKI	—REMOVED FROM LIST
ODD3	YANAGI	—REMOVED FROM LIST

MOMI CLASS

ODD4	HASHI	(NASI)	—REMOVED FROM LIST
ODD5	TAKE		—REMOVED FROM LIST
ODD6	KAYA		—REMOVED FROM LIST
ODD7	KURI		
ODD8	NIRE		—REMOVED FROM LIST
ODD9	AOI		—REMOVED FROM LIST
ODD10	KIKU		—REMOVED FROM LIST
ODD11	KAKI		—REMOVED FROM LIST
ODD12	TSUGA	(TUGA)	
ODD13	HAGI		—REMOVED FROM LIST
ODD14	SUSUKI		—REMOVED FROM LIST
ODD15	FUJI		—REMOVED FROM LIST
ODD16	ASHI	(ASI)	—REMOVED FROM LIST
ODD17	TSUTA	(TUTA)	—REMOVED FROM LIST
ODD18	HASU		

ODD19	HISHI	(HISI)	—REMOVED FROM LIST
ODD20	TADE		—REMOVED FROM LIST
ODD21	YOMOGI		—REMOVED FROM LIST
ODD22	SUMIRA		—REMOVED FROM LIST

WAKATAKE CLASS

ODD23	WAKATAKE	(EX NO. 2)
ODD24	KURETAKE	(EX NO. 4)
ODD25	SANAYE	(EX NO. 6)
ODD26	ASAGAO	(EX NO. 10)
ODD27	FUYO (HUYO)	(EX NO. 16)
ODD28	KARUKAYA	(EX NO. 18)
ODD29	YUGAO	(EX NO. 12) —REMOVED FROM LIST
ODD—	SAWARABI	(EX NO. 8) —FOUNDERED, 1932

NOTE—FROM 35 TO 40 OR SO DESTROYERS ARE CONSIDERED LOST, IDENTITY UNCERTAIN.

SUBMARINES
(ABOVE 1,000 TONS—SS)

SS1	I-151	(EX I-51, EX NO. 44)
SS2	I-152	(EX I-52, EX NO. 51)

I-153 CLASS
(FORMERLY I-53 CLASS)

SS3	I-153	(EX I-53, EX NO. 64)
SS4	I-154	(EX I-54, EX NO. 77)
SS5	I-155	(EX I-55, EX NO. 78)
SS6	I-156	(EX I-56)
SS7	I-157	(EX I-57)
SS8	I-158	(EX I-58)
SS9	I-159	(EX I-59)
SS10	I-60	—WAR LOSS
SS11	I-61	—SUNK BY COLLISION, 1941
SS12	I-162	(EX I-62)
SS13	I-63	—SUNK BY COLLISION, 1939
SS14	I-164	(EX I-64)

I-1 CLASS

SS15	I-1	(EX NO. 74)
SS16	I-2	(EX NO. 75)
SS17	I-3	(EX NO. 76)
SS18	I-4	

I-165 CLASS
(FORMERLY I-65 CLASS)

SS19	I-165	(EX I-65)
SS20	I-166	(EX I-66)
SS21	I-67	—FOUNDERED, 1940

SUBMARINES (Continued)

SS22	I-5
SS23	I-6

I-168 CLASS   (FORMERLY I-68 CLASS)

SS24	I-168	(EX I-68)
SS25	I-169	(EX I-69)
SS26	I-170	(EX I-70)
SS27	I-171	(EX I-71)
SS28	I-172	(EX I-72)
SS29	I-173	(EX I-73)
SS30	I-174	(EX I-74)
SS31	I-175	(EX I-75)

I-7 CLASS

SS32	I-7
SS33	I-8

I-9 CLASS

SS34	I-9	
SS35	I-10	
SS36	I-11	
SS37	I-12	
SS38	I-13	
SS39	I-14	
SS40	I-15	
SS41	I-16	
SS42	I-17	
SS43	I-18	
SS44	I-19	
SS45	I-20	
SS46	I-21	
SS47	I-22	
SS48	I-23	
SS49	I-24	
SS50	I-25	
SS51	I-26	
SS52	I-27	
SS53	I-28	—WAR LOSS
SS54	I-29	
SS55	I-30	
SS56	I-31	
SS57	I-32	
SS58	I-33	
SS59	I-34	
SS60	I-35	

SS61	I-36	
SS62	I-37	
SS63	I-38	
SS64	I-39	
SS65	I-41	
SS66	I-43	—BUILDING
SS67	I-45	—BUILDING
SS68	I-47	—BUILDING
SS69	I-49	—BUILDING

I-76 CLASS

SS70	I-76	
SS71	I-77	
SS72	I-78	
SS73	I-79	
SS74	I-80	
SS75	I-81	
SS76	I-82	
SS77	I-83	—BUILDING
SS78	I-84	—BUILDING
SS79	I-85	—BUILDING

I-101 CLASS

SS80	I-101	
SS81	I-102	
SS82	I-103	
SS83	I-104	
SS84	I-105	—BUILDING
SS85	I-106	—BUILDING
SS86	I-107	—BUILDING

I-176 CLASS

SS87	I-176	—BUILDING
SS88	I-177	—BUILDING
SS89	I-178	
SS90	I-179	
SS91	I-180	
SS92	I-181	
SS93	I-182	
SS94	I-185	

NOTE—POSITIVE IDENTIFICATION OF THE I-176 CLASS HAS YET TO BE ESTABLISHED

SUBMARINES		(BELOW 1,000 TONS — OSS)

RO-26 CLASS

OSS1	RO-26	(EX NO. 45) —REPORTED REMOVED FROM LIST
OSS2	RO-27	(EX NO. 58) —REPORTED REMOVED FROM LIST
OSS2	RO-27	(EX NO. 58) —REPORTED REMOVED FROM LIST
OSS3	RO-28	(EX NO. 62) —REPORTED REMOVED FROM LIST

RO-51 CLASS

OSS4	RO-51	(EX NO. 25) —REPORTED REMOVED FROM LIST
OSS5	RO-52	(EX NO. 26) —REPORTED REMOVED FROM LIST
OSS6	RO-53	(EX NO. 27) —REPORTED REMOVED FROM LIST
OSS7	RO-54	(EX NO. 28) —REPORTED REMOVED FROM LIST
OSS8	RO-55	(EX NO. 29) —REPORTED REMOVED FROM LIST
OSS9	RO-56	(EX NO. 30) —REPORTED REMOVED FROM LIST
OSS10	RO-57	(EX NO. 46)
OSS11	RO-58	(EX NO. 47)
OSS12	RO-59	(EX NO. 57)

RO-60 CLASS

OSS13	RO-60	(EX NO. 59)
OSS14	RO-61	(EX NO. 72) —WAR LOSS
OSS15	RO-62	(EX NO. 73)
OSS16	RO-63	(EX NO. 84)
OSS17	RO-64	
OSS18	RO-65	
OSS19	RO-66	
OSS20	RO-67	
OSS21	RO-68	

RO-33 CLASS

OSS22	RO-33
OSS23	RO-34
OSS24	RO-35
OSS25	RO-36
OSS26	RO-37

RO-100 CLASS

OSS27	RO-100	
OSS28	RO-101	
OSS29	RO-102	
OSS30	RO-103	
OSS31	RO-104	—BUILDING
OSS32	RO-105	—BUILDING
OSS33	RO-106	—BUILDING
OSS34	RO-107	—BUILDING

MINE-LAYING SUBMARINES

RO-29 CLASS

SM1	RO-29	(EX NO. 68) —REMOVED FROM LIST
SM2	RO-30	(EX NO. 69)
SM3	RO-31	(EX NO. 70)
SM4	RO-32	(EX NO. 71)

I-121 CLASS (FORMERLY I-21 CLASS)

SM5	I-121	(EX I-21; EX NO. 48)
SM6	I-122	(EX I-22; EX NO. 49)
SM7	I-123	(EX I-23; EX NO. 50)
SM8	I-124	(EX I-24)

NOTE—EIGHTEEN OR MORE SUBMARINES ARE CONSIDERED LOST; THE IDENTITY OF MOST UNITS LOST IS UNCERTAIN.

MINOR COMBATANT TYPES

CRUISERS, SECOND LINE (termed "Coast Defence Ships")

OCA1	**ASAMA**	
OCA2	**YAKUMO**	
OCA3	**AZUMA**	(ADUMA)

IWATE CLASS

OCA4	IWATE	
OCA5	IZUMO	(IDUMO)
OCA6	KASUGA	

MINE LAYERS

CM1	**TOKIWA**		(EX OCA)
CM2	**KATSURIKI**	(KATURIKI)	
CM3	**SHIRATAKA**	(SIRATAKA)	—ALSO FITTED AS AN AN
CM4	**ITSUKUSHIMA**	(ITUKUSIMA)	
CM5	**YAEYAMA**		—ALSO FITTED AS AN AN
CM6	**OKINOSHIMA**	(OKINOSIMA)	—WAR LOSS

HATSUTAKA CLASS

CM7	HATSUTAKA	(HATUTAKA)
CM8	AOTAKA	
CM9	WAKATAKA	
CM10	TSUGARU	(TUGARU)

MINE LAYERS (Continued)

SHIMUSHU CLASS

CM11	SHIMUSHU	(SIMUSU)
CM12	KUNAJIRI	
CM13	HACHIJO	
CM14	ISHIGAKI	(ISIGAKI)
CM15	MIYAKO	

MINE SWEEPERS

No. 1 CLASS

AM1	NO. 1
AM2	NO. 2
AM3	NO. 3
AM4	NO. 4
AM5	NO. 5
AM6	NO. 6

No. 7 CLASS

AM13	NO. 7
AM14	NO. 8
AM15	NO. 9
AM16	NO. 10
AM17	NO. 11
AM18	NO. 12

No. 13 CLASS

AM7	NO. 13
AM8	NO. 14
AM9	NO. 15
AM10	NO. 16
AM11	NO. 17
AM12	NO. 18

No. 19 CLASS

AM19	NO. 19
AM20	NO. 20
AM21	NO. 21
AM22	NO. 22
AM23	NO. 23
AM24	NO. 24

NOTE—TWELVE UNITS, DESIGN UNKNOWN, REPORTED BUILDING.

TORPEDO BOATS

CHIDORI CLASS

TB1	CHIDORI	(TIDORI)
TB2	MANAZURU	
TB3	TOMOZURU	
TB4	HATSUKARI	(HATUKARI)

OTORI CLASS

TB5	OTORI
TB6	HAYABUSA
TB7	HIYODORI
TB8	KASASAGI
TB9	HATO
TB10	SAGI
TB11	KARI
TB12	KIJI

NOTE—EIGHT UNITS, DESIGN UNKNOWN, REPORTED BUILDING.

GUNBOATS

PG1	YODO	
PG2	SAGA	
PG3	ASUGA	(EX-CHINESE MUNG CHI)
PG4	ATAKA	
PG5	HITONOSE	(EX-CHINESE MING SEN)

HASHIDATE CLASS

PG6	HASHIDATE	(HASIDATE)
PG7	UJI	

NOTE—FOUR UNITS, DESIGN UNKNOWN, REPORTED BUILDING.

RIVER GUNBOATS

PR1	TOBA

SETA CLASS

PR2	SETA
PR3	HOZU
PR4	HIRA
PR5	KATADA

ATAMI CLASS

PR6	ATAMI
PR7	FUTAMI

SUMIDA CLASS

PR8	SUMIDA	
PR9	FUSHIMI	(HUSIMI)
PR10	TATARA	(EX U. S. S. WAKE)
PR11	KARATSU	(KARATU) (EX U. S. S. LUZON)
PR12	HUI MO	(EX H. M. S. MOTH)

SUBMARINE CHASERS

PC1, 2	NOS. 1 AND 2
PC3–39	NOS. 3 TO 39
PC40–44	NOS. 51 TO 55
PC45–47	NOS. 101 TO 103

MOTOR TORPEDO-BOATS

OVER 50 UNITS ARE BELIEVED TO BE IN COMMISSION. DESIGN CLASSES UNKNOWN.

"CONVERTED GUNBOATS"

OVER 23 SMALL MERCHANT STEAMERS BELIEVED TO BE EMPLOYED AS GUNBOATS, INSUFFICIENT DATA FOR DESIGN CLASSIFICATION.

TRAWLERS

OVER 29 TRAWLERS SERVING IN THE NAVY, MOSTLY AS AUXILIARY MINESWEEPERS. AN UNDETERMINED NUMBER OF WHALE "KILLER BOATS" HAVE LIKEWISE BEEN TAKEN OVER.

AIRCRAFT AUXILIARIES

AUXILIARY AIRCRAFT CARRIERS

OTAKA CLASS

ACV1	OTAKA	(EX KASUGA MARU)
ACV2	UNYO	(EX YAWATA MARU)

NOTE—FOUR ADDITIONAL UNITS, INCLUDING THE CHUYO, ARE REPORTED FITTING OUT.

SEAPLANE TENDERS

KAMIKAWA MARU CLASS

AV1	KAMIKAWA MARU
AV2	KIYOKAWA MARU

KINUGASA MARU CLASS

AV3	KINUGASA MARU
AV4	KIYOSUMI MARU
AV5	FUJIKAWA MARU
AV6	YASUKAWA MARU
AV7	SOUYOU (SOYO) MARU
AV8	GOSHU MARU
AV9	NARUTO MARU
AV10	SANUKI MARU
AV11	SAN-YO MARU
AV12	KATSURAGI MARU
AV13	KOKITSU MARU
AV14	NITCHO MARU
AV15	MOGAMIGAWA MARU

NAVAL AUXILIARIES, MISCELLANEOUS AND UNCLASSIFIED TYPES

SUBMARINE TENDERS

AS1	KOMAHASHI	(KOMAHASI)

JINGEI CLASS

AS2	JINGEI	(ZINGEI)	
AS3	CHOGEI	(TYOGEI)	
AS4	TAIGEI		
AS5	MANZYU MARU		(EX-SANTOS)
AS6	RIO DE JANEIRO MARU		
AS7	YASUKUNI MARU		

HIE MARU CLASS

AS8	HIE MARU
AS9	HEIAN MARU
AS10	NAGOYA MARU
AS11	ARATAMA MARU
AS12	URAKAMI MARU
AS13	HINODE MARU
AS14	NISSO MARU

REPAIR SHIPS

AR1	ASAHI		(EX OBB)
AR2	AKASHI	(AKASI)	
AR3			—BUILDING

SALVAGE SHIPS

ARS1	KURIHASHI
ARS2	YODOBASHI
ARS3	SARUHASHI
ARS4	SHIRAGANE
ARS5	NAGAURA

HOSPITAL SHIPS

AH1	HIKAWA MARU
AH2	TAKASAGO MARU
AH3	ASARI MARU
AH4	URAL MARU
AH5	AMERICA MARU
AH6	MANILA MARU
AH7	RYUKO MARU

HOSPITAL SHIPS (Continued)

AH8	**BAIKAL MARU**
AH9	**SEATTLE MARU**
AH10	**HOKUSAN MARU**

FUEL-OIL TANKERS

AO1   SUNOSAKI

SHIRETOKO CLASS

AO2	SHIRETOKO	(SIRETOKO)
AO3	ERIMO	
AO4	SATA	
AO5	TSURIMI	(TURIMI)
AO6	SHIRIYA	(SIRIYA)
AO7	IRO	
AO8	ONDO	
AO9	HAYATOMO	
AO10	NARUTO	

—REPORTED WAR LOSS

TOA MARU CLASS

AO11	TOA MARU
AO12	KYOKUTO MARU

SAN PEDRO MARU CLASS

AO13	SAN PEDRO MARU
AO14	SAN DIEGO MARU

TONAN MARU CLASS

AO15	TONAN MARU NO. 2
AO16	TONAN MARU NO. 3

KENYO MARU CLASS

AO17	KENYO MARU
AO18	KOKUYO MARU

HOYO MARU CLASS

AO19	HOYO MARU	
AO20	KAIZYO MARU	
AO21	**AKEBONO MARU**	
AO22	**NISSHIN MARU NO. 2**	
AO23	**FUJISAN MARU**	
AO24	**OMUROSAN MARU**	
AO25	**GENATA**	(EX-DUTCH)

STORESHIPS

AF1	**MAMIYA**	
AF2	**KASHINO**	(KASINO)
AF3	**IRAKO**	

MUROTO CLASS

AF4	MUROTO	
AF5	NOJIMA	(NOZIMA)
AF6	**KOSEI MARU**	

CABLE LAYING SHIPS

HASHIMA CLASS

ARC1	HASHIMA	(HASIMA)
ARC2	TSURUSHIMA	(TURUSIMA)
ARC3	TATEISHI	(TATEISI)
ARC4	ODATE	

TARGET SHIP

SETTSU   (EX-BB)

ICE-BREAKER

OTOMARI

SURVEYING SHIPS

AGS1	**KOSHU**	
AGS2	**TSUKUSHI**	(TUKUSI)
AGS3	**SOYA**	

DISTRICT CRAFT

MIDGET SUBMARINES

5 TO 15 TON CLASS

NUMBER AVAILABLE AND BUILDING UNKNOWN.

40 TO 50 TON CLASS

NUMBER AVAILABLE AND BUILDING UNKNOWN.

ONI 41-42

COASTAL MINE LAYERS (CAN ALSO BE EMPLOYED AS AMC'S)

TOSHIMA CLASS

CMc1   TOSHIMA   (TOSIMA)
CMc2   KUROSHIMA   (KUROSIMA)
CMc3   KATOKU
CMc4   ASHIZAKI   (ASIZAKI)
CMc5   ENTO
CMc6   KATASHIMA   (KATASIMA)
CMc7   KUROKAMI
CMc8   ENOSHIMA   (ENOSIMA)
CMc9   KUROZAKI
CMc10   NINOSHIMA   (NINOSIMA)

TSUBAME CLASS

CMc11   TSUBAME   (TUBAME)   —ALSO FITTED AS AN AN
CMc12   KAMOME   —ALSO FITTED AS AN AN

NATSUSHIMA CLASS

CMc13   NATSUSHIMA   (NATUSIMA)
CMc14   NASAMI
CMc15   SARUSHIMA   (SARUSIMA)

SOKUTEN CLASS

CMc16   SOKUTEN
CMc17   SHIRAKAMI   (SIRAKAMI)
CMc18   KYOSAI
CMc19   NARIU
CMc20   UKISHIMA   (UKISIMA)

YURISHIMA CLASS

CMc21   YURISHIMA   (YURISIMA)
CMc22   NUWASHIMA   (NUWASIMA)
CMc23   MAESHIMA   (MAESIMA)
CMc24   MOROSHIMA   (MOROSIMA)
CMc25   HIRASHIMA   (HIRASIMA)
CMc26   TAKASHIMA   (TAKASIMA)
CMc27   ARAISAKI
CMc28   ISHIZAKI   (ISIZAKI)
CMc29   BOKO
CMc30   SAGISAKI
CMc31   SAISHU

ONI 41-42

NO.	DATE	SOURCE	SHIP	AMENDMENTS
1	1/43	OP 16- P 2	DUGUAY-TROUIN CL-6	SHIP ILLUSTRATED IS LAMOTTE-PICQUET, CL 8, A UNIT OF THE DUGUAY-TROUIN CLASS
2	9/9/43	OP 16- P 2	DD UN NO. 1	Information received by the Division of Naval Intelligence since issue of ONI 41-42 jacket dated March, 1943, covering appearance of ship referred to as DD UN No. 1 (destroyer unknown, number one) confirms previous reports that this vessel is one of the TERUTSUKI Class. The designation DD UN No. 1 will, therefore, be dropped in future ONI recognition publications, and ships built to this design will be designated as belonging to the TERUTSUKI Class (formerly spelled TERATSUKI). This class is believed to have included AKITSUKI, SUZUTSUKI, TERUTSUKI, HATSUTSUKI, WAKATSUKI and ARAZUKI. Additional information has confirmed the general accuracy of the profile and plan developed by the Division of Naval Intelligence and previously published in ONI serial F-20:3-42 (November 30, 1942) and in ONI 41-42. Further information indicates the following corrections and additions to data on these ships previously issued in ONI 41-42 and ONI 222.

TERUTSUKI (DD 111) BUILT—Mitsubishi Yard, Nagasaki.
COMMISSIONED—August 2, 1942.

ARMAMENT—

4 TWIN MOUNTS, dual purpose max. elevations 90°, train 180°.

RANGE—Estimated as being in excess of 16,000 yards.

MAIN BATTERY—Caliber has been reported as 3".94?

It is possible that these guns may be 5"/50's.

2-25 mm. AA TWIN MOUNTS

2 LIGHT MACHINE GUNS

1 QUADRUPLE TORPEDO TUBE MOUNT.

2 TWIN TUBE DEPTH CHARGE THROWERS, ASDIC GEAR FITTED.

All these ships are provided with DEGAUSSING EQUIPMENT and are believed to lack MINESWEEPING, PARAVANE OR RADAR GEAR.

COMPLEMENT—260-300.

BRIDGE, TURRET, TORPEDO TUBE PLATING—Believed to be unusually light.

NO.	DATE	SOURCE	SHIP	AMENDMENTS
3	9/43	OP-16- P-2	KUMA, NATORI CLASSES	AERIAL VIEWS OF KUMA AND NATORI CLASSES (PAGES 2 AND 3) HAVE BEEN INTERCHANGED.

BATTLESHIPS

↓ KONGO CLASS   ↑ FUSO CLASS →

JAPANESE BATTLESHIPS

DIVISION OF NAVAL INTELLIGENCE—IDENTIFICATION AND CHARACTERISTICS SECTION —JUNE, 1943

KONGO CLASS BB 1-4

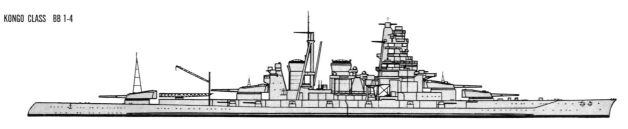

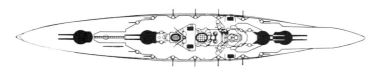

LENGTH— 704' OA   BEAM—95'
DISPLACEMENT—29,300 TONS (STANDARD)
MAIN BATTERY— 8–14"

Only class of BB's with two stacks. Note mainmast forward of No. 2 stack, 2A-1-1 main battery disposition. Pagoda foremast relatively low and massive, blending with No. 1 stack.

FUSO CLASS BB 5, 6

YAMASHIRO

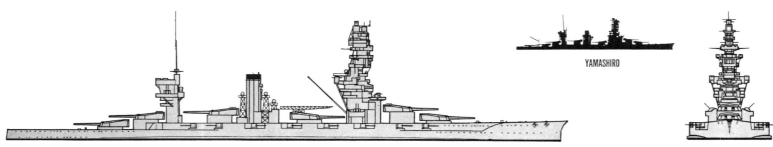

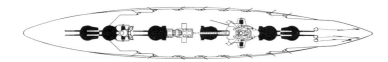

LENGTH—673' OA—665' WL   BEAM—94'
DISPLACEMENT—29,330 TONS (STANDARD)
MAIN BATTERY— 12–14"

Note distinctive 2A-1-1-2 main battery disposition, with turrets fore and aft of stack. Very tall, relatively slender pagoda foremast. Locations of catapults differentiate two ships of class.

ONI 41-42

ISE CLASS BB 7, 8

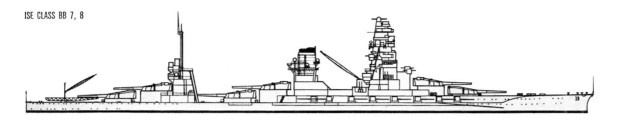

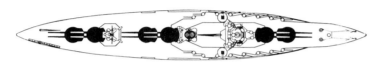

LENGTH— 683' OA   BEAM—94'
DISPLACEMENT—29,990 TONS (STANDARD)
MAIN BATTERY—12-14"

Note 2A-2-2 armament disposition, with super-imposed turrets between stack and mainmast. Hull breaks amidships, forward of stack.

NAGATO CLASS BB 9, 10

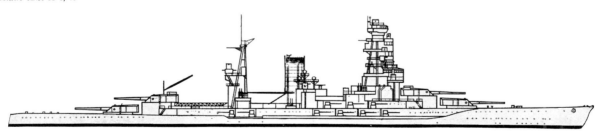

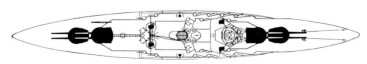

LENGTH— 700' OA   BEAM—95'
DISPLACEMENT—32,720 TONS (STANDARD)
MAIN BATTERY— 8-16"

2A-2 main battery disposition. Note that masts and stack are more closely grouped than in FUSO or ISE Classes.

↑ ISE CLASS FOLLOWED BY FUSO CLASS   ↓ NAGATO CLASS ↓

ONI 41-42

KONGO CLASS BB—1-4

DIVISION OF NAVAL INTELLIGENCE—IDENTIFICATION AND CHARACTERISTICS SECTION—NOVEMBER, 1942

HORIZON BEYOND THE SHIP

SHIP BEYOND THE HORIZON

LENGTH—704' OA
BEAM— 95'
DRAFT— 27' 6" (NORMAL)

DISPLACEMENT—29,300 TONS (STANDARD)—30,500 TONS (NORMAL)

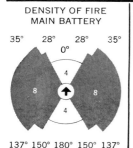

DENSITY OF FIRE MAIN BATTERY

35°   28°   28°   35°
      0°

4

8   8

4

137° 150° 180° 150° 137°

ARMAMENT

	MAX. ELEV.	RANGE
8–14" (45)	30°	30,000 YD.
14–6" (50) CASEMATES	25°	19,000 YD.
8–5" AA TWIN MOUNTS	85°	18,000 YD.

1 CATAPULT, 3 SCOUT OBSERVATION
NOTE: HIYEI, ONCE DEMILITARIZED; MAY HAVE WEAKER ORDNANCE.

PROTECTION

BELT—	6"–8" WITH 3" ENDS
TURRETS—	9"–10"
BARBETTES—	10"
CONNING TOWER—	10"
DECK—	2¾"–4"; 7" OVER VITALS

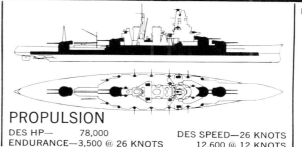

PROPULSION

DES HP— 78,000
ENDURANCE—3,500 @ 26 KNOTS

DES SPEED—26 KNOTS
12,600 @ 12 KNOTS

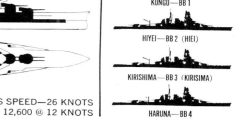

KONGO CLASS

KONGO—BB 1

HIYEI—BB 2 (HIEI)

KIRISHIMA—BB 3 (KIRISIMA)

HARUNA—BB 4

KONGO CLASS
—BB 1-4

DIVISION OF NAVAL INTELLIGENCE—IDENTIFICATION
AND CHARACTERISTICS SECTION —DECEMBER, 1942

PROFILE—
LOW PAGODA FOREMAST
TWO FLARED SINGLE
PIPE STACKS
HIGH TRIPOD MAINMAST
FOR'D OF AFT STACK
→

AERIAL—
TURRETS—
TWO SUPERIMPOSED
TWINS FOR'D
TWO TWINS AFT, SEPA-
RATED BY CATAPULT
←

END-ON—
HIGH, PYRAMIDAL
SUPERSTRUCTURE
EXTREMELY WIDE BEAM
↑

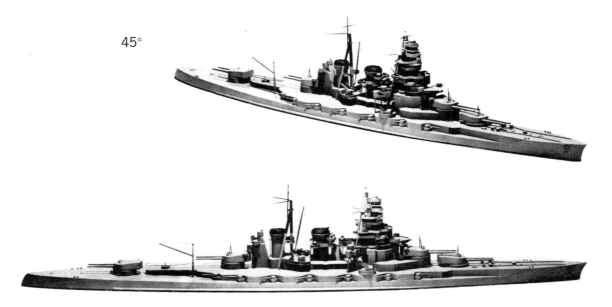

45°

90°

135°

ONI 41-42

0°

315°

270°

180°

225°

KONGO CLASS—BB 1-4

DIVISION OF NAVAL INTELLIGENCE—IDENTIFICATION AND CHARACTERISTICS SECTION· DECEMBER, 1942

0°   10°   20°   30°

75°   90°

135°   150°   165°   180°

240°   255°

300°   315°

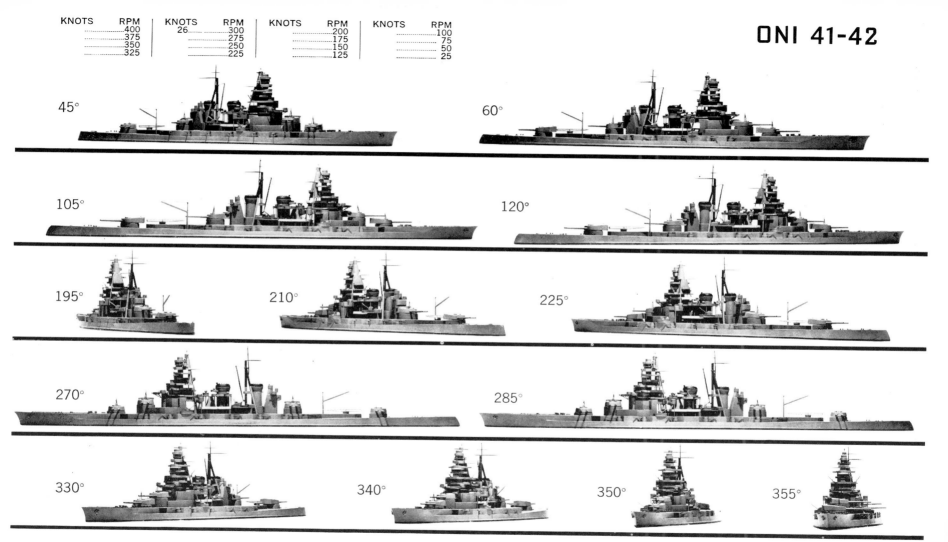

KONGO CLASS—BB1-4

DIVISION OF NAVAL INTELLIGENCE—IDENTIFICATION AND CHARACTERISTICS SECTION—NOVEMBER, 1942

		BEGUN	COMPLETED	MODERNIZED
KONGO—	BB1	1/17/11	8/16/13	1935–1937
HIYEI—	BB2	11/4/11	8/4/14	1938
KIRISHIMA—	BB3	3/17/12	4/19/15	1926–1930
HARUNA—	BB4	3/16/12	4/19/15	1929–1934

ONI 41-42

KONGO—12/19/38 ▼

↑ KIRISHIMA—12/19/38

HARUNA—1937 ▼

DIVISION OF NAVAL INTELLIGENCE—IDENTIFICATION AND CHARACTERISTICS SECTION—DECEMBER, 1942

HEIGHT OF OBSERVER

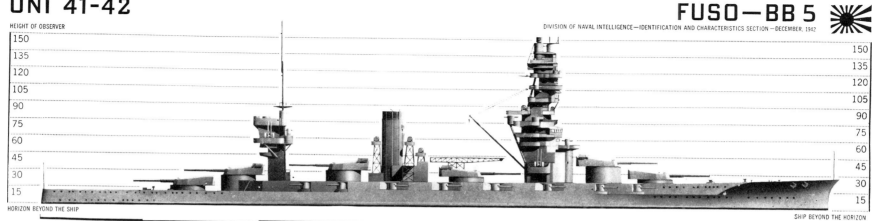

HORIZON BEYOND THE SHIP

SHIP BEYOND THE HORIZON

LENGTH—673' OA—665' WL
BEAM— 94'
DRAFT— 28'6" (NORMAL)

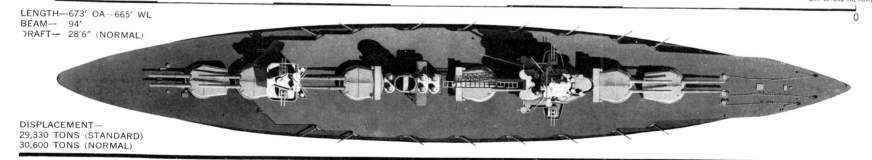

DISPLACEMENT—
29,330 TONS (STANDARD)
30,600 TONS (NORMAL)

DENSITY OF FIRE
MAIN BATTERY

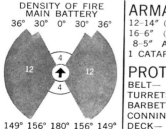

ARMAMENT

	MAX. ELEV.	RANGE
12–14" (45) TWIN TURRET	30°	30,000 YD.
16–6" (50) CASEMATES	25°	19,000 YD.
8–5" A. A. TWIN MOUNTS	85°	18,000 YD.
1 CATAPULT; 3 SCOUT OBSERVATION		

PROTECTION

BELT—	8–12" ENDS 4–5"
TURRETS—	8–12"
BARBETTES—	8–12"
CONNING TOWER—	6–12"
DECK—	2" 7" OVER VITALS

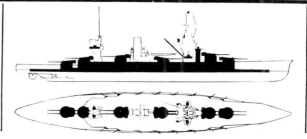

FUSO CLASS

FUSO (HUSO) BB 5

YAMASHIRO (YAMASIRO) BB 6

FUSO—BB 5

DIVISION OF NAVAL INTELLIGENCE—IDENTIFICATION
AND CHARACTERISTICS SECTION —DECEMBER, 1942

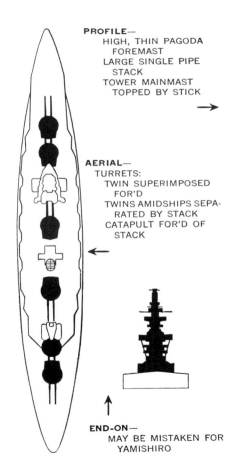

PROFILE—
  HIGH, THIN PAGODA
    FOREMAST
  LARGE SINGLE PIPE
    STACK
  TOWER MAINMAST
    TOPPED BY STICK →

AERIAL—
  TURRETS:
    TWIN SUPERIMPOSED
      FOR'D
    TWINS AMIDSHIPS SEPA-
      RATED BY STACK
    CATAPULT FOR'D OF
      STACK

END-ON—
  MAY BE MISTAKEN FOR
    YAMISHIRO

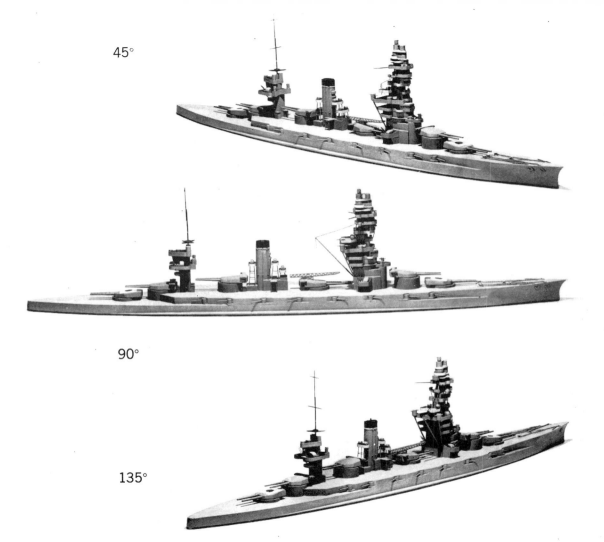

45°

90°

135°

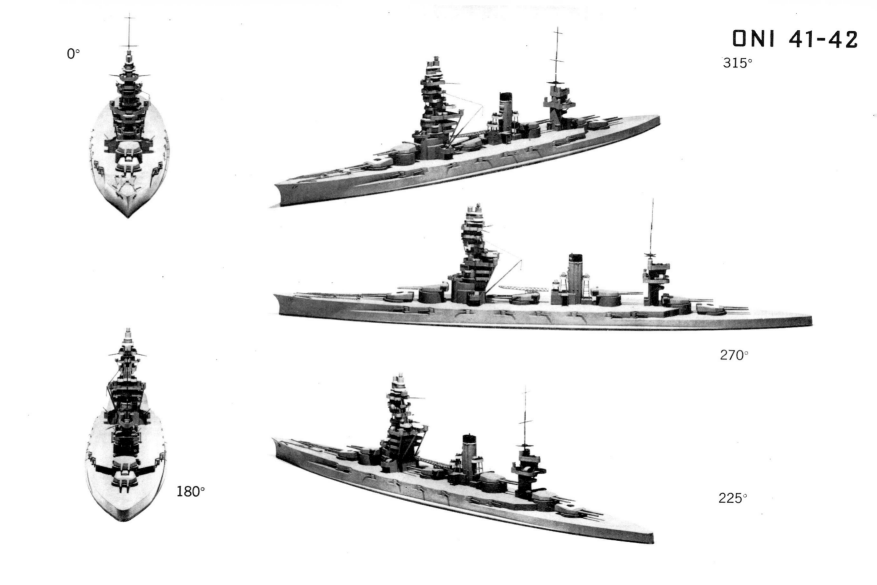

0°

315°

270°

180°

225°

FUSO—BB 5

DIVISION OF NAVAL INTELLIGENCE—IDENTIFICATION AND CHARACTERISTICS SECTION · DECEMBER, 1942

0°

10°

20°

30°

75°

90°

135°

150°

165°

180°

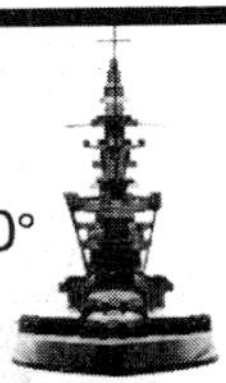

240°

255°

300°

315°

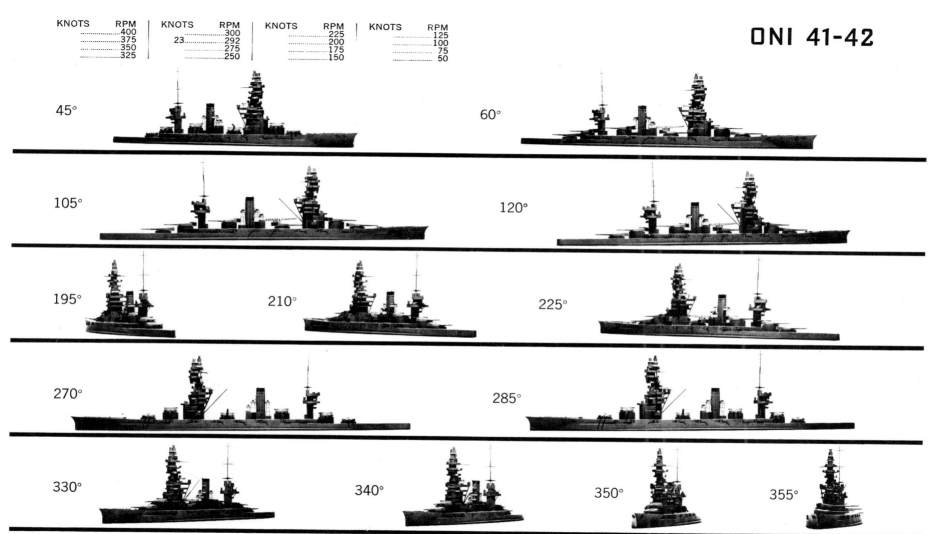

KNOTS   RPM   KNOTS   RPM   KNOTS   RPM   KNOTS   RPM

KNOTS	RPM	KNOTS	RPM	KNOTS	RPM	KNOTS	RPM
	400		300		225		125
	375	23	292		200		100
	350		275		175		75
	325		250		150		50

45°

60°

105°

120°

195°

210°

225°

270°

285°

330°

340°

350°

355°

FUSO—BB 5
DIVISION OF NAVAL INTELLIGENCE—IDENTIFICATION AND CHARACTERISTICS SECTION—DECEMBER, 1942

	BEGUN	COMPLETED	
FUSO —BB 5	3/11/12	11/8/15	MODERNIZED 1932-33
YAMASHIRO—BB 6			PROFILE MODIFIED

ONI 41-42

↑ 1935

↓ FUSO LEADING UNITS OF THE KONGO CLASS

HEIGHT OF OBSERVER

150	150
135	135
120	120
105	105
90	90
75	75
60	60
45	45
30	30
15	15

HORIZON BEYOND THE SHIP

SHIP BEYOND THE HORIZON

0

LENGTH—673' OA—665' WL
BEAM —94'
DRAFT—28'6" (NORMAL)

DISPLACEMENT
29,330 TONS (STANDARD)
30,600 TONS (NORMAL)

DENSITY OF FIRE MAIN BATTERY

36° 30° 0° 30° 36°

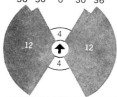

4
12   12
4

149° 156° 180° 156° 149°

ARMAMENT

	MAX. ELEV.	RANGE
12–14" (45) TWIN TURRETS	30°	30,000 YD.
16–6" (50) CASEMATES	25°	19,000 YD.
8–5" AA TWIN MOUNTS	85°	18,000 YD.
1 CATAPULT; 3 SCOUT OBSERVATION		

PROTECTION

BELT—	8–12" ENDS 4–5"
TURRETS—	8–12"
BARBETTES—	8–12"
CONNING TOWER—	6–12"
DECK—	2" 7" OVER VITALS

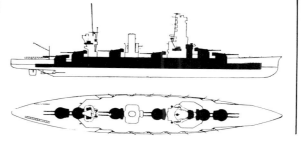

FUSO CLASS

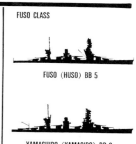

FUSO (HUSO) BB 5

YAMASHIRO (YAMASIRO) BB 6

YAMASHIRO
BB 6

DIVISION OF NAVAL INTELLIGENCE—IDENTIFICATION

AND CHARACTERISTICS SECTION —JANUARY, 1943

PROFILE—
 HIGH, SQUARE PAGODA
  FOREMAST
 HEAVY STACK SEARCH-
  LIGHT PLATFORM
 HIGH TOWER MAINMAST,
 TOPPED BY STICK

→

AERIAL—
 TURRETS:
  SUPERIMPOSED TWINS
   FOR'D
  SINGLE TWINS AMID-
   SHIPS (TRAINED AFT)
  SUPERIMPOSED TWINS
   AFT
 CATAPULT AFT

←

↑

END-ON—
 EASILY MISTAKEN FOR
 FUSO

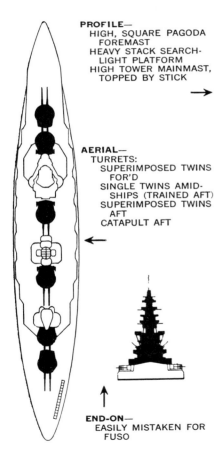

45°

90°

135°

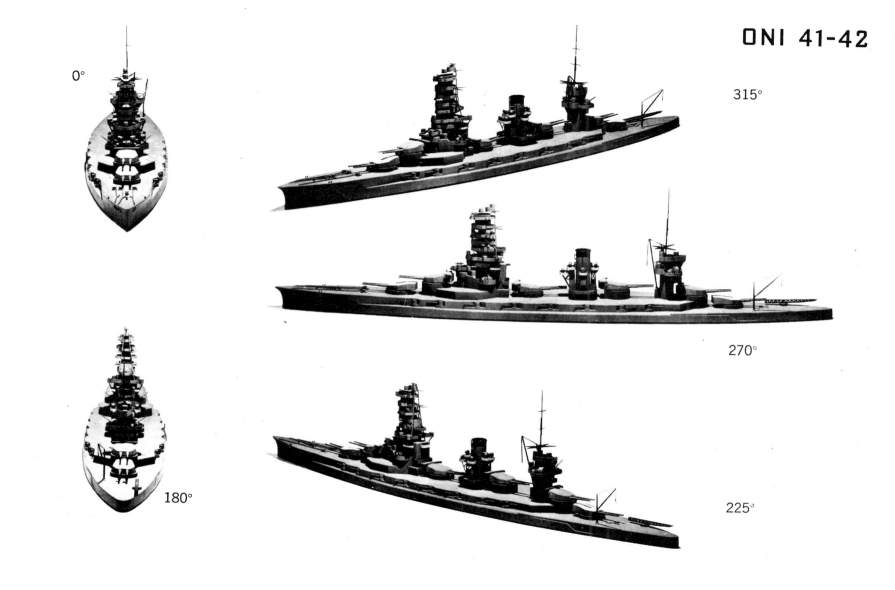

0°

315°

270°

180°

225°

YAMASHIRO—BB 6

DIVISION OF NAVAL INTELLIGENCE—IDENTIFICATION AND CHARACTERISTICS SECTION—JANUARY, 1943

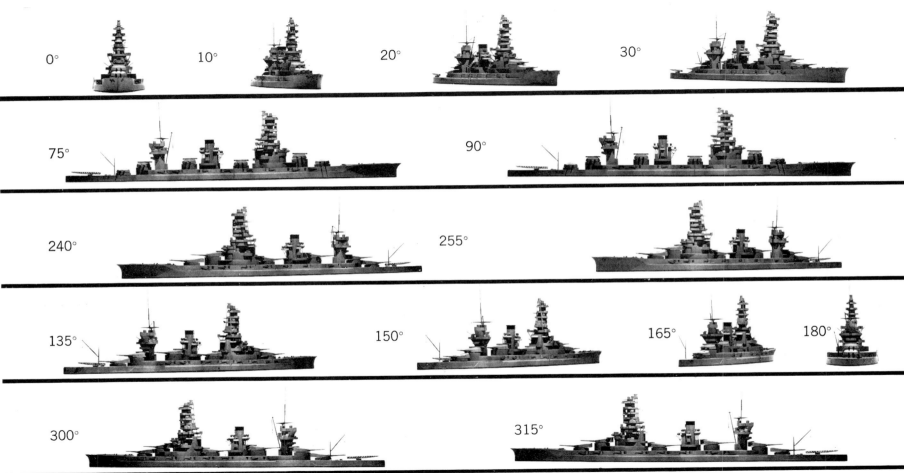

0° 10° 20° 30°

75° 90°

240° 255°

135° 150° 165° 180°

300° 315°

KNOTS	RPM	KNOTS	RPM	KNOTS	RPM	KNOTS	RPM
	400		300		225		125
	375	23	292		200		100
	350		275		175		75
	325		250		150		50

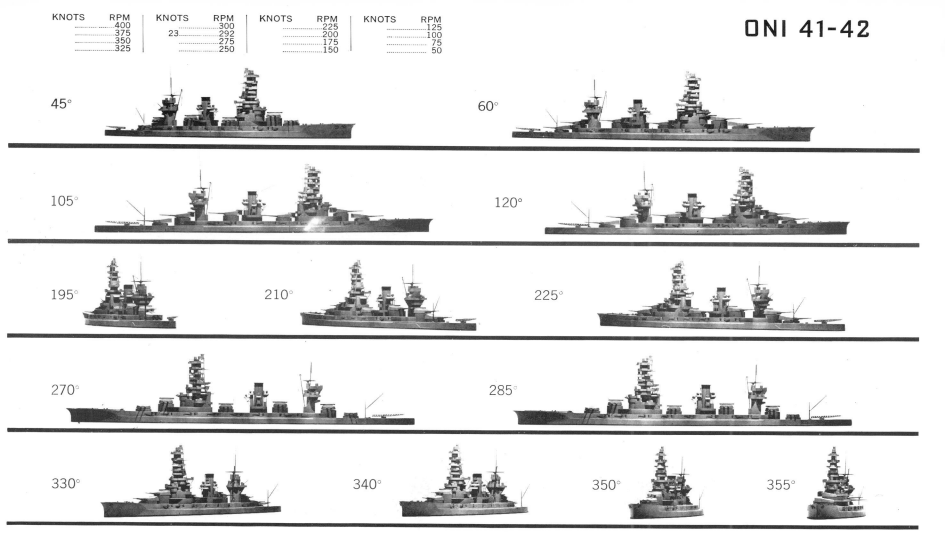

45°

60°

105°

120°

195°

210°

225°

270°

285°

330°

340°

350°

355°

YAMASHIRO—BB 6
DIVISION OF NAVAL INTELLIGENCE—IDENTIFICATION AND CHARACTERISTICS SECTION—DECEMBER, 1942

	BEGUN	COMPLETED	
YAMASHIRO—BB 6	11/20/13	3/31/17	MODERNIZED 1932–33

SISTERSHIP FUSO, BB 5, HAS MODIFIED PROFILE

ONI 41-42

↑ 1939   ↓ 1938   ↑ YAMASHIRO, 1938. FUSO BEHIND, KONGO CLASS BEYOND

ISE, HYUGA—BB 7, 8

DIVISION OF NAVAL INTELLIGENCE—IDENTIFICATION AND CHARACTERISTICS SECTION—OCTOBER, 1942

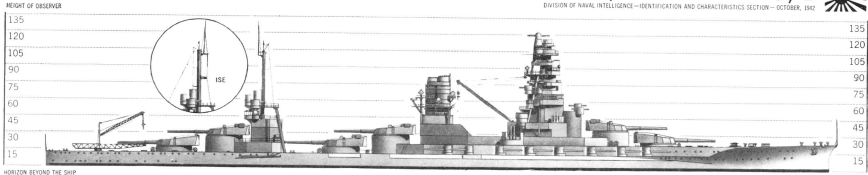

HEIGHT OF OBSERVER

ISE

HORIZON BEYOND THE SHIP

SHIP BEYOND THE HORIZON

LENGTH—683' OA—676' WL
BEAM—   94'
DRAFT—   28'8" (NORMAL)

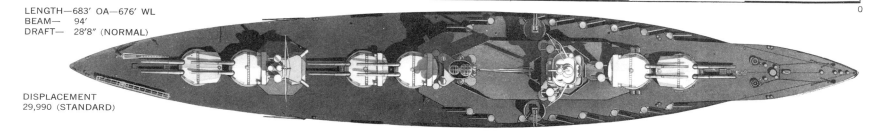

DISPLACEMENT
29,990 (STANDARD)

DENSITY OF FIRE MAIN BATTERY

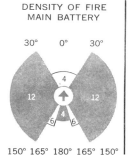

30°	0°	30°
	4	
12		12
	6 6	
150° 165° 180° 165° 150°		

ARMAMENT

	MAX. ELEV.	RANGE
12-14" (45) TWIN TURRETS	30°	30,000 YD.
16-5".5 (50) CASEMATES	25°	19,000 YD.
8-5" AA, 4-1" AA TWIN MOUNTS	85°	18,000 YD.
1 CATAPULT, 3 SEAPLANE SCOUTS		

PROTECTION

BELT—	8"-12"
TURRETS—	8"-12"
BARBETTES—	8"
CONNING TOWER—	12"-6"
DECK—	6¾"-
	2½"

PROPULSION

MACHINERY—	4 TURBINES
BOILERS—	8 KAMPON
FUEL—	OIL, 4,500 TONS
DES HP—	45,000
DES SPEED—	23 KNOTS
ENDURANCE—	4,200 @ 23 KNOTS
	12,600 @ 12 KNOTS

KNOTS	RPM
	420
	400
	350
23	318
	300
	275
	250
	245
	240
	220
	200
	160
	150
	120
	80

ISE CLASS
BB 7-8

DIVISION OF NAVAL INTELLIGENCE IDENTIFICATION

AND CHARACTERISTICS SECTION   DECEMBER, 1942

PROFILE—
PAGODA FOREMAST
POLE MAINMAST ON LOW
   TRIPOD
ONE SINGLE PIPE WITH
   SEARCHLIGHT PLATFORMS

→

45°

← **AERIAL—**
TWIN TURRETS—
   2 SUPERIMPOSED FOR'D
   2 SUPERIMPOSED
         AMIDSHIPS
   2 SUPERIMPOSED AFT
HULL BROKEN AMIDSHIPS

90°

↑
END-ON—
   FLARED PAGODA
         FOREMAST
   FLANKING SECONDARY
         MOUNTS

135°

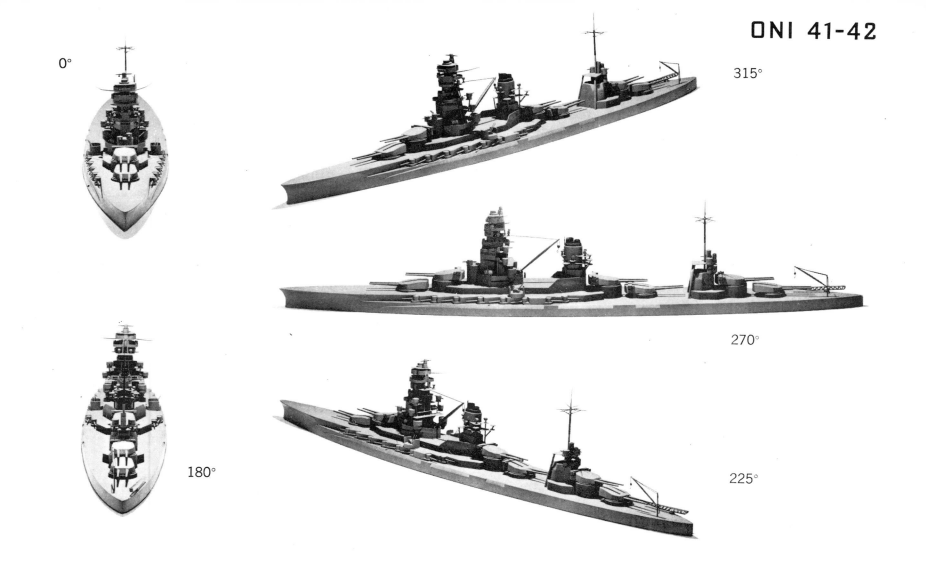

ONI 41-42

0°

315°

270°

180°

225°

ISE, HYUGA—BB 7, 8

DIVISION OF NAVAL INTELLIGENCE—IDENTIFICATION AND CHARACTERISTICS SECTION—NOVEMBER, 1942

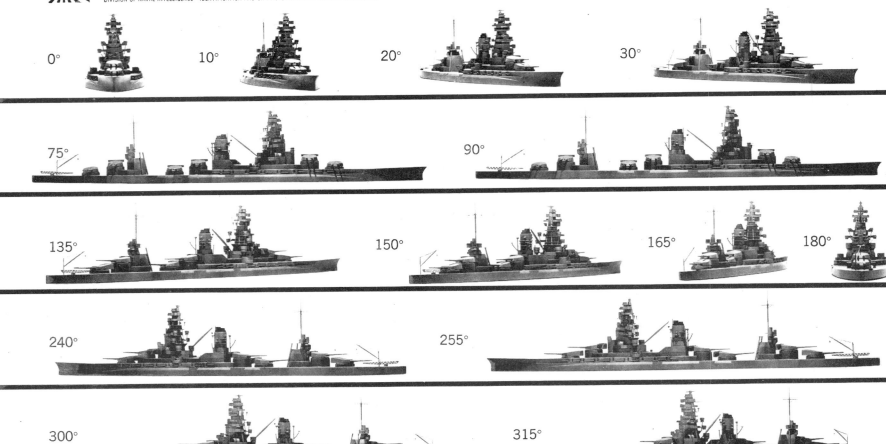

0°   10°   20°   30°

75°   90°

135°   150°   165°   180°

240°   255°

300°   315°

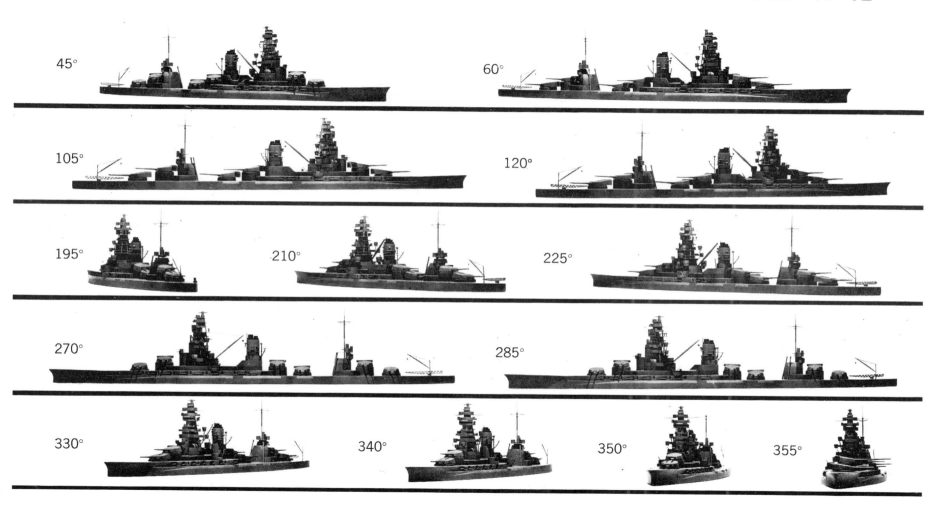

ISE, HYUGA—BB 7, 8

DIVISION OF NAVAL INTELLIGENCE—IDENTIFICATION AND CHARACTERISTICS SECTION—OCTOBER, 1942

		BEGUN	COMPLETED	MODERNIZED
ISE	—BB 7	5/10/15	12/15/17	
HYUGA	—BB 8	5/ 6/15	4/30/18	1935–37

ONI 41-42

ISE—DEC. 19, 1938 ↑

↓ HYUGA—OCT., 1938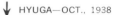

HEIGHT OF OBSERVER

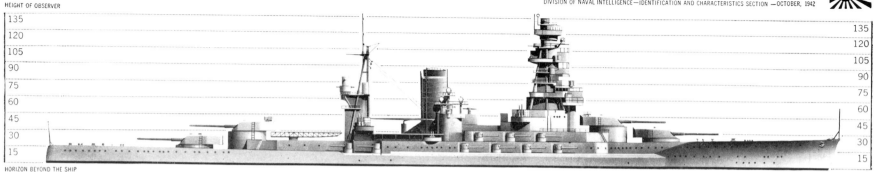

135	135
120	120
105	105
90	90
75	75
60	60
45	45
30	30
15	15

HORIZON BEYOND THE SHIP

LENGTH--700' OA
BEAM— 95'
DRAFT— 29'8" (NORMAL)

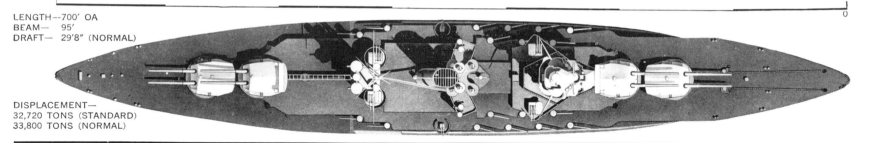

0

DISPLACEMENT—
32,720 TONS (STANDARD)
33,800 TONS (NORMAL)

DENSITY OF FIRE
MAIN BATTERY

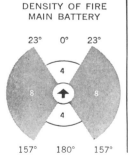

23°   0°   23°

4

8   8

4

157° 180° 157°

ARMAMENT

	MAX. ELEV.	RANGE
8-16" (45) TWIN TURRETS	35°	36,000 YD.
18-5.5 (50) CASEMATES	25°	19,000 YD.
8-5" AA TWIN SHIELD MOUNTS	85°	18,000 YD.
1 CATAPULT, 3 SEAPLANE SCOUTS		

PROTECTION

BELT—	13"
TURRETS—	14"
BARBETTES—	
CONNING TOWER—14"	
DECK—(OVER VITALS)	
	3½"-7"

PROPULSION

MACHINERY—	4 TURBINES
BOILERS—	21 KAMPON
FUEL—	OIL—5,000 TONS
DESIGNED HP—	80,000
DESIGNED SPEED—	26 KNOTS
ENDURANCE—	4700 @ 26 KTS
	12,000 @ 12 KTS

KNOTS	RPM
	420
	400
	350
26	330
	300
	275
	250
	245
	240
	220
	200
	160
	150
	120
	80

NAGATO
CLASS
BB 9-10

DIVISION OF NAVAL INTELLIGENCE—IDENTIFICATION

AND CHARACTERISTICS SECTION —DECEMBER, 1942

PROFILE—
 PAGODA FOREMAST
 LARGE S. P. STACK
 TRIPOD MAINMAST
 ENCLOSING LOW TOWER

AERIAL—
 TURRETS—
 TWIN SUPERIMPOSED
 FOR'D & AFT.
 STACK SEARCHLIGHT
 PLATFORMS
 CATAPULT AFT OF
 MAINMAST

END-ON—
 TRIPOD FRAMEWORK
 FOR PAGODA FOREMAST
 FREEBOARD BROKEN
 BY BLISTER, CASEMATES

45°

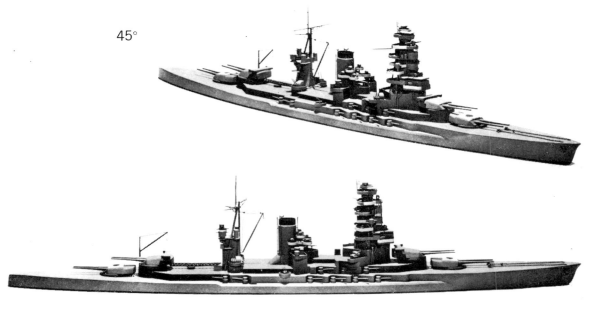

90°

135°

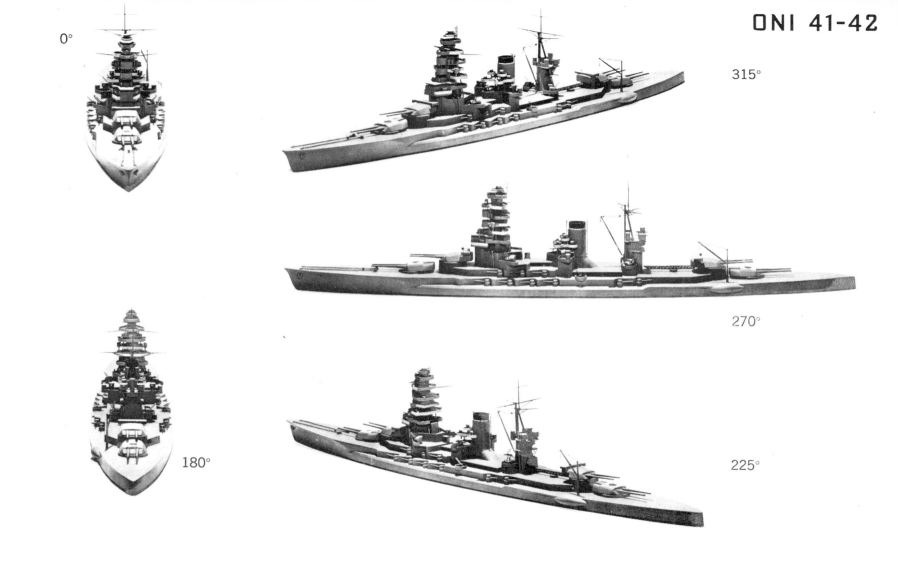

0°

315°

270°

180°

225°

ONI 41-42

NAGATO CLASS—BB 9-10

DIVISION OF NAVAL INTELLIGENCE—IDENTIFICATION AND CHARACTERISTICS SECTION—DECEMBER, 1942

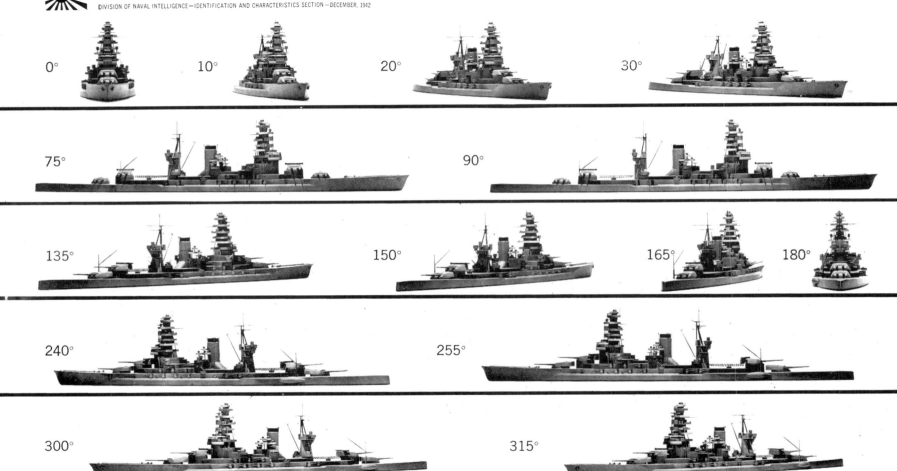

0° 10° 20° 30°

75° 90°

135° 150° 165° 180°

240° 255°

300° 315°

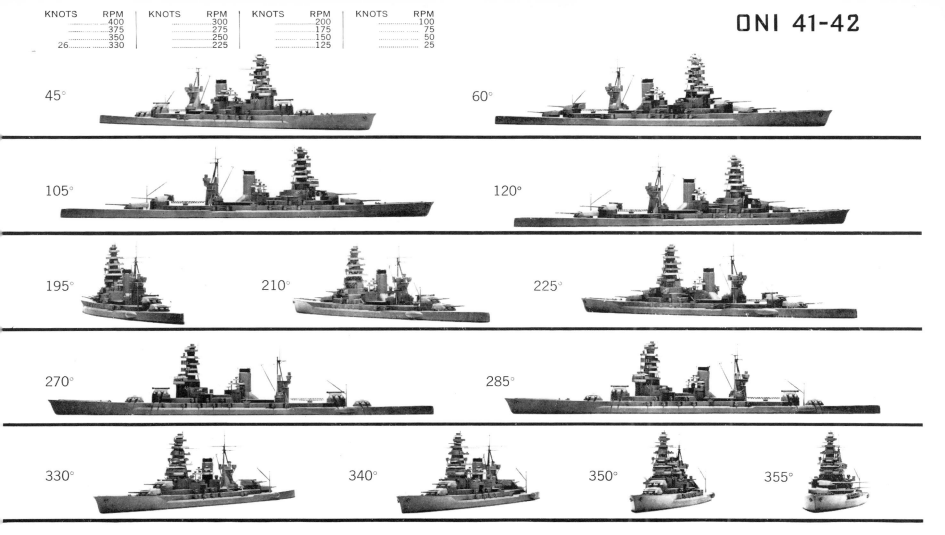

ONI 41-42

KNOTS	RPM	KNOTS	RPM	KNOTS	RPM	KNOTS	RPM
	400		300		200		100
	375		275		175		75
	350		250		150		50
26	330		225		125		25

45°

60°

105°

120°

195°

210°

225°

270°

285°

330°

340°

350°

355°

NAGATO CLASS—BB9-10

DIVISION OF NAVAL INTELLIGENCE—IDENTIFICATION AND CHARACTERISTICS SECTION—OCTOBER, 1942

	BEGUN	COMPLETED	MODERNIZED
NAGATO-BB9	8/28/17	11/25/20	1935
MUTSU –BB10	6/1 /18	10/24/21	1936

ONI 41-42

NAGATO-1938 ↓

↑ MUTSU–DEC. 1938

CARRIERS

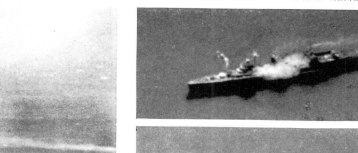

↑ SHOKAKU CLASS

HOSHO ↓ ↑ CHIYODA   MIZUHO (TOP)

HOSHO—CV1

ZUIHO CLASS—CV 9, 10—SILHOUETTE PROVISIONAL

CV—AIRCRAFT CARRIERS

Of the 10 Fleet Aircraft Carriers the Japanese had in operation prior to the outbreak of war 5 or more have been sunk—the Akagi, Kaga, Ryujo, Soryu, and Hiryu, while other units are believed sunk, but unverified.

SHOKAKU CLASS—CV 7, 8

EX-ARGENTINA MARU—CVE 1

SILHOUETTES ARE PROVISIONAL

OTAKA CLASS—CVE 2-4

CVE—ESCORT AIRCRAFT CARRIERS

These are the only units on which any appearance data is known. However, specific instances of the conversion of tenders, passenger ships, cargo hulls, and oilers have been reported.

XCVS—APV—CONVERTED MERCHANT SHIPS

KAMIKAWA MARU CLASS—XCVS 1, 3, 7, 9, TYPICAL

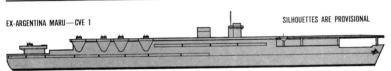

This category includes the 5 large Fleet Seaplane Tenders, the older converted freighters, and a miscellaneous assortment of merchant Ships. The dual function of all of these vessels is the supplying of Operational Seaplane Commands and the ferrying of aircraft.

CVS—SEAPLANE CARRIERS

↓ CHITOSE CLASS—CVS 3, 4   MIZUHO CLASS—CVS 5-7 →

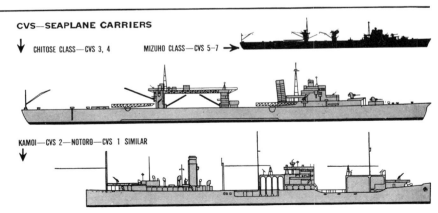

KAMOI—CVS 2—NOTORO—CVS 1 SIMILAR
↓

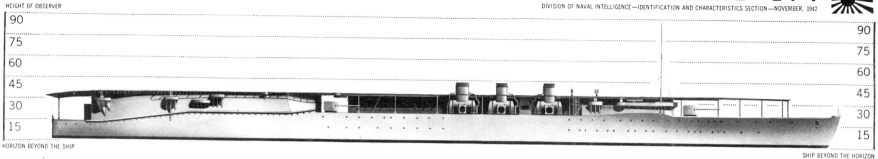

HEIGHT OF OBSERVER

90	90
75	75
60	60
45	45
30	30
15	15

HORIZON BEYOND THE SHIP

SHIP BEYOND THE HORIZON

0

LENGTH—540'6" OA—531' WL
BEAM —62'
DRAFT —20'3" (NORMAL)

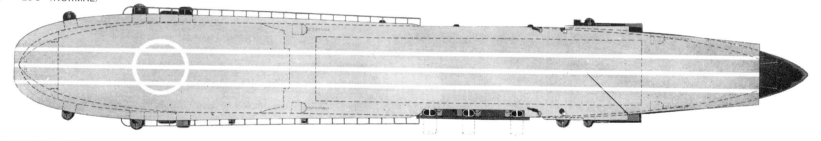

DISPLACEMENT—7,470 TONS (STANDARD)—9,500 TONS (NORMAL)

ARMAMENT

	MAX. ELEV.	RANGE
4-5"5 (50)	30°	19,000 YD.
?2-3" (40)	85°	6,000 YD.
-AAMG		

36 AIRCRAFT-12 FIGHTER
12 SCOUT OBSERVATION
12 TORPEDO BOMBER

PROPULSION

MACHINERY—	2 GEARED TURBINES
BOILERS—	8 KAMPON
FUEL—	OIL 1,500 TONS
DESIGNED HP—	30,000
DESIGNED SPEED—	26 KNOTS
ENDURANCE—	2,170 @ 26 KNOTS
	8,680 @ 12 KNOTS

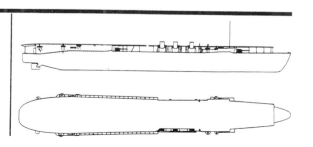

HOSHO—CV 1

DIVISION OF NAVAL INTELLIGENCE—IDENTIFICATION
AND CHARACTERISTICS SECTION —DECEMBER, 1942

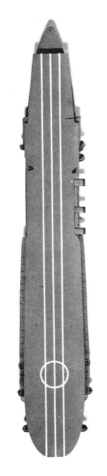

45°

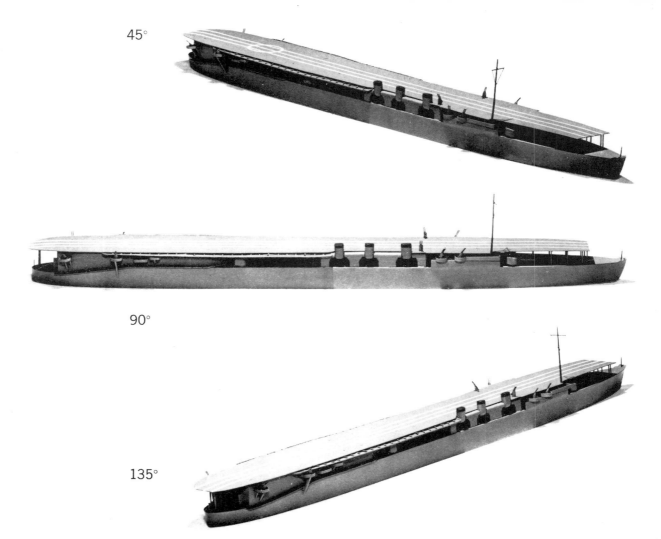

90°

135°

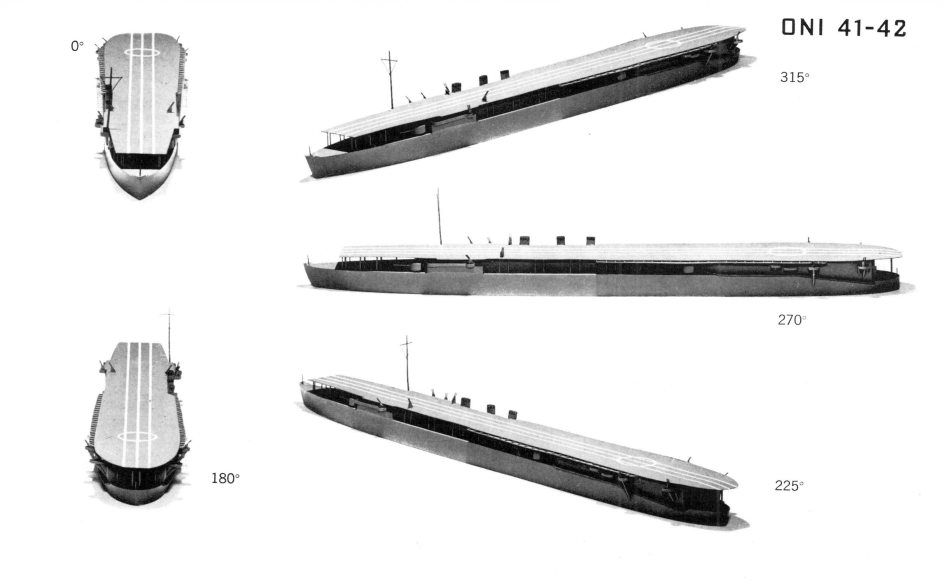

ONI 41-42

0°

315°

270°

180°

225°

HOSHO—CV1

DIVISION OF NAVAL INTELLIGENCE—IDENTIFICATION AND CHARACTERISTICS SECTION—NOVEMBER, 1942

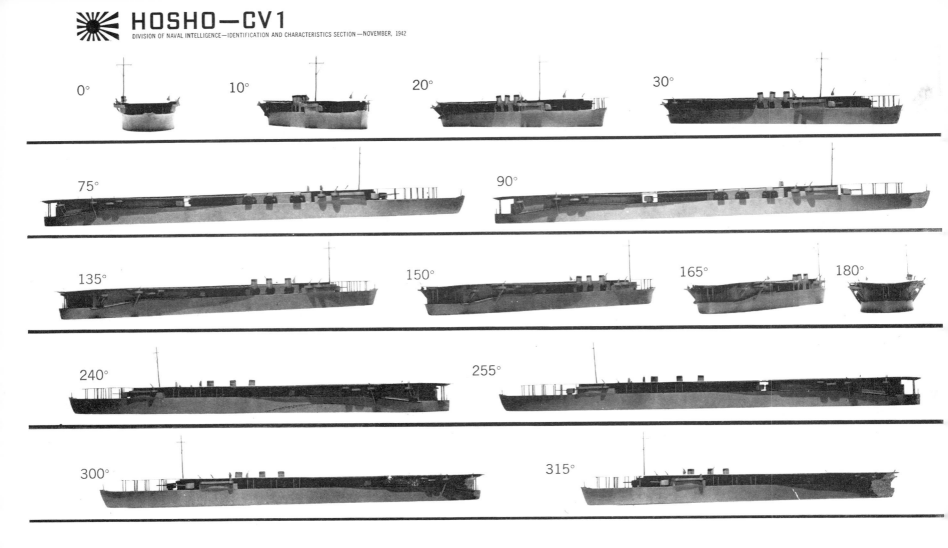

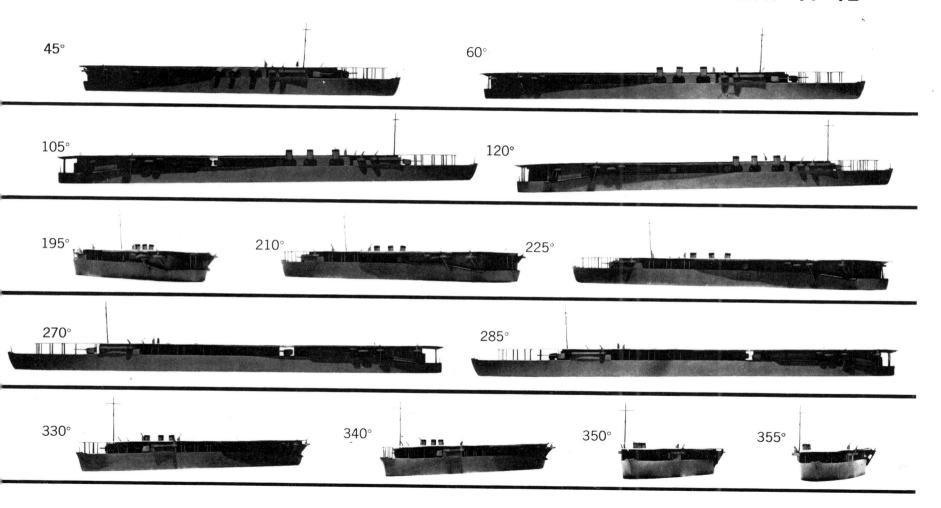

45°

60°

105°

120°

195°

210°

225°

270°

285°

330°

340°

350°

355°

↓ 1939

JAPAN'S FIRST CARRIER, ALSO FIRST BUILT AS A CARRIER

1939 ↓

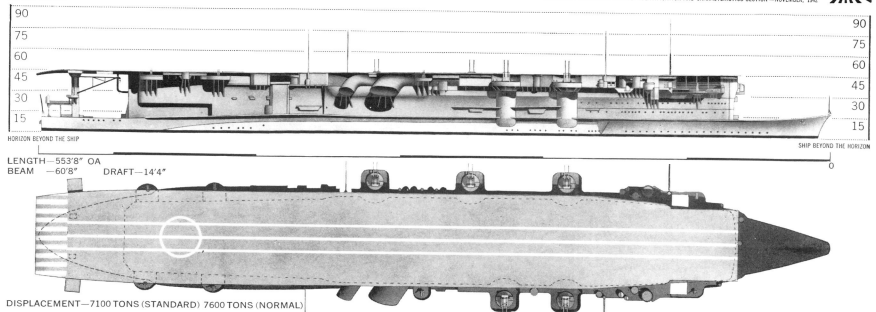

90
75
60
45
30
15

90
75
60
45
30
15

HORIZON BEYOND THE SHIP

SHIP BEYOND THE HORIZON

0

LENGTH—553'8" OA
BEAM   —60'8"   DRAFT—14'4"

DISPLACEMENT—7100 TONS (STANDARD) 7600 TONS (NORMAL)

ARMAMENT

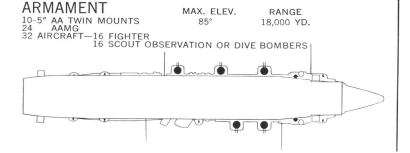

	MAX. ELEV.	RANGE
10-5" AA TWIN MOUNTS	85°	18,000 YD.
24 AAMG		

32 AIRCRAFT—16 FIGHTER
16 SCOUT OBSERVATION OR DIVE BOMBERS

PROPULSION

MACHINERY —2 TURBINES
BOILERS—   ? KAMPON
FUEL—   OIL 2000 TONS
DES HP—   40,000
DES SPEED— 25 KNOTS
ENDURANCE—3200 @ 25 KNOTS
           9500 @ 12 KNOTS

PROTECTION

BLISTER AND
COMPARTMENTATION

KNOTS	RPM
	400
	375
	350
	325
	300
	275
	250
	225
	200
	175
	150
	125
	100

RYUJO—CV 4

DIVISION OF NAVAL INTELLIGENCE—IDENTIFICATION
AND CHARACTERISTICS SECTION —DECEMBER, 1942

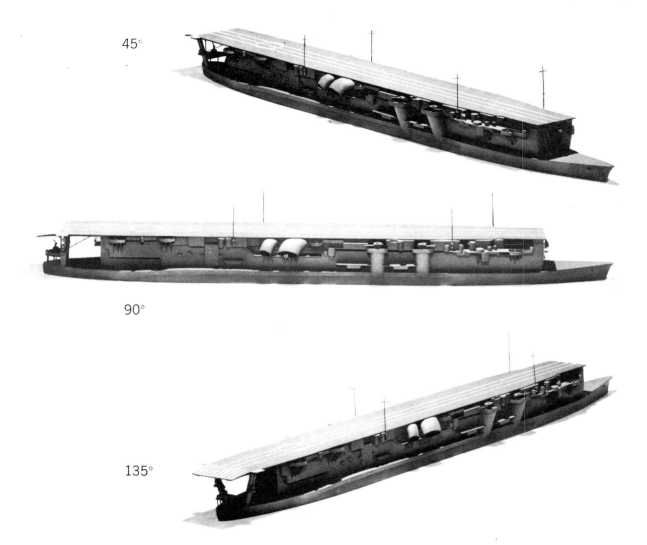

45°

90°

135°

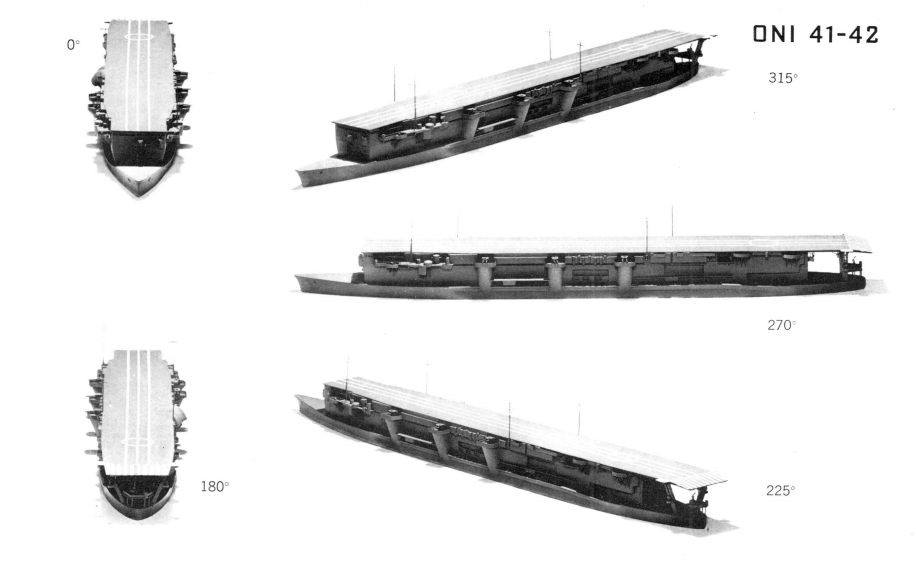

ONI 41-42

0°

315°

270°

180°

225°

RYUJO—CV4

DIVISION OF NAVAL INTELLIGENCE—IDENTIFICATION AND CHARACTERISTICS SECTION —NOVEMBER, 1942

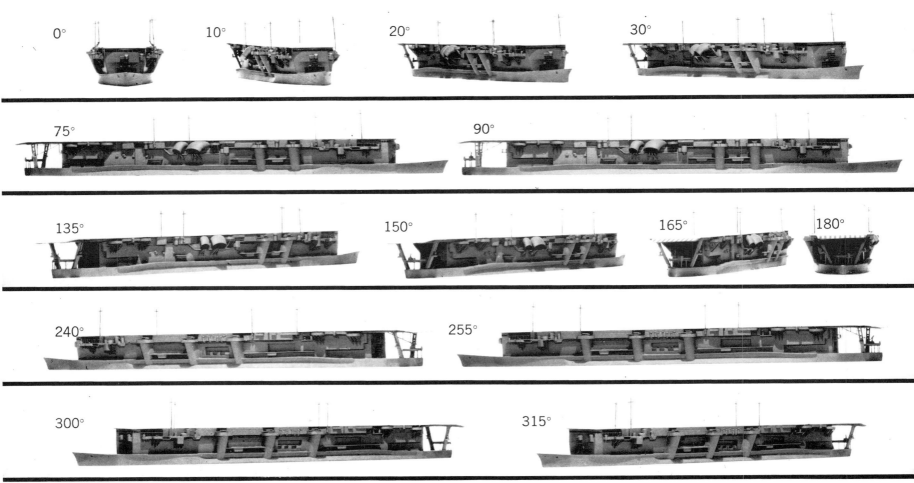

0°   10°   20°   30°

75°   90°

135°   150°   165°   180°

240°   255°

300°   315°

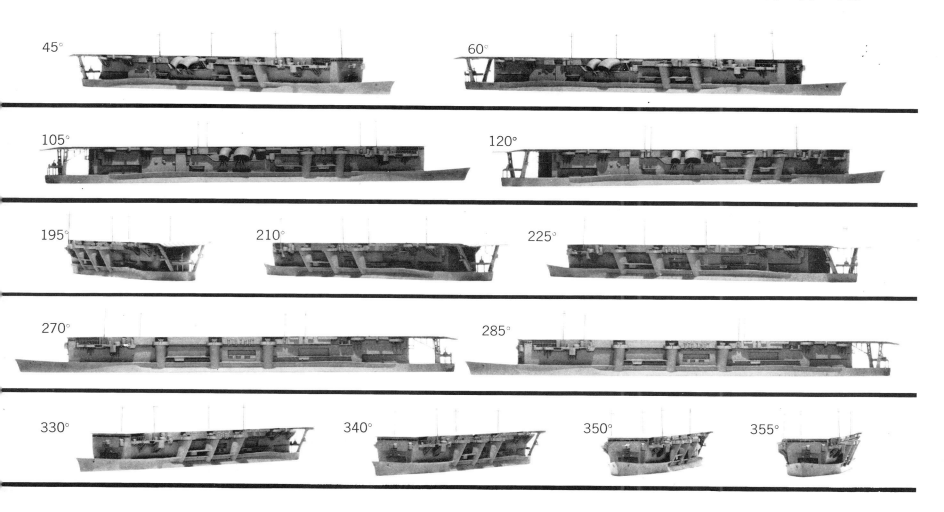

45°

60°

105°

120°

195°

210°

225°

270°

285°

330°

340°

350°

355°

RYUJO—CV 4

DIVISION OF NAVAL INTELLIGENCE—IDENTIFICATION AND CHARACTERISTICS SECTION—NOVEMBER, 1942

BEGUN—FEBRUARY 4, 1931. COMPLETED—1933
NOTE—ZUIHO, CONVERTED IN 1940, IS REPORTED TO RESEMBLE
RYUJO WITH THE ADDITION OF A MUCH HIGHER BOW.

ONI 41-42

↑ JUNE 6, 1935

1938 ↓

HEIGHT OF OBSERVER

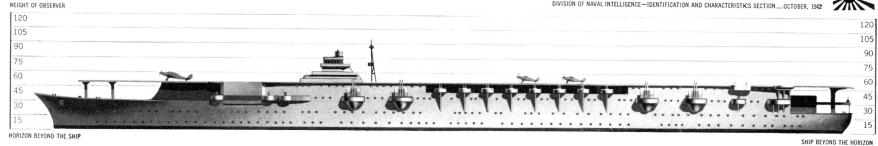

HORIZON BEYOND THE SHIP

SHIP BEYOND THE HORIZON

LENGTH—826' OA—792' WL
BEAM —93'
DRAFT —21' (MEAN)

★ BASED ON INCOMPLETE INFORMATION

DISPLACEMENT—
15,000 TONS (STANDARD)

ARMAMENT

	MAX. ELEV.	RANGE
16-5" TWIN MOUNTS	85°	18,000 YD.
AIRCRAFT-VF —18-21		
VOB OR VSB—18-21		
VTB —18-21		

PROPULSION

MACHINERY—	GEARED TURBINES
BOILERS—	
FUEL—	OIL—3500 TONS
DESIGNED HP—	
DESIGNED SPEED—	30 KNOTS (?)
ENDURANCE—	3900 @ 30(?) KNOTS
	14,000 @ 12 KNOTS

KNOTS	RPM
	420
	400
	350
	300
	275
	250
	245
	240
	220
	200
	160
	150
	120
	80

SHOKAKU CLASS—CV7-8

DIVISION OF NAVAL INTELLIGENCE—IDENTIFICATION AND CHARACTERISTICS SECTION—OCTOBER, 1942

SHOKAKU—CV7
ZUIKAKU— CV8

	BEGUN	COMPLETED
	12/11/37	8/ /40
	1938	1941

ONI 41-42

CORAL SEA—MAY 8, 1942

SHOKAKU CLASS CV 7, 8
RECENT REPORTS INDICATE—DISPLACEMENT 20,000 TONS (STANDARD)
—72 AIRCRAFT CARRIED

HITAKA CLASS CV 11, 12 (CONVERTED 1942)
LENGTH— 720'
ARMAMENT— 16-5" AA
AIRCRAFT— 48-60
DESIGNED SPEED—28 KNOTS
HITAKA (HIYO) CV 11 (EX-IZUMO MARU)
HAYATAKA (JUNYO) CV 12 (EX-KASHIWARA MARU)

ZUIHO CLASS CV 9, 10 (EX-AS TAKASAKI—CONVERTED 1940)
LENGTH— 660' O.A.
DISPLACEMENT— 15,000 (?) TONS (STANDARD)
DESIGNED SPEED—25 (?) KNOTS
AIRCRAFT— 36 PLANES CARRIED
SHOHO CV 10— REPORTED SUNK 5/7/42

↑ PROBABLY ZUIHO CLASS ↓

PHOTO 4/7/43

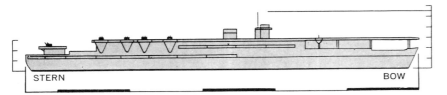

STERN   BOW

LENGTH—545' OA, 516' WL, 450' FLIGHT DECK
BEAM— 69' HULL, 74' FLIGHT DECK
DRAFT— 29' (MAXIMUM—PRE-CONVERSION)
        12,775 TONS (GROSS—PRE-CONVERSION)

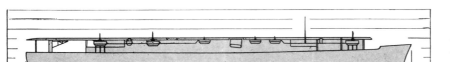

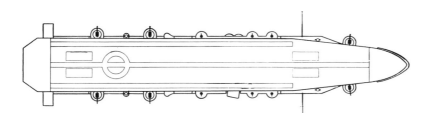

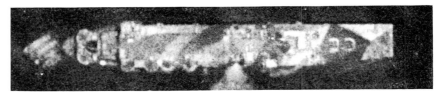

← **CVE 1—(EX-ARGENTINA MARU TYPE)**   COMPLETED 1939—CONVERTED 1942

ARMAMENT— 6 HEAVY AA MOUNTS
           5 AAMG MOUNTS

AIRCRAFT— 30 (?)

PROPULSION—(PRE-CONVERSION)—
            MACHINERY—   DIESEL
            FUEL—   OIL
            BRAKE HP—   16,500
            DESIGNED SPEED—21 KNOTS

OTAKA CLASS CVE 2-4

DIMENSIONS—   591' OA x 74' (PRE-CONVERSION)
               22,500 TONS (PRE-CONVERSION)
ARMAMENT—   6-5"(?) AA
AIRCRAFT—   48 PLANES CARRIED
DESIGNED SPEED—23 KNOTS
OTAKA CVE 2 (EX-KASUGA MARU)
UNYO CVE 3 (EX-YAWATA MARU)
CHUYO CVE 4 (EX-NITTA MARU)

CONVERSION COMPLETED 1941

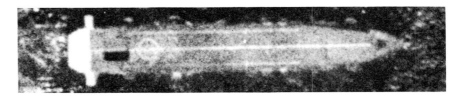

ONI 41-42

HEIGHT OF OBSERVER

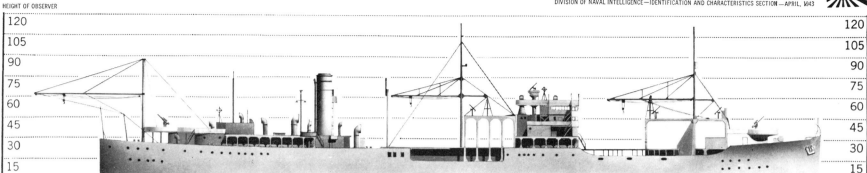

HORIZON BEYOND THE SHIP

SHIP BEYOND THE HORIZON

LENGTH—496' OA—478'6" P.P.
BEAM— 67'
DRAFT— 27'8" (MEAN)

DISPLACEMENT—17,000 TONS (STANDARD)—19,550 TONS (NORMAL)

ARMAMENT

	MAX. ELEV.	RANGE
2-5".5		
2-3".15 A.A.		
9 SEAPLANES		

PROPULSION

MACHINERY—	G.E. (Curtis) TURBINES AND ELECTRIC DRIVE
BOILERS—	4 YARROW
FUEL—	COAL, 2,500 TONS
DESIGNED HP—	8,000
DESIGNED SPEED—	15 KNOTS
ENDURANCE—	10,000 @ 10 KNOTS
	9,000 @ 15 KNOTS

KTS	RPM
	400
	375
	350
	325
	300
	275
	250
	225
	200
	150
	100
	50

KAMOI—CVS 2

DIVISION OF NAVAL INTELLIGENCE—IDENTIFICATION
AND CHARACTERISTICS SECTION —APRIL, 1943

MISTAKEN IDENTITY

KAMOI—CVS 2

NOTORO—CVS 1

TYPICAL JAPANESE TANKER

TYPICAL JAPANESE CARGO VESSEL

AE—USS NITRO, PYRO

AERIAL VIEWS

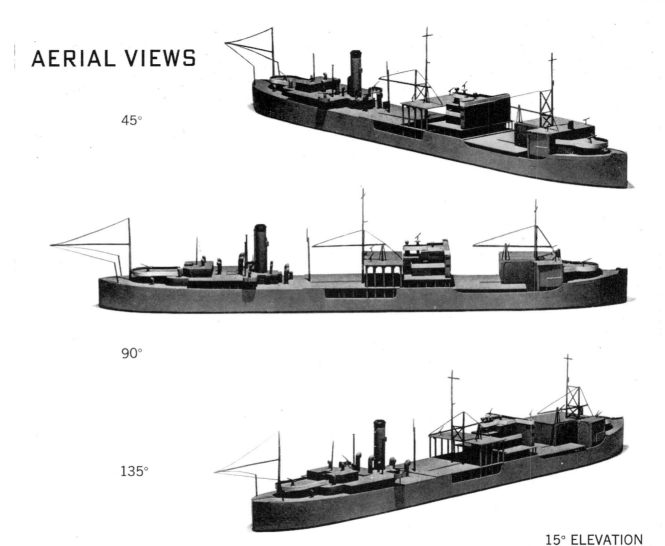

45°

90°

135°

15° ELEVATION

0°

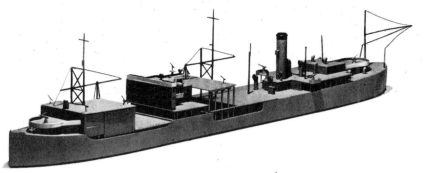

315°

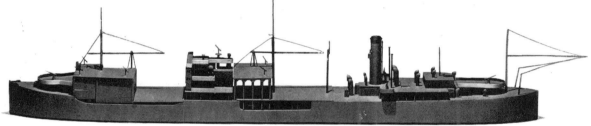

270°

180°

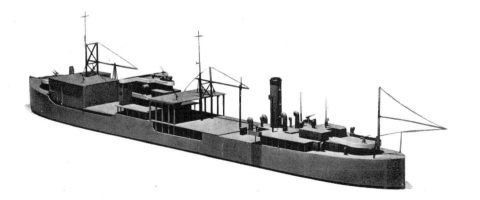

225°

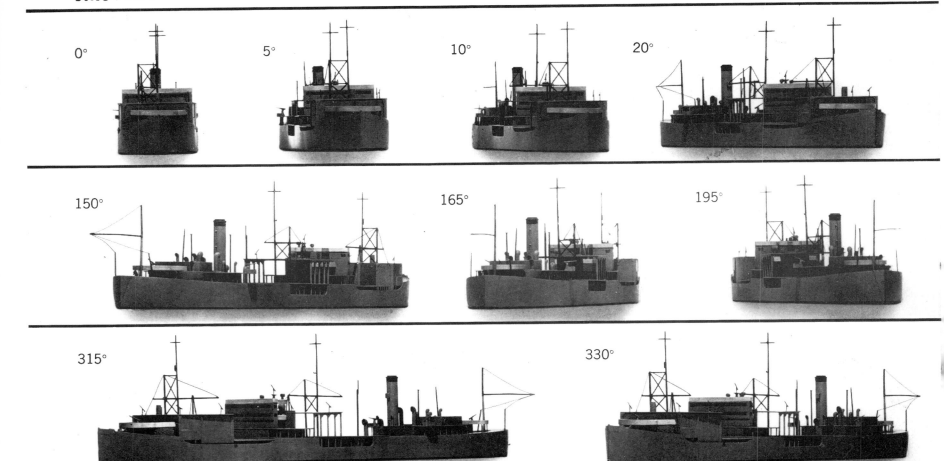

0°

5°

10°

20°

150°

165°

195°

315°

330°

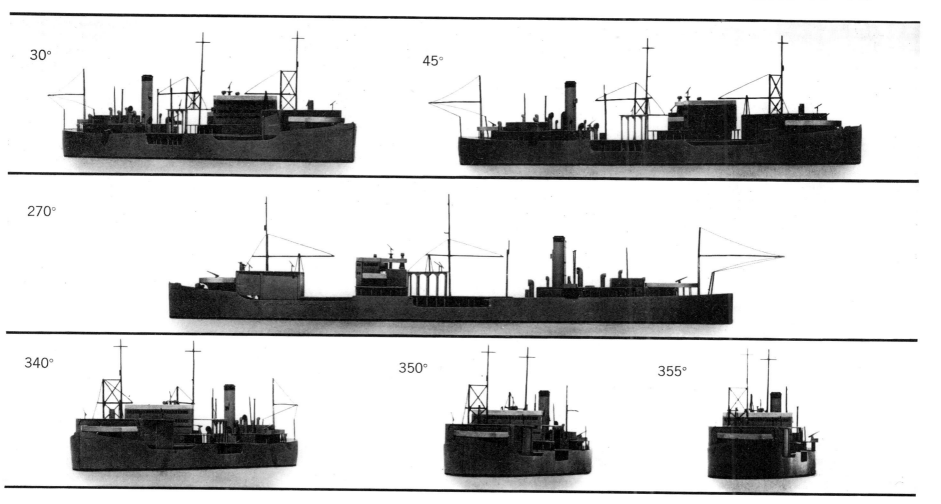

30°

45°

270°

340°

350°

355°

KAMOI—CVS 2

DIVISION OF NAVAL INTELLIGENCE—IDENTIFICATION AND CHARACTERISTICS SECTION—APRIL, 1943

BUILT FOR JAPAN BY THE N. Y. SHIPBUILDING CO. AS A TANKER.
COMPLETED 6/8/22, CONVERTED TO CVS—1932-33, MODERNIZED 1941

ONI 41-42

8/26/37 SHOWING OLD RIG

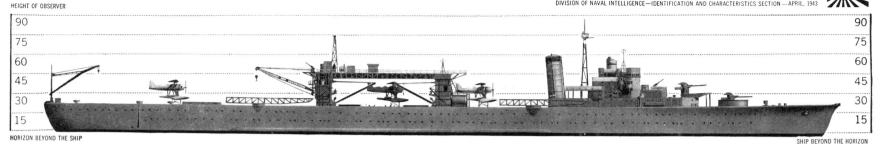

HEIGHT OF OBSERVER

90 · 75 · 60 · 45 · 30 · 15

90 · 75 · 60 · 45 · 30 · 15

HORIZON BEYOND THE SHIP

SHIP BEYOND THE HORIZON

0

LENGTH—597'5" OA
BEAM—   61'8"
DRAFT— 19' (MAXIMUM)

DISPLACEMENT—9,000 TONS (STANDARD)

ARMAMENT

	MAX. ELEV.	MAX. RANGE (HORIZONTAL)	MAX. RANGE (VERTICAL)
4–5" (50) AA	85°	19,000 YARDS	33,000 FEET
12 AAMG (TWINS)			
4 CATAPULTS; 16 SCOUT OBSERVATION			

PROPULSION

MACHINERY—	GEARED TURBINES
BOILERS—	TWO KAMPONS
FUEL—	OIL, 1,000 TONS
DESIGNED H. P.—	15,000
DESIGNED SPEED—	20 KNOTS
ENDURANCE—	11,000 MILES @ 10 KNOTS
	2,700 MILES @ 20 KNOTS

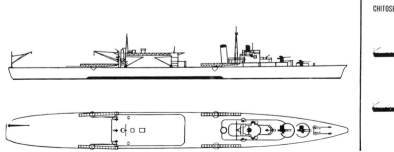

CHITOSE CLASS—

CHITOSE—CVS 3

CHIYODA—CVS 4

CHITOSE CLASS— CVS 3, 4

DIVISION OF NAVAL INTELLIGENCE—IDENTIFICATION
AND CHARACTERISTICS SECTION —APRIL, 1943

AERIAL— DECKED-OVER STRUCTURE AMIDSHIPS
(MIZUHO HAS SEPARATED STRUCTURES)

PROFILE— FLUSH HULL
TRIPOD MASTS
RAKED SINGLE PIPE STACK

END ON— MAY BE MISTAKEN FOR CA OR CL

MIZUHO ↑   ↑ CHITOSE

AERIAL VIEWS

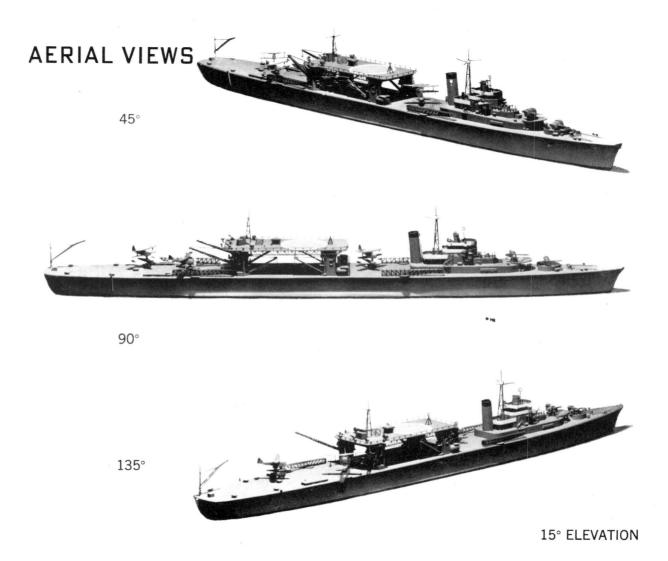

45°

90°

135°

15° ELEVATION

0°

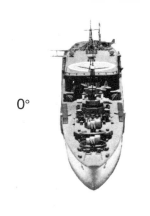

315°

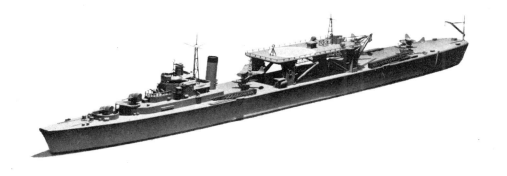

270°

180°

225°

0°

5°

10°

20°

150°

165°

195°

315°

330°

KNOTS	RPM	KNOTS	RPM	KNOTS	RPM	KNOTS	RPM
	400		300		200		100
	375		275		175		75
	350		250		150		50
	325		225		125		25

30°

45°

270°

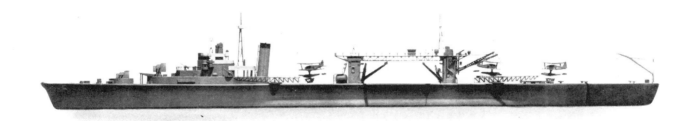

340°

350°

355°

CHITOSE CLASS—CVS 3, 4

DIVISION OF NAVAL INTELLIGENCE—IDENTIFICATION AND CHARACTERISTICS SECTION — APRIL, 1943

		BEGUN	COMPLETED
CHITOSE—	CVS 3	11/26/34	1/?/38
CHIYODA—	CVS 4	12/14/36	1938

ONI 41-42

HEIGHT OF OBSERVER

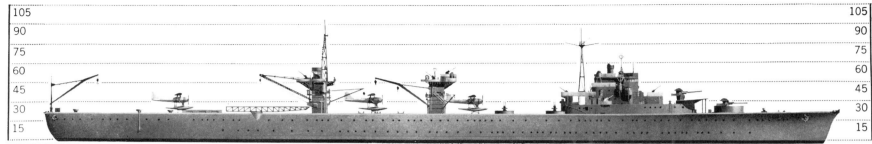

105	105
90	90
75	75
60	60
45	45
30	30
15	15

HORIZON BEYOND THE SHIP

SHIP BEYOND THE HORIZON

0

LENGTH—597'6" OA
BEAM—   61'8"
DRAFT— 19' (MAXIMUM)

DISPLACEMENT
9,000 TONS (STANDARD)

ARMAMENT

	MAX. ELEV.	MAX. RANGE (HORIZONTAL)	MAX. RANGE (VERTICAL)
4-5" (50) AA TWINS	85°	19,000 YARDS	33,000 FEET

12 AAMG TWINS
4 CATAPULTS, 20 SCOUT OBSERVATION

PROPULSION

MACHINERY—   GEARED TURBINES
BOILERS—   TWO KAMPONS
FUEL—   OIL, 1,000 TONS
DESIGNED HP—   15,000
DESIGNED SPEED—   20 KNOTS
ENDURANCE—   11,000 MILES @ 10 KNOTS
                  2,700 MILES @ 20 KNOTS

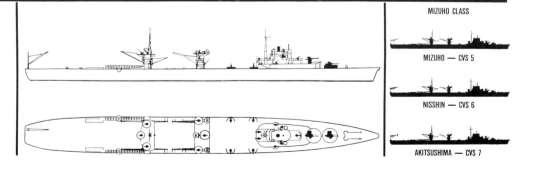

MIZUHO CLASS

MIZUHO — CVS 5

NISSHIN — CVS 6

AKITSUSHIMA — CVS 7

MIZUHO CLASS CVS 5-7

DIVISION OF NAVAL INTELLIGENCE—IDENTIFICATION
AND CHARACTERISTICS SECTION —APRIL, 1943

AERIAL VIEWS

45°

90°

135°

15° ELEVATION

MISTAKEN IDENTITY

CHITOSE CLASS—CVS 3-4

MIZUHO CLASS—CVS 5-7

0°

180°

315°

270°

225°

0° 5° 10° 20°

150° 165° 195°

315° 330°

KNOTS	RPM	KNOTS	RPM	KNOTS	RPM	KNOTS	RPM
......	400	......	300	......	200	......	100
......	375	......	275	......	175	......	75
......	350	......	250	......	150	......	50
......	325	......	225	......	125	......	25

30°

45°

270°

340°

350°

355°

MIZUHO CLASS—CVS 5-7

DIVISION OF NAVAL INTELLIGENCE—IDENTIFICATION AND CHARACTERISTICS SECTION—APRIL, 1943

MIZUHO— CVS5
NISSHIN— CVS6
AKITSUSHIMA—CVS7 BELIEVED BEGUN 1940

	BEGUN	COMPLETED
	1937	2/25/39
	1937	1941
		1942

ONI 41-42

ALL PHOTOS MIZUHO DATED APRIL, 1940.

CRUISERS

↑ MOGAMI CLASS

↑ NACHI CLASS

↓ ATAGO CLASS →

JAPANESE HEAVY CRUISERS

DIVISION OF NAVAL INTELLIGENCE—IDENTIFICATION AND CHARACTERISTICS SECTION —JUNE, 1943

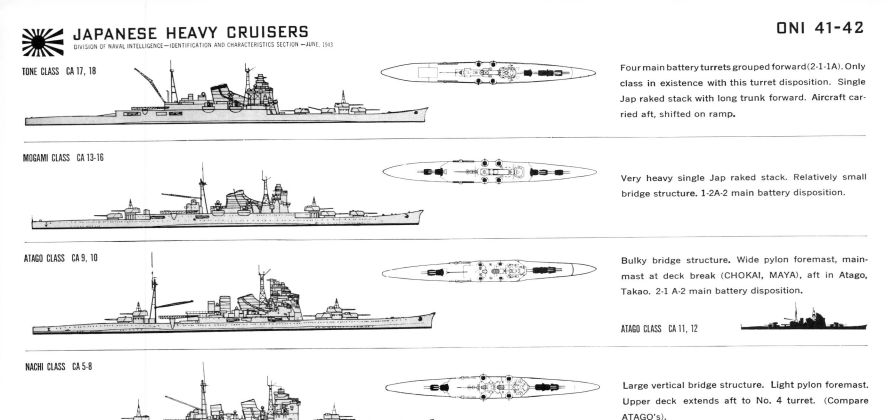

TONE CLASS   CA 17, 18

Four main battery turrets grouped forward (2-1-1A). Only class in existence with this turret disposition. Single Jap raked stack with long trunk forward. Aircraft carried aft, shifted on ramp.

MOGAMI CLASS   CA 13-16

Very heavy single Jap raked stack. Relatively small bridge structure. 1-2A-2 main battery disposition.

ATAGO CLASS   CA 9, 10

Bulky bridge structure. Wide pylon foremast, mainmast at deck break (CHOKAI, MAYA), aft in Atago, Takao. 2-1 A-2 main battery disposition.

ATAGO CLASS   CA 11, 12

NACHI CLASS   CA 5-8

Large vertical bridge structure. Light pylon foremast. Upper deck extends aft to No. 4 turret. (Compare ATAGO's).

AOBA CLASS   CA 3, 4

Flush deck. Note 2A-1 main battery disposition. Pole foremast. Irregular bridge structure. Catapult forward of No. 3 turret.

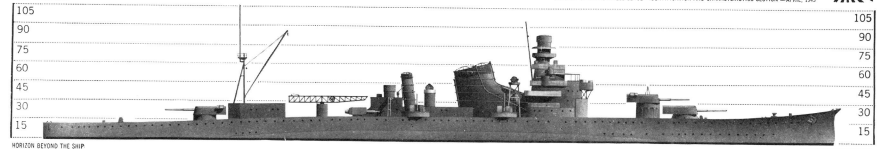

105	105
90	90
75	75
60	60
45	45
30	30
15	15

HORIZON BEYOND THE SHIP

SHIP BEYOND THE HORIZON

0

LENGTH—595' OA
BEAM— 50'9"
DRAFT— 14'9" (MEAN)

DISPLACEMENT
7,100 TONS (STANDARD)
7,500 TONS (NORMAL)

DENSITY OF FIRE
MAIN BATTERY

29°   0°   29°

4

6   ↑   6

2

151°   180°   151°

ARMAMENT

	MAX. ELEV.	RANGE (HORIZONTAL)	RANGE (VERTICAL)
6–8" (50) TWINS	30°	28,000 YD.	
4–4.7 (50) AA	85°	19,000 YD.	25,000 FT.
10 MG			
12–21" TORPEDO TUBES			
1 CATAPULT; 2 SCOUT OBSERVATION PLANES			

PROPULSION

MACHINERY—	GEARED TURBINE
BOILERS—	TWELVE YARROW
FUEL—	OIL, 1,800 TONS; COAL, 400 TONS
DESIGNED HP—	95,000
DESIGNED SPEED—	33 KNOTS*
ENDURANCE—	8,000 MILES @ 10 KNOTS
	1,740 MILES @ 33 KNOTS

*SPEED PROBABLY REDUCED BY BULGES.

PROTECTION

BELT—2" (AMIDSHIPS)
DECK—2"

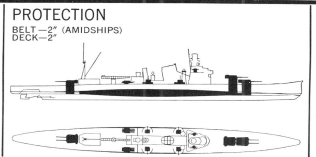

FURUTAKA CLASS

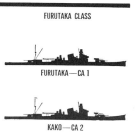

FURUTAKA—CA 1

KAKO—CA 2

FURUTAKA CLASS CA1,2

DIVISION OF NAVAL INTELLIGENCE—IDENTIFICATION AND CHARACTERISTICS SECTION —APRIL, 1943

PROFILE ➡️

TOWER BRIDGE, STICK FORE-MAST, TRIPOD MAINMAST

JAP RAKED STACK FORWARD, RAKED SINGLE PIPE AFT.

⬅️

AERIAL

SUPERIMPOSED TWIN TURRETS FORWARD

SINGLE TWIN AFT

CATAPULT AMIDSHIPS

MISTAKEN IDENTITY

FURUTAKA CLASS—CA1, 2

AOBA CLASS—CA3, 4

NACHI CLASS—CA5-8

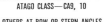

ATAGO CLASS—CA9, 10

OTHERS AT BOW OR STERN ANGLES

AERIAL VIEWS

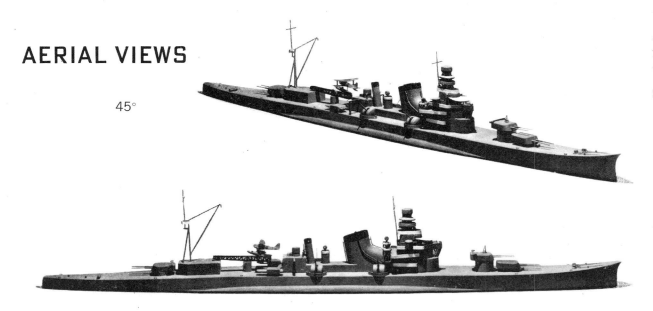

45°

90°

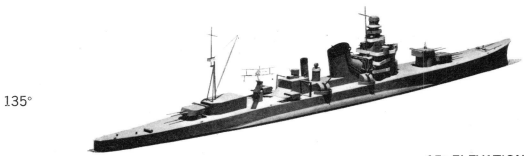

135°

15° ELEVATION

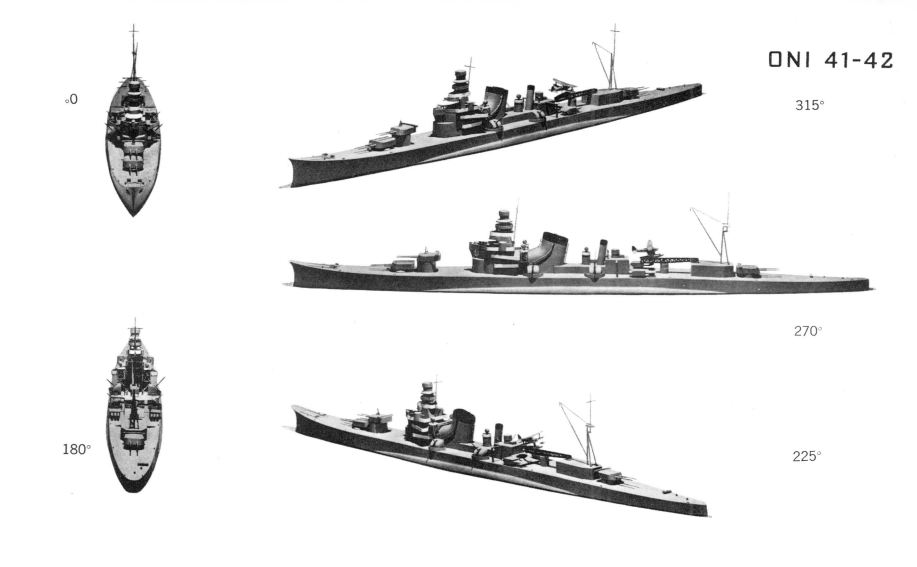

ONI 41-42

°0

315°

270°

180°

225°

0°

5°

10°

20°

150°

165°

195°

300°

330°

ONI 41-42

30°

45°

270°

340°

350°

355°

FURUTAKA CLASS—CA 1,2

DIVISION OF NAVAL INTELLIGENCE—IDENTIFICATION AND CHARACTERISTICS·SECTION —APRIL, 1943

	BEGUN	COMPLETED
FURUTAKA—CA1	12/5/22	3/31/26
KAKO— CA2	11/17/22	7/20/26

MODERNIZED IN 1939, BULGES ADDED.

ONI 41-42

HEIGHT OF OBSERVER

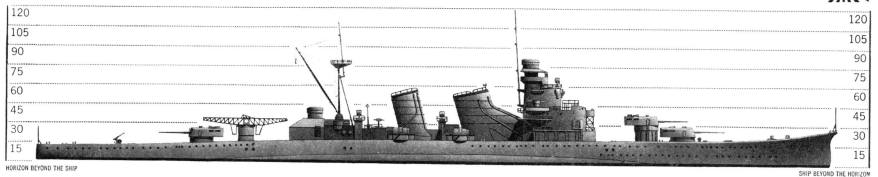

120		120
105		105
90		90
75		75
60		60
45		45
30		30
15		15

HORIZON BEYOND THE SHIP

SHIP BEYOND THE HORIZON

LENGTH—598' OA—594' WL
BEAM —50'9"
DRAFT —19' (MAXIMUM)
14'9" (MEAN)

O

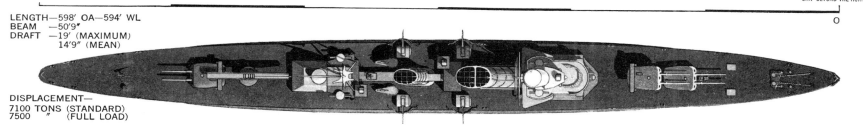

DISPLACEMENT—
7100 TONS (STANDARD)
7500 " (FULL LOAD)

DENSITY OF FIRE MAIN BATTERY

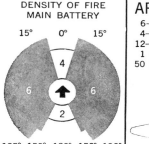

15°	0°	15°
	4	
6	⬆	6
	2	

135° 150° 180° 150° 135°

ARMAMENT

	MAX. ELEV.	RANGE
6-8" 50 CAL. TWIN TURRETS	35°	32,600 YD
4-4.7 50 CAL. AA—SINGLE MOUNTS	85°	21,000 YD
12-21" TORPEDO TUBES—TWIN MOUNTS		
1 CATAPULT—2 SEAPLANE SCOUTS		
50 MINES—MOORED TYPE		

PROTECTION

BELT—2"-3"
TURRETS—1"
BARBETTES—
CONNING TOWER—
DECK—2" (OVER VITALS)

PROPULSION

MACHINERY—4 GEARED TURBINES
BOILERS—12 KAMPON
FUEL—OIL—1800 TONS
DESIGNED HP—95,000
DESIGNED SPEED—33 KTS
ENDURANCE—1120 @ 33 KTS
5040 @ 15 KTS

KNOTS	RPM
	420
	400
33	370
	350
	300
	275
	250
	245
	240
	220
	200
	160
	150
	120
	80

AOBA CLASS
CA 3-4

DIVISION OF NAVAL INTELLIGENCE—IDENTIFICATION
AND CHARACTERISTICS SECTION —DECEMBER, 1942

PROFILE—
  STACKS—
    JAP RAKED FOR'D
    RAKED SINGLE PIPE AFT
    HEAVY, STEPPED BRIDGE
    STICK FOREMAST, TRIPOD
    MAINMAST

→

AERIAL—
  TURRETS—
    2 SUPERIMPOSED TWINS
      FOR'D
    SINGLE TWIN AFT
    HIGH, PROMINENT
    CATAPULT AFT

←

↑

END-ON—
  HIGH, NARROW BRIDGE
  HEAVY CONTROL TOWER

EASILY MISTAKEN FOR **NACHI**

45°

90°

135°

0°

270°

180°

225°

AOBA CLASS—CA 3-4

DIVISION OF NAVAL INTELLIGENCE—IDENTIFICATION AND CHARACTERISTICS SECTION · DECEMBER, 1942

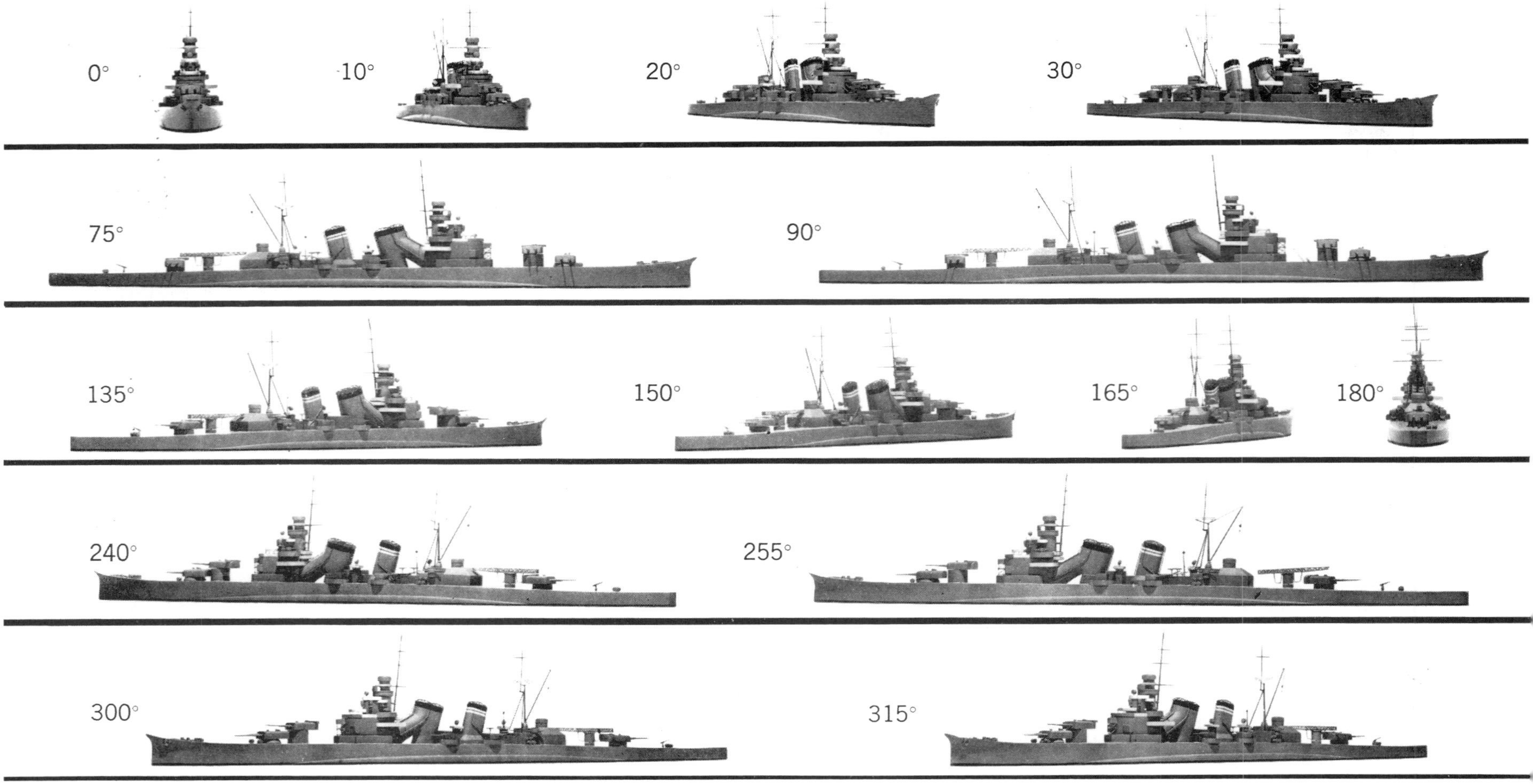

0° 10° 20° 30°

75° 90°

135° 150° 165° 180°

240° 255°

300° 315°

ONI 41-42

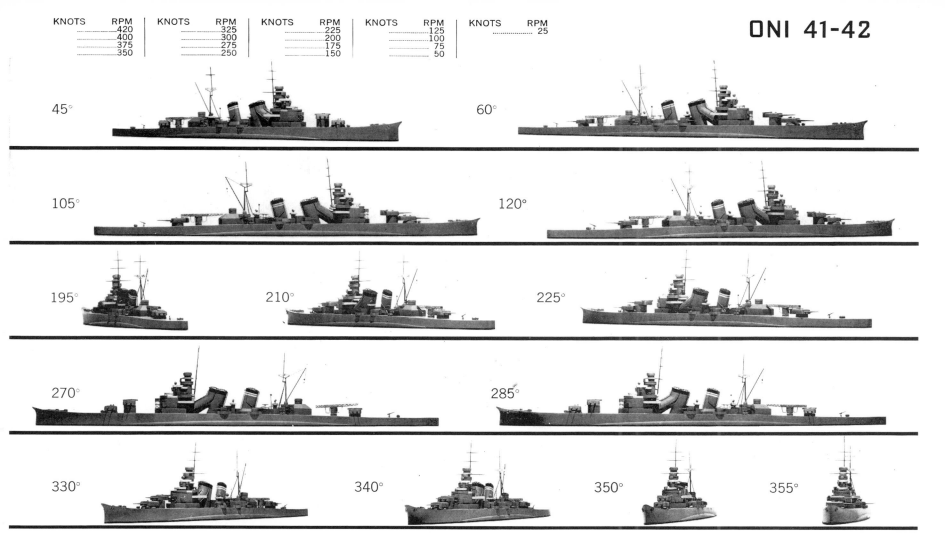

45°   60°

105°   120°

195°   210°   225°

270°   285°

330°   340°   350°   355°

AOBA CLASS—CA3-4

DIVISION OF NAVAL INTELLIGENCE—IDENTIFICATION AND CHARACTERISTICS SECTION — OCTOBER, 1942

	BEGUN	COMPLETED
AOBA —	2/4/24	9/20/27
KINUGASA —	1/23/24	9/30/27

ONI 41-42

1933 ↑

HEIGHT OF OBSERVER

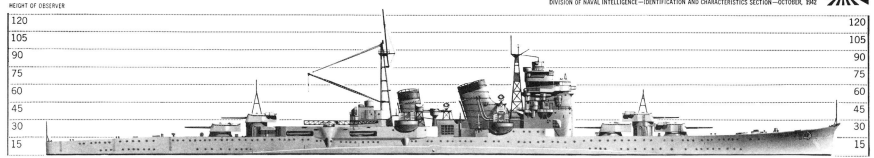

120	120
105	105
90	90
75	75
60	60
45	45
30	30
15	15

HORIZON BEYOND THE SHIP

SHIP BEYOND THE HORIZON

0

LENGTH—656' OA
BEAM— 62'4"
DRAFT— 16'6" (MEAN)

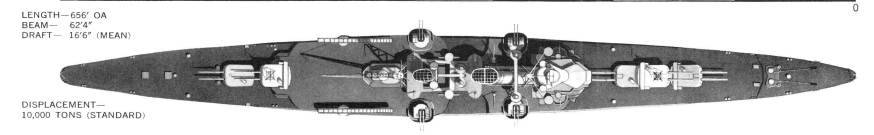

DISPLACEMENT—
10,000 TONS (STANDARD)

DENSITY OF FIRE
MAIN BATTERY

46° 21° 0° 21° 46°

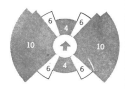

135° 156° 180° 156° 135°

ARMAMENT

	MAX. ELEV.	RANGE
10-8" 50 CAL TWIN TURRETS	35°	32,600 YD.
8-4".7 50 CAL AA TWIN SHIELD MOUNTS	85°	21,000 YD·
8-21" TORPEDO TUBES—(TWIN MOUNTS)		
2 CATAPULTS—4 SEAPLANE SCOUTS		
DEPTH CHARGES CARRIED		

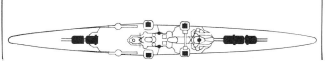

PROTECTION

BELT—   3"–4"
TURRETS—
BARBETTES—
CONNING TOWER—3"
DECK—   1¼"–2"–3" (OVER VITALS)

KNOTS	RPM
	420
	400
	350
	300
	275
	250
	245
	240
	220
	200
	160
	150
	120
	80

DES HP—100,000
DES SPD—33 KTS
ENDURANCE—
2800 @ 33 KTS
10,000 @ 15 KTS

NACHI CLASS
CA 5-8

DIVISION OF NAVAL INTELLIGENCE—IDENTIFICATION

AND CHARACTERISTICS SECTION —DECEMBER, 1942

IDENTIFICATION

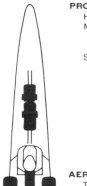

PROFILE—
　HIGH BRIDGE
　MASTS—
　　PYLON FORE
　　TRIPOD MAIN
　STACKS—
　　NO. 1 JAP RAKED
　　NO. 2 S.P. RAKED

AERIAL—
　TURRETS—
　　3 TWINS FOR'D
　　2 TWINS AFT
　SECONDARIES MOUNTED
　ON SPONSONS

END-ON—
　HIGH, NARROW BRIDGE
　PROMINENT SPONSONS

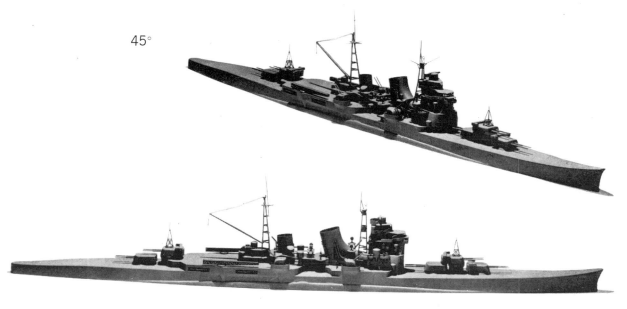

45°

90°

135°

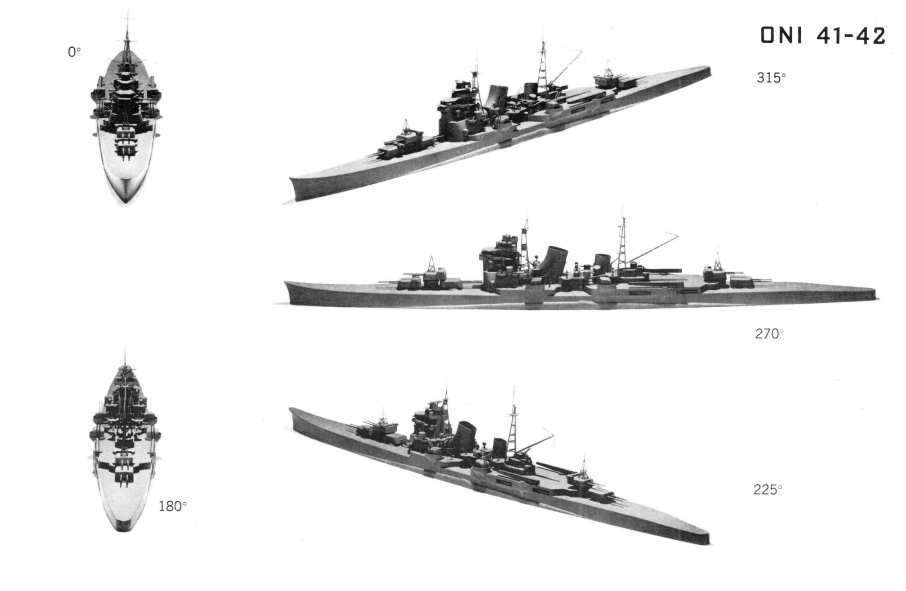

ONI 41-42

0°

180°

315°

270°

225°

NACHI CLASS—CA 5-8

DIVISION OF NAVAL INTELLIGENCE—IDENTIFICATION AND CHARACTERISTICS SECTION —NOVEMBER, 1942

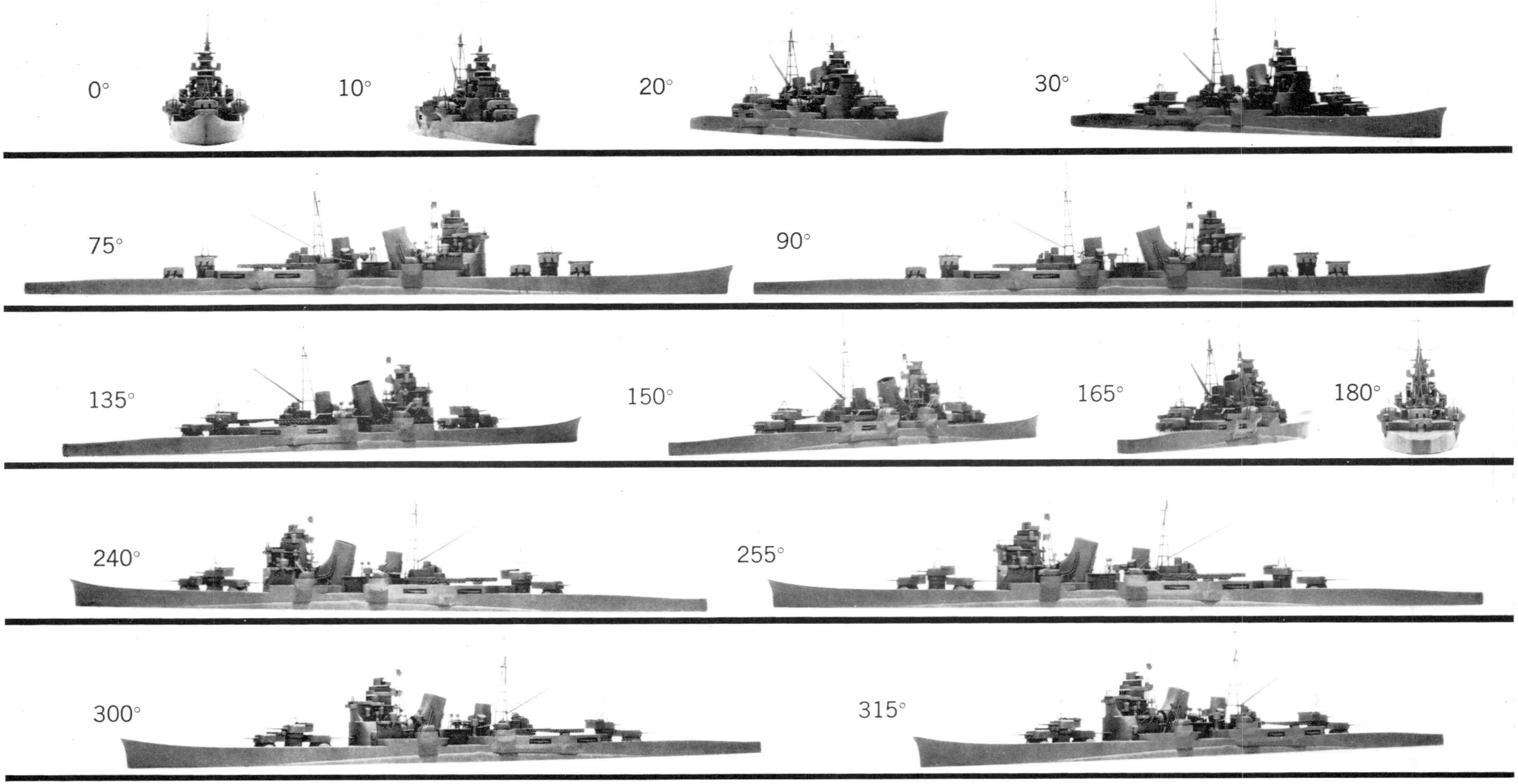

0° 10° 20° 30°

75° 90°

135° 150° 165° 180°

240° 255°

300° 315°

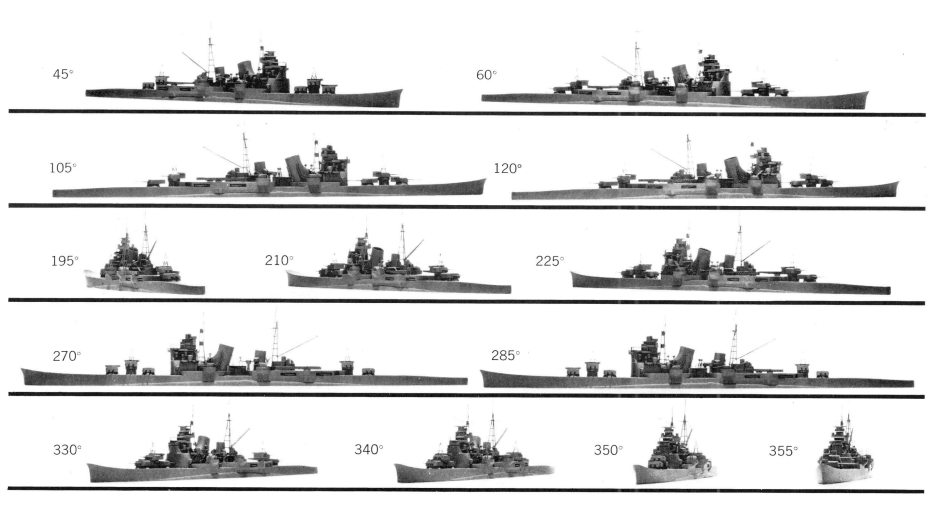

45°

60°

105°

120°

195°

210°

225°

270°

285°

330°

340°

350°

355°

NACHI CLASS—CA 5-8

DIVISION OF NAVAL INTELLIGENCE—IDENTIFICATION AND CHARACTERISTICS SECTION—OCTOBER, 1942

	BEGUN	COMPLETED		BEGUN	COMPLETED
NACHI— CA5	11/26/24	11/26/28	MYOKO— CA7	10/25/24	7/31/29
HAGURO—CA6	3/16/25	4/25/29	ASHIGARA—CA8	4/11/25	8/20/29

ONI 41-42

↓ DEC. 1940   ↑ DEC. 1940   ↓ MAY 1938

HEIGHT OF OBSERVER

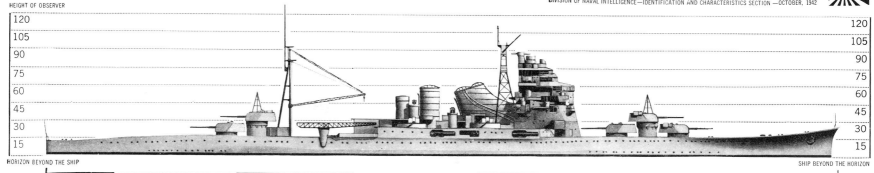

120	120
105	105
90	90
75	75
60	60
45	45
30	30
15	15

HORIZON BEYOND THE SHIP

SHIP BEYOND THE HORIZON

0

LENGTH—657'0" OA—650'0" WL
BEAM—   62'4"
DRAFT—   19'8" (MAXIMUM)
         16'5" (MEAN)

DISPLACEMENT—
9,850 TONS (STANDARD)

DENSITY OF FIRE
MAIN BATTERY

64° 41° 0° 41° 64°

142° 161° 180° 161° 142°

ARMAMENT

	MAX. ELEV.	RANGE
10–8" 50 CAL TWIN TURRETS	35°	32,600 YD.
4-4".7 50 CAL AA	85°	21,000 YD.
8-21" TORPEDO TUBES		
2 CATAPULTS—4 SEAPLANE SCOUTS		

IT IS REPORTED THAT THE 4-4".7 BATTERY IS TO
BE REPLACED BY 8-4".7 50 CAL AA GUNS IN TWIN
SHIELD MOUNTS

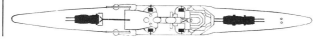

PROTECTION

BELTS—	3"—4"
TURRETS—	3"
BARBETTES—	2½"—3½"
CONNING TOWER—	
DECK—	3"—5"

KNOTS	RPM
	420
	400
	350
	300
	275
	250
	245
	220
	200
	160
	150
	120
	80

DES SPEED DES HP
33 KTS   100,000

ATAGO CLASS—CA9-10

DIVISION OF NAVAL INTELLIGENCE—IDENTIFICATION AND CHARACTERISTICS SECTION —OCTOBER, 1942

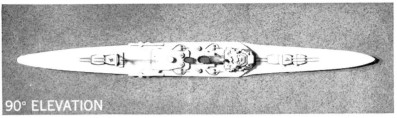

90° ELEVATION

PROFILE—PYLON FOREMAST, HEAVY BRIDGE TRIPOD MAINMAST STACKS—JAP RAKE FOR'D UPRIGHT SINGLE PIPE AFT

AERIAL—TURRETS—THREE TWINS FOR'D TWO TWINS AFT AMIDSHIPS—SECONDARY

END ON—FLARED HULL FULL WIDTH PYRAMID SUPERSTRUCTURE

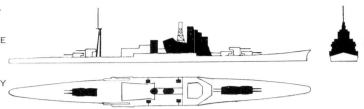

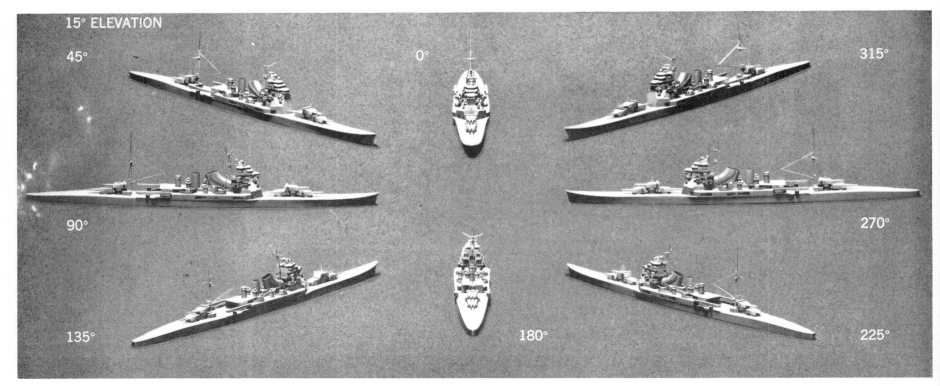

15° ELEVATION

45° 0° 315°

90° 270°

135° 180° 225°

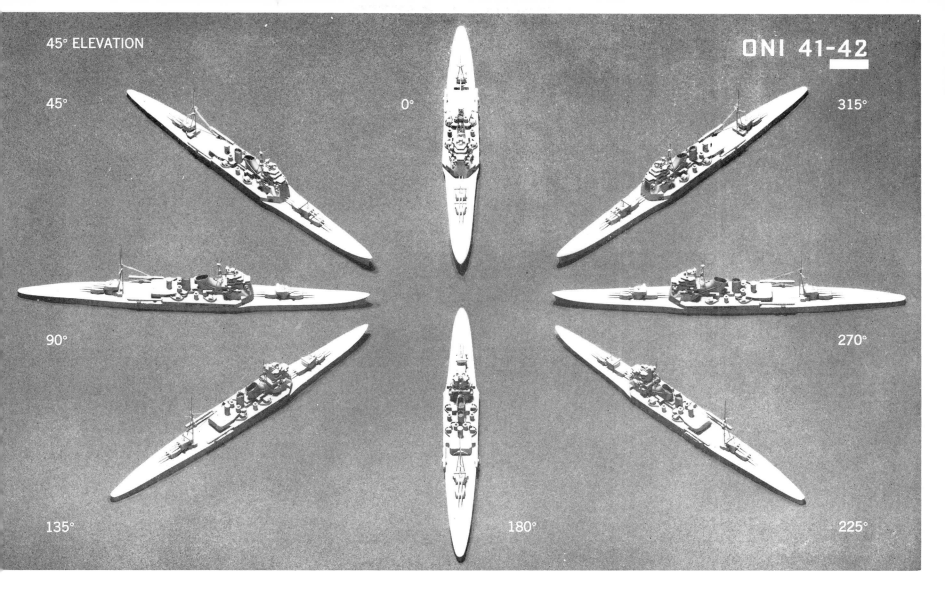

45°

0°

315°

90°

270°

135°

180°

225°

ATAGO CLASS—CA 9-10

DIVISION OF NAVAL INTELLIGENCE—IDENTIFICATION AND CHARACTERISTICS SECTION—OCTOBER, 1942

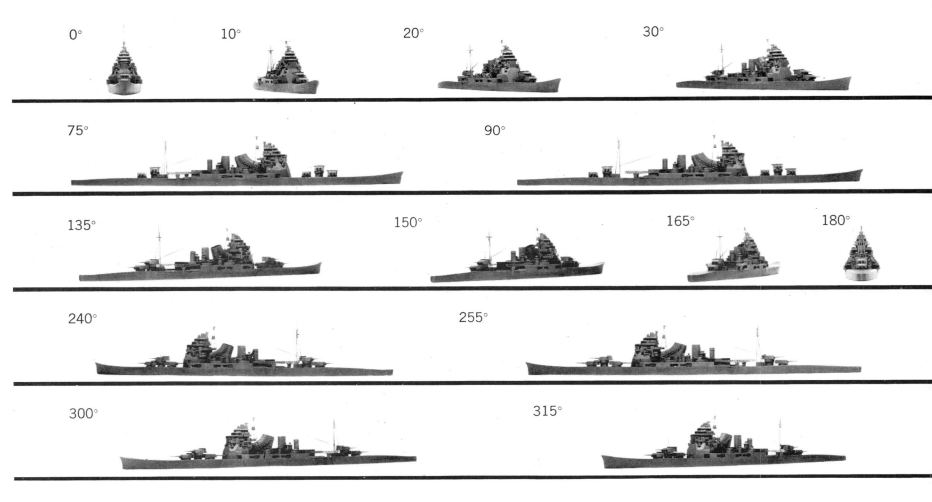

0° 10° 20° 30°

75° 90°

135° 150° 165° 180°

240° 255°

300° 315°

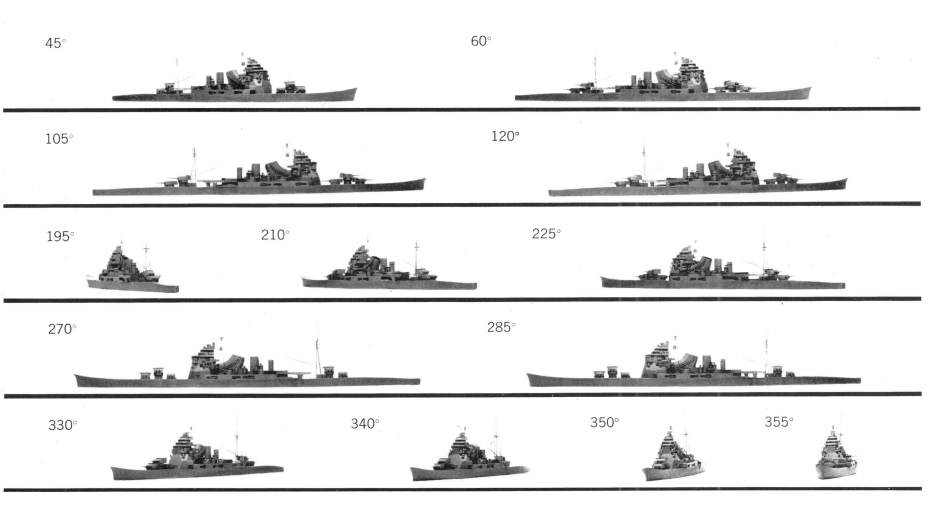

45°

60°

105°

120°

195°

210°

225°

270°

285°

330°

340°

350°

355°

ATAGO CLASS—CA9-10

DIVISION OF NAVAL INTELLIGENCE—IDENTIFICATION AND CHARACTERISTICS SECTION · OCTOBER, 1942

ATAGO—CA9
TAKAO—CA10
TWO OTHER UNITS—CHOKAI (TYOKAI), MAYA—RETAIN ORIGINAL PROFILE

	BEGUN	COMPLETED
ATAGO—CA9	4/28/27	3/30/32
TAKAO—CA10	4/28/27	5/31/32

ONI 41-42

1941 ↓   TAKAO—1941 ↑   ↓ ATAGO OLD RIG

CHOKAI (TYOKAI)—MAYA

ATAGO CLASS—CA11-12

DIVISION OF NAVAL INTELLIGENCE—IDENTIFICATION AND CHARACTERISTICS SECTION —OCTOBER, 1942

HEIGHT OF OBSERVER

HORIZON BEYOND THE SHIP

SHIP BEYOND THE HORIZON

LENGTH—657'0" OA—650'0" WL
BEAM —62'4"
DRAFT —19'8" (FULL LOAD)
         16'5" (MEAN)

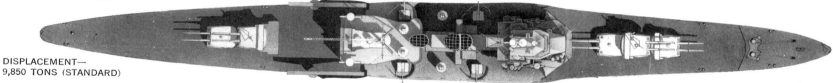

DISPLACEMENT—
9,850 TONS (STANDARD)

↓ JUNE, 1940

ARMAMENT

	MAX. ELEV.	RANGE
10–8" 50 CAL TWIN TURRETS	35°	32,600
4–4.7 50 CAL AA SINGLE SHIELD MOUNTS	85°	21,000
8–21" TORPEDO TUBES		
2 CATAPULTS—4 SEAPLANE SCOUTS		

PROTECTION

BELT	—3"–4"
TURRETS	—3"
BARBETTES	—2½"–3½"
DECK	—3"–5"

PROPULSION

MACHINERY	—8 GEARED TURBINES
FUEL	—OIL—2400 TONS
DESIGNED HP	—100,000
DESIGNED SPD.	—33 KTS.

ATAGO CLASS—CA11-12
DIVISION OF NAVAL INTELLIGENCE—IDENTIFICATION AND CHARACTERISTICS SECTION—OCTOBER, 1942

	BEGUN	COMPLETED
CHOKAI—CA11	3 /26/28	6/30/32
MAYA —CA12	12/4 /28	6/30/32

TWO OTHER UNITS—ATAGO, TAKAO HAVE MAINMAST AFT

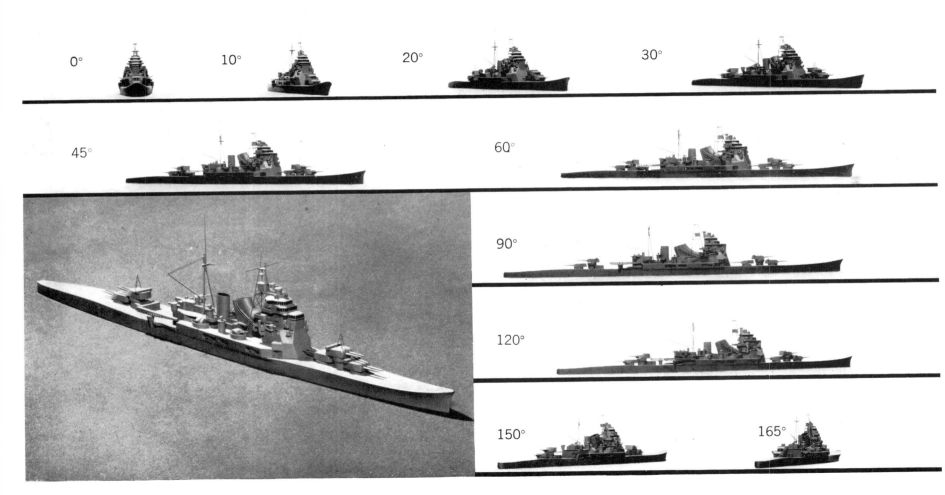

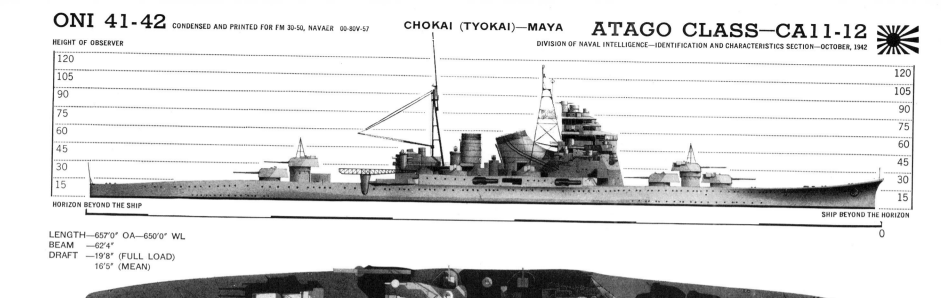

HEIGHT OF OBSERVER

HORIZON BEYOND THE SHIP

SHIP BEYOND THE HORIZON

LENGTH—657'0" OA—650'0" WL
BEAM —62'4"
DRAFT —19'8" (FULL LOAD)
        16'5" (MEAN)

DISPLACEMENT—
9,850 TONS (STANDARD)

↓ JUNE, 1940

ARMAMENT

10–8" 50 CAL TWIN TURRETS
4–4.7" 50 CAL AA SINGLE SHIELD MOUNTS
8–21" TORPEDO TUBES
2 CATAPULTS—4 SEAPLANE SCOUTS

	MAX. ELEV.	RANGE
	35°	32,600
	85°	21,000

PROTECTION

BELT   —3"–4"
TURRETS   —3"
BARBETTES—2½"–3½"
DECK   —3"–5"

PROPULSION

MACHINERY   —8 GEARED TURBINES
FUEL   —OIL—2400 TONS
DESIGNED HP —100,000
DESIGNED SPD.—33 KTS.

ATAGO CLASS-CA 11-12

DIVISION OF NAVAL INTELLIGENCE—IDENTIFICATION AND CHARACTERISTICS SECTION—AUGUST, 1943

	BEGUN	COMPLETED
CHOKAI (TYOKAI)—CA11	3/26/28	6/20/32
MAYA —CA12	12/4/28	6/30/32

ALL PHOTOS ARE OF **CHOKAI** JUNE, 1940

ONI 41-42

HEIGHT OF OBSERVER

HORIZON BEYOND THE SHIP

SHIP BEYOND THE HORIZON

LENGTH—639'8" OA—630' WL
BEAM —59'9"
DRAFT —14'9" (MEAN)

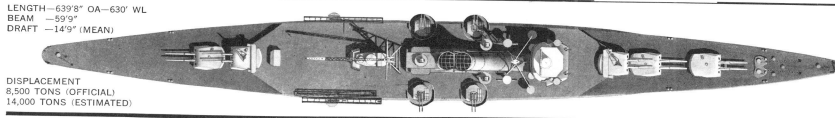

DISPLACEMENT
8,500 TONS (OFFICIAL)
14,000 TONS (ESTIMATED)

DENSITY OF FIRE
MAIN BATTERY

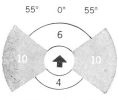

55°   0°   55°

6

10   10

4

125°   180°   125°

ARMAMENT

		MAX. ELEV.	RANGE
10–8"	50 CAL TWIN TURRETS	35°	32,600 YD.
8–5"	50 CAL AA TWIN SHIELD MOUNTS	85°	18,000 YD.
4–3"	40 CAL AA (REPORTED)	85°	9,000 YD.

12–21" TORPEDO TUBES (TRIPLE MOUNTS)
2 CATAPULTS—4 SEAPLANE SCOUTS
DEPTH CHARGES CARRIED

PROTECTION   PROPULSION

BELT—2½"
TURRETS—
BARBETTES—
CONNING TOWER—
DECKS—2"
    (OVER VITALS)

MACHINERY—4 (MAIN)—2 (CRUIS-
    ING) GEARED TURBINES
BOILERS—8 OR 10 KAMPON
FUEL—OIL—2400 TONS
DESIGNED HP—90,000
DESIGNED SPEED—33 KTS
ENDURANCE—2,800 @ 33 KTS
    10,000 @ 15 KTS

KNOTS	RPM
	420
	400
	350
	300
	290
	275
	250
	245
	240
	220
	200
	160
	150
	120
	80

33

MOGAMI
CLASS
CA 13-16

DIVISION OF NAVAL INTELLIGENCE - IDENTIFICATION
AND CHARACTERISTICS SECTION - DECEMBER, 1942

PROFILE– →
OVERSIZE J. R. STACK
UNDERSIZE TOWER
BRIDGE
TRIPOD FOREMAST
TRIPOD MAINMAST

AERIAL–
TURRETS
FOR'D–TWIN SINGLE
AND SUPERIMPOSED
AFT–TWIN SUPERIMPOSED
←

END-ON–
PROMINENT SPONSONS
LOW, SLENDER BRIDGE

45°

90°

135°

0°

180°

315°

270°

225°

MOGAMI CLASS—CA 13-16

DIVISION OF NAVAL INTELLIGENCE—IDENTIFICATION AND CHARACTERISTICS SECTION—NOVEMBER, 1942

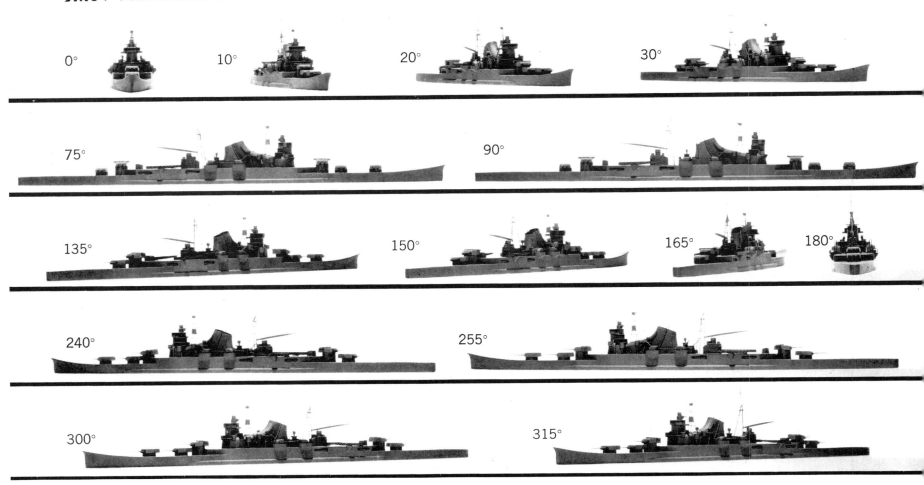

0°   10°   20°   30°

75°   90°

135°   150°   165°   180°

240°   255°

300°   315°

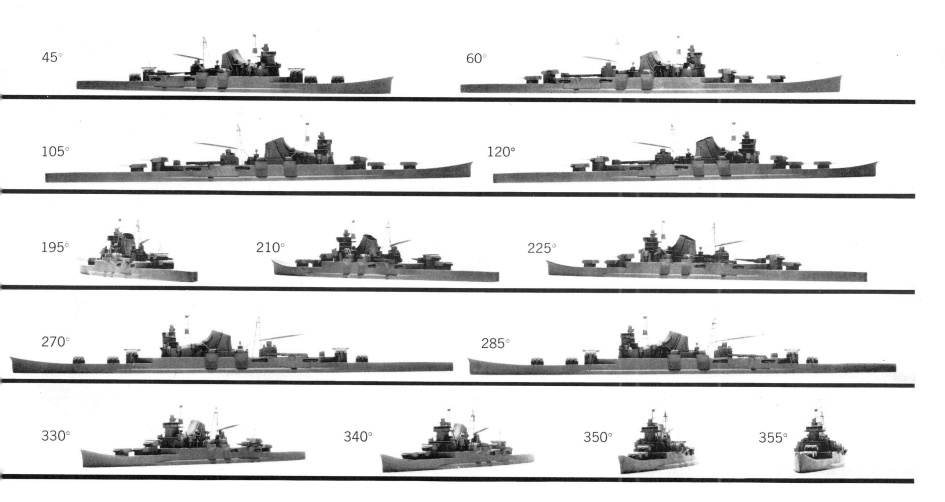

ONI 41-42

45° 60°

105° 120°

195° 210° 225°

270° 285°

330° 340° 350° 355°

	BEGUN	COMPLETED			
MOGAMI—CA13	10/27/31	7/28/35	SUZUYA —CA15	12/11/33	1936
MIKUMA—CA14	SUNK		KUMANO—CA16	4/ 4/34	10/31/37

KUMANO—DEC. 19, 1938 ↓

SUZUYA—DEC. 19, 1938 ↑

KUMANO—OCT. 1938 ↓

PHOTOS SHOW OLD TRIPLE TURRETS, PREVIOUS TO 1938-39 REFIT

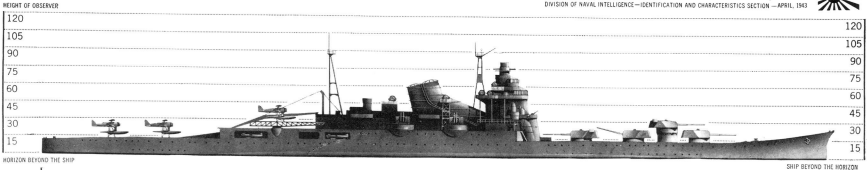

HEIGHT OF OBSERVER

120		120
105		105
90		90
75		75
60		60
45		45
30		30
15		15

HORIZON BEYOND THE SHIP

SHIP BEYOND THE HORIZON

0

LENGTH—658' (E) OA—614'3" WL
BEAM— 65' (E)
DRAFT— 14'7" (MEAN)

DISPLACEMENT
12,000 TONS STANDARD (E)

DENSITY OF FIRE
MAIN BATTERY

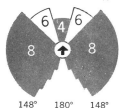

45° 15° 0° 15° 45°

6 | 4 | 6

8 | | 8

148° 180° 148°

ARMAMENT

	MAX. ELEV.	RANGE
8-8" (50)	45°?	32,800 YD.
8-5" (50) AA	85°	19,000 YD.
8-3" (40) AA (?)	85°	9,000 YD.

6 SCOUT OBSERVATION; 2 CATAPULTS
12-24" TORPEDO TUBES

PROPULSION

MACHINERY—	FOUR GEARED TURBINE ENGINES
BOILERS—	EIGHT KAMPON
FUEL—	OIL, 2,400 TONS
DESIGNED HP—	90,000
CRUISING SPEED—	15 KNOTS
MAXIMUM SPEED—	33 KNOTS
PROPELLERS—	FOUR
SEARCHLIGHTS—	THREE

PROTECTION

BRIDGES—LIGHT STEEL

BELT— 2.5"
DECK— 2"

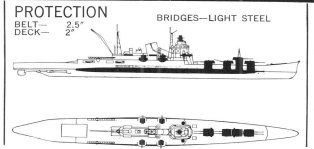

TONE CLASS

TONE—CA 17

CHIKUMA—CA 18

TONE CLASS
CA 17, 18

DIVISION OF NAVAL INTELLIGENCE—IDENTIFICATION
AND CHARACTERISTICS SECTION —APRIL, 1943

AERIAL
FOUR TWIN TURRETS FOR'D
AIRCRAFT RAMP AFT
CRUISER HULL, BROKEN UP-
WARDS.

PROFILE
TOWER BRIDGE
TRIPOD FOREMAST & MAIN-
MAST
LARGE JAP RAKED STACK

MISTAKEN IDENTITY

TONE CLASS—CA 17, 18

MOGAMI CLASS—CA 13-16

DD UNKNOWN 1 CLASS

AERIAL VIEWS

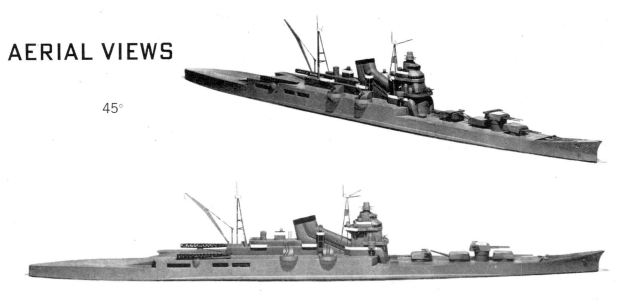

45°

90°

135°

15° ELEVATION

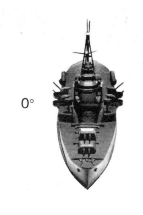

0°

180°

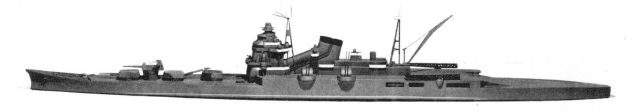

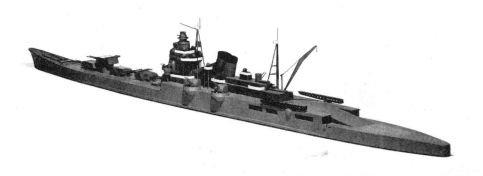

ONI 41-42

315°

270°

225°

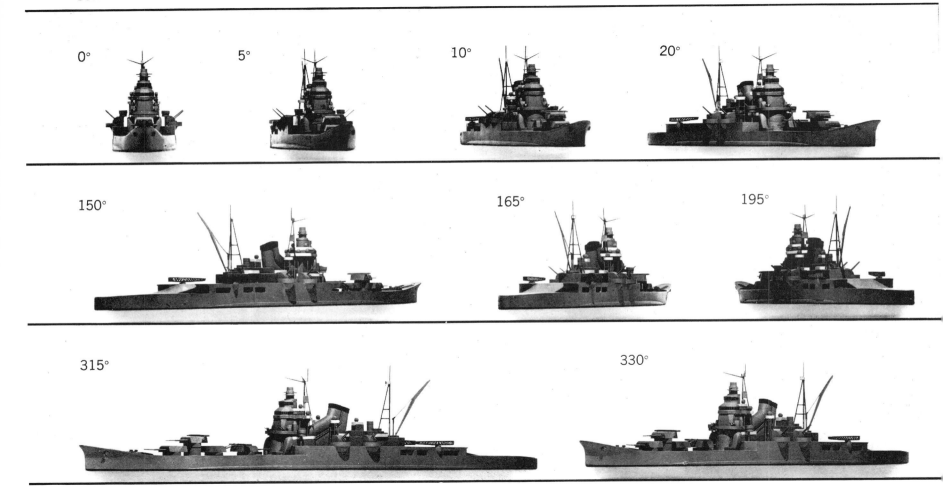

KNOTS	RPM	KNOTS	RPM	KNOTS	RPM	KNOTS	RPM
	400		290		200		100
	375		275		175		75
	350		250		150		50
	325		225		125		25

30°

45°

270°

340°

350°

355°

TONE CLASS—CA 17, 18

DIVISION OF NAVAL INTELLIGENCE—IDENTIFICATION AND CHARACTERISTICS SECTION — APRIL, 1943

		BEGUN	COMPLETED
TONE—	CA17	12/1/34	11/20/38
CHIKUMA—CA18		10/1/35	3/?/39

ONI 41-42

 SANTA CRUZ, 10/26/42

TENRYU CLASS CL 1, 2

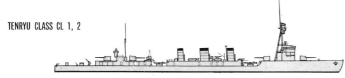

Hull broken forward. 1A–1–1–1 main battery disposition. No. 2 turret just abaft bridge structure. Stacks of unequal size. Tripod foremast, pole mainmast. Very small box-like bridge structure.

KUMA CLASS CL 3-7

Deck well between foremast and No. 1 stack. 1–1 A–1–1–1 main battery disposition. Prominent catapult forward of tripod mainmast. Relatively low bridge. Flared stacks on Kuma, OI only.

NATORI CLASS CL 8-13

Similar to KUMA's. Bridge somewhat higher. No flare to stack tops. Note aft deckhouse differences to Kuma. Some units have cutter bows, others hooked.

SENDAI CLASS CL 15-17

No. 1, 2 and 4 stacks thin, heavy No. 3 stack. 1–1A–1–1–1 main battery disposition. Prominent catapult abaft mainmast, reverse tripod between No. 4 and No. 5 turrets. Bows vary as in Natori's.

YUBARI CLASS CL 14

Very heavy Jap raked stack. Long deck structure forward of bridge. Hull broken forward at bridge. No. 3 turret situated over separate deckhouse aft.
Note general destroyer lines.

↑ KUMA CLASS　　　　　　　　　　　　　　　　YUBARI ↓　　　　↑ SENDAI CLASS　　　　　　　　　　　NATORI CLASS ↓

ONI 41-42

HEIGHT OF OBSERVER

120		120
105		105
90		90
75		75
60		60
45		45
30		30
15		15

HORIZON BEYOND THE SHIP

SHIP BEYOND THE HORIZON

LENGTH—468' OA
BEAM —40'9"
DRAFT —13'3" (NORMAL)

0

DISPLACEMENT—3,230 TONS (STANDARD)—3,500 TONS (NORMAL)

DENSITY OF FIRE
MAIN BATTERY

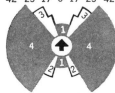

42° 25° 17° 0° 17° 25° 42°

148° 162° 180° 162° 148°

ARMAMENT

	MAX. ELEV.	RANGE
4-5"5 (50)	25°	19,000 YDS.
1-3" (40)	85°	9,000 YDS.
6-21" TORPEDO TUBES, TRIPLE MOUNTS		
DEPTH CHARGES AND MINES CARRIED		

PROPULSION

MACHINERY—	CURTIS-PARSONS
BOILERS—	10 KAMPON
FUEL—	COAL AND OIL, 900 TONS
DESIGNED HP—	51,000
DESIGNED SPEED—	31 KNOTS; 33 KNOTS ON TRIAL
ENDURANCE—	1,250 @ 31 KNOTS
	6,000 @ 10 KNOTS

PROTECTION

BELT—	2"	TURRETS—
BARBETTES—		CONNING TOWER—
DECK—		

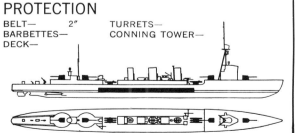

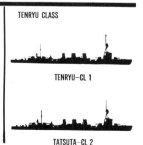

TENRYU CLASS

TENRYU—CL 1

TATSUTA—CL 2

TENRYU CLASS—CL 1-2

DIVISION OF NAVAL INTELLIGENCE—IDENTIFICATION AND CHARACTERISTICS SECTION—DECEMBER, 1942

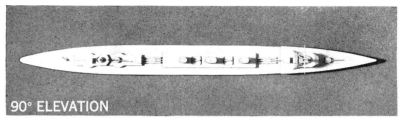

90° ELEVATION

PROFILE—3 RAKING SINGLE PIPES
CRUISER HULL, BROKEN FOR'D
TRIPOD FOREMAST,
STICK MAINMAST

AERIAL—TURRETS—
1 FOR'D OF
FOREMAST, 1 AFT
1 FOR'D OF
MAINMAST, 1 AFT
NO CATAPULT

END-ON—LOW, NARROW BOX
BRIDGE
HIGH PROMINENT
FOREMAST

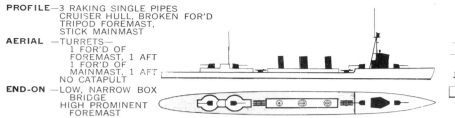

15° ELEVATION

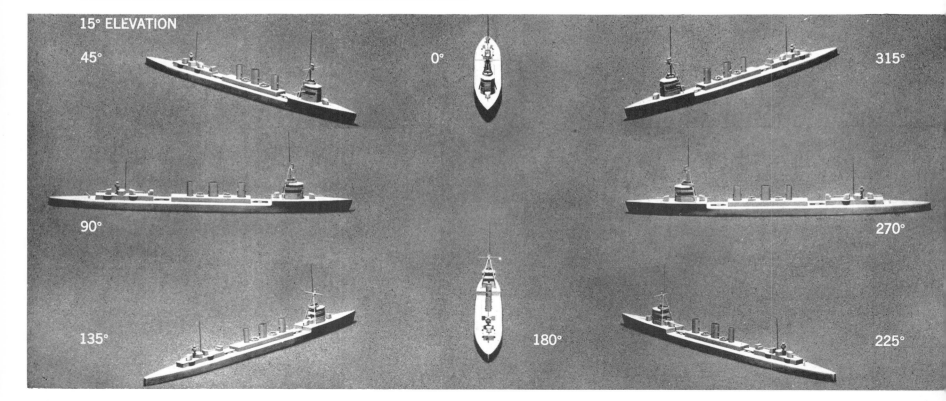

45°   0°   315°

90°   270°

135°   180°   225°

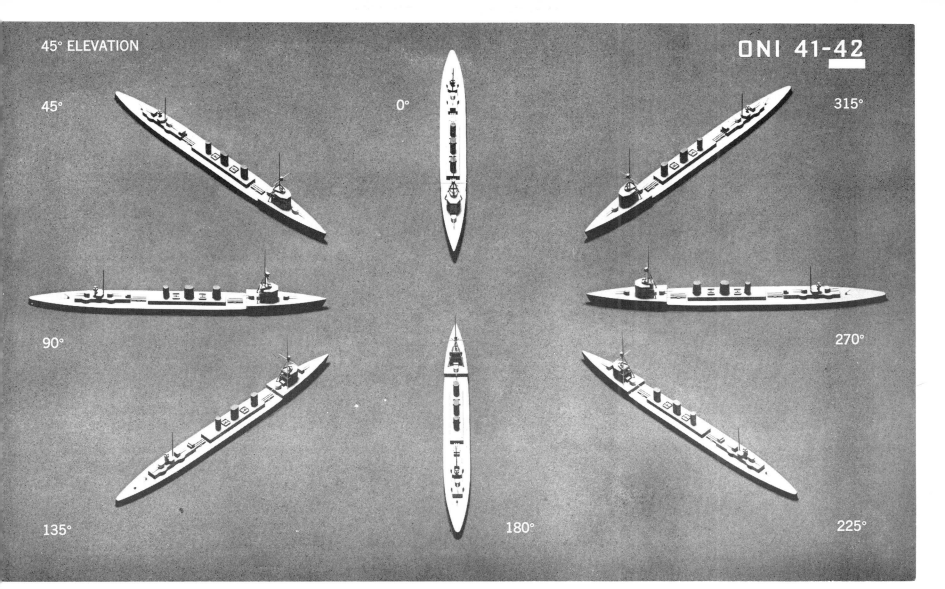

45° ELEVATION

ONI 41-42

45°

0°

315°

90°

270°

135°

180°

225°

TENRYU CLASS—CL 1-2

DIVISION OF NAVAL INTELLIGENCE—IDENTIFICATION AND CHARACTERISTICS SECTION—OCTOBER, 1942

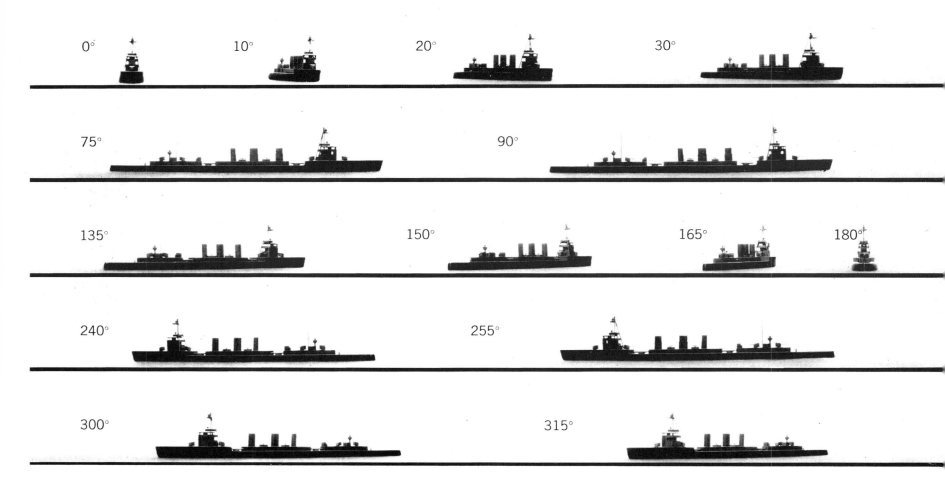

0°   10°   20°   30°

75°   90°

135°   150°   165°   180°

240°   255°

300°   315°

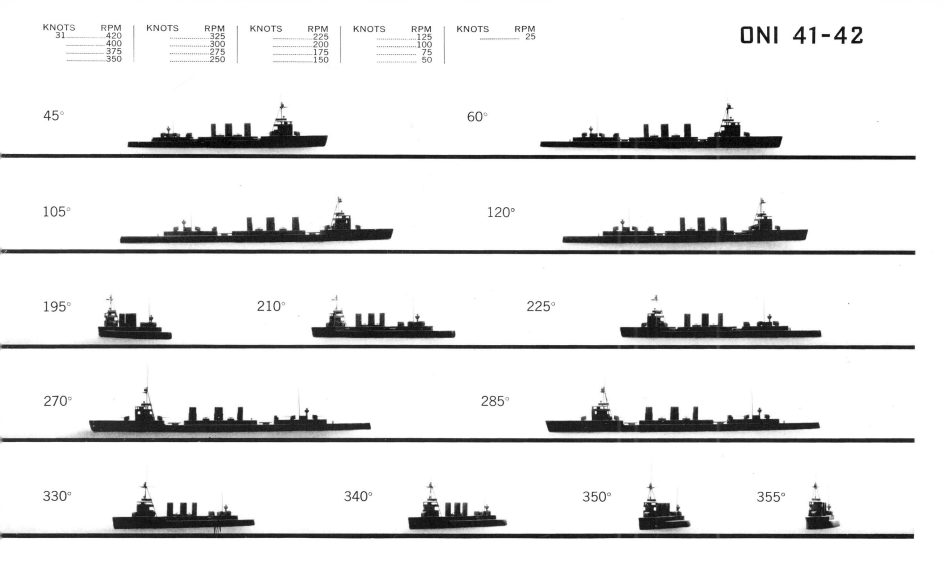

45°

60°

105°

120°

195°

210°

225°

270°

285°

330°

340°

350°

355°

TENRYU CLASS—CL 1, 2

DIVISION OF NAVAL INTELLIGENCE—IDENTIFICATION AND CHARACTERISTICS SECTION—DECEMBER, 1942

	BEGUN	COMPLETED
TENRYU –CL 1	5/17/17	11/20/19
TATSUTA–CL 2	7/24/17	3/31/19

ONI 41-42

↓ TATSUTA—6/21/35   ↑ TENRYU—1935

KUMA CLASS—CL3-7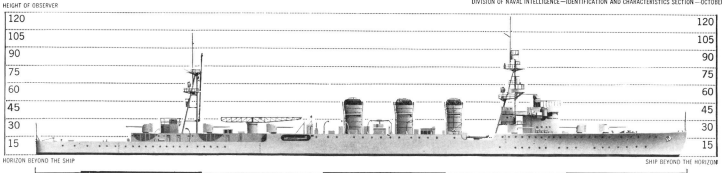

HEIGHT OF OBSERVER

120		120
105		105
90		90
75		75
60		60
45		45
30		30
15		15

HORIZON BEYOND THE SHIP

SHIP BEYOND THE HORIZON

0

LENGTH—535' OA—529' WL
BEAM —47'3"
DRAFT —15'9" (MEAN)

DISPLACEMENT
5,100 TONS (STANDARD)

DENSITY OF FIRE MAIN BATTERY

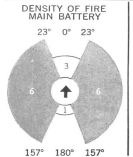

23°   0°   23°

3

6   ↑   6

1

157°   180°   157°

ARMAMENT

	MAX. ELEV.	RANGE
7-5".5 50 CAL	15°	20,000 YD.
2-3".15 AA		

8-21" TORPEDO TUBES TWIN MOUNTS

80 MINES—LAUNCHING TRACKS

1 CATAPULT—1 SEAPLANE SCOUT

24 DEPTH CHARGES—2 PROJECTORS

PROTECTION

BELT—1¾"
TURRETS—1" TO 1½"
CONNING TOWER—2"
DECK—2" OVER VITALS
UNDERWATER PROTECTION VERY GOOD

KNOTS	RPM
33	439
	420
	400
	350
	300
	275
	250
	245
	240
	220
	200
	160
	150
	120
	80

DES. SPEED	DES. HP
33 KTS	70,000

KUMA CLASS—CL3-7

DIVISION OF NAVAL INTELLIGENCE—IDENTIFICATION AND CHARACTERISTICS SECTION — OCTOBER, 1942

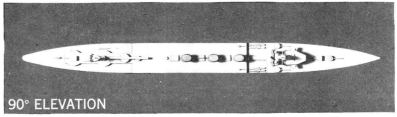

90° ELEVATION

MISTAKEN IDENTITY

KUMA CLASS

NATORI CLASS

NOTE—ONLY KUMA AND KISO HAVE FLARED STACKS AS SHOWN BELOW

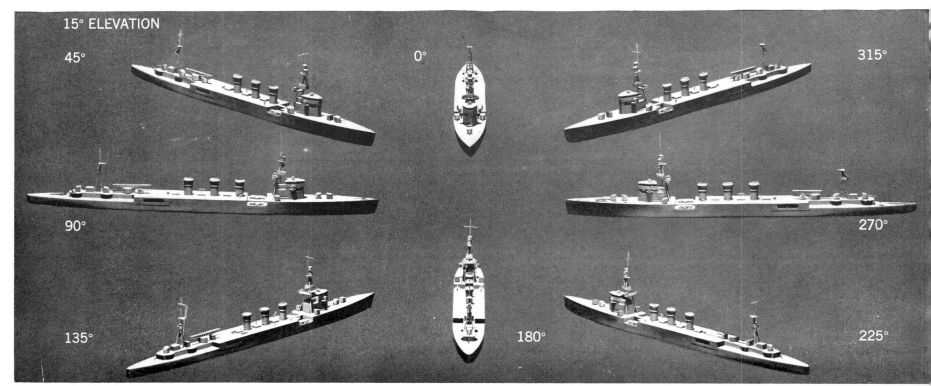

15° ELEVATION

45°

0°

315°

90°

270°

135°

180°

225°

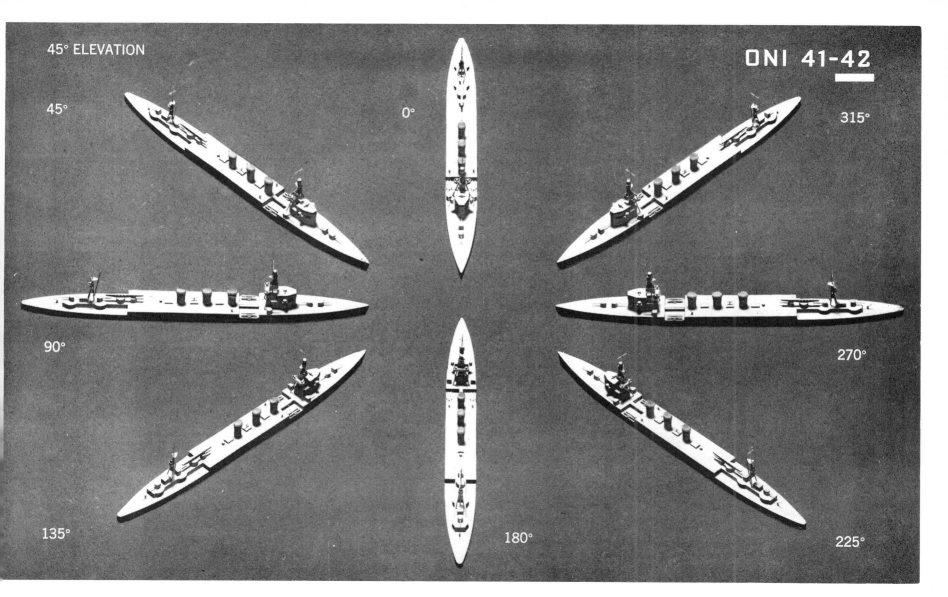

45° ELEVATION

ONI 41-42

45°

0°

315°

90°

270°

135°

180°

225°

KUMA CLASS—CL3-7

DIVISION OF NAVAL INTELLIGENCE—IDENTIFICATION AND CHARACTERISTICS SECTION—OCTOBER, 1942

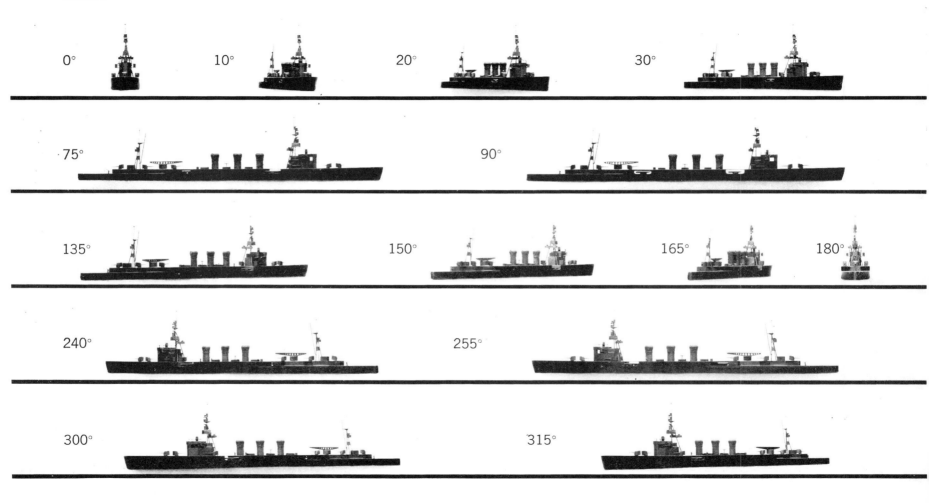

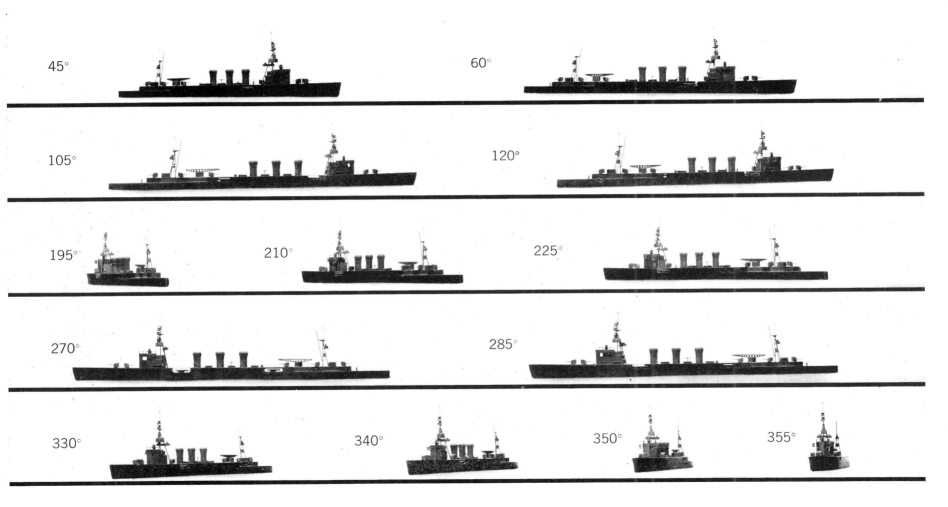

45°

60°

105°

120°

195°

210°

225°

270°

285°

330°

340°

350°

355°

KUMA CLASS—CL3-7

DIVISION OF NAVAL INTELLIGENCE—IDENTIFICATION AND CHARACTERISTICS SECTION—OCTOBER, 1942

SISTER SHIPS	BEGUN	COMPLETED
KUMA—CL3	8/29/18	8/31/20
TAMA—CL4	8/10/18	1/29/21
KITAKAMI—CL5	9/1 /19	4/15/21
KISO —CL6	6/10/19	5/4 /21
OI —CL7	11/24/19	1/29/21

ONI 41-42

JUNE 1935 ↓

1937 ↑

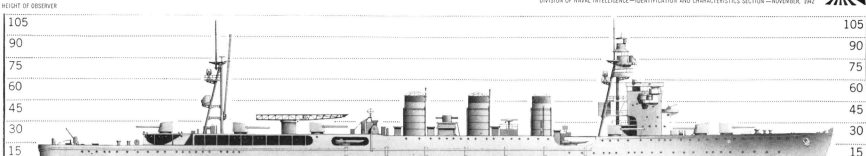

105		105
90		90
75		75
60		60
45		45
30		30
15		15

HORIZON BEYOND THE SHIP

SHIP BEYOND THE HORIZON

0

LENGTH—535' OA
BEAM— 47' 3"
DRAFT— 15' 10½" (NORMAL)

DISPLACEMENT—
5,170 TONS (STANDARD)
5,570 TONS (NORMAL)

DENSITY OF FIRE
MAIN BATTERY
19° 0° 19°

147° 180° 147°

ARMAMENT

	MAX. ELEV.	RANGE
7–5"5 (50)	30°	19,000 YD.
3–3" (40) AA	85°	9,000 YD.
8–21" TORPEDO TUBES TWIN MOUNTS		
80 MINES, 24 DEPTH CHARGES		
1 CATAPULT, 1 SCOUT OBSERVATION		

PROPULSION

MACHINERY—4 CURTIS-PARSONS   BOILERS—8 OIL, 4 COAL
FUEL—   COAL-300 TONS; OIL-1,260 TONS
DESIGNED HP—   90,000   ENDUR.—1,500 @ 33 KNOTS
DESIGNED SPEED—33 KNOTS   8,500 @ 10 KNOTS

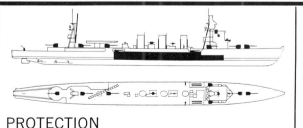

PROTECTION

BELT—2"   TURRETS—   BARBETTES—
CONNING TOWER—2"   DECK—2"

6—NATORI CLASS

NATORI —CL 8
NAGARA —CL 9
KINU —CL 10
YURA —CL 11
ISUZU —CL 12
ABUKUMA —CL 13

NATORI CLASS—CL 8-13

DIVISION OF NAVAL INTELLIGENCE—IDENTIFICATION AND CHARACTERISTICS SECTION—DECEMBER, 1942

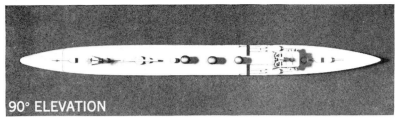

90° ELEVATION

PROFILE—STACKS—3 S. P.
      MASTS —TRIPOD FORE
            TRIPOD MAIN

AERIAL —GUNS—
      2 SINGLE FOR'D
      2 ABREAST BRIDGE
      3 AFT
      CATAPULT FOR'D OF
      MAINMAST

END-ON —HIGH BOX BRIDGE
      NARROW BEAM, LOW FREEBOARD

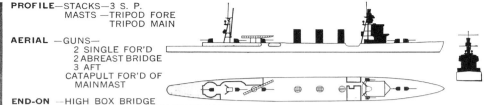

15° ELEVATION

45°   0°   315°

90°   270°

135°   180°   225°

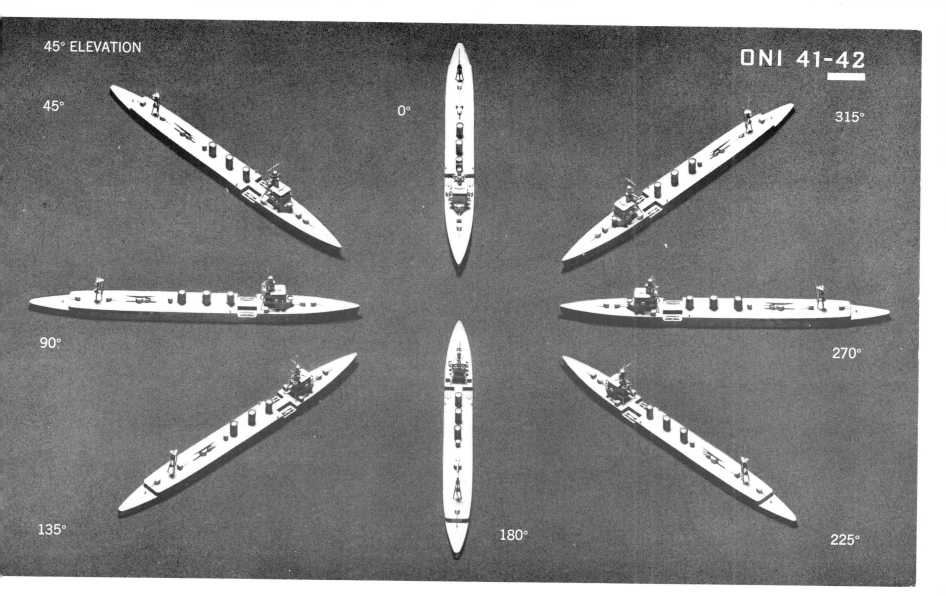

45° ELEVATION

ONI 41-42

45°

0°

315°

90°

270°

135°

180°

225°

NATORI CLASS—CL 8-13

DIVISION OF NAVAL INTELLIGENCE—IDENTIFICATION AND CHARACTERISTICS SECTION —OCTOBER, 1942

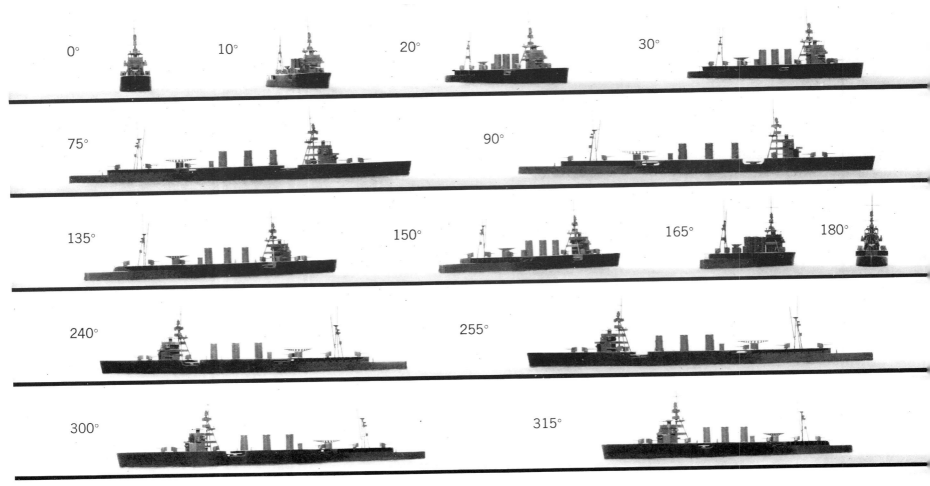

0°　　10°　　20°　　30°

75°　　90°

135°　　150°　　165°　　180°

240°　　255°

300°　　315°

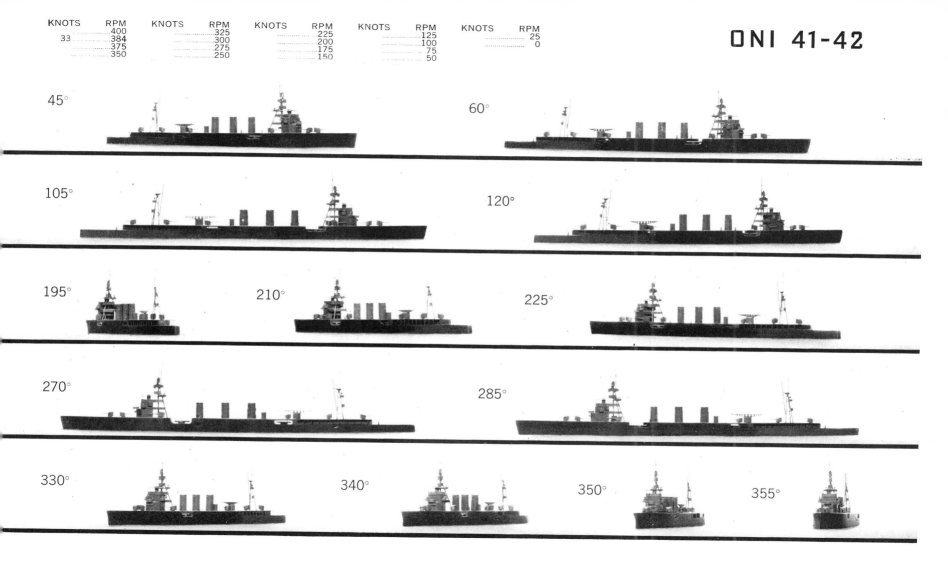

KNOTS   RPM   KNOTS   RPM   KNOTS   RPM   KNOTS   RPM   KNOTS   RPM

KNOTS	RPM	KNOTS	RPM	KNOTS	RPM	KNOTS	RPM	KNOTS	RPM
	400		325		225		125		25
33	384		300		200		100		0
	375		275		175		75		
	350		250		150		50		

45°

60°

105°

120°

195°

210°

225°

270°

285°

330°

340°

350°

355°

	BEGUN	COMPLETED			BEGUN	COMPLETED
NATORI CL 8	12/14/20	9/15/22	YURA	CL11	5/21/21	3/20/23
NAGARA CL 9	9/9/20	4/21/22	ISUZU	CL12	8/10/20	8/15/23
KINU CL10	1/17/21	11/10/22	ABUKUMA	CL13	1/8/21	5/26/25

SEVERAL OF THIS CLASS ARE REPORTED SUNK

↑ YURA 1937 ↓

NAGARA 1937 ↓

HEIGHT OF OBSERVER

105	105
90	90
75	75
60	60
45	45
30	30
15	15

HORIZON BEYOND THE SHIP

SHIP BEYOND THE HORIZON

0

LENGTH—463' OA—459' WL
BEAM— 39'6"
DRAFT— 11'8" (MEAN)

DISPLACEMENT—2,890 TONS (STANDARD)—3,100 TONS (NORMAL)

DENSITY OF FIRE MAIN BATTERY

29°   0°   29°

3

6   ⬆   6

3

137° 160° 180° 160° 137°

ARMAMENT

	MAX. ELEV.	MAX. RANGE (HORIZONTAL)	MAX. RANGE (VERTICAL)
6–5".5 (50)	45°	20,000 YARDS	
1–3" (40)	85°	9,000 YARDS	20,000 FEET
4–21" TORPEDO TUBES	50 MINES		

PROPULSION

MACHINERY— GEARED TURBINES
BOILERS— EIGHT KAMPON
FUEL— OIL, 820 TONS
DESIGNED H.P.—57,000   DESIGNED SPEED—33 KNOTS
ENDURANCE— 5,500 MILES @ 10 KNOTS—1,400 MILES @ 33 KNOTS

PROTECTION

BELT—2"
DECK—2"

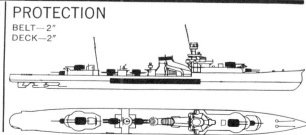

YUBARI— CL 14

DIVISION OF NAVAL INTELLIGENCE—IDENTIFICATION
AND CHARACTERISTICS SECTION —APRIL. 1943

PROFILE— →

DESTROYER HULL,
BROKEN AMIDSHIPS
LARGE JAP-RAKED STACK

←**AERIAL—**

TWIN SHIELDS SUPER-
IMPOSING SINGLES,
FOR'D AND AFT
(NOTE BLAST SHIELDS)
AMIDSHIPS TWIN TORPEDO
TUBES

END-ON—

EASILY CONFUSED WITH
DESTROYERS

MISTAKEN IDENTITY

THIS SHIP HAS CONSISTENTLY BEEN REPORTED FOR THE—
CA—MOGAMI CLASS
TONE CLASS
CL—KATORI CLASS
DD—UN NO. 1 AND OTHER DESTROYER CLASSES.
TORPEDO BOATS AND MINESWEEPERS.

YUBARI CL-14

AERIAL VIEWS

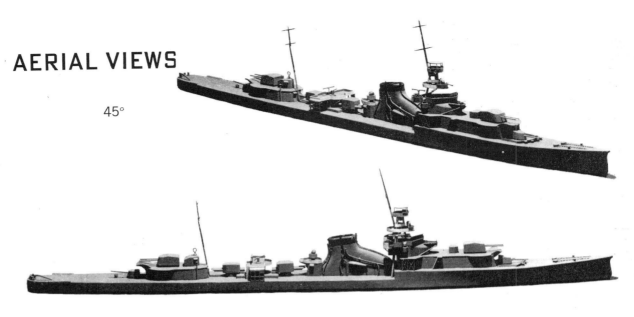

45°

90°

135°

15° ELEVATION

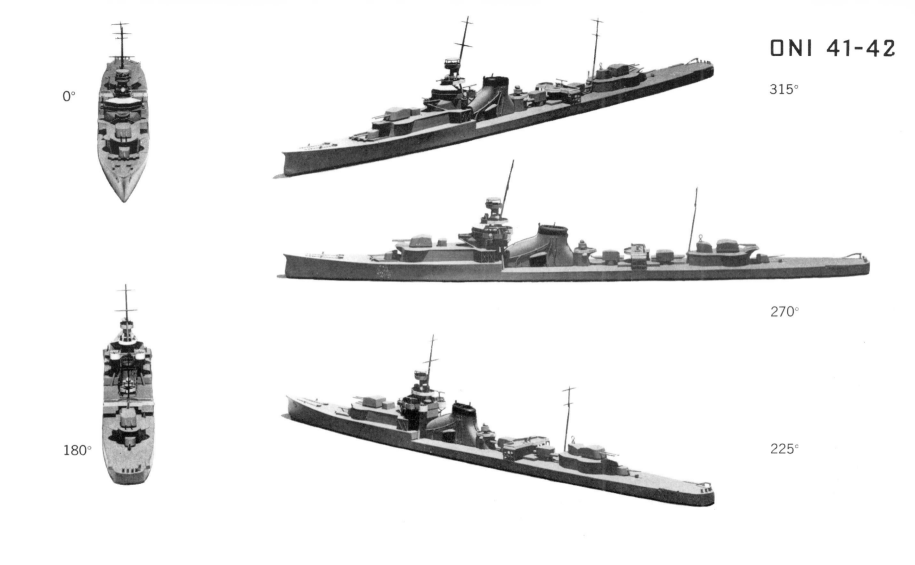

ONI 41-42

0°

180°

315°

270°

225°

0° 5° 10° 20°

150° 165° 195°

315° 330°

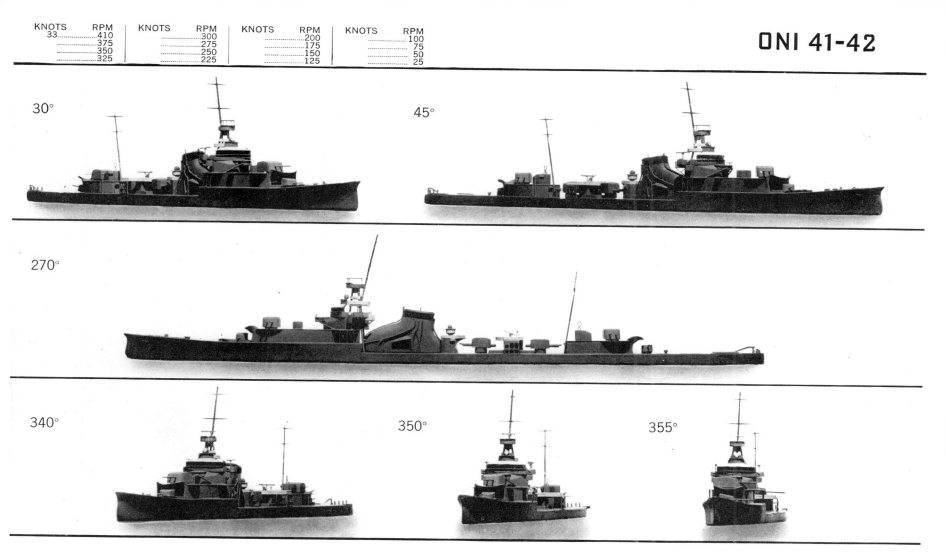

KNOTS	RPM	KNOTS	RPM	KNOTS	RPM	KNOTS	RPM
33	410		300		200		100
	375		275		175		75
	350		250		150		50
	325		225		125		25

30°

45°

270°

340°

350°

355°

YUBARI—CL 14

DIVISION OF NAVAL INTELLIGENCE—IDENTIFICATION AND CHARACTERISTICS SECTION—APRIL, 1943

BEGUN
6/5/22

COMPLETED
7/21/23

ONI 41-42

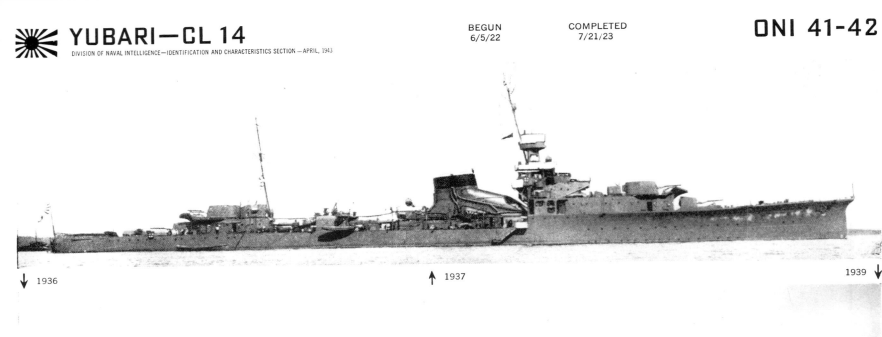

↓ 1936   ↑ 1937   1939 ↓

ONI 41-42

SENDAI CLASS—CL15-17

DIVISION OF NAVAL INTELLIGENCE—IDENTIFICATION AND CHARACTERISTICS SECTION—NOVEMBER, 1942

HEIGHT OF OBSERVER

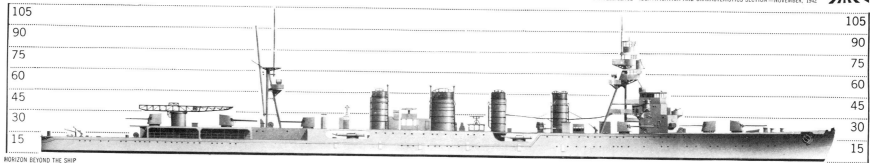

HORIZON BEYOND THE SHIP

SHIP BEYOND THE HORIZON

LENGTH—535' OA
BEAM— 47'3"
DRAFT— 15'11" (NORMAL)

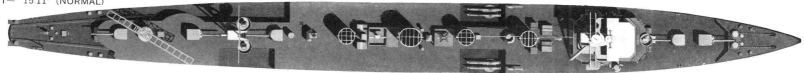

DISPLACEMENT—5,195 TONS (STANDARD)—5,595 TONS (NORMAL)

DENSITY OF FIRE
MAIN BATTERY

31° 21° 0° 21° 31°

3

6   6

3

145° 159° 180° 159° 145°

ARMAMENT

	MAX. ELEV.	RANGE
7–5″5 (50)	25°	19,000 YD.
2–3″ (40)	85°	9,000 YD.

8–21″ TORPEDO TUBES, TWIN MOUNTS
80 MINES
1 CATAPULT, 1 SCOUT OBSERVATION

PROPULSION

MACHINERY—4 CURTIS PARSONS   BOILERS—16 KAMPON
FUEL—OIL 1500 TONS—COAL
DES HP—   90,000   ENDURANCE—1300 @ 33 KNOTS
DES SPEED—33 KNOTS   7800 @ 10 KNOTS

PROTECTION

BELTS— 2″   TURRETS—   BARBETTES—
        CONNING TOWER—2″   DECK—

SENDAI CLASS

SENDAI CL 15

JINTSU CL 16 (ZINTU)

NAKA CL 17

SENDAI CLASS—CL 15-17

DIVISION OF NAVAL INTELLIGENCE—IDENTIFICATION AND CHARACTERISTICS SECTION—NOVEMBER, 1942

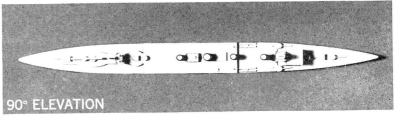

90° ELEVATION

PROFILE—4 SINGLE PIPE STACKS (FOR'D STACK MAY BE HIGH ON SOME) TRIPOD FOREMAST TRIPOD MAINMAST

AERIAL—TORPEDO WELL BETWEEN FOR'D STACKS
GUNSHIELDS: 2 FOR'D
               2 ABREAST BRIDGE
               3 AFT
CATAPULT AFT OF MAINMAST

END-ON—MAY EASILY BE MISTAKEN FOR NATORI OR KUMA CLASS SHIPS

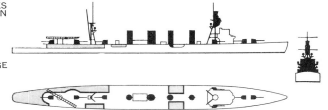

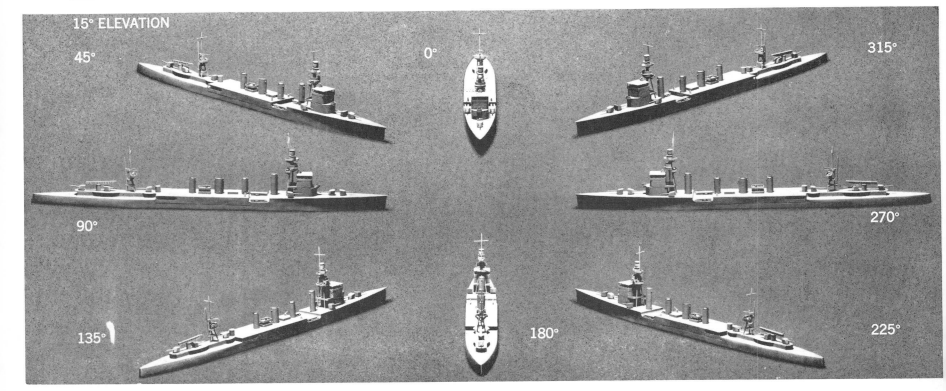

15° ELEVATION

45°

0°

315°

90°

270°

135°

180°

225°

45° ELEVATION

ONI 41-42

0°

45°

315°

90°

270°

135°

180°

225°

SENDAI CLASS—CL 15-17

DIVISION OF NAVAL INTELLIGENCE—IDENTIFICATION AND CHARACTERISTICS SECTION—OCTOBER, 1942

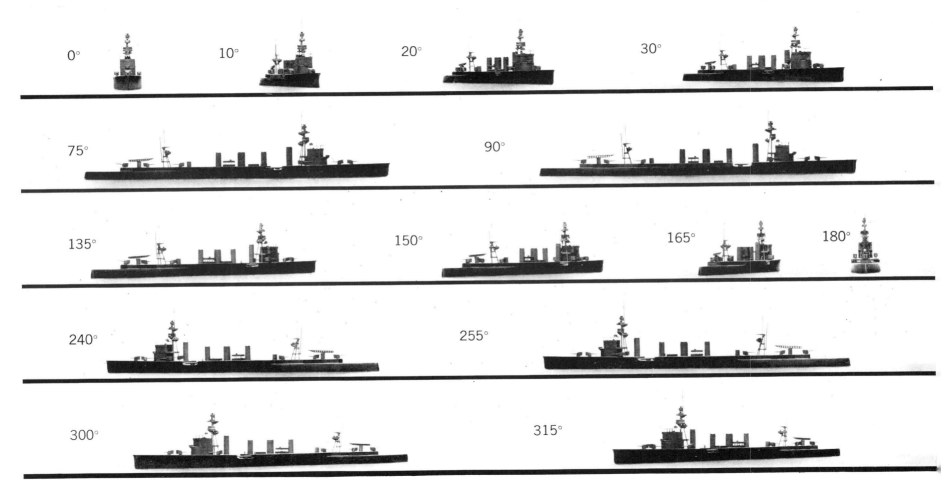

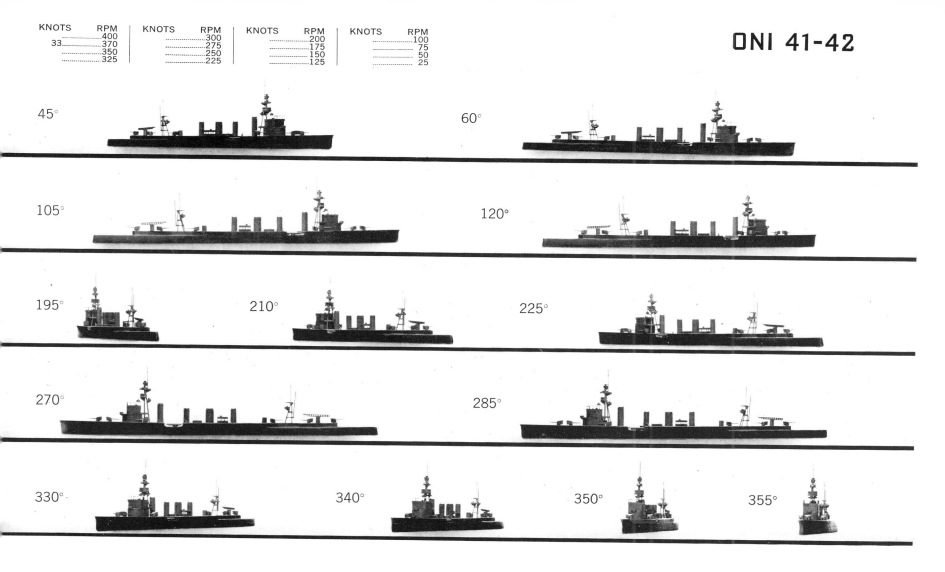

KNOTS RPM
..............400
33..............370
..............350
..............325

KNOTS RPM
..............300
..............275
..............250
..............225

KNOTS RPM
..............200
..............175
..............150
..............125

KNOTS RPM
..............100
..............75
..............50
..............25

45°

60°

105°

120°

195°

210°

225°

270°

285°

330°

340°

350°

355°

SENDAI CLASS—CL 15-17

DIVISION OF NAVAL INTELLIGENCE—IDENTIFICATION AND CHARACTERISTICS SECTION—NOVEMBER, 1942

		BEGUN	COMPLETED
SENDAI	CL15	2/16/22	4/29/24
JINTSU	CL16	8/4/22	7/31/25
NAKA	CL17	6/10/22	11/30/25

ONI 41-42

SENDAI 8/37   NOTE CUTTER BOW—JINTSU, NAKA HAVE HOOKED BOW

SENDAI 8/37

JINTSU—NAKA HAS MAINMAST TRIPOD REVERSED

SENDAI 8/16/37

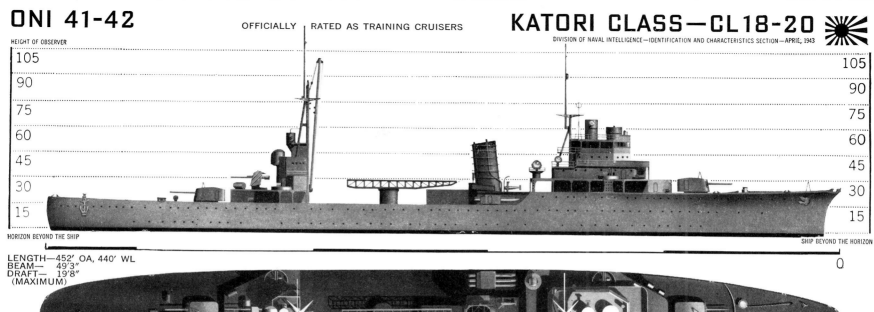

HEIGHT OF OBSERVER

105 · 90 · 75 · 60 · 45 · 30 · 15

HORIZON BEYOND THE SHIP

SHIP BEYOND THE HORIZON

0

LENGTH—452' OA, 440' WL
BEAM— 49'3"
DRAFT— 19'8"
(MAXIMUM)

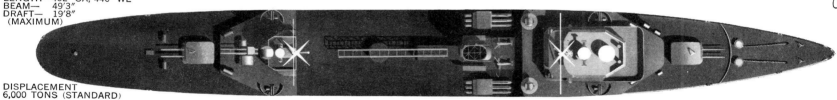

DISPLACEMENT
6,000 TONS (STANDARD)

DENSITY OF FIRE
MAIN BATTERY

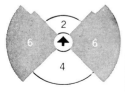

49° 42° 0° 42° 49°

6   2   6
    4
135° 180° 135°

ARMAMENT

ARMAMENT	MAX. ELEV.	MAX. RANGE (HORIZONTAL)	MAX. RANGE (VERTICAL)
4-5″.5 (50)	30°	19,000 YARDS	
2-5″ (50)	85°	18,000 YARDS	20,000 FEET

4-21″ TORPEDO TUBES
1 CATAPULT—1 SCOUT OBSERVATION

PROPULSION

DESIGNED HP— 8,000
DESIGNED SPEED—18 KNOTS (ANNOUNCED)

PROTECTION

DEGAUSSING EQUIPMENT SEEN ON KASHII
2″ DECK REPORTED

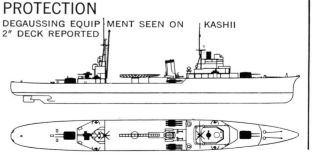

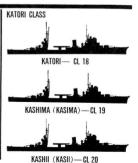

KATORI— CL 18

KASHIMA (KASIMA)—CL 19

KASHII (KASII)—CL 20

KATORI CLASS
—CL 18-20

DIVISION OF NAVAL INTELLIGENCE—IDENTIFICATION
AND CHARACTERISTICS SECTION —APRIL, 1943

READY RECOGNITION

PROFILE →
CRUISER HULL, BROKEN
AMIDSHIPS (NOTE
EXTREME FREEBOARD)
HEAVY ISLAND SUPER-
STRUCTURES, TOPPED
BY TRIPODS
RAKED SINGLE-PIPE
STACK

AERIAL
TURRETS—
SINGLE TWIN FORWARD
SUPERIMPOSED TWINS
AFT
AMIDSHIPS CATAPULT

END-ON
MAY BE MISTAKEN FOR
OTHER CL's OR CA's ↓

AERIAL VIEWS

45°

90°

135°

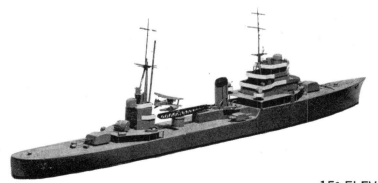

15° ELEVATION

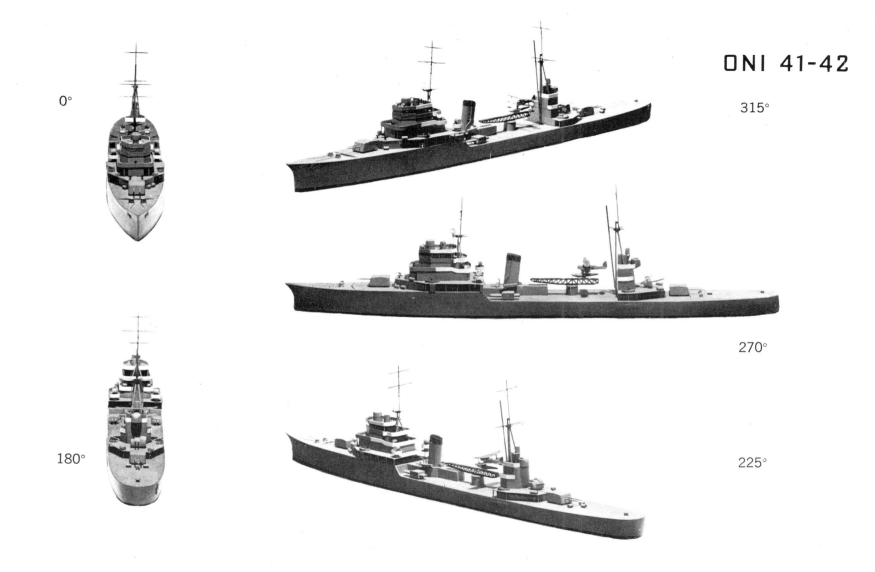

ONI 41-42

0°

315°

180°

270°

225°

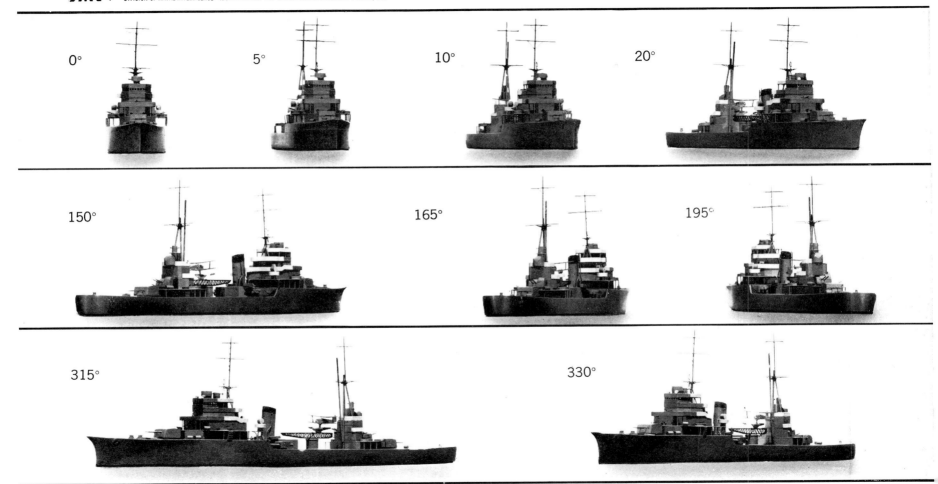

0° 5° 10° 20°

150° 165° 195°

315° 330°

KNOTS	RPM	KNOTS	RPM	KNOTS	RPM	KNOTS	RPM
	400		300		200		100
	375		275		175		75
	350		250		150		50
	325		225		125		25

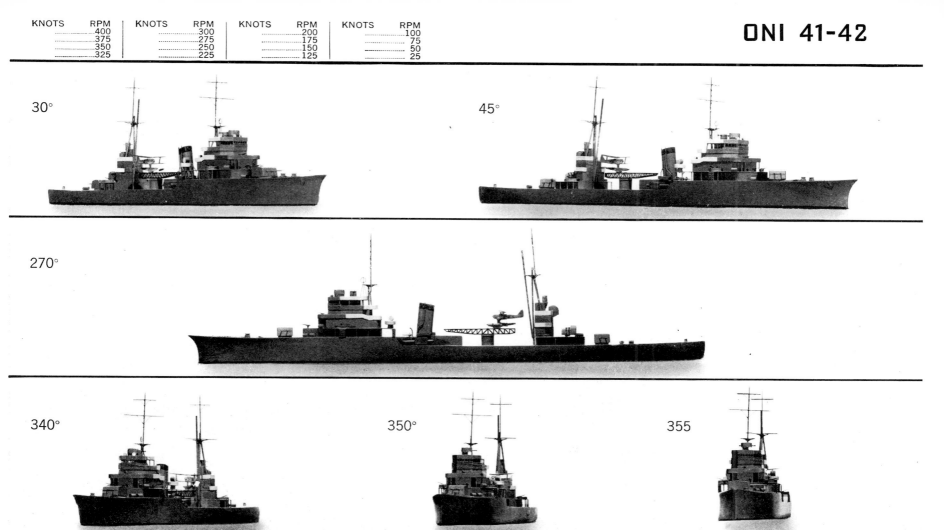

30°

45°

270°

340°

350°

355

KATORI CLASS—CL 18-20

DIVISION OF NAVAL INTELLIGENCE—IDENTIFICATION AND CHARACTERISTICS SECTION—APRIL, 1943

		BEGUN	COMPLETED
KATORI—	CL 18	1938	4/15/40
KASHIMA (KASIMA)—	CL 19	1938	5/15/40
KASHII (KASII)—	CL 20	1938	1941

ONI 41-42

↑ JUNE 28, 1940

↓ SEPT., 1940 ↑

DESTROYERS

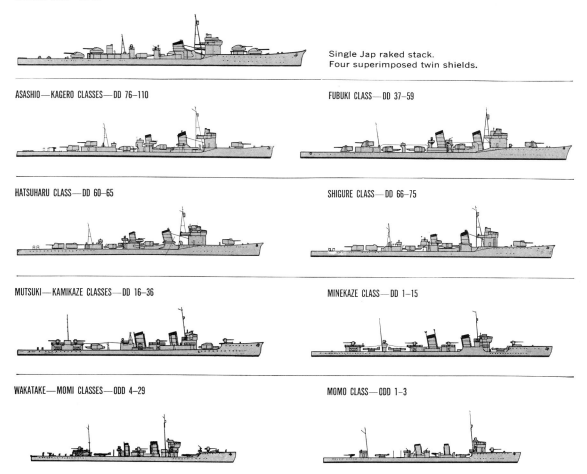

TERUTSUKI CLASS—DD 111

Single Jap raked stack.
Four superimposed twin shields.

ASASHIO—KAGERO CLASSES—DD 76—110

FUBUKI CLASS—DD 37—59

HATSUHARU CLASS—DD 60—65

SHIGURE CLASS—DD 66—75

MUTSUKI—KAMIKAZE CLASSES—DD 16—36

MINEKAZE CLASS—DD 1—15

WAKATAKE—MOMI CLASSES—ODD 4—29

MOMO CLASS—ODD 1—3

Japanese destroyers fall into two distinct groups:
The first-line DD's all have two high, raking stacks (except Terutsuki), tall bridges, tripod masts and enclosed gun shields.

The second-line DD's have shorter, broader stacks, low bridges, and pole masts. The distinctive feature is the forecastle torpedo-tube well.

ASASHIO—KAGERO CLASSES—DD 76—110
Like other classes, two raked, single-pipe stacks.
Torpedo tubes between and aft of stacks.
Superimposed twin shields aft.

FUBUKI CLASS—DD 37—59
Differs from other classes by having two sets of tubes abaft 2nd stack.
Stack and torpedo blast shield variances split class into three groups.

HATSUHARU CLASS—DD 60—65
Similar to Asashio class with aft gun shields placed on deck.
Note extreme rake to stacks, heavy bridge.

SHIGURE CLASS—DD 66—75
Quadruple torpedo mounts differentiate this class from Hatsuharu (triples)—otherwise identical.

MUTSUKI—KAMIKAZE CLASSES—DD 16—36
Two raked, combined stacks.
Shielded torpedo tubes.
Note large aft deckhouse supporting two guns and main-mast.
Kamikaze has two torpedo nests aft.

MINEKAZE CLASS—DD 1—15
Distinctive 1A 1—1—1 gun arrangement. Note three torpedo nests, separated aft by mainmast.

WAKATAKE—MOMI CLASSES—ODD 4—29
Distinguished by smaller raked single-pipe stack aft and 1A—1—1 gun disposition.
Minelayer version has no torpedo tubes, sloping stern.

MOMO CLASS—ODD 1—3
May be recognized by hull break abaft bridge and short, raked, single-pipe stacks.

↑ HATSUHARU CLASS   ↓ MUTSUKI CLASS ↑   KAMIKAZE CLASS ↓

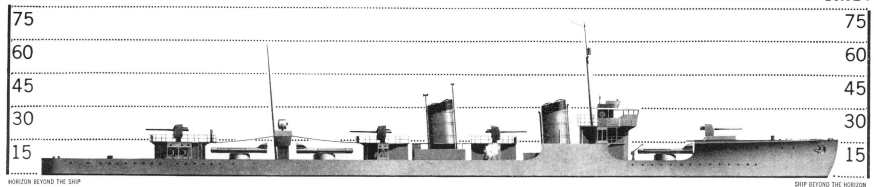

HORIZON BEYOND THE SHIP

SHIP BEYOND THE HORIZON

LENGTH—336'6" OA
BEAM— 29'3"
DRAFT— 9'6" (MEAN)

0

DISPLACEMENT—1215 TONS (STANDARD) 1345 (NORMAL)

ARMAMENT

	MAX. ELEV.	RANGE (HORIZONTAL)
4-4.7" SHIELDS	45°	19,000 YDS

2-1" AA
6–21" TORPEDO TUBES 10 TORPEDOES CARRIED
50–MINES; 14?–DEPTH CHARGES
2 ?-30" SEARCHLIGHTS
FITTED FOR MINESWEEPING

PROPULSION

MACHINERY— 4 PARSONS
BOILERS— 4 KAMPON   FUEL—   OIL 315 TONS
DESIGNED HP—38,500   DESIGNED SPEED—34 KNOTS
ENDURANCE— 4,100 @ 15 KNOTS —900 @ 34 KNOTS

PROTECTION—SPLINTER PROTECTION FOR BRIDGE AND GUNS

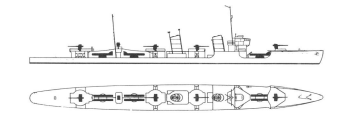

15 MINEKAZE CLASS

MINEKAZE CLASS DD—1-15

DIVISION OF NAVAL INTELLIGENCE - IDENTIFICATION
AND CHARACTERISTICS SECTION — JUNE, 1943

PROFILE

MAY BE DISTINGUISHED FROM OTHER JAP DD's BY MAINMAST BETWEEN AFT TUBE NESTS.

MISTAKEN IDENTITY

MINEKAZE CLASS DD—1-15

FARRAGUT—DD (U.S.)

AM 1-6 (JAPAN)

RAVEN—AM (U.S.)

BRITISH 2-STACKER DD

ALSO—   LA RIOJA—DD (ARGENTINA)
          ALDEA—DD (CHILE)
          ANTIOQUIA—DD (COLOMBIA)

AERIAL VIEWS

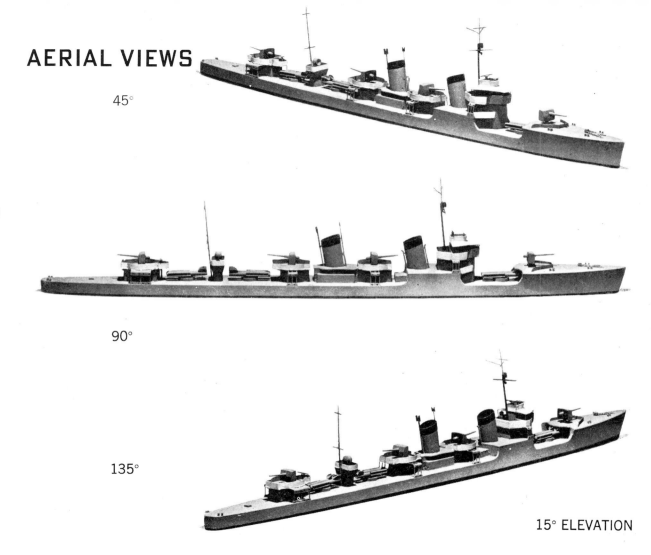

45°

90°

135°

15° ELEVATION

0°

180°

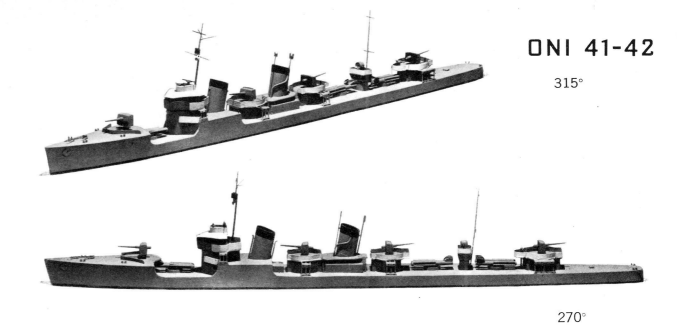

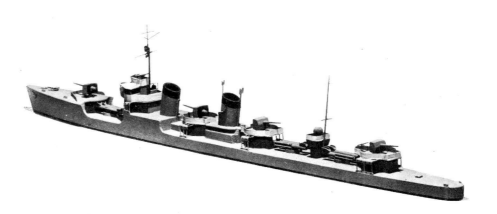

ONI 41-42

315°

270°

255°

0°
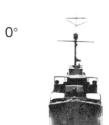

5°

10°

20°

150°

165°

195°

315°

330°

KNOTS	RPM	KNOTS	RPM	KNOTS	RPM	KNOTS	RPM
34	417		300		200		100
	375		275		175		75
	350		250		150		50
	325		225		125		25

30°

45°

270°

340°

350°

355°

MINEKAZE CLASS—DD 1-15

DIVISION OF NAVAL INTELLIGENCE—IDENTIFICATION AND CHARACTERISTICS SECTION —JUNE, 1943

ONI 41-42

	COMPLETED
MINEKAZE DD-1	1920
OKIKAZE DD-2	1920
SHIMAKAZE DD-3	1920
SAWAKAZE DD-4	1920
HAKAZE DD-5	1920
YAKAZE DD-6	1920
AKIKAZE DD-7	1921
YUKAZE DD-8	1921
HOKAZE DD-9	1921
SHIOKAZE DD-10	1921
TACHIKAZE DD-11	1921
NADAKAZE DD-12	1921
NAMIKAZE DD-13	1922
NUMAKAZE DD-14	1922
NOKAZE DD-15	1922

↑ 1938

↓ HOKAZE—1939

YUKAZE 8/26/37 ↓

HEIGHT OF OBSERVER

HORIZON BEYOND THE SHIP

SHIP BEYOND THE HORIZON

LENGTH—336'6" OA—331' WL
BEAM— 30'
DRAFT— 9'10" (MEAN)

DISPLACEMENT—1,315 TONS (STANDARD)—1,445 TONS (NORMAL)

ARMAMENT

	MAX. ELEV.	RANGE (HORIZONTAL)
4-4".7 (45) AA	45°	19,000 YDS
2-1".4 AA		

6-21" TORPEDO TUBES (TRIPLE MOUNTS)   (DD 16-24—TWIN MOUNTS)
FITTED FOR MINESWEEPING
50(?)-MINES, 14 DEPTH CHARGES

PROPULSION

MACHINERY—   FOUR PARSONS DOUBLE SHAFT GEARED TURBINES.
BOILERS—   FOUR KAMPON   FUEL—   OIL, 350 TONS
DESIGNED HP—   38,500
DESIGNED SPEED—34 KNOTS
PROPELLERS—   2

PROTECTION

SPLINTER PROTECTION ON BRIDGES, MAIN BATTERY AND TORPEDO
TUBES. WELL COMPARTMENTED. CAN REMAIN AFLOAT AND ON EVEN
KEEL WITH THREE OF LARGEST COMPARTMENTS FLOODED.

DD 25-36

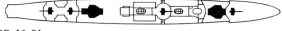

DD 16-24

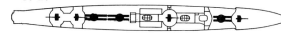

12 MUTSUKI CLASS DD 25-36

9 KAMIKAZE CLASS DD 16-24

MUTSUKI CLASS DD 25-36

DIVISION OF NAVAL INTELLIGENCE IDENTIFICATION
AND CHARACTERISTICS SECTION — JUNE, 1943

**JAPANESE SECOND LINE
DESTROYERS**

MINEKAZE CLASS—DD 1-15

KAMIKAZE CLASS—DD 16-24

MUTSUKI CLASS—DD 25-36

MOMI CLASS—ODD 4-22   WAKATAKE CLASS—ODD 23-29

AERIAL VIEWS

45°

90°

135°

15° ELEVATION

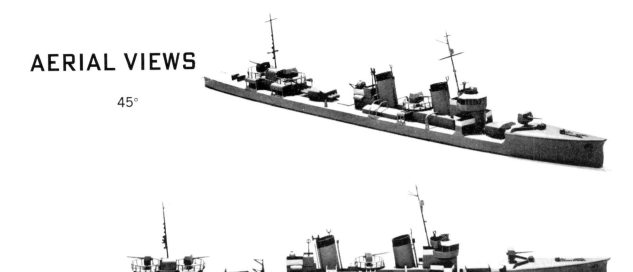

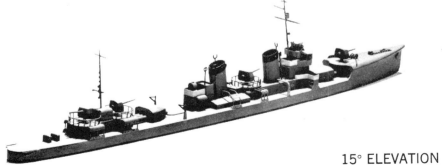

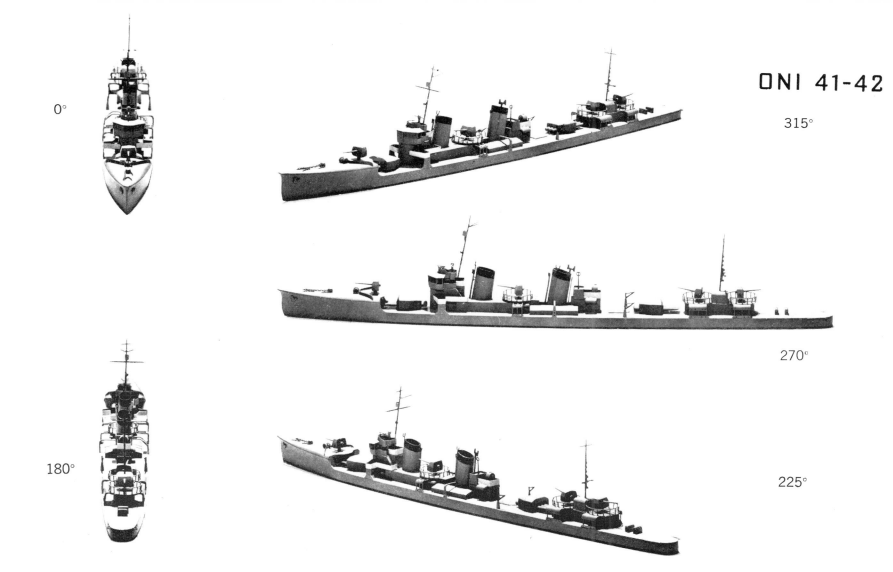

ONI 41-42

0°

180°

315°

270°

225°

MUTSUKI CLASS—DD 25-36

DIVISION OF NAVAL INTELLIGENCE—IDENTIFICATION AND CHARACTERISTICS SECTION — FEBRUARY. 1943

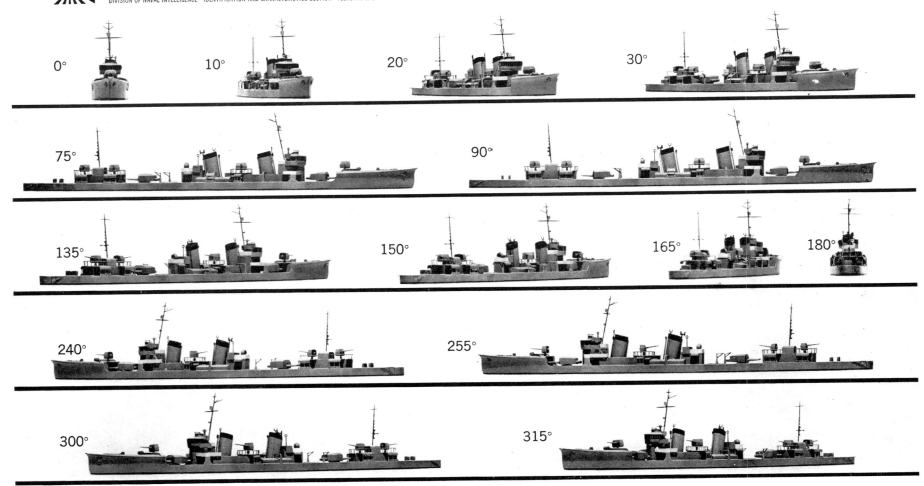

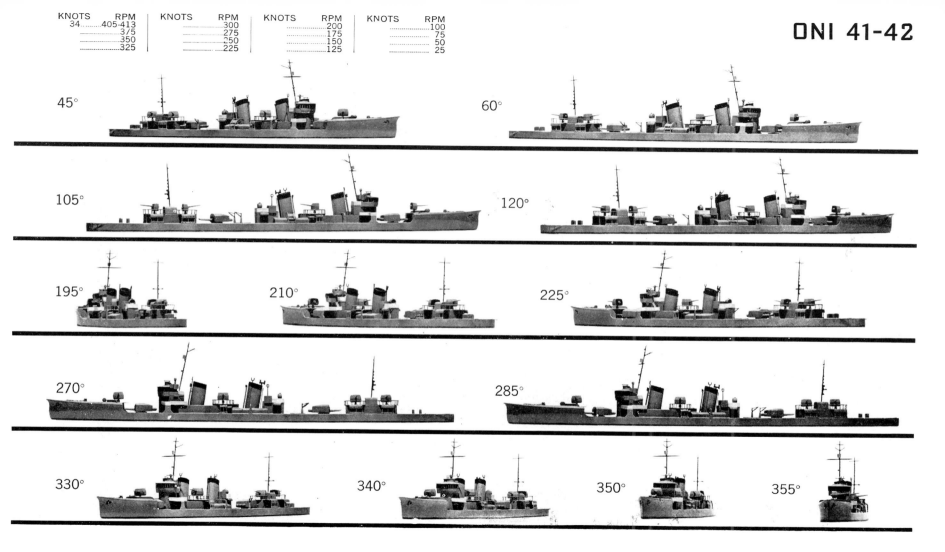

KNOTS   RPM   KNOTS   RPM   KNOTS   RPM   KNOTS   RPM
34 405-413 300 200 100
.................3/5 275 175 75
.................350 250 150 50
.................325 225 125 25

45°

60°

105°

120°

195°   210°   225°

270°   285°

330°   340°   350°   355°

MUTSUKI CLASS—DD 25-36

DIVISION OF NAVAL INTELLIGENCE—IDENTIFICATION AND CHARACTERISTICS SECTION —JUNE, 1943

		COMPLETED			COMPLETED
MUTSUKI—	DD 25	3/25/26	KAMIKAZE—	DD 16	28/12/22
SATSUKI—	DD 26	11/15/25	ASAKAZE—	DD 17	16/ 6/23
KISARAGI—	DD 27	12/21/25	HARUKAZE—	DD 18	31/ 5/23
YAYOI—	DD 28	8/28/26	MATSUKAZE—	DD 19	5/ 4/24
UZUKI—	DD 29	9/14/26	ASANAGI—	DD 20	29/12/24
FUMITSUKI—	DD 30	7/ 3/26	HATAKAZE—	DD 21	30/ 8/24
KIKUTSUKI—	DD 31	11/20/26	OITE—	DD 22	30/10/25
MINATSUKI—	DD 32	3/22/27	HAYATE—	DD 23	21/12/25
NAGATSUKI—	DD 33	4/30/27	YUNAGI—	DD 24	24/ 4/25
MIKATSUKI—	DD 34	5/ 7/27			
MOCHITSUKI—	DD 35	10/31/27			
YUZUKI—	DD 36	7/25/27			

 NAGATSUKI 1/15/41   SATSUKI 8/18/37

← 9/11/42   HATAKAZE (KAMIKAZE CLASS) 5/40

DIVISION OF NAVAL INTELLIGENCE—IDENTIFICATION AND CHARACTERISTICS SECTION—NOVEMBER, 1942

ARMAMENT

	MAX. ELEV.	RANGE
6-5" (50) TWIN TURRETS	85°	18,000 YD.

2-AAMG
9-21" TORPEDO TUBES, TRIPLE MOUNTS
14 DEPTH CHARGES
SOME FITTED FOR MINELAYING

PROPULSION

MACHINERY— 2 PARSONS
BOILERS— 4 KAMPON
FUEL— OIL, 500 TONS
DESIGNED HP— 40,000
DESIGNED SPEED— 34 KNOTS
ENDURANCE— 1100 @ 34 KNOTS
4700 @ 15 KNOTS

LENGTH—379'6" OA
BEAM— 33'9"
DRAFT— 9'9" (NORMAL)

HEIGHT OF OBSERVER

75 · 60 · 45 · 30 · 15

HORIZON BEYOND THE SHIP

SHIP BEYOND THE HORIZON

DISPLACEMENT—1,700 TONS (STANDARD)—1,850 TONS (NORMAL)

← FUBUKI   MURAKUMO ↑   ISONAMI 1934 ↓

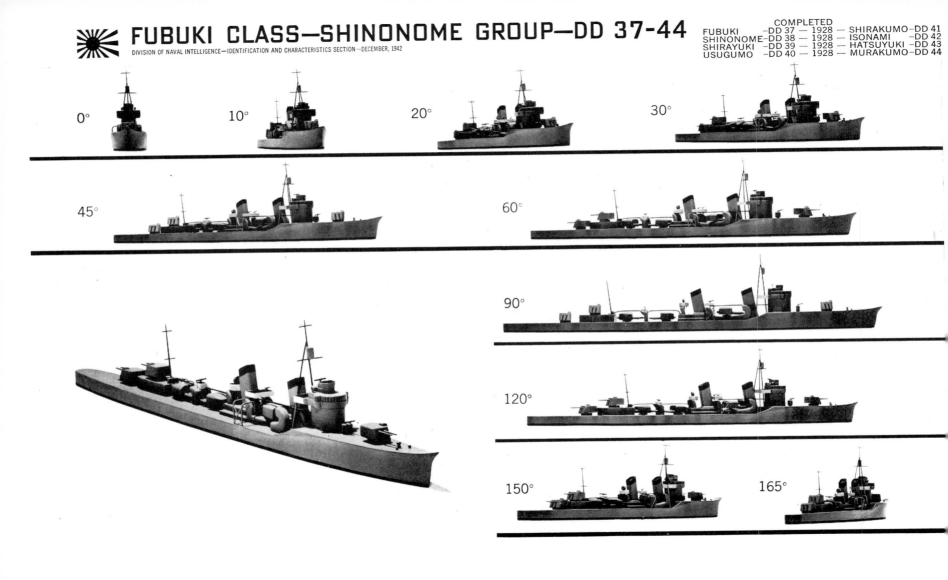

FUBUKI CLASS—SHINONOME GROUP—DD 37-44

DIVISION OF NAVAL INTELLIGENCE—IDENTIFICATION AND CHARACTERISTICS SECTION—DECEMBER, 1942

COMPLETED		
FUBUKI	—DD 37 — 1928 —	SHIRAKUMO–DD 41
SHINONOME	–DD 38 — 1928 —	ISONAMI –DD 42
SHIRAYUKI	–DD 39 — 1928 —	HATSUYUKI –DD 43
USUGUMO	–DD 40 — 1928 —	MURAKUMO–DD 44

0°

10°

20°

30°

45°

60°

90°

120°

150°

165°

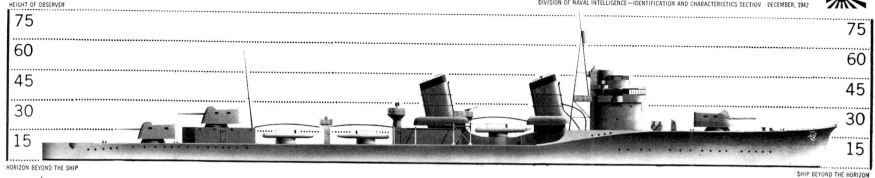

HEIGHT OF OBSERVER

75 · 60 · 45 · 30 · 15

75 · 60 · 45 · 30 · 15

HORIZON BEYOND THE SHIP

SHIP BEYOND THE HORIZON

0

LENGTH—379'6" OA
BEAM —33'9"
DRAFT —9'9" (NORMAL)

DISPLACEMENT—1,700 TONS (STANDARD)—1,850 TONS (NORMAL)

ARMAMENT

	MAX. ELEV.	RANGE
6-5" (50)	85°	18,000 YD.
2-AAMG		
9-21" TORPEDO TUBES, TRIPLE MOUNTS		
14 DEPTH CHARGES		

PROPULSION

MACHINERY—	2 PARSONS
BOILERS—	4 KAMPON
FUEL—	OIL, 500 TONS
DESIGNED HP—	40,000
DESIGNED SPEED—	34 KNOTS
ENDURANCE—	1,100 @ 34 KNOTS
	4,700 @ 15 KNOTS

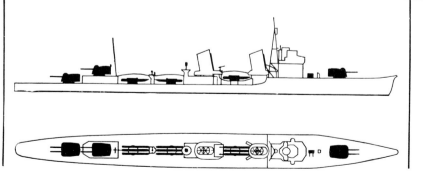

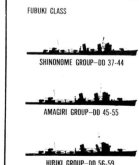

FUBUKI CLASS

SHINONOME GROUP—DD 37-44

AMAGIRI GROUP—DD 45-55

HIBIKI GROUP—DD 56-59

FUBUKI— DD 45-55

DIVISION OF NAVAL INTELLIGENCE—IDENTIFICATION
AND CHARACTERISTICS SECTION —DECEMBER, 1942

PROFILE—
STACKS—2 RAKED COMBINED
MASTS —TRIPOD FORE
STICK MAIN
UNDULATING DECK LINE
HULL BROKEN FORWARD

AERIAL—
TURRETS—TWIN SINGLE FOR'D
TWIN SUPERIMPOSED AFT

END-ON—
NOTE VARIATIONS OF
FUBUKI BRIDGES

SHINONOME GROUP—
FREESTANDING CURVED VENTILATORS.
TORPEDO CREW SHIELDS.

AMIGIRI GROUP—
COLLAR VENTILATORS ON STACKS.
NO TORPEDO CREW PROTECTION.

HIBIKI GROUP—
THIN FORWARD STACK.
COLLAR VENTILATORS ON STACKS.
TORPEDO CREW SHIELDS.

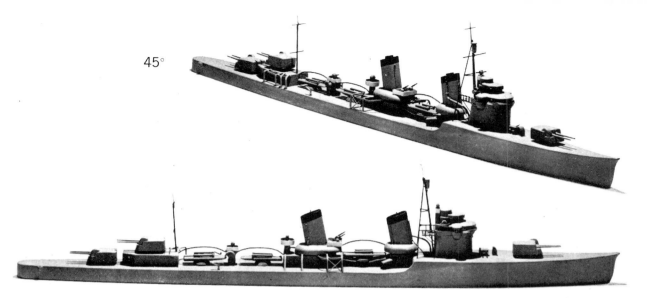

45°

90°

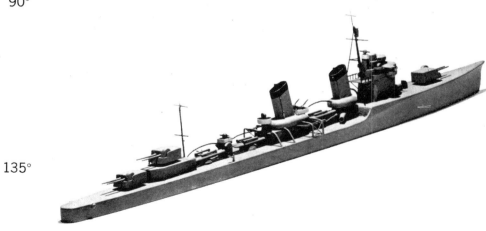

135°

0°

315°

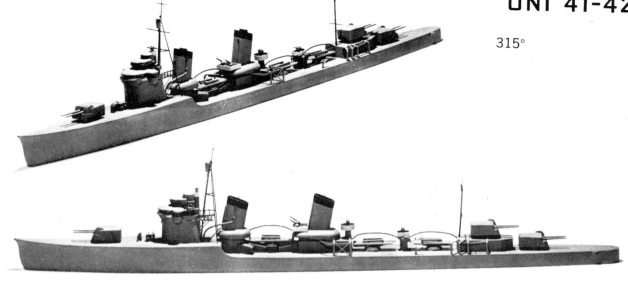

270°

180°

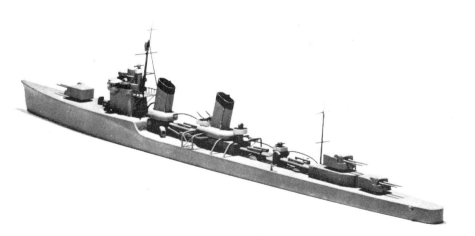

225°

FUBUKI CLASS—AMAGIRI GROUP—DD 45-55

DIVISION OF NAVAL INTELLIGENCE—IDENTIFICATION AND CHARACTERISTICS SECTION—NOVEMBER, 1942

0° 10°  20°  30°

75° 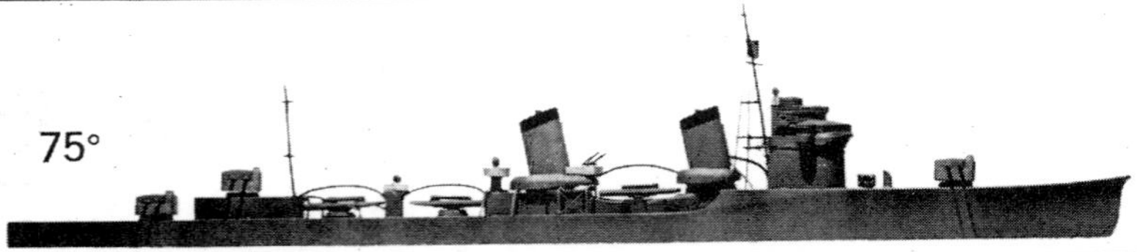 90°

135°  150°  165°  180°

240°  255°

300°  315°

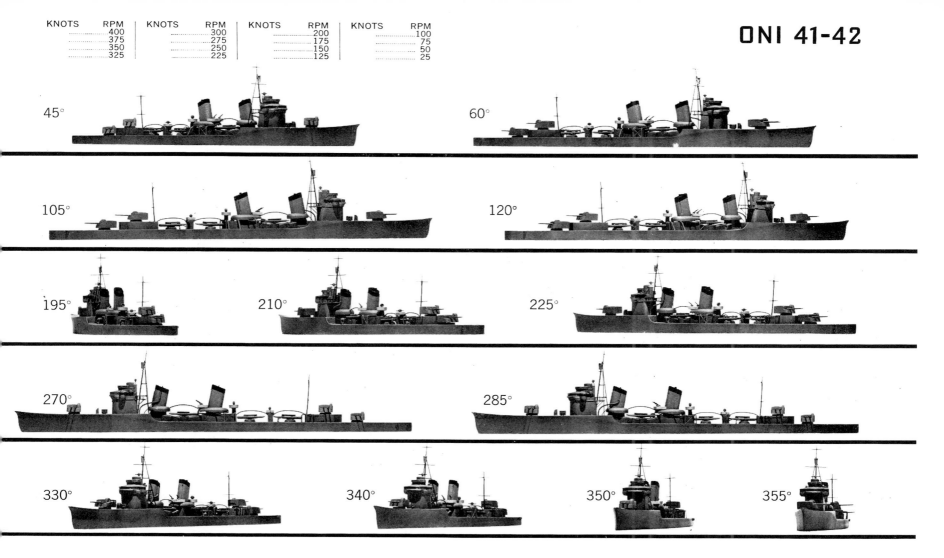

KNOTS .... RPM
.... 400
.... 375
.... 350
.... 325

KNOTS .... RPM
.... 300
.... 275
.... 250
.... 225

KNOTS .... RPM
.... 200
.... 175
.... 150
.... 125

KNOTS .... RPM
.... 100
.... 75
.... 50
.... 25

ONI 41-42

45°

60°

105°

120°

195°

210°

225°

270°

285°

330°

340°

350°

355°

FUBUKI CLASS—AMAGIRI GROUP—DD 45-55

DIVISION OF NAVAL INTELLIGENCE—IDENTIFICATION AND CHARACTERISTICS SECTION —DECEMBER, 1942

ONI 41-42

	BEGUN	COMPLETED	
DD 45—AMAGIRI	11/28/28	11/10/30	(SIKINAMI)
DD 46—SHIKINAMI	7/6/28	12/24/29	
DD 47—AYANAMI	1/20/28	4/30/30	
DD 48—ASAGIRI	12/12/28	6/30/30	
DD 49—URANAMI	4/28/27	6/30/29	
DD 50—YUGURI	4/1/29	12/3/30	(USIO)
DD 52—USHIO	12/24/29	11/14/31	
DD 53—OBORO	11/29/29	10/31/31	
DD 54—AKEBONO	10/25/29	7/31/31	
DD 55—SAZANAMI	2/21/30	5/19/32	

↑ OBORO

↑ SHIKINAMI

URANAMI ↓

FUBUKI CLASS—HIBIKI GROUP—DD 56-59

DIVISION OF NAVAL INTELLIGENCE—IDENTIFICATION AND CHARACTERISTICS SECTION — DECEMBER, 1942

ARMAMENT

	MAX. ELEV.	RANGE
6-5" (50) TWIN TURRETS	85°	18,000 YD.
2-AAMG		
9-21" TORPEDO TUBES, TRIPLE MOUNTS		
14 DEPTH CHARGES		

PROTECTION

GUN HOUSES, SPLINTER SHIELDS,
& TORPEDO-CREW SHIELDS

PROPULSION

MACHINERY—	2 PARSONS
BOILERS—	4 KAMPON
FUEL—	OIL, 500 TONS
DESIGNED HP—	40,000
DESIGNED SPEED—	34 KNOTS
ENDURANCE—	1100 @ 34 KNOTS
	4700 @ 15 KNOTS

HEIGHT OF OBSERVER

HORIZON BEYOND THE SHIP

SHIP BEYOND THE HORIZON

LENGTH—379'6" OA
BEAM— 33'9"
DRAFT— 9'9" (NORMAL)

DISPLACEMENT—1,700 TONS (STANDARD)—1,850 TONS (NORMAL)

↑ IKAZUCHI

FUBUKI CLASS—HIBIKI GROUP—DD 56-59

DIVISION OF NAVAL INTELLIGENCE—IDENTIFICATION AND CHARACTERISTICS SECTION —DECEMBER, 1942

	BEGUN	COMPLETED	ALSO SPELLED
AKATSUKI–DD56	2/17/30	11/30/32	AKATUKI
IKAZUCHI–DD57	3/ 7/30	8/15/32	IKADUTI
INAZUMA –DD58	3/ 7/30	11/15/32	INADUMA
HIBIKI –DD59	2/21/30	3/31/32	

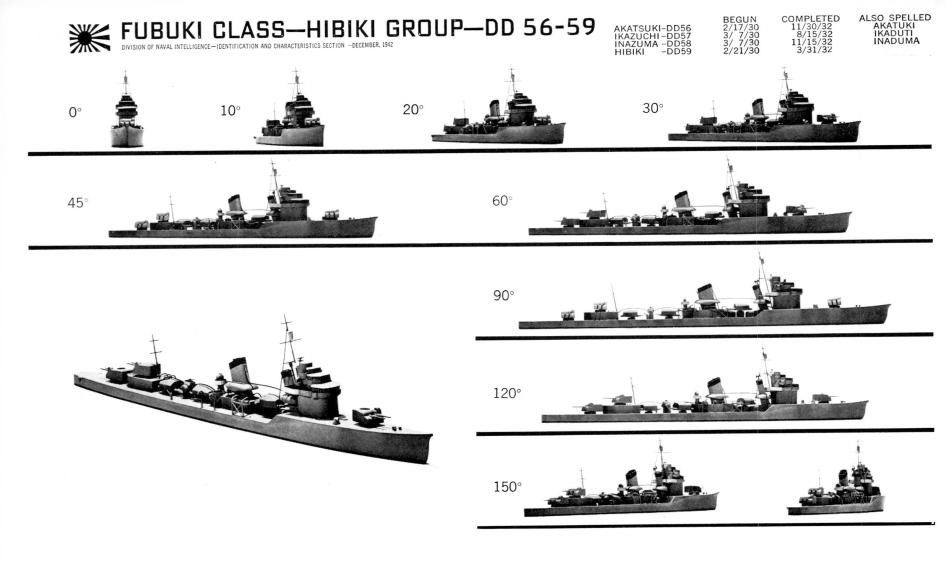

0°   10°   20°   30°

45°   60°

90°

120°

150°

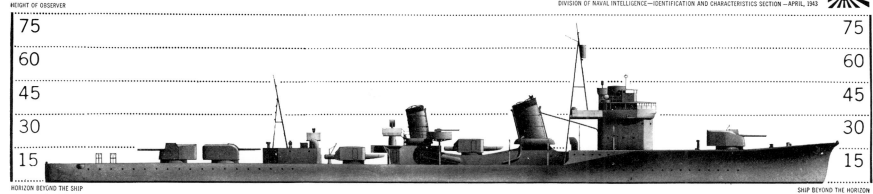

HORIZON BEYOND THE SHIP

SHIP BEYOND THE HORIZON

LENGTH—344'0" OA
BEAM— 32'6"
DRAFT— 8'9" (MEAN)

DISPLACEMENT
1368 (STANDARD)

ARMAMENT
	MAX. ELEV.	RANGE
5-5" (50)	45°	19,000 YDS.

2 AAMG
6-21" TORPEDO TUBES, TRIPLE MOUNTS.   —14 DEPTH CHARGES
ORIGINALLY FITTED WITH SUPERFIRING GUNHOUSES FORWARD AND
ONE AFT. TO IMPROVE STABILITY THE HIGH SINGLE MOUNT FORWARD
WAS MOVED AFT, THE BRIDGE CUT DOWN, AND TORPEDO BATTERY
REDUCED.

PROPULSION
MACHINERY— GEARED TURBINES
BOILERS—   3 KAMPON
FUEL—   OIL, 500 TONS
DES HP—   37,000   DES SPEED—34 KNOTS
ENDURANCE— 1020 @ 34 KNOTS —6000 @ 15 KNOTS
PROPELLERS— 2

PROTECTION
LIGHT SPLINTER PROTECTION (1/8") FOR GUN   HOUSES AND TOR-
PEDO CONTROL STATIONS. ELECTRIC WELDING   USED.

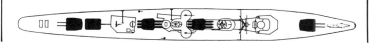

6 HATSUHARU CLASS

HATSUHARU—	DD 60
HATSUSHIMO—	DD 61
NENOHI—	DD 62
WAKABA—	DD 63
ARIAKE—	DD 64
YUGURE—	DD 65

HATSUHARU CLASS DD 60-65

DIVISION OF NAVAL INTELLIGENCE-IDENTIFICATION
AND CHARACTERISTICS SECTION-APRIL, 1943

MISTAKEN IDENTITY

FIRST LINE DESTROYERS

AFT TURRETS FLUSH

HATSUHARU CLASS—DD 60-65

SHIGURE CLASS—DD 66-75

AFT TURRETS SUPERIMPOSED

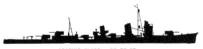

ASASHIO CLASS—DD 76-85

FUBUKI CLASS—DD 37-59

AERIAL VIEWS

45°

90°

135°

15° ELEVATION

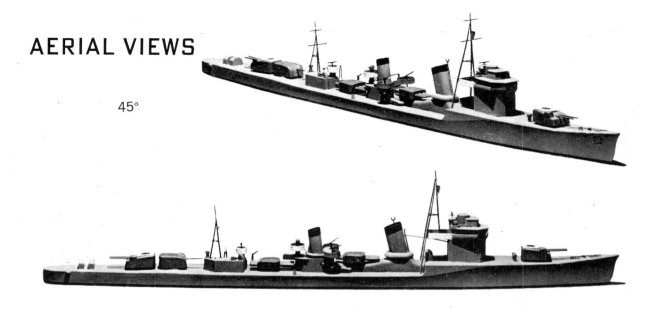

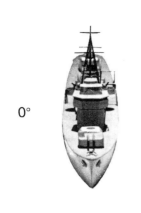

0°

180°

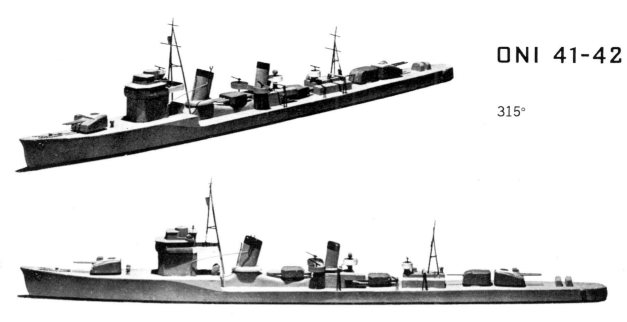

315°

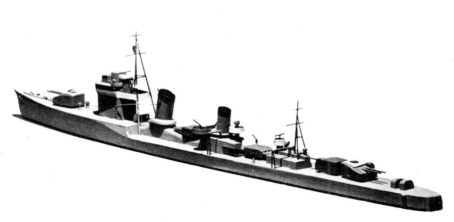

270°

225°

ONI 41-42

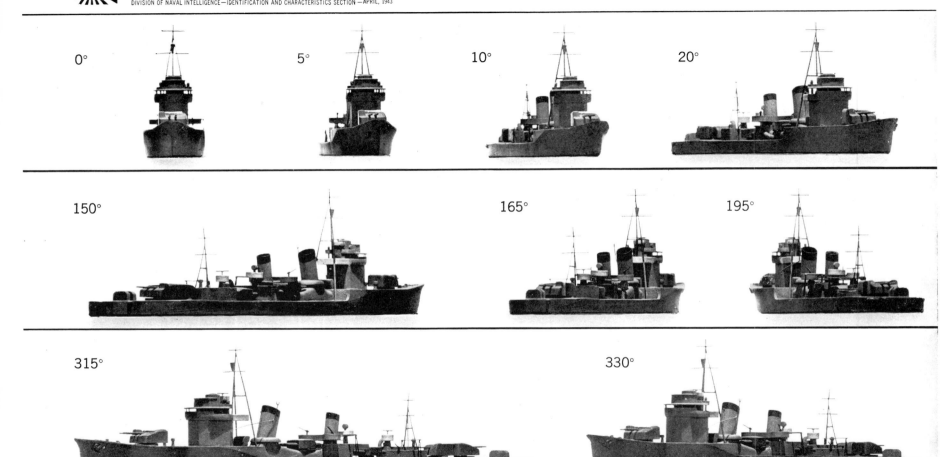

0° 5° 10° 20°

150° 165° 195°

315° 330°

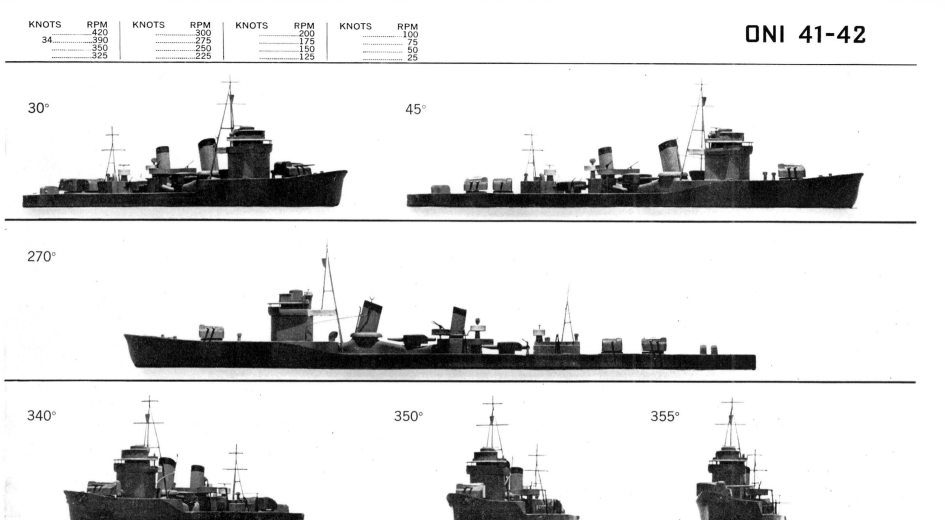

30°

45°

270°

340°

350°

355°

HATSUHARU CLASS—DD 60-65

DIVISION OF NAVAL INTELLIGENCE—IDENTIFICATION AND CHARACTERISTICS SECTION—APRIL, 1943

	BEGUN	COMPLETED		BEGUN	COMPLETED
HATSUHARU —DD60	5/14/31	9/30/33	WAKABA—DD63	12/12/31	10/31/34
HATSUSHIMO—DD61	1/31/33	9/27/34	ARIAKE —DD64	1/14/33	3/25/35
NENOHI —DD62	12/15/31	9/30/33	YUGURE—DD65	4/ 9/33	3/30/35

↓ NENOHI—8/18/37   ↑ 1941—YUGURE—8/16/37 ↑   HATSUSHIMO—8/18/37 ↓

ONI 41-42

SHIGURE CLASS—DD 66-75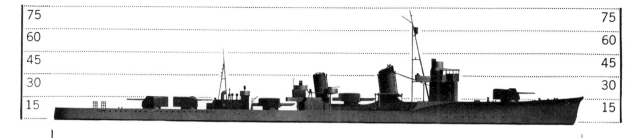

DIVISION OF NAVAL INTELLIGENCE—IDENTIFICATION AND CHARACTERISTICS SECTION—APRIL, 1943

ARMAMENT

5– 5″ (50) AA (2 TWINS AND 1 SINGLE)
2   AAMG
8–21″ TORPEDO TUBES (QUADS)
?   MINES   16 DEPTH CHARGES

PROPULSION

MACHINERY—   GEARED TURBINES
BOILERS—   FOUR KAMPON
FUEL—   OIL, 500
DESIGNED HP—   37,000
DESIGNED SPEED—34 KNOTS
ENDURANCE—   6,000 MILES @ 15 KNOTS
                1,020 MILES @ 34 KNOTS

LENGTH—341′3″ OA 335′5″ WL
BEAM—   31′9″
DRAFT—   9′3″ (MEAN)

DISPLACEMENT—1,368 TONS (STANDARD

10 SHIGURE CLASS—DD 66-75

↓ SAMIDARE—SEPTEMBER 1937

KAWAKAZE ↓

SHIGURE CLASS—DD 66-75

DIVISION OF NAVAL INTELLIGENCE—IDENTIFICATION AND CHARACTERISTICS SECTION—APRIL, 1943

		BEGUN	COMPLETED				
SHIGURE—	DD 66	12/ 9/33	9/ 7/36	SAMIDARE—	DD 71	12/19/34	2/ 3/37
SHIRATSUYU—	DD 67	11/14/33	8/20/36	YAMAKAZE—	DD 72	5/25/35	5/ ?/37
MURASAME—	DD 68	2/ 1/34	1/ 7/37	SUZUKAZE—	DD 73	7/ 7/35	5/ ?/37
YUDACHI—	DD 69	10/16/34	11/1/36	KAWAKAZE—	DD 74	4/25/35	5/ ?/37
HARUSAME—	DD 70	2/ 3/35	9/ ?/37	UMIKAZE—	DD 75	4/ 5/35	5/31/37

0°   10°   20°   30°

45°   60°

90°

120°

150°   165°

ARMAMENT

5– 5″ (50) AA (2 TWINS AND 1 SINGLE)
2   AAMG
8–21″ TORPEDO TUBES (QUADS)
?   MINES   16 DEPTH CHARGES

PROPULSION

MACHINERY—   GEARED TURBINES
BOILERS—   FOUR KAMPON
FUEL—   OIL, 500
DESIGNED HP—   37,000
DESIGNED SPEED—34 KNOTS
ENDURANCE—   6,000 MILES @ 15 KNOTS
    1,020 MILES @ 34 KNOTS

10 SHIGURE CLASS—DD 66-75

↓ SAMIDARE—SEPTEMBER 1937

LENGTH—341′3″ OA 335′5″ WL
BEAM— 31′9″
DRAFT— 9′3″ (MEAN)

DISPLACEMENT—1,368 TONS (STANDARD)

KAWAKAZE ↓

		BEGUN	COMPLETED
SHIGURE—	DD 66	12/9/33	9/7/36
SHIRATSUYU—	DD 67	11/14/33	8/20/36
MURASAME—	DD 68	2/1/34	1/7/37
YUDACHI—	DD 69	10/16/34	11/1/36
HARUSAME—	DD 70	2/3/35	9/?/37
SAMIDARE—	DD 71	12/19/34	2/3/37
YAMAKAZE—	DD 72	5/25/35	5/?/37
SUZUKAZE—	DD 73	7/7/35	5/?/37
KAWAKAZE—	DD 74	4/25/35	5/?/37
UMIKAZE—	DD 75	4/5/35	5/31/37

↑ YAMAKAZE—9/38   ↓ SAMIDARE—8/16/37—SHANGHAI   ↓ YUDACHI—8/16/37—SHANGHAI ↓

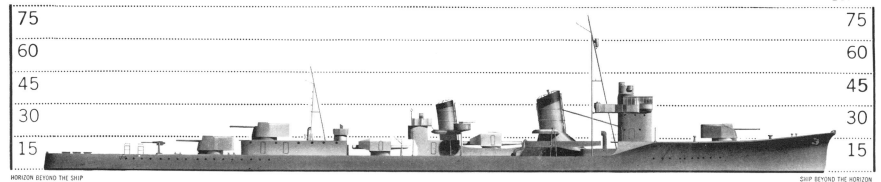

75	75
60	60
45	45
30	30
15	15

HORIZON BEYOND THE SHIP

SHIP BEYOND THE HORIZON

0

LENGTH—361'6" OA, 356'2" WL
BEAM— 33'4"
DRAFT— 9'0" (MEAN)

DISPLACEMENT
1,500 TONS (STANDARD)

ARMAMENT

MAX. ELEV. MAX. RANGE

6–5" TWIN MOUNTS
2 M.G.
8–21" TORPEDO TUBES (POSSIBLY 24")
14 (?) DEPTH CHARGES

PROPULSION

MACHINERY— GEARED TURBINES
BOILERS— THREE KAMPON
FUEL— OIL, 500 TONS
DESIGNED HP— 38,000
DESIGNED SPEED—34 KNOTS
ENDURANCE— 5,700 MILES @ 10 KNOTS
960 MILES @ 34 KNOTS

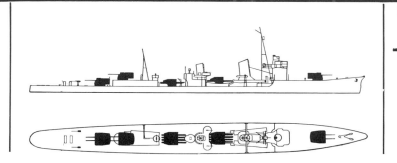

10 ASASHIO CLASS—DD 76-85

KAGERO CLASS—DD 86-117
BELIEVED SIMILAR

ASASHIO CLASS
DD 76-85

DIVISION OF NAVAL INTELLIGENCE—IDENTIFICATION
AND CHARACTERISTICS SECTION—APRIL, 1943

MISTAKEN IDENTITY

2-STACK DESTROYERS
JAPANESE

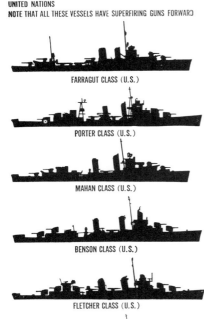

ASASHIO CLASS

UNITED NATIONS
NOTE THAT ALL THESE VESSELS HAVE SUPERFIRING GUNS FORWARD

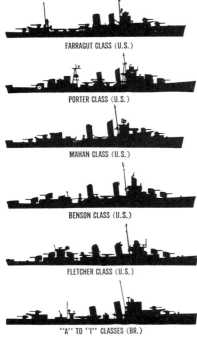

FARRAGUT CLASS (U.S.)

PORTER CLASS (U.S.)

MAHAN CLASS (U.S.)

BENSON CLASS (U.S.)

FLETCHER CLASS (U.S.)

"A" TO "I" CLASSES (BR.)

AERIAL VIEWS

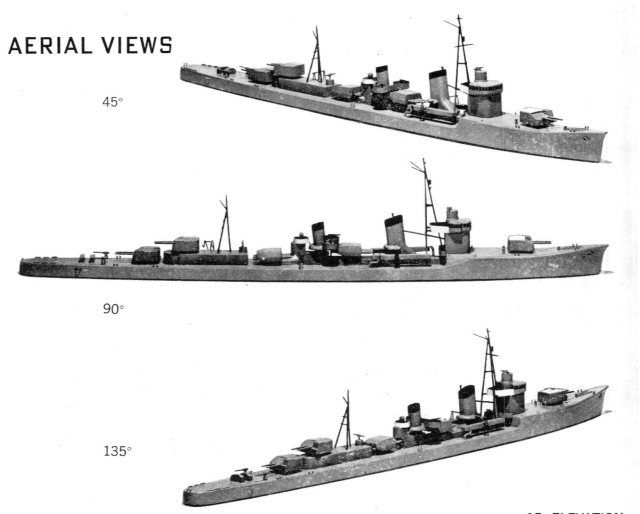

45°

90°

135°

15° ELEVATION

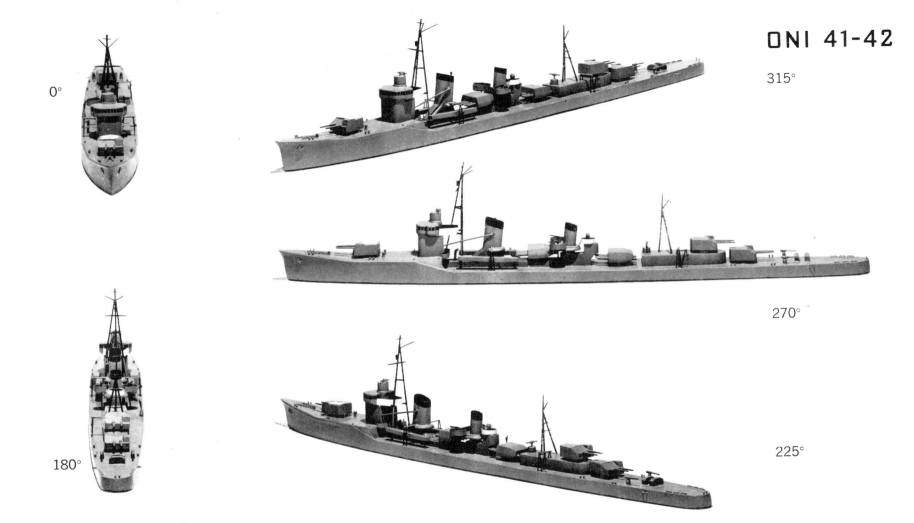

ONI 41-42

0°

180°

315°

270°

225°

DIVISION OF NAVAL INTELLIGENCE—IDENTIFICATION AND CHARACTERISTICS SECTION—APRIL, 1943

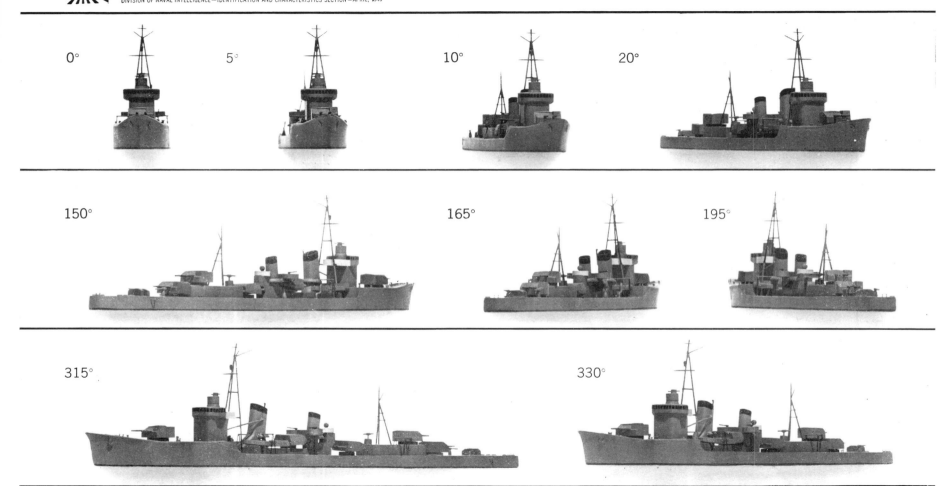

0°   5°   10°   20°

150°   165°   195°

315°   330°

KNOTS	RPM	KNOTS	RPM	KNOTS	RPM	KNOTS	RPM
	400		300		200		100
	375		275		175		75
	350		250		150		50
	325		225		125		25

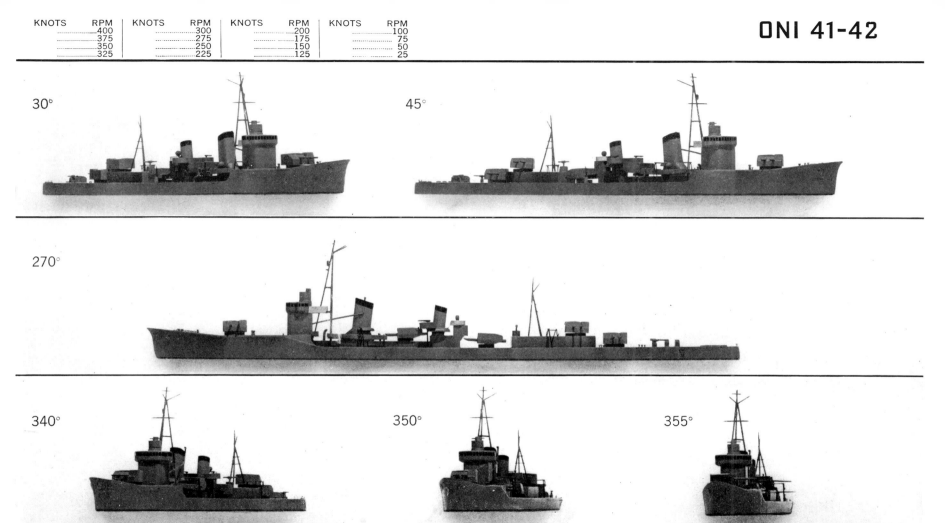

30°

45°

270°

340°

350°

355°

ARASHIO 12/38   ASAGUMO 11/38 ↓

		BEGUN	COMPLETED	
ASASHIO—	DD 76	9/ 7/35	8/31/37	
ARASHIO—	DD 77	10/ 1/35	11/37	
OSHIO—	DD 78	8/ 5/36	10/31/37	
MICHISHIO—	DD 79	11/ 5/35	11/37	
ASAGUMO—	DD 80	12/23/36	3/38	REPORTED WAR LOSS
YAMAGUMO—	DD 81	11/ 4/36	3/38	REPORTED WAR LOSS
MINEGUMO—	DD 82	1937	1938	
NATSUGUMO—	DD 83	7/ 1/36	2/10/38	
KASUMI—	DD 84	12/ 1/36	6/28/39	
ARARE—	DD 85	3/ 5/37	4/15/39	

ONI 41-42

HEIGHT OF OBSERVER

DD UN-1 CLASS*

DIVISION OF NAVAL INTELLIGENCE—IDENTIFICATION AND CHARACTERISTICS SECTION·—MARCH. 1943

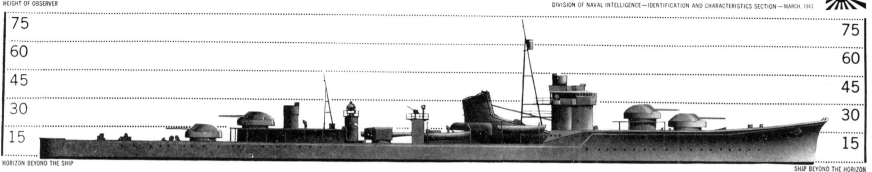

75	75
60	60
45	45
30	30
15	15

HORIZON BEYOND THE SHIP

SHIP BEYOND THE HORIZON

LENGTH—405' OA
BEAM —37'
DRAFT —?

0

DISPLACEMENT—2,300 TONS (STANDARD)

ARMAMENT

8-5" (50) DUAL PURPOSE TWINS
? SMALL AA GUNS
3-21" OR 24".5 TORPEDO TUBES
ONE OR MORE SETS OF RELOADS

PROPULSION

DESIGNED SPEED—34 KNOTS (E)
THIS DATA ESTIMATED FROM PHOTOGRAPHIC
MATERIAL AND DESIGN TRENDS.

DESIGN AND ARMAMENT SUGGESTS ESCORT OR SCREENING DUTIES

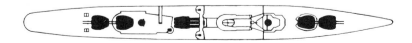

DD UN-1 CLASS

DIVISION OF NAVAL INTELLIGENCE—IDENTIFICATION
AND CHARACTERISTICS SECTION —APRIL. 1943

AERIAL VIEWS

MISTAKEN IDENTITY

DD UNKNOWN 1

CA MOGAMI CLASS

CL YUBARI

TB CHIDORI, OTORI CLASSES

ALSO—TB—TRAD CLASS (THAI)
PG—PING HAI, NING HAI (EX-CHINESE)

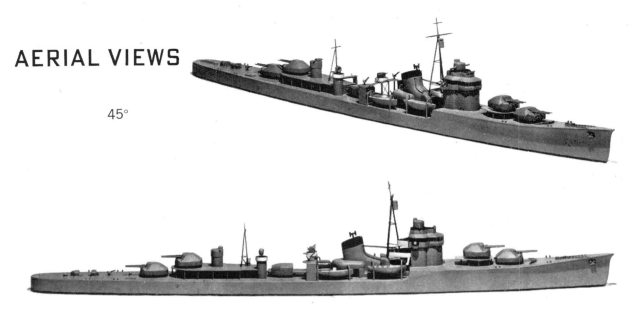

45°

90°

135°

15° ELEVATION

0°

180°

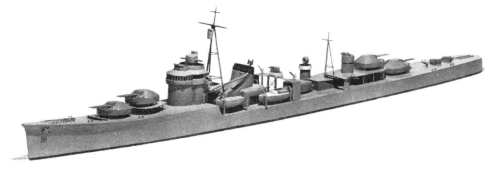

ONI 41-42

315°

270°

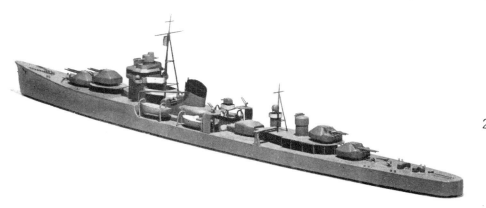

225°

0°  5°  10°  20°

150°  165°  195°

315°  330°

KNOTS	RPM	KNOTS	RPM	KNOTS	RPM	KNOTS	RPM
	400		300		200		100
	375		275		175		75
	350		250		150		50
	325		225		125		25

30°

45°

270°

340°

350°

355°

PHOTOS TAKEN IN EMPRESS AUGUSTA BAY, SWP 9/29/42

ONI 41-42

HEIGHT OF OBSERVER

MOMI CLASS—ODD-4-22
IDENTICAL IN APPEARANCE

WAKATAKE CLASS—ODD-23-29

DIVISION OF NAVAL INTELLIGENCE—IDENTIFICATION AND CHARACTERISTICS SECTION —JUNE, 1943

75	75
60	60
45	45
30	30
15	15

HORIZON BEYOND THE SHIP

SHIP BEYOND THE HORIZON

0

LENGTH—287′ OA; 282′ WL
BEAM— 26′6″
DRAFT— 8′3″ (NORMAL)

DISPLACEMENT—770 (M)—820 (W) TONS STANDARD

ARMAMENT

	MAX. ELEV.	MAX. RANGE (HORIZONTAL)
3–4″.7 (45)	40°	19,000 YARDS

2–AAMG
4–21″ TORPEDO TUBES
10 DEPTH CHARGES
SOME HAVE BEEN CONVERTED FOR MINELAYING

PROPULSION

MACHINERY— PARSONS GEARED TURBINE
BOILERS— 3 KAMPON
FUEL— OIL —275 TONS
DESIGNED HP—21,500
MAX. SPEED— 31.5 KNOTS

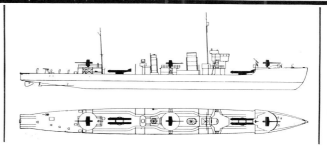

7 WAKATAKE CLASS—ODD-23-29

19 MOMI CLASS—ODD-4-22

WAKATAKE CL.
ODD-23-29

DIVISION OF NAVAL INTELLIGENCE—IDENTIFICATION
AND CHARACTERISTICS SECTION—AUGUST, 1943

MISTAKEN IDENTITY—

AERIAL VIEWS

WAKATAKE CLASS—ODD 23-29
MOMI CLASS —ODD 4-22

MINEKAZE CLASS—DD 1-15

KAMIKAZE CLASS—DD 16-24

MUTSUKI CLASS—DD 25-36

AERIAL VIEWS

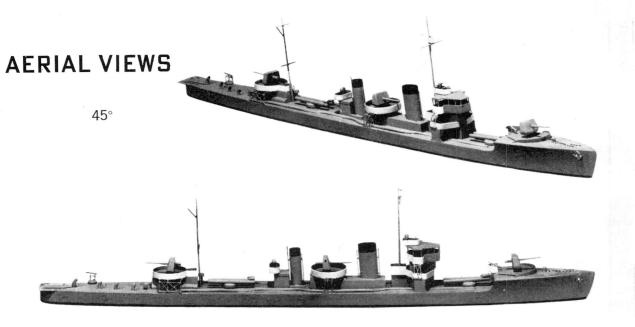

45°

90°

135°

15° ELEVATION

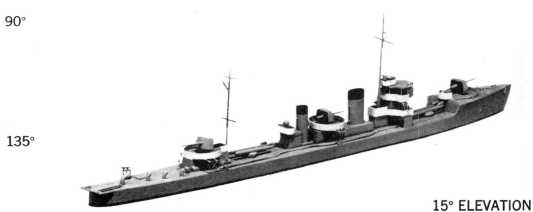

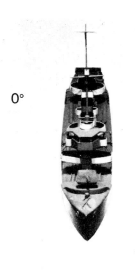

0°

180°

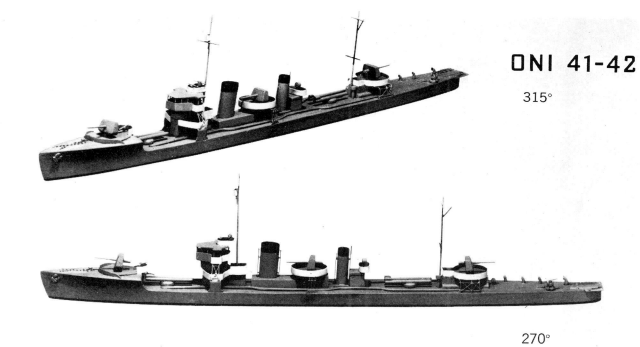

ONI 41-42

315°

270°

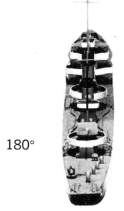

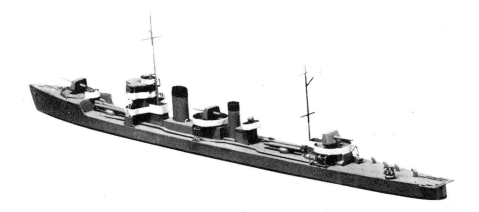

225°

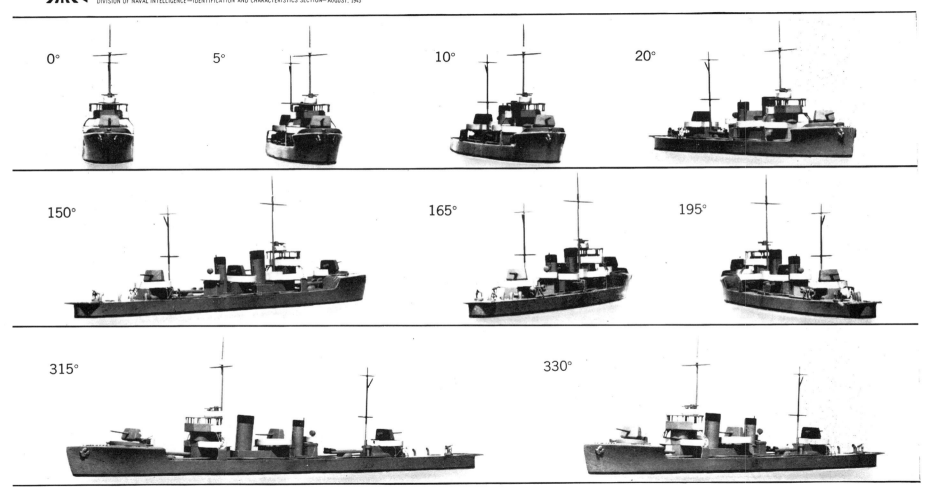

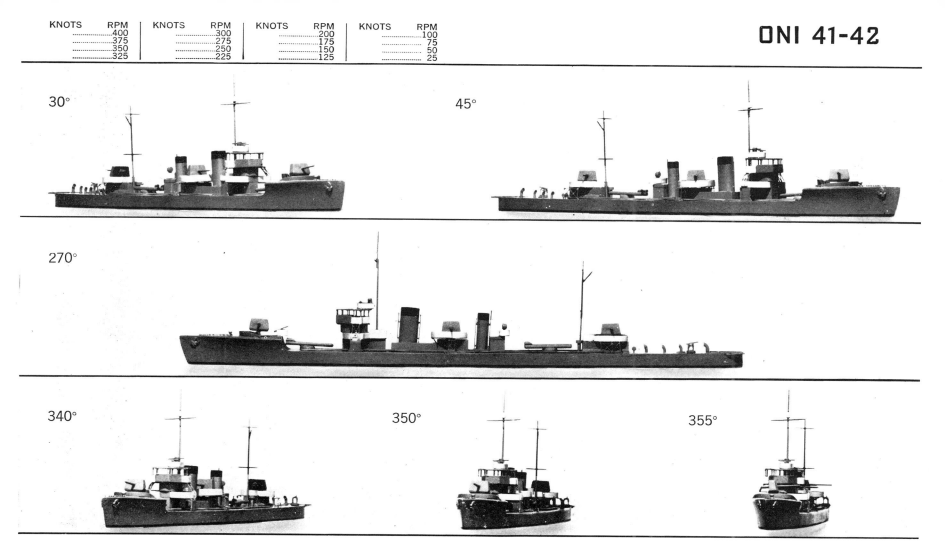

KNOTS	RPM	KNOTS	RPM	KNOTS	RPM	KNOTS	RPM
	400		300		200		100
	375		275		175		75
	350		250		150		50
	325		225		125		25

30°

45°

270°

340°

350°

355°

WAKATAKE CLASS—ODD-23-29		COMPLETED
ODD-23	WAKATAKE	1922
ODD-24	KURETAKE	1922
ODD-25	SANAYE	1923
ODD-26	ASAGAO	1923
ODD-27	FUYO	1923
ODD-28	KARUKAYA	1923
ODD-29	YUGAO	1924

MOMI CLASS—ODD-4-22 COMPLETED 1919–1923

ODD- 4	NASHI	ODD-14	SUSUKI
ODD- 5	TAKE	ODD-15	FUJI
ODD- 6	KAYA	ODD-16	ASHI
ODD- 7	KURI	ODD-17	TSUTA
ODD- 8	NIRE	ODD-18	HASU
ODD- 9	AOI	ODD-19	HISHI
ODD-10	KIKU	ODD-20	TADE
ODD-11	KAKI	ODD-21	YOMOGI
ODD-12	TSUGA	ODD-22	SUMIRA
ODD-13	HAGI		

↑ KURI—8/18/37   HASU—8/18/37 ↓

HAGI—10/36 ↓

I-151 CLASS

	I-151	I-152
LENGTH—	300'	330'11"
BEAM—	28'11"	25'1"
DRAFT—	15'1"	16'10"

	SURFACE	SUBMERGED
DISPLACEMENT—(STANDARD)	1,390 TONS	2,000 TONS

ARMAMENT—
1-4".7/40
TT—8-21" (6 BOW, 2 STERN)

MAX. RANGE (HORIZONTAL)
10,800 YDS.
TORPEDOES 20   COMPLEMENT—60

PROPULSION—	I-151	I-152
MACHINERY—	4—SULZER DIESELS	2—SULZER DIESELS
	4—MOTORS	2—MOTORS
FUEL—	470 TONS OIL	470 TONS OIL
SURFACE H.P.—	5200	6000
SUBMERGED H.P.—	2600	1800
SUBMERGED SPEED—9		
SURFACE SPEED—	I-151—17 KTS	R.P.M.—340 RADIUS—6100
	I-152—20 KTS	R.P.M.—300
		AT MINIMUM SPEED —25,450
PROPELLERS—	I-151—4 I-152—2	

I-151—SS 1—COMPLETED 1924
I-152—SS 2—COMPLETED 1925

SS 3-14

DIVISION OF NAVAL INTELLIGENCE—IDENTIFICATION AND CHARACTERISTICS SECTION—AUGUST, 1943

I-153 CLASS

LENGTH— 331'
BEAM— 26'
DRAFT— 16'

	SURFACE	SUBMERGED
DISPLACEMENT—	(STANDARD) 1,635 TONS	2,100 TONS

ARMAMENT—	MAX. ELEV.	MAX. RANGE (HOR.)	MAX. RANGE (VERT.)
1-4.7/40		10,800 YD.	
1-3" AA (?)	85°	9,000 YD.	20,000 FT.
2-AAMG			

TORPEDO TUBES— 8-21" (6 BOW, 2 STERN)—TORPEDOES 20
COMPLEMENT— 70-85
PROPULSION—
    MACHINERY— 2 DIESELS—SULZER—2 MOTORS
    FUEL— OIL—255 TONS
    SURFACE HP— 6,000
    SUBMERGED HP— 1,800   RADIUS—6,700
    SURFACE SPEED— 19 KTS   12 KNOTS— 8,640
    SUBMERGED SPEED—9 KTS   MINIMUM—29,500

I-153 CLASS   COMPLETED 1927–1930

I-153—SS 3
I-154—SS 4
I-155—SS 5
I-156—SS 6
I-157—SS 7
I-158—SS 8
I-159—SS 9
I-160—SS 10
I-161—SS 11
I-162—SS 12
I-163—SS 13
I-164—SS 14

NOTE—2 PERISCOPES IN CONTROL ROOM, 1 IN CONNING TOWER

I-1 CLASS   SS 15-18

LENGTH—320'   BEAM—30'3"   DRAFT—15'9"

DISPLACEMENT—(STANDARD) SURFACE—1,955 TONS   SUBMERGED—2,480 TONS

ARMAMENT   MAX. ELEV.   MAX RANGE (HORIZONTAL)

2-5"5/50 (ONE MAY BE REMOVED)   15°   17,000 YD. (?)

2-AAMG

TT 6-21" (4 BOW, 2 STERN)   TORPEDOES—15

1-AIRCRAFT (COLLAPSIBLE)

PROPULSION—MACHINERY—2 M.A.N. DIESELS, 2 MOTORS

BOILERS—KAMPON   FUEL—OIL—520 TONS

SURFACE HP—6,000   SUBMERGED HP—3,600

SURFACE SPEED—17   R.P.M.—387-450—RADIUS—9,850

SUBMERGED SPEED—9   12 KNOTS—   15,600

I-1 CLASS   COMPLETED—1926-29

I-1—SS 15, I-2—SS 16, I-3—SS 17, I-4—SS 18

NOTES—

SEAPLANE HOUSED IN TWO HULL COMPARTMENTS ABAFT CONNING TOWER

DOUBLE HULL—NET CUTTERS (I-2, I-3)

I-165—CLASS   SS 19-21

LENGTH—320'7" WL   BEAM—26'11"   DRAFT—15'10"

DISPLACEMENT—(STANDARD) SURFACE—1,638 TONS   SUBMERGED—2,100 TONS

ARMAMENT—   1-4"   1-AAMG

                 TT—6-21" (4 BOW—2 STERN)

PROPULSION—   MACHINERY—2 M.A.N. DIESELS—2 MOTORS

SURFACE HP—   6,000   SUBMERGED HP—1,800

SURFACE SPEED—   19 KTS   @ RADIUS—6,700

SUBMERGED SPEED—9 KTS

I-165 CLASS   COMPLETED—1932

I-165—SS 19,   I-166—SS 20,   I-167—SS 21

NOTES—

3 SEPARATE HULLS

HYDROPHONE LISTENING GEAR—12.5 MILE RANGE

EQUIPPED WITH NET CUTTERS

I-5 CLASS SS 22, 23, 32, 33

LENGTH—	I-5	I-6	I-7-8
	319'11" WL	309'5" WL	343'8" WL
BEAM—	30'3"	29'8"	30'
DRAFT—	15'9"	15'5"	14'5"

DISPLACEMENT (STANDARD) TONS	SURFACE	SUBMERGED
	I-5-1900	I-5-2500
	I-6-1900	I-6-2600
	I-7-8-1950	I-7-8-2600

ARMAMENT	MAX. RANGE
1-5"/50 I-5-6	19,000 YD.
1-5".5/50 I-7	20,000 YD.
2-5".5/50 I-8	20,000 YD.

2-AAMG
TT—6-21"   TORPEDOES 15
1-AIRCRAFT (COLLAPSIBLE)
COMPLEMENT—   60
PROPULSION—
   MACHINERY—   2 M.A.N. DIESELS—2 MOTORS
   BOILERS—   KAMPON
   SURFACE H.P.—   6,000   SUBMERGED H.P.—2642-2800
   SUBMERGED SPEED—9 KTS
   SURFACE SPEED—   17 KTS   R.P.M. 350   RADIUS 9,850
                                                 AT MINIMUM SPEED 34,870

(2) I-5 CLASS	COMPLETED
I-5 SS 22	(1932)
I-6 SS 23	(1935)
I-7 SS 32	(1937)
I-8 SS 33	(1938)

NOTE—SEAPLANE HOUSED IN TUBULAR HANGAR ABAFT CONNING TOWER

I 168 CLASS SS 24-31

LENGTH—331'5" WL
BEAM—   27'
DRAFT— 13'
DISPLACEMENT STANDARD (SURFACE) 1,400 TONS

ARMAMENT	MAX. RANGE (HORIZONTAL)
1-4" I 168-170	
1-4".7/40 I 171-175	10,200 YD.

2 AAMG
TT—6-21" (4 BOW, 2 STERN)   15 TORPEDOES—MINES (?)
COMPLEMENT—   60
PROPULSION—
   MACHINERY—   2 DIESELS
   FUEL—OIL—   500 TONS
   DES. H.P.—   6,000
   SUBMERGED H.P.—   1,800
   SUBMERGED SPEED—9 KTS
   SURFACE SPEED—   20 KTS   RADIUS-5,350
                                           MINIMUM SPEED 25,400

I 168 CLASS	COMPLETED (1934-1938)
I 168 (ex I-68) SS 24	
I 169 (ex I-69) SS 25	
I 170 (ex I-70) SS 26	
I 171 (ex I-71) SS 27	
I 172 (ex I-72) SS 28	
I 173 (ex I-73) SS 29	
I 174 (ex I-74) SS 30	
I 175 (ex I-75) SS 31	

NOTE—FITTED WITH MINE TRIPPING AND CUTTING GEAR

ONI 41-42

I-9 CLASS 9-41—COMPLETED 1940-41

SS 43-49 STiLL COMPLETING

LENGTH—343'8" WL

BEAM— 29'10"

DRAFT— 14'5" (MEAN)

DISPLACEMENT—2,180 TONS SURFACE (STANDARD)

2,600 TONS SUBMERGED

ARMAMENT—   MAX. ELEV.   MAX. RANGE (HORIZONTAL)   MAX. RANGE (VERTICAL)

1-5".5   20,000 YARDS

2-AAMG

8-21" TORPEDO TUBES—20 TORPEDOES CARRIED

1 OR 2 AIRCRAFT (HOUSED IN TWIN HULL COMPARTMENTS ABAFT C. T.)

NOTE—SOME BELIEVED **TO CARRY** 2-MAN MIDGET SUBMARINES (SEE CUT)

PROPULSION—

DESIGNED H.P.— 6,000-9,000/ (SURFACE)

DESIGNED SPEED—20 KNOTS SURFACE, 9 KNOTS SUBMERGED

RADIUS—   5,300 MILES @ 20 KTS

25,480 MILES MAXIMUM

I 9-41 COMPLETED 1940-1941

I 43-48 BUILDING

PROBABLY I-22, 27, OR 29 PHOTOGRAPHED AT ST. NAZAIRE 9/29/42

HANGAR FOR MIDGET SS CENSORED (BELOW), RECONSTRUCTED (ABOVE).

I-76 CLASS— SS 70-79—NO DATA

I-76-82 BELIEVED COMPLETED, OTHERS BUILDING

RO-26 CLASS OSS 1-3

LENGTH—243'6"(OA)   BEAM—20'1"   DRAFT—12'3"

	SURFACE	SUBMERGED
DISPLACEMENT (STANDARD) TONS	746	1,000

ARMAMENT   MAX. ELEV.   MAX. RANGE (HORIZONTAL)   MAX. RANGE (VERTICAL)
1-3"15 DP   85°   9,000 YARDS   20,000 FEET
1-AAMG
TT-4-21" (BOW)

COMPLEMENT—45

PROPULSION
   MACHINERY—   2 SULZER DIESELS 2 MOTORS
   FUEL—   75 TONS OIL
   SUBMERGED HP—   1,200   SURFACE HP—2,600
   SUBMERGED SPEED—10 KTS RADIUS 3,860
   SURFACE SPEED—   16 KTS

RO-26 CLASS RO-26 OSS 1, RO-27 OSS 2, RO-28 OSS 3   COMPLETED 1923-24

NOTE—THESE SHIPS MAY BE USED FOR TRAINING

I-101 CLASS SS 80-86 NO DATA

I-101—SS 80
I-102—SS 81
I-103—SS 82 (1942)
I-104—SS 83
I-105—SS 84 (BUILDING)
I-106—SS 85 (BUILDING)
I-107—SS 86 (BUILDING)

I-176 CLASS SS 87-94 NO DATA

I-176—SS 87 (BUILDING)
I-177—SS 88 (BUILDING)
I-178—SS 89 PROJECTED
I-179—SS 90 PROJECTED
I-180—SS 91 PROJECTED
I-181—SS 92 PROJECTED
I-182—SS 93 PROJECTED
I-185—SS 94 PROJECTED

RO 51 CLASS OSS 4-12
LENGTH—**RO 51-56**—231'7" OA   RO 57-59—250' PP
BEAM— 23'6"   DRAFT—13'
DISPLACEMENT (STANDARD) TONS   SURFACE   SUBMERGED
     RO 51-56—893   1,082
     RO 57-59—889

ARMAMENT   MAX. ELEV.   MAX. RANGE (HOR.)   MAX. RANGE (VER.)
   1—3".15 DP   85°   9,000 YDS.   20,000 FT.
   RO 51-56 TT—6-18" (BCW —TORPEDOES, 12
   RO 57-59 TT—4-21" (BOW —TORPEDOES, 8
COMPLEMENT—65
PROPULSION—MACHINERY—2 DIESELS—VICKERS 12 CYL.—4 MOTORS
   FUEL—65 TONS—OIL
   SURFACE HP— 2,400   SUBMERGED HP—1,200
   SURFACE SPEED— 17 KTS
   SUBMERGED SPEED—10 KTS

RO 51 CLASS   COMPLETED 1922-1923
   RO-57 OSS 10, RO-58 OSS 11, RO-59, OSS 12

NOTE—OSS 4-9 MAY BE USED FOR TRAINING

RO 60 CLASS OSS 13-21
LENGTH—250' (P.P.)—BEAM-24'3"—DRAFT-12'4"
DISPLACEMENT—(STANDARD) TONS   SURFACE   SUBMERGED
   988   1,300
ARMAMENT   MAX. ELEVATION   MAX. RANGE (HOR.)   MAX. RANGE (VER.)
   1— 3" AA   85°   9,000 YDS.   20,000 FEET
     3".15 DP
   TT—6-21" (4 BOW 2 STERN OR ALL BOW)
COMPLEMENT—47
PROPULSION—MACHINERY—DIESEL—2 VICKERS SOLID INJECTION
   FUEL—75 TONS OIL
   SURFACE HP—2,400   SUBMERGED HP—1,800
   SURFACE SPEED— 16 KTS
   SUBMERGED SPEED—10 KTS
   MAX. SUSTAINED— 13 KTS   RADIUS 4,670

RO 60 CLASS   COMPLETED 1923-1926
   RO 62 OSS 15   RO 65 OSS 18
   RO 63 OSS 16   RO 67 OSS 20
   RO 64 OSS 17   RO 68 OSS 21

NOTES—DOUBLE HULLS
   2 PERISCOPES 60MM TAPERED HEAD
   CLEARING WIRES—NO NET CUTTERS
   TWO TELESCOPIC RADIO MASTS
   (NOTE VARIATION IN GUN MOUNTS)

RO-33 CLASS—OSS 22-26 ↑

LENGTH—239'6" OA   BEAM—22'   DRAFT—10'8"

DISPLACEMENT—(STANDARD)   SURFACE—700 TONS

ARMAMENT	MAX. ELEV.	MAX. RANGE (HOR.)	MAX. RANGE (VERT.)
1–3".15 DP	85°	9,000 YDS.	20,000 FT.
1–MG			
TT—4–21" (BOW)			

PROPULSION—

MACHINERY—   DIESELS

BOILERS—

SURFACE HP—   2,600

SUBMERGED HP—   1,300

SURFACE SPEED—   16.9 KNOTS

SUBMERGED SPEED—10 KNOTS

RO-33 CLASS   COMPLETED 1935-1942

RO-33   OSS 22

RO-34   OSS 23

RO-37   OSS 26

RO-100 CLASS—OSS 27-34   NO DATA   COMPLETED 1942

RO-100   OSS 27

RO-101   OSS 28

RO-102   OSS 29

RO-103   OSS 30

RO-104   OSS 31—BUILDING

RO-105   OSS 32—BUILDING

RO-106   OSS 33—BUILDING

RO-107   OSS 34—BUILDING

RO-29 CLASS SM 1-4

LENGTH—243'6" OA
BEAM— 20'9"
DRAFT— 12'3"

	SURFACE	SUBMERGED
DISPLACEMENT—(STANDARD)	655 TONS	1,000? TONS

ARMAMENT—
  1-4.7"/40   MAX. RANGE
  1-3 POUNDER   10,800 YDS.
  TT—4-21" (BOW)—TORPEDOES 8
  MINES-42

COMPLEMENT—43

PROPULSION—
  MACHINERY—   2 FIAT DIESELS
  FUEL—   60 TONS OIL
  SURFACE HP—   1,300
  SUBMERGED HP— 1,200
  SURFACE SPEED— 13 KTS
  SUBMERGED SPEED—10 KTS   RPM—385

(3) **RO-29 CLASS**   COMPLETED—1924-1927

  RO-29 **SM 1** — MAY BE USED FOR TRAINING
  RO-30 **SM 2**
  RO-31 **SM 3**
  RO-32 **SM 4**

I-121 CLASS SM 5-8

LENGTH—279'6" (P.P.)
BEAM— 24'7"
DRAFT— 14'1"

	SURFACE	SUBMERGED
DISPLACEMENT—(STANDARD) TONS	1,142	1,470

ARMAMENT   MAX. ELEV.   MAX. RANGE (HORIZONTAL)
  1-5.5"/50   15°   16,000 YD (E)
  1-AAMG
  TT—4-21" (BOW)—TORPEDOES 20
  MINES—42 —2 TUBES

COMPLEMENT—70

PROPULSION—
  MACHINERY—   2 M. A. N. DIESELS
  SURFACE HP—   2,400
  SUBMERGED HP— 1,200
  SURFACE SPEED— 14 KTS
  SUBMERGED SPEED—9.5 KTS

I-121 CLASS   COMPLETED—1927-1928

I-121	SM 5	ex I 21
I-122	SM 6	ex I 22
I-123	SM 7	ex I 23
I-124	SM 8	ex I 24

NOTES—
  3 TAPERED-HEAD PERISCOPES.

AUXILIARIES

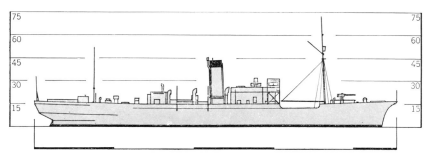

KOMABASHI—AS 1   1914

DIMENSIONS— 227' OA x 35' x 17'8"
DISPLACEMENT—1,125 TONS (STANDARD)—1,230 TONS (NORMAL)

ARMAMENT	MAX. ELEV.	MAX. RANGE (HORIZONTAL)	MAX. RANGE (VERTICAL)
2–3"			
2–3" AA	85°	9,000 YARDS	20,000 FEET
2–12 PDR.			

MACHINERY—RECIPROCATING—TRIPLE EXPANSION   FUEL—COAL
DESIGNED HP—1,824   MAXIMUM SPEED—14 KNOTS @ 118 R.P.M.

TAIGEI—AS 4   1934

DIMENSIONS— 647'4" WL x 59'2" x 17'
DISPLACEMENT—10,000 TONS (STANDARD)

ARMAMENT	MAX. ELEV.	MAX. RANGE (HORIZONTAL)	MAX. RANGE (VERTICAL)
4–5" (50) AA	85°	19 000 YARDS	33,000 FEET
2 CATAPULTS—3 SCOUT OBSERVATION			

MACHINERY— FOUR DIESELS   FUEL—   OIL
DESIGNED HP—13,000   MAXIMUM SPEED—20 KNOTS

MAY BE CONVERTED INTO AN ACV

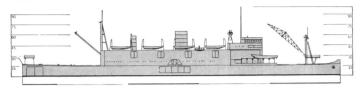

LENGTH—448' OA   BEAM—57'   DRAFT— —

DISPLACEMENT—7,500 TONS

ARMAMENT—   2-4" (?) AA   ?-AAMG   2-SEARCHLIGHTS

CAPACITY—   APP. 140 LCI—8,600 TROOPS
             10 LAUNCHES, 4 DESPATCH BOATS

PROTECTION—   SPLINTER ONLY

PROPULSION—   MACHINERY—
             BOILERS—   FUEL—
             DESIGNED HP—   DESIGNED SPEED—18 KTS.

COMPLETED—1937   SISTERSHIPS REPORTED, UNVERIFIED

THIS SHIP HAS TAKEN PART IN MANY JAPANESE
COMBINED OPERATIONS—SEE ONI 225-J "JAPANESE
LANDING OPERATIONS AND EQUIPMENT" FOR FURTHER TREATMENT

PHOTOS—SHANGHAI, NOV. 13, 1937

ONI 41-42

AGS—AG

DIVISION OF NAVAL INTELLIGENCE—IDENTIFICATION AND CHARACTERISTICS SECTION —JUNE, 1943

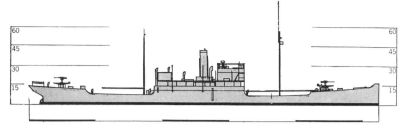

SURVEYING VESSELS

KOSHU—AGS-1   (EX-GERMAN—COMPLETED 1904)

DIMENSIONS—264' OA—252'6" (PP) x 36'2" x 22'3" (MEAN)

DISPLACEMET—2,080 TONS (STANDARD)—2,270 TONS (NORMAL)
ARMAMENT—   2—3"   ?—AAMG
MACHINERY—   TRIPLE EXPANSION
DESIGNED HP—   800
DESIGNED SPEED—10.3 KNOTS

TSUKUSHI (TUKUSI)—AGS-2—COMPLETED 1941

SOYA—   AGS-3—COMPLETED 1942

DISPLACEMENT—2,000 TONS (E)

←**OTOMARI—ICE BREAKER**—BEGUN 6/24/21; COMPLETED—11/7/21

DIMENSIONS—200' (PP) x 50' x 21' (MEAN)
DISPLACEMENT—2,330 TONS (STANDARD)
ARMAMENT—   1- 3"
                ?-AAMG
DESIGNED HP—
DESIGNED SPEED—13 KNOTS

SETTSU—TARGET VESSEL—
COMPLETED AS OBB—1912; CONVERTED—1935
DIMENSIONS—500' OA x 84' x 23' 3" (MEAN)
DISPLACEMENT—16,130 TONS (STANDARD)
ARMAMENT—   NONE
DESIGNED HP—
MAXIMUM SPEED—14.5 KNOTS

NOTE CENTER STACK REMOVED

YODO—PG-1— NOW LISTED AS SURVEYING VESSEL — SEE PG-GUNBOATS PAGES

JINGEI CLASS—AS 2, 3

DIVISION OF NAVAL INTELLIGENCE—IDENTIFICATION AND CHARACTERISTICS SECTION —JUNE, 1943

LENGTH—380'0" OA
        374'0" WL
BEAM— 53'0"
DRAFT— 19'6" (MEAN)
DISPLACEMENT—
5,160 TONS (STANDARD)
8,500 TONS (NORMAL)

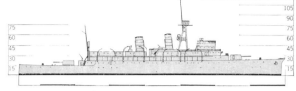

	MAX. ELEV.	MAX. RANGE
ARMAMENT— 4-5".5	30°	19,000 YDS.
2-3" AA	85°	9,000 YDS.
?-AAMG		
1-SCOUT OBSERVATION	2-SEARCHLIGHTS	

PROPULSION—MACHINERY— GEARED TURBINES
        BOILERS—6 KAMPON   FUEL—OIL, 1,295 TONS
        DESIGNED HP—8,400   DESIGNED SPEED—16 KNOTS @ 126 R.P.M.

	BEGUN	COMPLETED
AS-2 JINGEI (ZINGEI)	9/16/22	8/30/23
AS-3 CHOGEI (TYOGEI)	3/16/22	8/ 2/24

ONI 41-42

JAPANESE MERCHANT AUXILIARIES

THIS SECTION MAY BE USED IN CONNECTION WITH ONI 208-J
JAPANESE MERCHANT SHIPS, ISSUED IN TASK BINDER SIZE

DIVISION OF NAVAL INTELLIGENCE—IDENTIFICATION AND CHARACTERISTICS SECTION—AUGUST, 1943

NOTE—HULLS WHITE WITH BROAD GREEN STRIPE—RED CROSS ON GREEN STRIPE AND STACK—BRIDGE OR DECK AFT OF FUNNELS ILLUMINATED AT NIGHT

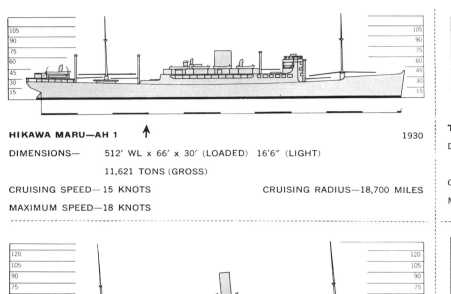

HIKAWA MARU—AH 1 ↑   1930

DIMENSIONS—   512' WL x 66' x 30' (LOADED) 16'6" (LIGHT)

                11,621 TONS (GROSS)

CRUISING SPEED—15 KNOTS   CRUISING RADIUS—18,700 MILES

MAXIMUM SPEED—18 KNOTS

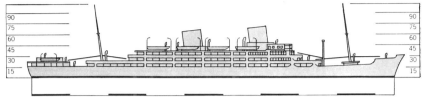

TAKASAGO MARU—AH 2 ↑   1936

DIMENSIONS—   463' WL x 61' x 27' (LOADED)

                9,347 TONS (GROSS)

CRUISING SPEED—16 KNOTS

MAXIMUM SPEED—19 KNOTS

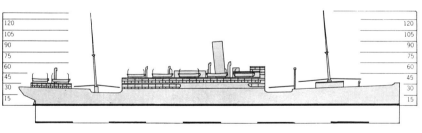

ASAHI MARU—AH 3 ↑   1914

DIMENSIONS—   483' WL x 59' 6" x 27' (LOADED)

                9,326 TONS (GROSS)

CRUISING SPEED—15 KNOTS

MAXIMUM SPEED—18 KNOTS   FORMERLY A 2-STACKER

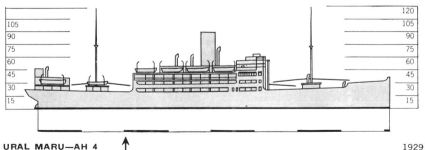

URAL MARU—AH 4 ↑   1929

DIMENSIONS—   406' WL x 55' x 23' (LOADED)

                6,374 TONS (GROSS)

CRUISING SPEED—15½ KNOTS

MAXIMUM SPEED—18½ KNOTS

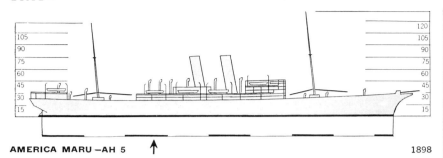

AMERICA MARU—AH 5 ↑   1898

DIMENSIONS—   423' WL x 51' x 27' (LOADED)

                6,070 TONS (GROSS)

CRUISING SPEED—14 KNOTS

MAXIMUM SPEED—15 KNOTS

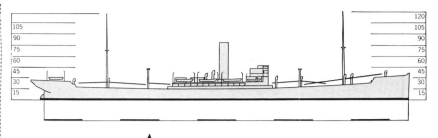

MANILA MARU—AH 6 ↑   **ARABIA MARU—AH 15**   1920

DIMENSIONS—   475' WL x 61' x 28' (LOADED)

                9,486 TONS (GROSS)

CRUISING SPEED—14 KNOTS   CRUISING RADIUS—8,000 MILES

MAXIMUM SPEED—16 KNOTS

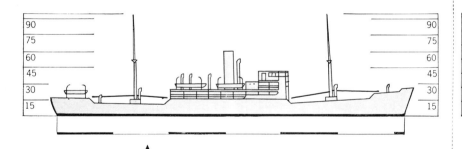

RYUKO MARU—AH 7 ↑   1938

DIMENSIONS—   298' WL x 45' x 21' (LOADED)

                2,962 TONS (GROSS)

CRUISING SPEED—11½ KNOTS   CRUISING RADIUS—6,000 MILES

MAXIMUM SPEED—14 KNOTS   SISTERSHIP—XPG-DAIDO MARU

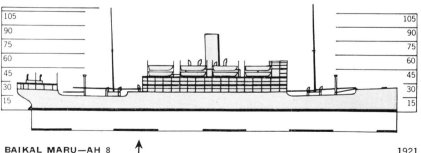

BAIKAL MARU—AH 8 ↑   1921

DIMENSIONS—   400' WL x 50' x 23' (LOADED)

                5,266 TONS (GROSS)

CRUISING SPEED— 15 KNOTS

MAXIMUM SPEED—18 KNOTS

ONI 41-42

INTERNATIONAL AH MARKING IS ILLUSTRATED BELOW

AH—HOSPITAL SHIPS

DIVISION OF NAVAL INTELLIGENCE—IDENTIFICATION AND CHARACTERISTICS SECTION —JUNE, 1943

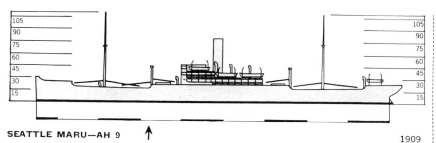

SEATTLE MARU—AH 9 ↑   1909

DIMENSIONS—   420' (WL) x 49' 6" x 26' (MAXIMUM)
                  5770 TONS (GROSS)

MAXIMUM SPEED—13.5 KNOTS

SISTERSHIP OPERATED AS **AP** WITH 1350 TROOP CAPACITY

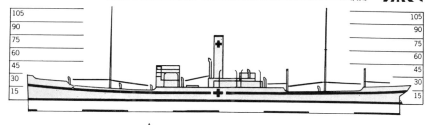

HOKUSIN MARU—AH 10 ↑   1920

DIMENSIONS—   407' (WL) x 51' x 26' (MAXIMUM), 9' (LIGHT)
                  5819 TONS (GROSS)

NOMINAL HP—   559

MAXIMUM SPEED—13.5 KNOTS

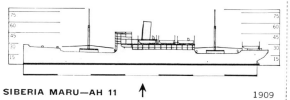

SIBERIA MARU—AH 11 ↑   1909

DIMENSIONS—   351' (WL) x 44' x 19' (MAXIMUM),
                                    12' 6" LIGHT
                  3461 TONS (GROSS)

NOMINAL HP—   643

MAXIMUM SPEED—14.5 KNOTS

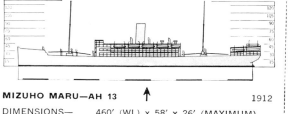

MIZUHO MARU—AH 13 ↑   1912

DIMENSIONS—   460' (WL) x 58' x 26' (MAXIMUM)
                  8506 TONS (GROSS)

NOMINAL HP—   1134

MAXIMUM SPEED—17 KNOTS

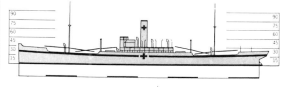

CHICAGO MARU—AH 14 ↑   1910

DIMENSIONS—   405' (WL) x 51' x 25' 6" (MAXIMUM)
                                    10' (LIGHT)
                  5800 TONS (GROSS)

NOMINAL HP—

MAXIMUM SPEED—14.5 KNOTS

KOHOKU MARU—AH 12   1915

DIMENSIONS—   285' (WL) x 43' x 20' (MAXIMUM)

DISPLACEMENT—   2578 TONS (GROSS)

NOMINAL HP—   267

MAXIMUM SPEED—13 KNOTS   APPEARANCE UNKNOWN

NOTES—

AH—HOSPITAL SHIPS

DIVISION OF NAVAL INTELLIGENCE—IDENTIFICATION AND CHARACTERISTICS SECTION —JUNE, 1943

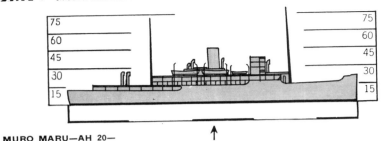

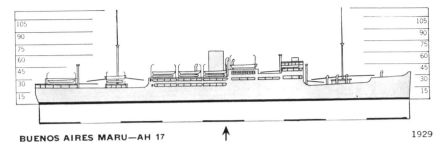

MURO MARU—AH 20—

DIMENSIONS—	230′ WL x 37′ x 28′ (LOADED)
	1,607 TONS (GROSS)
MACHINERY—	DIESEL
MAXIMUM SPEED—15½ KNOTS	

BUENOS AIRES MARU—AH 17   1929

DIMENSIONS—	461′ WL x 62′ x 26′ (LOADED)
	9,626 TONS (GROSS)
CRUISING SPEED— 15 KNOTS	
MAXIMUM SPEED— 17 KNOTS	

SISTERSHIP—XAS 2

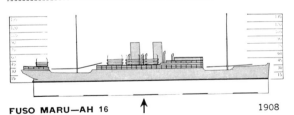

FUSO MARU—AH 16   1908

DIMENSIONS—	475′ WL x 57′6″ x 28′ (LOADED)
	8,196 TONS (GROSS)
CRUISING SPEED— 15 KNOTS	
MAXIMUM SPEED— 17 KNOTS	

YOSHINO MARU—AH 18   1906

DIMENSIONS—	463′ WL x 57′ x 28′ (LOADED)
	8,990 TONS (GROSS)
CRUISING SPEED— 13 KNOTS	
MAXIMUM SPEED— 15 KNOTS	

MIKASA MARU—AH 19

DIMENSIONS—	325′ WL x 46′ x 21′ (LOADED)
	3,143 TONS (GROSS)
CRUISING SPEED— 12½ KNOTS	
MAXIMUM SPEED— 15 KNOTS	

NOTE—

ALMOST ALL OF THESE **AH** HAVE SISTERSHIPS IN OTHER
AUXILIARY CAPACITY OR IN MERCHANT SERVICE. ANY
VARIATIONS IN APPEARANCE, HOWEVER SLIGHT, IS OF
IMPORTANCE, AND SHOULD BE NOTED.

ONI 41-42

SHIPS AND DESIGNATIONS BELOW SUPERSEDE CVS—
AV LISTING IN ONI 41-42—12/42

CVS—XCVS

DIVISION OF NAVAL INTELLIGENCE—IDENTIFICATION AND CHARACTERISTICS SECTION—JULY, 1943

CVS—1 NOTORO (COMPLETED AS AO ERIMO CLASS 1920—MODERNIZED 1934)

LENGTH— 470' 9" OA	BEAM—58'	DRAFT—26' 6"

DISPLACEMENT—14,050 TONS (STANDARD)

ARMAMENT	MAX. ELEV.	MAX. RANGE
2-4".7	40°	19,000 YARDS
2-3" AA	85°	9,000 FEET
1-CATAPULT—16 AIRCRAFT CARRIED		

PROPULSION
MACHINERY— TRIPLE EXPANSION RECIPROCATING
BOILERS— 4 MIYABARA
DESIGNED HP—5850   FUEL—   OIL, 1000 TONS
                                    DESIGNED SPEED—12 KNOTS
ENDURANCE— 6100 MILES @ 12 KNOTS

KAMIKAWA MARU CLASS—XCVS-1, 3, 7, 9

LENGTH— 508' OA; 479' WL	BEAM—62'	DRAFT—29' (MAX.)
6853 TONS (GROSS)		

ARMAMENT	MAX. ELEV.	MAX. RANGE
2-5" AA	85°	18,000 FEET
?-AAMG		
2-SEARCHLIGHTS	1-CATAPULT	13 SEAPLANES CARRIED

PROPULSION
MACHINERY— DIESEL ENGINES   FUEL—   OIL, 2800 TONS
DESIGNED HP—7600   MAXIMUM SPEED—21 KNOTS

ENDURANCE— 10,000 @ 21 KNOTS —20,000 @ 15 KNOTS

XCVS 1—KAMIKAWA MARU	COMPLETED 1937
XCVS 3—KUNIKAWA MARU	CONVERTED 1939-40
XCVS 7—KIMIKAWA MARU	
XCVS 9—KIYOKAWA MARU	

SISTERSHIP HIROKAWA MARU HAS PAIRED KINGPOSTS IMMEDIATELY
ABAFT SUPERSTRUCTURE

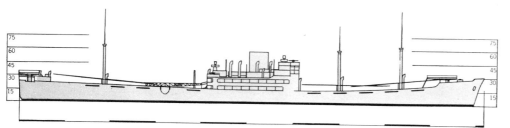

XCVS—CONVERTED SEAPLANE CARRIERS

DIVISION OF NAVAL INTELLIGENCE—IDENTIFICATION AND CHARACTERISTICS SECTION—JULY, 1943

FOR FURTHER TREATMENT OF THESE AND SISTER-
SHIPS, SEE ONI 208-J; JAPANESE MERCHANT SHIPS;
ALL CARRY 13 AIRCRAFT, ARE ARMED WITH 2-5" AA.

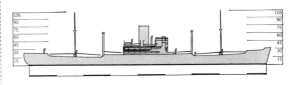

← **YASUKAWA MARU—XCVS 2**   1930

LENGTH—	455' WL
BEAM—	62'
DRAFT—	26' 6" (MAXIMUM)
	6,710 TONS (GROSS)
CRUISING SPEED—	13 KNOTS
MAXIMUM SPEED—	16 KNOTS

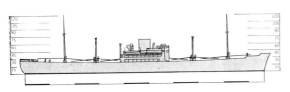

SANUKI MARU CLASS—XCVS 4, 8

LENGTH—	479' WL
BEAM—	62'
DRAFT—	28' (MAXIMUM)
	7,150 TONS (GROSS)
ARMAMENT—	4-5" (?)
CRUISING SPEED—	16 KNOTS
MAXIMUM SPEED—	19 KNOTS
XCVS—4 SANUKI MARU	COMPLETED 1939
XCVS—8 SAGARA MARU	COMPLETED 1940

SANYO MARU—XCVS 5   1930

LENGTH—	446' WL
BEAM—	60' 6"
DRAFT—	28' (MAXIMUM)
	8,360 TONS (GROSS)
DESIGNED SPEED—	16 KNOTS
MAXIMUM SPEED—	18 KNOTS

OKITSU MARU—XCVS 6   1939

LENGTH—	461' OA
BEAM—	58' 6"
DRAFT—	26' (MAXIMUM)
	6486-6667 TONS (GROSS)
CRUISING SPEED—	14 KNOTS
MAXIMUM SPEED—	17.5 KNOTS

ONI 41-42

FOR FURTHER TREATMENT OF THESE VESSELS
AND THEIR SISTERSHIPS SEE ONI 208-J—
JAPANESE MERCHANT VESSELS.

APV—AIRCRAFT TENDERS

DIVISION OF NAVAL INTELLIGENCE—IDENTIFICATION AND CHARACTERISTICS SECTION—JULY, 1943

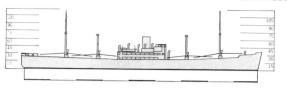

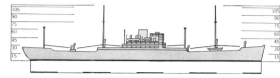

GOSHU MARU—APV 1　　　COMPLETED 1938

LENGTH—　　443' WL
BEAM—　　　60'
DRAFT—　　28' (MAXIMUM)
　　　　　　8,592 TONS (GROSS)
ARMAMENT—　MAY MOUNT UP TO 6-5"
CRUISING SPEED—15 KNOTS
MAXIMUM SPEED—17 KNOTS

FUJIKAWA MARU CLASS—APV 2, 5

LENGTH—　　436' WL
BEAM—　　　59'
DRAFT—　　26' (MAXIMUM)
　　　　　　6,850 TONS (GROSS)
ARMAMENT—　(?) 4-5" AA
CRUISING SPEED—13.5 KNOTS
MAXIMUM SPEED—16 KNOTS　　COMPLETED
APV 2—FUJIKAWA (HUZIKAWA) MARU　　1938
APV 5—MOGAMIGAWA MARU　　　　　1934
SISTERSHIPS TO XCM—TENYO MARU

KAMOGAWA MARU CLASS—APV 3, 4

LENGTH—　　456' OA
BEAM—　　　58'
DRAFT—　　26' (MAXIMUM)
　　　　　　6,440 TONS (GROSS)
CRUISING SPEED—14 KNOTS
MAXIMUM SPEED—17 KNOTS　　COMPLETED
APV 3—KAMOGAWA MARU　　　　　1938
APV 4—KEIYO MARU　　　　　　　1937

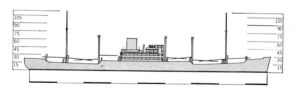

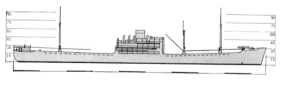

LYONS MARU—APV 6　　　1920

LENGTH—　　445' WL
BEAM—　　　58'
DRAFT—　　27' (MAXIMUM)
　　　　　　7,000 TONS (GROSS)
CRUISING SPEED—12 KNOTS
MAXIMUM SPEED—14.5 KNOTS

NARUTO MARU—APV 7　　　1934

LENGTH—　　470' OA
BEAM—　　　62'
DRAFT—　　27'5" (MAXIMUM)
　　　　　　7,150 TONS (GROSS)
CRUISING SPEED—15 KNOTS
MAXIMUM SPEED—19 KNOTS

SISTERSHIP TO XCL-1—NOSHIRO MARU

KINUGASA MARU CLASS—NO LONGER LISTED

LENGTH—　　453' WL
BEAM—　　　61'
DRAFT—　　28' (LOADED)
　　　　　　8,500 TONS (GROSS)
ARMAMENT—　2-5" AA—13 (VO) AIRCRAFT
CRUISING RADIUS—34,000 MILES
CRUISING SPEED—16.5 KNOTS
MAXIMUM SPEED—19 KNOTS
KINUGASA MARU—AV 3　　1934-36
KIYOSUMI MARU—AV 4

ARC—CABLE LAYING SHIPS

DIVISION OF NAVAL INTELLIGENCE—IDENTIFICATION AND CHARACTERISTICS SECTION —JUNE, 1943

HASHIMA CLASS—ARC 1, 2

DISPLACEMENT—2,000 TONS (?)

HASHIMA—   ARC 1 (CONVERTED 1940)
TSURUSHIMA— ARC 2 (CONVERTED 1940)

TATEISHI CLASS—ARC 3, 4

TATEISHI—ARC 3 (COMPLETED 1942)
ODATE— ARC 4 (COMPLETED 1942)

1923

NANYO MARU—ARC 5 ↑
DIMENSIONS—   344'6" WL x 44' x 21' (LOADED)
DISPLACEMENT— 3,605 TONS (GROSS)

CRUISING SPEED—10 KNOTS
MAXIMUM SPEED—12 KNOTS

NOMINAL HP—276

1937

TOYO MARU—ARC 7 ↑

DIMENSIONS—   335' WL x 46' x 20'6" (LOADED)

DISPLACEMENT— 3,719 TONS (GROSS)

CRUISING SPEED—12½ KNOTS

MAXIMUM SPEED— 15 KNOTS

NOMINAL HP—500

THESE SHIPS MAY ALSO BE EMPLOYED AS

SUBMARINE TENDERS, MINE LAYERS OR SWEEPERS

NET LAYERS, BOOM TENDERS, ESCORT VESSELS

FOR FURTHER TREATMENT SEE
ONI 208-J JAPANESE MERCHANT VESSELS

1906

OGASAWARA MARU—ARC 6 ↑
DIMENSIONS—   243'2" WL x 34' x 16'6" (LOADED)
DISPLACEMENT— 1,392 TONS (GROSS)
CRUISING SPEED—10 KNOTS   NOMINAL HP—176
MAXIMUM SPEED—12 KNOTS   FUEL   —COAL

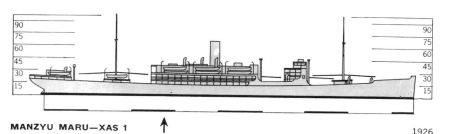

MANZYU MARU—XAS 1   1926

DIMENSIONS—   430' WL, 449' OA   56'   25' (LOADED)
                7,267 TONS (GROSS)

CRUISING SPEED— 14 KNOTS
MAXIMUM SPEED—16.5 KNOTS

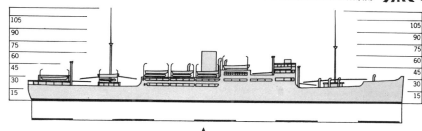

RIO DE JANEIRO MARU—XAS 2   1930

DIMENSIONS—   461' WL   62'   26' (LOADED)
                9,626 TONS (GROSS)

ARMAMENT—   (?)–6"

CRUISING SPEED— 15 KNOTS
MAXIMUM SPEED—17 KNOTS

SISTERSHIP—AH–BUENOS AIRES MARU

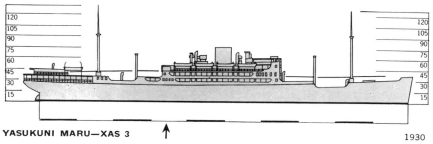

YASUKUNI MARU—XAS 3   1930

DIMENSIONS—   507' WL, 531' OA   64'   29' (LOADED) 15' (LIGHT)
                11,930 TONS (GROSS)

ARMAMENT—   (?)–5" AA
CRUISING SPEED— 16 KNOTS
MAXIMUM SPEED—18 KNOTS

EIGHT WATERTIGHT BULKHEADS EXTEND TO UPPER DECK

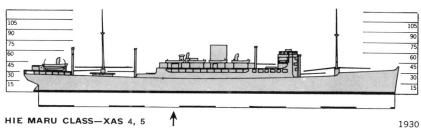

HIE MARU CLASS—XAS 4, 5   1930

DIMENSIONS—   510' WL, 535' OA   66'   30' (LOADED) 16' 6" (LIGHT)
                11,620 TONS (GROSS)
ARMAMENT—   (?)–6"
CRUISING SPEED— 15 KNOTS
MAXIMUM SPEED—18 KNOTS @ 104 R.P.M.
XAS 4—HIE MARU   XAS 5—HEIAN MARU
SISTERSHIP—AH–HIKAWA MARU
NINE WATERTIGHT BULKHEADS EXTEND TO UPPER DECK.

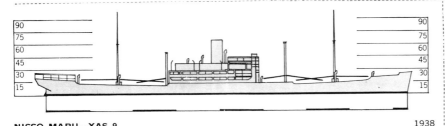

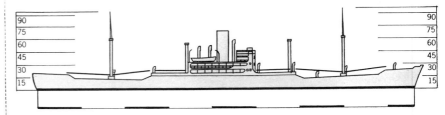

NAGOYA MARU—XAS 6   1932

DIMENSIONS—   407' WL x 56' x 26' (LOADED) 9' (LIGHT)

6,072 TONS (GROSS)

CRUISING SPEED—12 KNOTS @ 12,000 MILES RADIUS

MAXIMUM SPEED—13.5 KNOTS

FOR FURTHER TREATMENT OF THESE AND SISTERSHIPS SEE ONI 208-J—JAPANESE MERCHANT VESSELS

ARATAMA MARU—XAS 7   1938

DIMENSIONS—   446' 6" WL x 59' x 27' (LOADED) 11' (LIGHT)

6,780 TONS (GROSS)

CRUISING SPEED—13 KNOTS @ 110 R.P.M. @ 25,000 MILE RADIUS

MAXIMUM SPEED—16 KNOTS

URAGAMI MARU—XAS 8   1941

4,250 TONS (GROSS)

NISSO MARU—XAS 9   1938

DIMENSIONS—   420' WL x 57' x 27' (LOADED) 10' 6" (LIGHT)

6,510 TONS (GROSS)

CRUISING SPEED—14 KNOTS @ 11,700 MILES RADIUS

MAXIMUM SPEED—17 KNOTS

SOYO MARU—XAS 10   1930

DIMENSIONS—   415' WL x 56' x 25' (LOADED)

6,081 TONS (GROSS)

CRUISING SPEED—12 KNOTS

MAXIMUM SPEED—15 KNOTS

THIS SHIP WAS PREVIOUSLY LISTED AS AN AVP

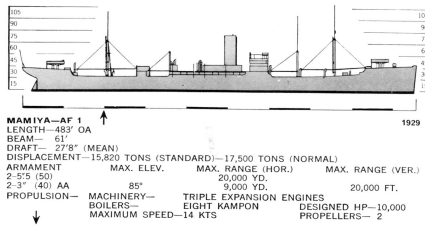

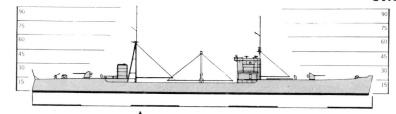

MAMIYA—AF 1

1929

LENGTH—483' OA
BEAM— 61'
DRAFT— 27'8" (MEAN)
DISPLACEMENT—15,820 TONS (STANDARD)—17,500 TONS (NORMAL)

ARMAMENT	MAX. ELEV.	MAX. RANGE (HOR.)	MAX. RANGE (VER.)
2-5"5 (50)		20,000 YD.	
2-3" (40) AA	85°	9,000 YD.	20,000 FT.

PROPULSION— MACHINERY— TRIPLE EXPANSION ENGINES
BOILERS— EIGHT KAMPON DESIGNED HP—10,000
MAXIMUM SPEED—14 KTS PROPELLERS— 2

KASHINO CLASS—AF 2, 3

KASHINO—AF 2 (1940)
IRAKO— AF 3 (1941)

LENGTH—400' OA
BEAM—
DRAFT— 16' —23'
DISPLACEMENT—7,000 TONS (E)

ARMAMENT— 2-3" AA 2-AAMG
SEARCHLIGHTS—3 RANGE FINDERS—3

THESE SHIPS MAY APPEAR WITHOUT STACK, BEING DIESEL DRIVEN

DIVISION OF NAVAL INTELLIGENCE—IDENTIFICATION AND CHARACTERISTICS SECTION — JUNE, 1943

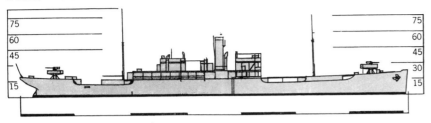

MUROTO CLASS—AF 4, 5 ↑

LENGTH—345' OA

BEAM— 50'

DRAFT— 23'11" (MEAN)

DISPLACEMENT—8,215 TONS (STANDARD) 8,751 TONS (NORMAL)

ARMAMENT—	MAX. ELEV.	MAX. RANGE (HOR.)	MAX. RANGE (VER.)
2-4."7 (45)	45°	19,000 YDS.	
2-3" AA	85°	9,000 YDS.	20,000 FT.

PROPULSION FUEL—   COAL, 877 TONS
              DESIGNED HP—2,640   MAXIMUM SPEED—12.5 KNOTS

AF 4—NOSHIMA (1919) EX-COLLIERS
AF 5—MUROTO (1918)

*SHURI MARU (SYURI MARU)—XAF 2—NO LONGER LISTED ↑   1928

DIMENSIONS—260' WL x 39' x 20' (LOADED)

DISPLACEMENT—1,857 TONS (GROSS)

CRUISING SPEED— 10 KNOTS
MAXIMUM SPEED—13 KNOTS

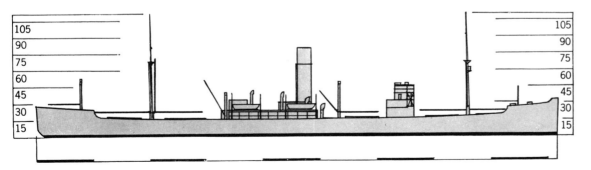

← *KOSEI MARU—XAF 1   1920

DIMENSIONS—450'2" WL x 58'3" x 29' (LOADED)

DISPLACEMENT—8,223 TONS (GROSS)

CRUISING SPEED— 11 KNOTS

MAXIMUM SPEED—13 KNOTS

*FOR COMPLETE TREATMENT SEE ONI 208-J JAPANESE
MERCHANT VESSELS

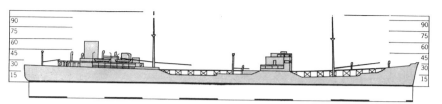

KYOKUTO MARU—XAO 1

DIMENSIONS— 500' (WL) x 65' x 29'6" (MAXIMUM), 11' (LIGHT)
10,052 TONS (GROSS)
CAPACITY— 93,000 BARRELS
BRAKE HP— 8,000
MAXIMUM SPEED—19 KNOTS
SISTERSHIP **TOA MARU** FORMERLY ON NAVY LIST

THIS LIST SUPERSEDES DESIGN CLASS LISTINGS. SHIPS NOT HEREIN NOTED ARE ASSUMED TO HAVE RETURNED TO MERCHANT STATUS. FOR FURTHER DATA, SEE ONI-208-J.

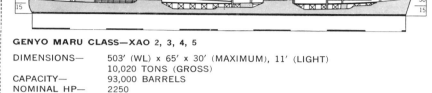

GENYO MARU CLASS—XAO 2, 3, 4, 5

DIMENSIONS— 503' (WL) x 65' x 30' (MAXIMUM), 11' (LIGHT)
10,020 TONS (GROSS)
CAPACITY— 93,000 BARRELS
NOMINAL HP— 2250
MAXIMUM SPEED—19-20 KNOTS

		COMPLETED
EX-GENYO MARU—	XAO 2—	1937
EX-TOEI MARU—	XAO 3—	1938
EX-KOKUYO MARU—	XAO 4—	1938
EX-KENYO MARU—	XAO 5—	1939

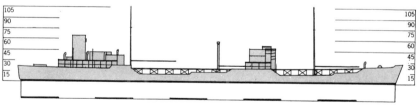

FUJISAN (HUZISAN) MARU—XAO 6   1931

DIMENSIONS— 512' (OA) x 65' x 28' (MAXIMUM), 10' (LIGHT)

9525 TONS (GROSS)

ARMAMENT— 2-5" (?)

CAPACITY— 93,000 BARRELS

NOMINAL HP— 1857

MAXIMUM SPEED—19 KNOTS

SINKOKU MARU—XAO 7   1940

DIMENSIONS— 500' (WL) x 65' x 29'6" (MAXIMUM), 11' (LIGHT)

10,020 TONS (GROSS)

CAPACITY— 93,000 BARRELS

NOMINAL HP— ?

MAXIMUM SPEED—19 KNOTS

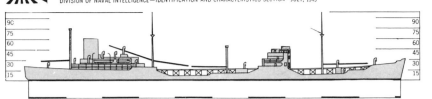

NIPPON MARU—XAO 8   1936

DIMENSIONS—   524' (OA) x 65' x 29'6" (MAXIMUM), 11' (LIGHT)

9,974 TONS (GROSS)

CAPACITY—   103,000 BARRELS

NOMINAL HP—   2115

MAXIMUM SPEED—19 KNOTS

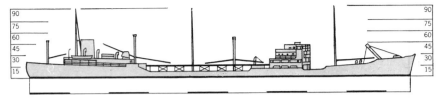

HOYO MARU CLASS—XAO 9, 10

DIMENSIONS—   494' (OA) x 61' x 30' (MAXIMUM), 10' (LIGHT)

8,692 TONS (GROSS)

CAPACITY—   95,000 BARRELS

NOMINAL HP—   1163

MAXIMUM SPEED—18 KNOTS   COMPLETED

HOYO MARU—   XAO 9   1936

KAIZYO MARU—   XAO 10   1937

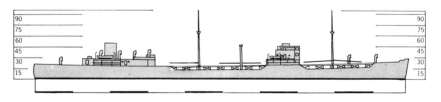

TEIYO MARU—XAO 11   1931

DIMENSIONS—   511' (OA) x 64' x 31' (MAXIMUM), 11'6" (LIGHT)

9,850 TONS (GROSS)

CAPACITY—   92,000 BARRELS

NOMINAL HP—   2340

MAXIMUM SPEED— 18 KNOTS

SAN PEDRO, SAN DIEGO, TONAN NOS. 2 & 3, AKEBONO, NISSHIN NO. 2, AND OMUR-
OSAN MARUS, FORMERLY LISTED, NO LONGER CARRIED AS NAVAL AUXILIARIES.

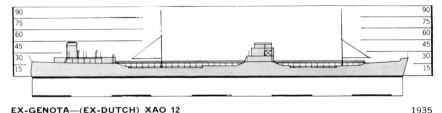

EX-GENOTA—(EX-DUTCH) XAO 12   1935

DIMENSIONS—   463' WL x 59'3" x 33'9" (MAXIMUM)

7,983 TONS (GROSS)

CAPACITY—   ?

NOMINAL HP—   502

MAXIMUM SPEED—11.5 KNOTS

ONI 41-42

XCL—ARMED MERCHANT CRUISERS
FOR FURTHER INFORMATION SEE
ONI 208—RAIDER SUPPLEMENT

XCL-XAM

DIVISION OF NAVAL INTELLIGENCE—IDENTIFICATION AND CHARACTERISTICS SECTION—JULY, 1943

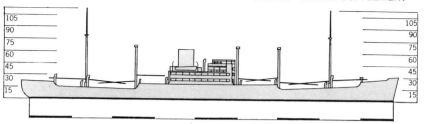

NOSHIRO MARU—XCL 1   1934

DIMENSIONS— 470' OA (450' WL) x 62' x 27'6" (MAX.) 11' (LiGHT)
    7150 TONS (GROSS)
ARMAMENT— 2–5" AA   ? AAMG
NOMINAL HP—1851   MAX. SPEED—18.5 KNOTS

SISTERSHIP TO **APV 7—NARUTO MARU**

KONGO MARU CLASS—XCL 2, 10

DIMENSIONS—477' OA (453' WL) x 61' x 28' (MAX.) 12' (LIGHT)
    8500 TONS (GROSS)
ARMAMENT— 2–5.5 AA (?) 2 AIRCRAFT CARRIED
BRAKE HP—   7000   MAX. SPEED—20 KNOTS

KONGO MARU—XCL 2   COMPLETED 1936
KIYOZUMI MARU—XCL 10   COMPLETED 1934

AIKOKU MARU CLASS—XCL 4, 9

DIMENSIONS— 527' OA (498' WL) x 66' x 29' (MAX.)
    10,500 TONS (GROSS)
ARMAMENT— 2–5.5 AA   2 AIRCRAFT CARRIED
DESIGNED HP—?   MAX. SPEED—21.5 KNOTS

AIKOKU MARU—XCL 4   COMPLETED 1940
HOKOKU MARU—XCL 9   COMPLETED 1941

AKAGI MARU CLASS—XCL 5-7

DIMENSIONS— 485' OA (462' WL) x
    62' x 28' (MAX.) 12' (LIGHT)
    7390 TONS (GROSS)
ARMAMENT— 2–5.5 (?) 2 AIRCRAFT CARRIED
NOMINAL HP—8000
MAX. SPEED— 19 KNOTS @ 118 RPM

AKAGI— XCL 5   COMPLETED 1936
ASAKA— XCL 6   COMPLETED 1937
AWATA—XCL 7   COMPLETED 1937

CHOKAI MARU—XAM   1932

DIMENSIONS—300' (WL) 43' x 19'6" (MAX.)
    2681 TONS (GROSS)
ARMAMENT— 2–5.5 (?)
MACHINERY— DIESEL
NOMINAL HP—270
MAX. SPEED— 13.5 KNOTS

SEICHO MARU—XCL 8   7500 TONS GROSS
OTHER DATA UNKNOWN

47 EX-WHALE "KILLER BOATS"—EMPLOYED AS OUT-POST VESSELS, NET-LAYERS OR NET-TENDERS

TYPICAL CHARACTERISTICS—

LENGTH—	120'
TONNAGE—	264 (GROSS)
ARMAMENT—	1-3" BOW
	?-AAMG
HORSEPOWER—	900-1300
MAXIMUM SPEED—13.5 KNOTS	

28 EX-NORWEGIAN "KILLER BOATS" — CHARACTER-ISTICS, APPEARANCE SIMILAR

20 EX-TUNA BOATS

TYPICAL CHARACTERISTICS—

LENGTH—	110'
TONNAGE—	250 (GROSS)
ARMAMENT—	1-3" BOW
	1-3" (?) STERN
	5-20mm MG
	?-DEPTH CHARGES
MAXIMUM SPEED—25 KNOTS	

XAM—COASTAL MINESWEEPERS (CONVERTED TRAWLERS)—34 OR MORE

TYPICAL CHARACTERISTICS—TONNAGE— 220-320 (GROSS)
ARMAMENT— 1-3" BOW—1-3" (?) STERN—?-AAMG
MAXIMUM SPEED—12 KNOTS

		BUILT	GROSS TONNAGE
XAM 134—	ATAKA MARU	1921	275
	AMOY MARU—No. 1-4	—	—
XAM 35, 36—	BANSHU MARU—No. 51, 52	1921	234
XAM 133—	HAGOROMO MARU—No. 133	1920	234
XAM 34—	HATAKA MARU—No. 6, 7	1922-1923	257-263
XAM 43, 44—	HINODO MARU—No 17, 18	1919	235
	KOHO MARU—No. 1, 2	—	—
XAM 31, 32—	MISAGO MARU—No. 1, 3	1920-21	265
XAM 42—	RANSAN MARU	—	—
XAM 45—	RIKUZEN MARU	1920	221
XAM 46—	TAMURE MARU	1920	235
XAM 23—	TAIKO MARU	—	—
XAM 132—	TAKASAGO MARU	1921	275
XAM 163, 164, 136—	TAMASONO MARU—No. 1-3	1920	316
XAM 41—	TSUKUSHI MARU	1920	220
XAM 131—	TORISHIMA MARU	1922	256
XAM 162—	YOSHIDO MARU	1920	220
XAM 161—	SONOBE MARU	1920	220
	TAME MARU—No. 3, 5	1936	258
	CHOKAI MARU—(SEE XCL-XCM)	1932	2658
XAM 101-104—	NO DATA		

AUXILIARIES

ONI 41-42

COMPLETED 1922-23

ARMAMENT—	MAX. ELEV.	MAX. RANGE
2-4.7 (45)	40°	19,000 YARDS
?-AAMG		
?-MINES AND DEPTH CHARGES		

PROPULSION—

MACHINERY—	PARSONS GEARED TURBINES
BOILERS—	3 KAMPON
FUEL—	OIL, 275 TONS
DESIGNED HP—	21,500
MAXIMUM SPEED—	31.5 KNOTS (PRE-CONVERSION)

NOTE:—DESTROYER CONVERSION TO DM DUTY PROB-
ABLY OCCURS IN ALL **ODD** CLASSES—NAMES AND
NUMBERS UNKNOWN

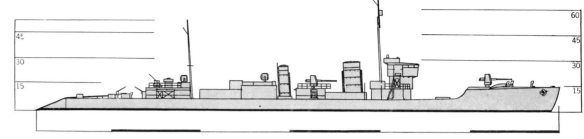

LENGTH—292' OA
BEAM— 26'6"
DRAFT— 8'3" (MEAN)

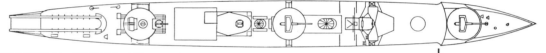

DISPLACEMENT—820 TONS (STANDARD); 900 TONS (NORMAL)   PHOTO—9/6/42 ↓ NOTE CINDERSCREEN

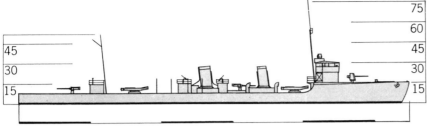

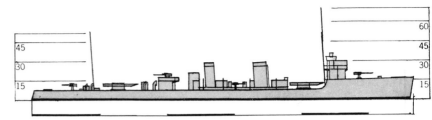

MOMO CLASS—ODD-1-3   COMPLETED 1916–1918

(MANCHUKUAN HAI WEI ALSO OF THIS TYPE)

DIMENSIONS—   275' (PP) x 25' x 7'9" (MEAN)
DISPLACEMENT— 835 TONS (NORMAL)
ARMAMENT—   3-4".7 (45)
               2-AAMG
               6-18" TORPEDO TUBES
               FITTED FOR MINE-SWEEPING
DESIGNED HP—   16,000
DESIGNED SPEED—31.5 KNOTS

URAKAZE—COMPLETED 1915 AS SISTERSHIP TO ITALIAN AUDACE

DIMENSIONS—   285' OA x 27'6" x 9'6" (MAX.)
DISPLACEMENT— 629 TONS
ARMAMENT—   1-4".7
               4-12 PDR
               4-21" TORPEDO TUBES
DESIGNED HP—   22,000
DESIGNED SPEED—28 KNOTS

THIS SHIP WAS PHOTOGRAPHED DURING THE TOKYO RAID, 4/18/42

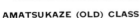

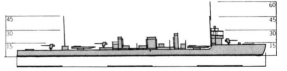

AMATSUKAZE (OLD) CLASS   COMPLETED 1916

DIMENSIONS—   326'6" OA x 28 x 9'3"

DISPLACEMENT— 1,227 TONS (MAX.)

ARMAMENT—   4-4".7 (40)
               2-AAMG
               6-18" TORPEDO TUBES

DESIGNED HP—   27,000

DESIGNED SPEED— 34 KNOTS

TANIKAZE (OLD) CLASS   COMPLETED 1917–1918

DIMENSIONS—   320' OA x 29'3" x 9'6"

DISPLACEMENT— 1,300 TONS (MAX.)

ARMAMENT—   3-4".7 (45)
               2-AAMG
               6-21" TORPEDO TUBES

DESIGNED HP—   28,000

DESIGNED SPEED— 34 KNOTS

KABA (OLD) CLASS   COMPLETED 1915
DIMENSIONS—   274' OA x 24' x 7'11"
DISPLACEMENT—665 TONS
ARMAMENT—   1-4".7   4-12 PDR (2 AA)
               4-18" TORPEDO TUBES
DESIGNED HP—   9,500   DESIGNED SPEED—30 KNOTS

EX-THRACIAN—BRITISH "S" CLASS   COMP. 3/23/22
BLOWN UP AT HONG KONG; SALVAGED BY JAPANESE
DIMENSIONS—   276½' OA x 26'10" x 10'10" (MEAN)
DISPLACEMENT—905 TONS (STANDARD)
FORMER ARMAMENT—3-4"   1-12 PDR AA
                1-2 PDR 4-21" TORPEDO TUBES

HEIGHT OF OBSERVER

60	60
45	45
30	30
15	15

HORIZON BEYOND THE SHIP

SHIP BEYOND THE HORIZON

0

LENGTH—268'6" OA
BEAM— 25'10"
DRAFT— 6'9" (MEAN)

DISPLACEMENT—527-595 TONS (STANDARD)

ARMAMENT

	MAX. ELEV.	MAX. RANGE (HORIZONTAL)
3–4"7	85°	19,000 YDS.
1-2-AAMG		
3–21" TORPEDO TUBES	10(?) DEPTH CHARGES	

PROPULSION

MACHINERY— 2 PARSONS GEARED TURBINES
BOILERS— 2 KAMPON
FUEL— OIL 100-150 TONS
DESIGNED HP— 7,000-9000
DESIGNED SPEED—26-28 KNOTS

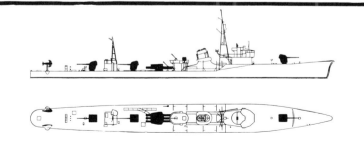

4 CHIDORI CLASS

8 OTORI CLASS

TB 1-4

DIVISION OF NAVAL INTELLIGENCE—IDENTIFICATION
AND CHARACTERISTICS SECTION —JUNE, 1943

MISTAKEN IDENTITY
(SEE #13 CLASS AM 7–12)

CHIDORI–OTORI CLASSES TB 1-12

YUBARI   CL 13

DD TERATSUKI CLASS

AM #13, CLASS   AM 7-12

SIMS CLASS (US)   DD

"J" CLASS (GB)   DD

AERIAL VIEWS

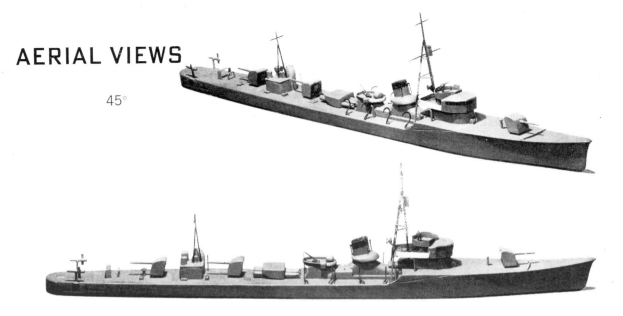

45°

90°

135°

15° ELEVATION

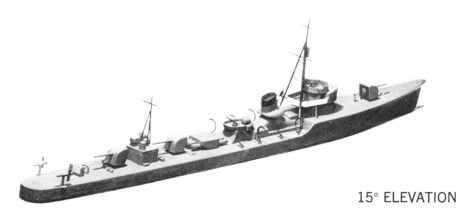

0°

180°

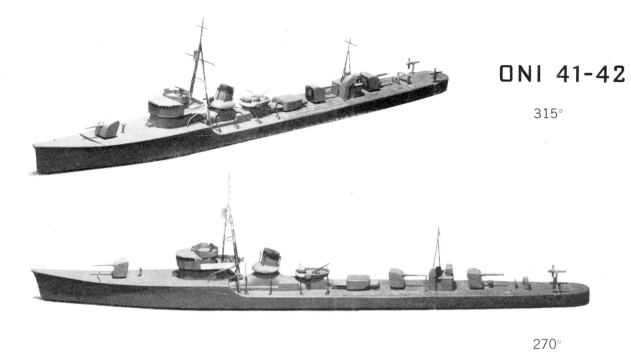

ONI 41-42

315°

270°

225°

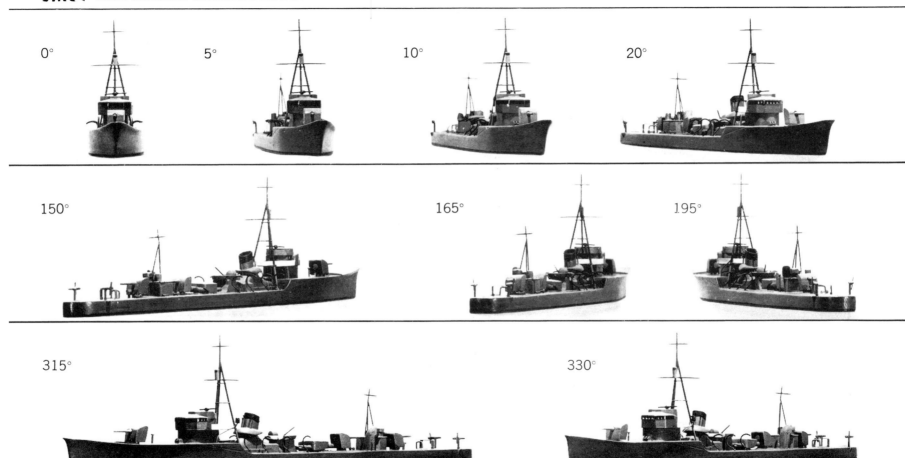

0° 5° 10° 20°

150° 165° 195°

315° 330°

KNOTS	RPM	KNOTS	RPM	KNOTS	RPM	KNOTS	RPM
....	400	....	300	....	200	....	100
....	375	....	275	....	175	....	75
....	350	....	250	....	150	....	50
....	325	....	225	....	125	....	25

30°

45°

270°

340°

350°

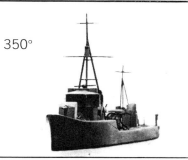

355°

CHIDORI CLASS		BEGUN	COMPLETED
CHIDORI—	TB 1	10/13/31	11/20/33
MANAZURU—	TB 2	12/22/31	11/31/34
TOMOZURU—	TB 3	11/11/32	2/24/34
HATSUKARI—	TB 4	4/ 6 /33	7/15/34
OTORI CLASS			
OTORI—	TB 5	11/ 8 /34	10/10/36
HAYABUSA—	TB 6	12/19/34	12/27/36
HIYODORI—	TB 7	11/26/34	12/20/36
KASASAGI—	TB 8	3/ 4 /35	1/15/37
HATO—	TB 9	5/28/36	8/ 7 /37
SAGI—	TB 10	5/20/36	7/31/37
KARI—	TB 11	5/11/36	9/20/37
KIJI—	TB 12	10/24/35	7/31/37

↓ HATSUKARI—TB 4   8/18/37

↑ HATO—TB 9—12/1/39   OTORI—TB 5—8/18/37 ↓

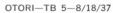

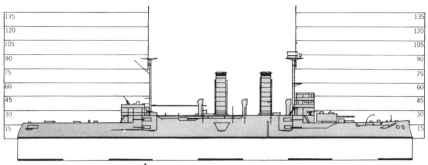

TOKIWA—CM 1 EX-OCA

DIMENSIONS—442' OA x 67' x 24'4" (MEAN)

DISPLACEMENT—9,240 TONS (STANDARD)

ARMAMENT	MAX. ELEV	MAX RANGE (HOR.)	MAX RANGE (VER)
2–8" (40)	20°	16,000 YD.	
8–6" (40)	20'	14,200 YD	
1–3" (40)	85	9,000 YD	20 000 FT
2–3" (40)	45ᶜ	9,000 YD.	

450 MINES CARRIED

COMPLETED 1898   **REFITTED AS CM**—1929

PROTECTION
BELT—	3½" TO 7"	DECK—2"	TURRETS—6"
CASEMATES—6'		CONNING TOWER—14"	

PROPULSION
MACHINERY—   TWO RECIPROCATING TRIPLE EXPANSION
BOILERS—   SIXTEEN MIYABARA
FUEL—   COAL, 1,400 TONS
DESIGNED HP—   18,248
MAXIMUM SPEED—21 KNOTS @ 153 R.P.M.

KATSURIKI—CM 2   **COMPLETED 1917**

DIMENSIONS—260'1" OA x 39' x 13'6" (MEAN)

DISPLACEMENT—1,540 TONS (STANDARD) 2,000 TONS (NORMAL)

ARMAMENT	MAX ELEV.	MAX. RANGE (HOR.)	MAX RANGE (VER.)
3–3" (40) AA	85ᶜ	9,000 YD	20,000 FT.

PROPULSION
MACHINERY—   TWO SETS TRIPLE EXPANSION RECIPROCATING
FUEL—   COAL, 80 TONS
DESIGNED HP—   1,800
MAXIMUM SPEED—13 KNOTS

SHIRATAKA—CM-3

DIVISION OF NAVAL INTELLIGENCE—IDENTIFICATION AND CHARACTERISTICS SECTION — JUNE, 1943

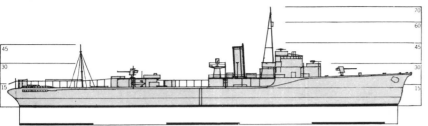

BEGUN—11/24/27; COMPLETED—4/9/29
LENGTH—259'10" WL   BEAM—37'9"   DRAFT—9'2" (NORMAL)
DISPLACEMENT—1345 TONS (STANDARD); 1405 TONS (NORMAL)

*ARMAMENT	MAX. ELEV.	MAX. RANGE (HORIZONTAL)	MAX. RANGE (VERTICAL)
2-3?—4".7 (50) AA	85°	19,000 YARDS	25,000 FEET
1— AAMG TWIN			
?— MINES			

EQUIPPED FOR NETLAYING, MINESWEEPING
PROPULSION
MACHINERY—2 TRIPLE EXPANSION RECIPROCATING
BOILERS—2 KAMPON   FUEL—OIL
DES. HP—2,200   MAX. SPEED—16 KNOTS
PROPELLERS—2
1/38 ↓   *PROFILE, PHOTOS SHOW OLD MOUNTS

ONI 41-42

BEGUN 2/2/28   COMPLETED 12/26/29

LENGTH—   339' OA; 329' WL
BEAM—   42'
DRAFT—   10'1" (MEAN)
DISPLACEMENT—1,970 TONS (STANDARD); 2,020 TONS (NORMAL)

ARMAMENT—	MAX. ELEV.	MAX. RANGE (HOR)	MAX. RANGE (VER.)
3-5.5 (50)	30°	20,000 YARDS	
2-3" (40) AA	85°	9,000 YARDS	20,000 FEET

2-D.C. GUNS, ?-DEPTH CHARGES
2-SEARCHLIGHTS
MINES–250 LARGE OR 500 SMALL

PROPULSION—
MACHINERY—   DIESEL
FUEL—   OIL, 300 TONS
DESIGNED HP—   3,000
MAXIMUM SPEED—16 KNOTS
RADIUS—   5,000 MILES @ 16 KNOTS
PROPELLERS—   3

NOTES: UPPER DECK USED FOR MINE STOWAGE.
       FOUR LINES OF MINELAYING RAILS EXTEND FROM FORECASTLE TO
       STERN

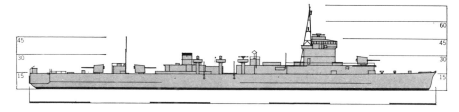

↓ 1937

↑ 1930

CM 5—YAEYAMA

DIVISION OF NAVAL INTELLIGENCE—IDENTIFICATION AND CHARACTERISTICS SECTION—JULY, 1943

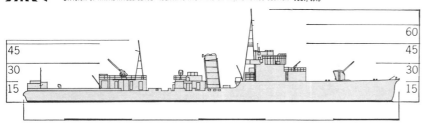

LENGTH— 280'6" OA   BEAM—34'8"   DRAFT—8'1" (MEAN)

DISPLACEMENT—1,135 TONS (STANDARD)

ARMAMENT—

	MAX. ELEV.	MAX. RANGE
2-4".7 AA	85°	21,000 YARDS
2-3" AA	85°	9,000 YARDS
?-AAMG		
?-MINES, DEPTH CHARGES		
EQUIPPED FOR MINESWEEPING, NET LAYING		

PROPULSION— MACHINERY—DIESEL
BOILERS—
FUEL—
DESIGNED HP—4800
DESIGNED SPEED—20 KNOTS

BEGUN—8/2/30   COMPLETED—8/31/32

ONI 41-42

OKINOSHIMA—CM 6

DIVISION OF NAVAL INTELLIGENCE—IDENTIFICATION AND CHARACTERISTICS SECTION —JUNE, 1943

ARMAMENT

	MAX. ELEV.	MAX. RANGE
4–5.5 (50) TWINS	30°	20,000 YDS. HOR.
2–3″ AA	85°	9,000 YDS. HOR.
		20,000 FT. VER.

4–AAMG

?–MINES

1–CATAPULT—2 SCOUT OBSERVATION PLANES

PROPULSION

MACHINERY—	GEARED TURBINES
BOILERS—	4 KAMPON
FUEL—	OIL
DESIGNED HP—	9,000
MAXIMUM SPEED—	20 KNOTS
PROPELLERS—	2

↓ 9/3/38

HEIGHT OF OBSERVER

HORIZON BEYOND THE SHIP

SHIP BEYOND THE HORIZON

LENGTH—405′ OA; 386′6″ WL
BEAM— 51′3″
DRAFT— 16′6″ (MEAN)

DISPLACEMENT—4400 TONS (STANDARD)

10/20/37 ↓

OKINOSHIMA—CM 6

DIVISION OF NAVAL INTELLIGENCE—IDENTIFICATION AND CHARACTERISTICS SECTION — JUNE, 1943

OKINOSHIMA
REPORTED SUNK

BEGUN
27/9/34

COMPLETED
30/9/36

ONI 41-42

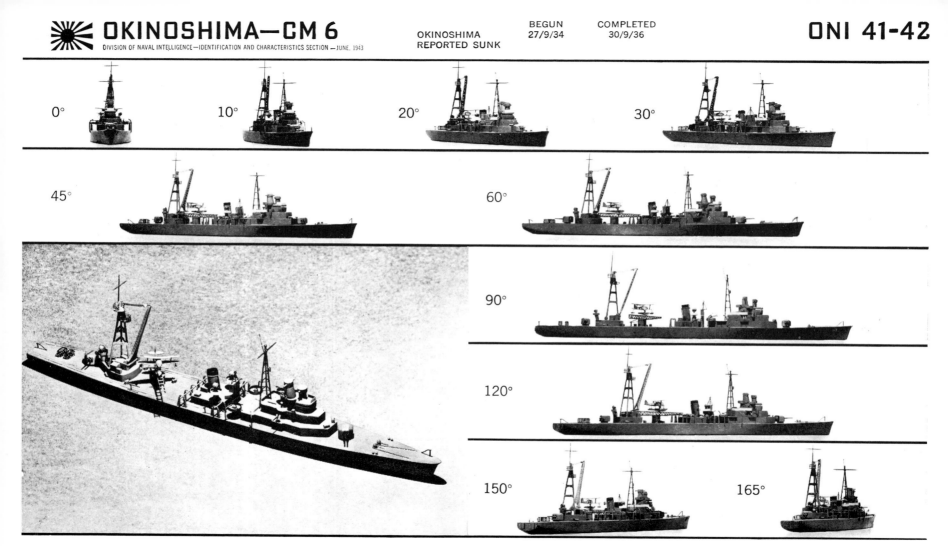

0° 10° 20° 30°

45° 60°

90°

120°

150° 165°

YAKUMO—OCA 2　　　　　　COMPLETED 1900, MODERNIZED 1935

LENGTH—434' OA
BEAM— 64' 3"
DRAFT— 23' 9" (MEAN)

DISPLACEMENT—9,010 TONS (STANDARD); 9,645 TONS (NORMAL)

ARMAMENT	MAX. ELEV.	MAX. RANGE (HOR.)	MAX. RANGE (VER.)
4-8" (40)	15°	16,000 YARDS	
8-6" (40)	20°	14,200 YARDS	
4-3" (40)	85°	9,000 YARDS	
1-3" (40) AA	85°	9,000 YARDS	20,000 FEET

2-18" TORPEDO TUBES

PROTECTION
CONNING TOWER—10"
BELT— 7" MAXIMUM (AMIDSHIPS); 3.5" ENDS;
　　　　5" SIDES ABOVE BELT
DECK— 2.5"
TURRETS— 6"
CASEMATES— 6"

PROPULSION
MACHINERY— 2 TRIPLE EXPANSION RECIPROCATING
BOILERS— SIX YARROW
FUEL— 1,200 TONS COAL
DESIGNED HP— 7,000
MAXIMUM SPEED— 16 KNOTS @ 120 R.P.M.

IWATE CLASS—OCA 4, 5

IWATE—OCA 4　　　　　　COMPLETED 1901, MODERNIZED 1935
IZUMO—OCA 5　　　　　　COMPLETED 1900, MODERNIZED 1935

LENGTH—434' OA
BEAM— 68' 6"
DRAFT—26' 3" (MEAN)

DISPLACEMENT—9,180 TONS (STANDARD); 9,826 TONS (NORMAL)

ARMAMENT	MAX. ELEV.	MAX. RANGE (HOR.)	MAX. RANGE (VER.)
4-8" (40)	15°	16,000 YARDS	
14-6" (40)	20°	14,200 YARDS	
4-3"	85°	9,000 YARDS	
1-3" AA	85°	9,000 YARDS	20,000 FEET

4-18" TORPEDO TUBES
1 SCOUT OBSERVATION PLANE

PROTECTION
CONNING TOWER— 14"
BELT— 7" MAXIMUM (AMIDSHIPS); 3.5" ENDS
DECK— 2.5"
TURRETS— 6"

PROPULSION
MACHINERY— 2 TRIPLE EXPANSION RECIPROCATING
BOILERS— SIX YARROW (IWATE);
　　　　TWENTY-FOUR BELLEVILLE (IZUMO)
FUEL— 1,400 TONS COAL
DESIGNED HP— 7,000 (IWATE); 14,700 (IZUMO)
MAXIMUM SPEED—20.7 KNOTS (IZUMO); 16 KNOTS @ 145 R.P.M. (IWATE)

FUJI—(EX-OBB)   COMPLETED 1897

DIMENSIONS—   374' OA x 73' x 21' 10" (MEAN)
DISPLACEMENT—   9,179 TONS (STANDARD)
ARMAMENT—   4-12", 10-6", 16-12 PDR
DESIGNED HP—   13,500
DESIGNED SPEED—18.2 KNOTS

SHIKISHIMA—(EX-OBB)   COMPLETED 1900

DIMENSIONS—   438' OA x 75' 6" x 21' 8" (MEAN)
DISPLACEMENT—   11,275 TONS (STANDARD)
ARMAMENT—   4-12", 14-6", 20-12 PDR
DESIGNED HP—   14,500
DESIGNED SPEED—18.6 KNOTS

ASAMA—(EX-OCA-1)   COMPLETED 1899

DIMENSIONS—   442' OA x 67' 1" x 24' 4" (MEAN)
DISPLACEMENT—9,240 TONS (STANDARD)—9,885 TONS (NORMAL)

ARMAMENT—	MAX. ELEV.	MAX. RANGE (HORIZONTAL)	MAX. RANGE (VERTICAL)
4- 8" (40)	15°	16,000 YARDS	
12- 6" (40)	20°	14,200 YARDS	
4- 3" (40)	85°	7,000 YARDS	
1- 3" (40) AA	85°	9,000 YARDS	20,000 FEET

4-18" TORPEDO TUBES; 18 EIGHTEEN INCH AND 4 FOURTEEN INCH TORPEDOES CARRIED

PROTECTION—
CONNING TOWER—10"
BELT—   7" MAXIMUM (AMIDSHIPS); 3.5" ENDS
DECK—   2"   TURRETS—6"   CASEMATES—6"

PROPULSION—
MACHINERY—   RECIPROCATING   FUEL—   1,400 TONS, COAL
DESIGNED HP—18,000   MAXIMUM SPEED—21 KNOTS

AZUMA—(EX-OCA-3)   COMPLETED 1900

DIMENSIONS—   452' 5" OA x 59' 6" x 25' (MAXIMUM)
DISPLACEMENT—8,640 TONS (STANDARD); 9,277 TONS (NORMAL)

ARMAMENT—	MAX. ELEV.	MAX. RANGE (HORIZONTAL)	MAX. RANGE (VERTICAL)
4- 8" (40)	13.5°	16,000 YARDS	
12- 6" (40)	20°	14,200 YARDS	
4- 3" (40)	85°	9,000 YARDS	
1- 3" (40) AA	85°	9,000 YARDS	20,000 FEET

4-18" TORPEDO TUBES; 18 EIGHTEEN AND 4 FOURTEEN INCH TORPEDOES CARRIED

PROTECTION—
CONNING TOWER—10"
BELT—   7" MAXIMUM (AMIDSHIPS); 3.5" ENDS; 5" SIDES ABOVE BELT
DECK—   2.5"   TURRETS—6"   CASEMATES—6"

PROPULSION—
MACHINERY—RECIPROCATING TRIPLE EXPANSION
BOILERS—   TWENTY-FOUR BELLEVILLE   FUEL—1,200 TONS, COAL
DESIGNED HP—9,400   MAXIMUM SPEED—16 KNOTS

SHIMUSHU CLASS—CM 11-15

LENGTH—200' OA   BEAM—   DRAFT—
DISPLACEMENT—1,200? TONS (STANDARD)

ARMAMENT	MAX. ELEV.	MAX. RANGE (HOR.)	MAX. RANGE (VER.)
3-4".7 AA	85°	21,000 YD.	25,000 FT.
4-AAMG	12-DEPTH CHARGES	?-MINES	

EQUIPPED FOR MINESWEEPING
1-SEARCHLIGHT
MAXIMUM SPEED—12 KNOTS

SHIMUSHU CLASS—CM 11-18

	BEGUN	COMPLETED
CM 11—SHIMUSHU	1938-39	1940-41
CM 12—KUNAJIRI	1938-39	1940-41
CM 13—HACHIJO	1938-39	1940-41
CM 14—ISHIGAKI	1938-39	1940-41
CM 15—ETORUFU	1940	1942
CM 16—MATSUWA	1940	1942
CM 17—SADO	1940	1942
CM 18—IKI	1940	1942

HATSUTAKA CLASS—CM 7-10

APPEARANCE UNKNOWN

LENGTH—240'7" OA
BEAM— 25'10"
DRAFT— 8'5" (MAXIMUM)

DISPLACEMENT—2,000 TONS (NORMAL)

ARMAMENT	MAX. ELEV.	MAX. RANGE (HOR.)
2(?)-4".7 (50)	30°	16,300 YD.
? —MINES, DEPTH CHARGES		

PROPULSION
MACHINERY—   DIESEL
FUEL—   OIL
DESIGNED HP—   9,000
MAXIMUM SPEED—20 KNOTS

HATSUTAKA CLASS—CM 7-10

		BEGUN	COMPLETED
CM-7	HATSUTAKA	1937-38	1942
CM-8	AOTAKA	1937-38	1942
CM-9	WAKATAKA	1937-38	1942
CM-10	TSUGARU	1937-38	1942

XCM-1—EX-TENYO MARU

COMPLETED—1935

DIMENSIONS— 436' WL x 59' x 26' (LOADED)
DISPLACEMENT—6,850 TONS (GROSS)
ARMAMENT—   UNKNOWN   MAY MOUNT UP TO 6—5" OR 6" GUNS
PROPULSION— NET HP—840   MAXIMUM SPEED—16 KNOTS
FOR SILHOUETTE, SEE SISTERSHIPS, APV-2, 5

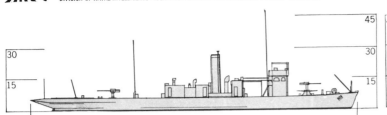

TOSHIMA CLASS—CMc 1-10

LENGTH—150' OA   BEAM—25'   DRAFT—7'6" (MEAN)
DISPLACEMENT—430 TONS (STANDARD)

ARMAMENT—	MAX. ELEV.	MAX. RANGE (HOR.)	MAX. RANGE (VER.)
2-3" (40) AA	85°	9,000 YARDS	20,000 FEET

120 MINES (ESTIMATED)
PROPULSION—
DESIGNED HP—700   DESIGNED SPEED—12 KNOTS
ENDURANCE— 430 MILES @ 12 KNOTS

TOSHIMA—	CMc 1	KATASHIMA— CMc 6
KUROSHIMA—	CMc 2	KUROKAMI— CMc 7
KATOKU—	CMc 3	ENOSHIMA— CMc 8
ASHIKAZI—	CMc 4	KUROZAKI— CMc 9
ENTO—	CMc 5	N'NOSHIMA— CMc 10
		COMPLETED—(1915-1920)

TSUBAME CLASS—CMc 11, 12

LENGTH—206'8" OA   BEAM—23'6"   DRAFT—6'4" (MEAN)
DISPLACEMENT—450 TONS (STANDARD)—570 TONS (NORMAL)

ARMAMENT—	MAX. ELEV.	MAX. RANGE (HORIZONTAL)	MAX. RANGE (VERTICAL)
1-3" (40) AA	85°	9,000 YARDS	20,000 FEET
1-M.G.			

?-MINES
PROPULSION
MACHINERY   —TWO RECIPROCATING TRIPLE EXPANSION
DESIGNED HP—   2,500
DESIGNED SPEED—19 KNOTS

	BEGUN	COMPLETED
TSUBAME—CMc 11	9/28	6/29
KAMOME— CMc 12	10/28	7/29/29

NOTE: EQUIPPED FOR NET-LAYING

DIVISION OF NAVAL INTELLIGENCE—IDENTIFICATION AND CHARACTERISTICS SECTION —JUNE, 1943

NATSUSHIMA CLASS—CMc13-15

LENGTH—237'0" OA—225'2" WL
BEAM— 24'6"
DRAFT— 5'8" (MAXIMUM)

DISPLACEMENT—443 TONS (STANDARD)

ARMAMENT	MAX. ELEV.	MAX RANGE (HOR.)	MAX. RANGE (VER.)
2-3" (40) AA	85°	9,000 YD.	20,000 FT.
1-AAMG			
45 MINES			

PROPULSION
MACHINERY—TWO SETS OF DIESELS   FUEL—   OIL
DES. HP—   2,300 (SARUSHIMA 2,100)   MAX. SPEED—19 KNOTS

	BEGUN	COMPLETED
NATSUSHIMA—CMc 13	12/24/31	11/33
NASAMI—CMc 14	1932	8/20/34
SARUSHIMA—CMc 15	1932	8/20/34

NOTE—NASAMI EQUIPPED FOR MINESWEEPING

↑ NATSUSHIMA

SARUSHIMA ↓

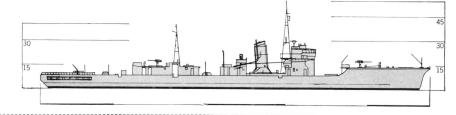

SOKUTEN CLASS—CMc 16-20

APPEARANCE UNKNOWN

LENGTH—240'7" OA
BEAM— 25'10"
DRAFT— 8'5" (MAXIMUM)

DISPLACEMENT—720 TONS (STANDARD)

ARMAMENT	MAX. ELEV.	MAX. RANGE (HOR.)	MAX. RANGE (VER.)
2-4".7 (50)	85°	17,500 YD.	25,000 FT.
?-AAMG, DEPTH CHARGES, MINES			

PROPULSION
MACHINERY—   DIESELS
FUEL—   OIL
DESIGNED HP—   3,600
DESIGNED SPEED—20 KNOTS

	BEGUN	COMPLETED
SOKUTEN— CMc 16	1937	8/22/39
SHIRAKAMI—CMc 17	9/3/37	1939
KYOSAI— CMc 18	1938	1939
NARIU— CMc 19	1938	8/28/39
UKISHIMA— CMc 20	1938	1939

YURISHIMA CLASS—CMc 21-31   APPEARANCE & CHARACTERISTICS UNKNOWN

DISPLACEMENT—700 TONS (E)

	TAKASHIMA—CMc 26
YURISHIMA— CMc 21	ARAISAKI— CMc 27
NUWASHIMA—CMc 22	ISHIZAKI— CMc 28
MAESHIMA— CMc 23	BOKO— CMc 29 COMPLETED—1941-1942
MOROSHIMA—CMc 24	SAGISAKI— CMc 30
HIRASHIMA— CMc 25	SAISHU— CMc 31

COMPLETED 1934

PC-1 CLASS—NO. 1, 2

DIMENSIONS—	210'6" WL x 19'9" x 5' (MAXIMUM)
DISPLACEMENT—	300 TONS (STANDARD)
ARMAMENT—	4-AAMG
	1-D. C. GUN
	?-DEPTH CHARGES
DESIGNED HP—	3400
DESIGNED SPEED—	24 KNOTS

COMPLETED 1938-42

PC-3-39 CLASS—NO. 3-39

DIMENSIONS—	176' WL x 18'2" x 6'6" (MAXIMUM)
DISPLACEMENT—	270 TONS (STANDARD)
ARMAMENT—	4-AAMG
	1-D. C. GUN
	?-DEPTH CHARGES
DESIGNED HP—	3200
DESIGNED SPEED—	20 KNOTS

COMPLETED 1937-42

PC—40-44 CLASS—NO. 51-55

DIMENSIONS—	144'4" OA x 15'3" x 5'6" (MAXIMUM)
DISPLACEMENT—	170 TONS (STANDARD)
ARMAMENT—	4-AAMG
	?-D.C. GUNS
	?-DEPTH CHARGES
DESIGNED HP—	3000
MAXIMUM SPEED—	33 KNOTS

→

PC 45-47 CLASS—NO. 101-103   COMPLETED 1939-42

NO DATA—APPEARANCE UNKNOWN

PC 40-47—ALSO DESIGNATED AS XPC—SPECIAL SUBCHASERS

ONI 41-42

DIVISION OF NAVAL INTELLIGENCE—IDENTIFICATION AND CHARACTERISTICS SECTION — JUNE, 1943

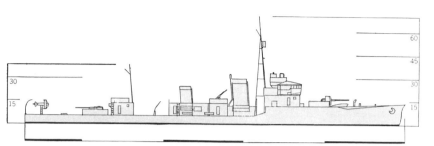

LENGTH—235' OA   BEAM—26'4"   DRAFT—7'6"

DISPLACEMENT— 615 TONS (STANDARD); 700 TONS (NORMAL)

		MAX. ELEV.	MAX. RANGE
ARMAMENT—	2-4.7"	30°	17,500 YARDS
	1-3" AA	85°	9,000 YARDS
	?-AAMG		
	2-D. C. GUNS		10 MINES CARRIED

PROPULSION—

MACHINERY—   TRIPLE EXPANSION RECIPROCATING

BOILERS—   3 KAMPON

FUEL—   COAL, 180 TONS

DESIGNED HP—   4,000

MAXIMUM SPEED— 20 KNOTS

			BEGUN	COMPLETED
NO. 1	AM	1	5/10/22	6/30/23
NO. 2	AM	2	4/13/22	6/30/23
NO. 3	AM	3	8/ 1 /22	6/30/23
NO. 4	AM	4	12/ 1 /23	4/29/25
NO. 5	AM	5	3/25/28	2/25/29
NO. 6	AM	6	STRICKEN FROM LIST	

NOTE—POLE FOREMAST ON **AM 1-4**, TRIPOD ON NO. 5
    PRONOUNCED DESTROYER APPEARANCE.

NO. 7 CLASS—AM 13-18

LENGTH—235' OA; 229'6" WL

BEAM —25'8"

DRAFT —7'8" (MAXIMUM)

DISPLACEMENT—630 TONS (STANDARD)

ARMAMENT	MAX. ELEV.	MAX. RANGE (HOR.)
3-4".7	30°	19,000 YARDS
2-AAMG		
?-MINES, DEPTH CHARGES		
1-SEARCHLIGHT		

PROPULSION
MACHINERY—	TRIPLE EXPANSION RECIPROCATING
BOILERS—	3 KAMPON
FUEL—	COAL
DESIGNED HP—	3850
DESIGNED SPEED—	20 KNOTS
BEGUN—1937-38;	COMPLETED—1938-39

NO. 19 CLASS—AM 19-24—APPEARANCE UNKNOWN

DIMENSIONS— 217'11" (WL) x 25'4" x 6'7" (MEAN)

DISPLACEMENT—492 TONS (STANDARD)

ARMAMENT	MAX. ELEV.	MAX. RANGE (HORIZONTAL)
2-4".7	30°	19,000 YARDS
?-AAMG		
?-MINES, DEPTH CHARGES		

PROPULSION
MACHINERY—	TRIPLE EXPANSION RECIPROCATING
FUEL—	COAL
DESIGNED HP—	3200
DESIGNED SPEED—19 KNOTS	

BEGUN—1939-41; COMPLETED—1941-42

ONI 41-42

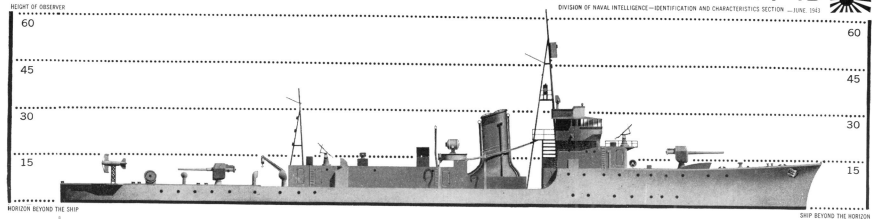

HEIGHT OF OBSERVER

60
45
30
15

HORIZON BEYOND THE SHIP

SHIP BEYOND THE HORIZON

0

LENGTH—236'9" OA; 232'3" WL (NO. 17, 18—218' OA)
BEAM— 25'
DRAFT— 6' 1" (NORMAL)

DISPLACEMENT—492-511 TONS (STANDARD)

ARMAMENT

2-4".7
2-AAMG
?-MINES

	MAX. ELEV.	MAX. RANGE (HORIZONTAL)
	30°	19,000 YDS.

PROPULSION

MACHINERY— T.E. RECIPROCATING
BOILERS—
DESIGNED HP—3200

FUEL— COAL
DESIGNED SPEED—20 KNOTS

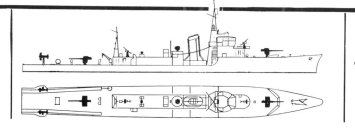

6—NO. 13 CLASS—AM 7-12

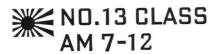

NO.13 CLASS
AM 7-12

DIVISION OF NAVAL INTELLIGENCE—IDENTIFICATION
AND CHARACTERISTICS SECTION —JUNE, 1943

MISTAKEN IDENTITY
(SEE CHIDORI CLASS)

NO. 13 CLASS AM 7-12   (AM 13-18 SIMILAR)

CHIDORI—OTORI CLASSES—TB 1-12

SHIMUSHU CLASS CM 11-15

TB—TRAD CLASS (THAI)

DE (US)

PG-HASHIDATE CLASS   ALSO—CMC AND PC TYPES

AERIAL VIEWS

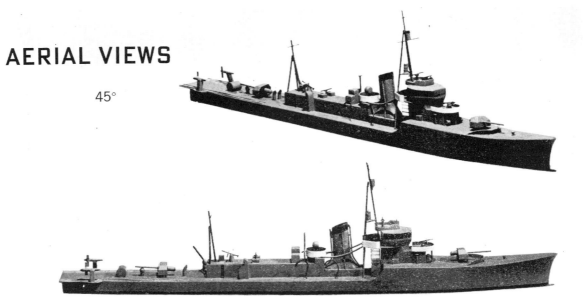

45°

90°

135°

15° ELEVATION

0°

180°

ONI 41-42

315°

270°

225°

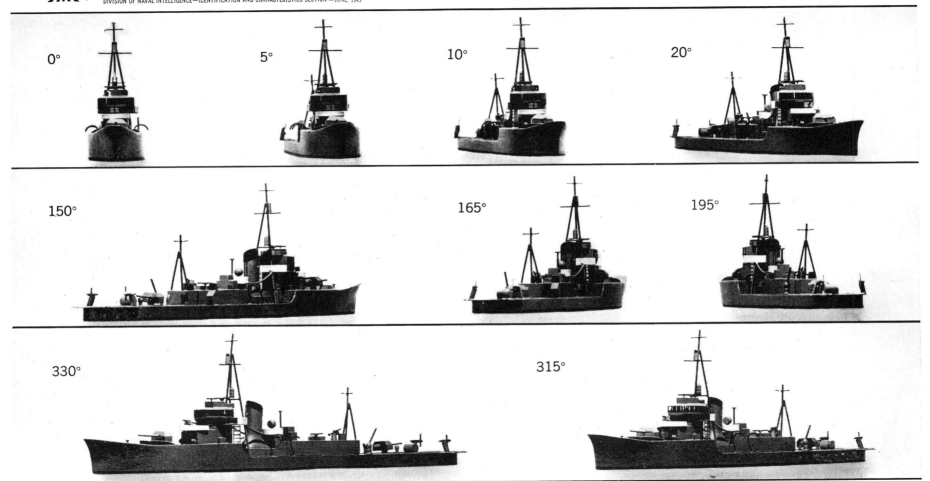

0°   5°   10°   20°

150°   165°   195°

330°   315°

KNOTS	RPM	KNOTS	RPM	KNOTS	RPM	KNOTS	RPM
	400		300		200		100
	375		275		175		75
	350		250		150		50
	325		225		125		25

30°

45°

270°

340°

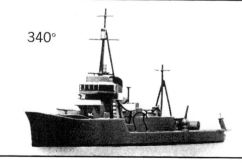

350°

355°

NO. 13 CLASS—AM 7-12

DIVISION OF NAVAL INTELLIGENCE—IDENTIFICATION AND CHARACTERISTICS SECTION —JUNE, 1943

COMPLETED

NO. 13—AM 7—1933	NO. 16—AM 10—1936
NO. 14—AM 8—1933	NO. 17—AM 11—1936
NO. 15—AM 9—1934	NO. 18—AM 12—1941

ONI 41-42

4/8/38

4/8/33

NO. 16—1/31/39

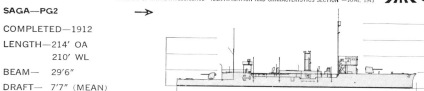

SAGA—PG2

COMPLETED—1912

LENGTH—214' OA
210' WL

BEAM— 29'6"

DRAFT— 7'7" (MEAN)

DISPLACEMENT—685 TONS (STANDARD); 780 TONS (NORMAL)

ARMAMENT	MAX. ELEV.	MAX. RANGE (HOR.)	MAX. RANGE (VERT.)
1-4.7" (40)		10,800 YDS.	
3-3" AA	85°	9,000 YDS.	20,000 FT.
?-AAMG			

PROPULSION
MACHINERY— TRIPLE EXPANSION RECIPROCATING
BOILERS— 2 KAMPON
FUEL— COAL, 200 TONS
DESIGNED HP— 1,600
MAXIMUM SPEED—15 KNOTS @ 279 R.P.M.

YODO—PG 1

LENGTH—300' OA; 280' PP   BEAM— 32' 1"   COMPLETED—1908
DRAFT— 11' (MEAN)

DISPLACEMENT—1,320 TONS (STANDARD); 1,450 TONS (NORMAL)

ARMAMENT	MAX. ELEV.	MAX. RANGE (HOR.)	MAX. RANGE (VERT.)
2-3" AA	85°	9,000 YDS.	20,000 FT.
2-AAMG			
2-18" TORPEDO TUBES			

PROPULSION
MACHINERY —TRIPLE EXPANSION RECIPROCATING
BOILERS— 4-MIYABARA   FUEL—COAL, 420 TONS
DESIGNED HP—6,500   MAXIMUM SPEED—22 KNOTS
RIG AS SURVEY SHIP—PRESENT STATUS UNKNOWN AS SURVEY SHIP

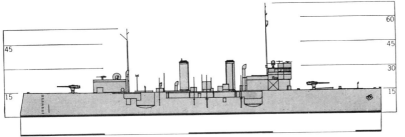

ASUGA—PG 3

COMPLETED 1915 (EX CHINESE MUNG CHI)

LENGTH—215'6" OA   BEAM—29'6"   DRAFT—11'6" (MEAN)

DISPLACEMENT—860 TONS (STANDARD)

ARMAMENT—MAX. ELEV.	MAX. RANGE (HORIZONTAL)	MAX. RANGE (VERTICAL)
2–3" (40) 85°	9,000 YARDS	20,000 FEET
1–20 MM. AAMG		
2–50 MM. AAMG		

PROPULSION

MACHINERY —RECIPROCATING   FUEL—COAL, 150 TONS

DESIGNED HP—1,350   MAXIMUM SPEED—13 KNOTS

NOW CLASSIFIED AS MISCELLANEOUS DUTY BOAT

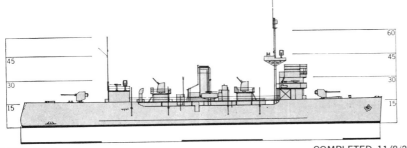

ATAKA—PG 4

COMPLETED 11/8/22

LENGTH—222' OA   BEAM—32'   DRAFT—7'6" (MEAN)

DISPLACEMENT—725 TONS (STANDARD); 820 (NORMAL)

ARMAMENT	MAX. ELEV.	MAX. RANGE (HORIZONTAL)	MAX. RANGE (VERTICAL)
2–4.7 (45)	40°	19,000 YARDS	
2(?)–3" (40) AA	85°	9,000 YARDS	20,000 FEET
6–AAMG			

PROPULSION

MACHINERY—TRIPLE EXPANSION—RECIPROCATING   BOILERS—2 KAMPON

FUEL—COAL   DESIGNED HP—1,700

MAXIMUM SPEED—16 KNOTS   EQUIPPED FOR SUBMARINE SALVAGE WORK

PRESENT ARMAMENT UNKNOWN

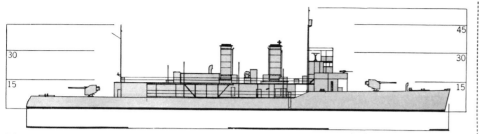

PG—5 HITONOSE

(EX-CHINESE MING SEN)

LENGTH—210' OA—207' WL
BEAM— 27'
DRAFT— 6'6" (MAXIMUM)
DISPLACEMENT—600 TONS (STANDARD); 464 TONS (NORMAL)

*ARMAMENT—(OLD)	MAX. ELEV.	MAX. RANGE
2-3" AA	85°	9,000 YARDS
2-AAMG		

PROPULSION—
FUEL— COAL
DESIGNED HP— 2400
DESIGNED SPEED—16 KNOTS; 18 KNOTS MAXIMUM

BEGUN—5/5/31   COMPLETED—11/12/31
*PRESENT ARMAMENT UNKNOWN   PHOTO—1938? NOTE NO ARMAMENT VISIBLE

PG—EX-CHINESE YAT SEN

(NEW NAME UNKNOWN)

LENGTH—275' OA, 268' WL   BEAM—32'   DRAFT—11'0" (MAXIMUM)
DISPLACEMENT—1600 TONS (STANDARD); 1650 TONS (NORMAL)

*ARMAMENT—(OLD)	MAX. ELEV.	MAX. RANGE
1-6"		25,000 YARDS
1-5.5		16,000 YARDS
4-3" AA		
2-AAMG		

PROPULSION
FUEL— COAL, 300 TONS
DESIGNED HP—4000   DESIGNED SPEED—16 KNOTS
BEGUN—2/30;   COMPLETED—12/30

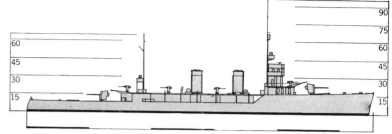

DIVISION OF NAVAL INTELLIGENCE—IDENTIFICATION AND CHARACTERISTICS SECTION —JUNE, 1943

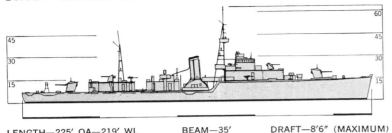

LENGTH—225' OA—219' WL   BEAM—35'   DRAFT—8'6" (MAXIMUM)

DISPLACEMENT—1,200 TONS (STANDARD)

ARMAMENT—   MAX. ELEV.   MAX. RANGE (HOR.)   MAX. RANGE (VER.)
2-4.7 (50)   85°   19,000 YARDS   25,000 FEET
2-1.4 AA TWINS
5-AAMG
12 DEPTH CHARGES   2 SEARCHLIGHTS—36"

PROTECTION—
GUN SHIELDS—¼"   DEGAUSSING EQUIPMENT

PROPULSION—
DESIGNED HP—3,600 (?)   MAXIMUM SPEED—20 KNOTS

	BEGUN	COMPLETED
HASHIDATE—PG-6	1938-39	1941
UJI— PG-7	1938-39	1941

NOTE BRIDGE VARIATION

↓ UJI—8/7/41

↑ HASHIDATE—7/5/41   UJI ↓

KASUGA (EX-OCA-6)—COMPLETED 1904

DIMENSIONS—367'2" OA x 61'11" x 25'3" (MAXIMUM) 23'11" (MEAN)

DISPLACEMENT—7,080 TONS (STANDARD); 7,700 TONS (NORMAL)

ARMAMENT—	MAX. ELEV.	MAX. RANGE (HORIZONTAL)	MAX. RANGE (VERTICAL)
1–10" (45)	18°	17,950 YARDS	
2– 8" (45)	20°	18,800 YARDS	
14– 6" (45)	25°	18,900 YARDS	
4– 3"	85°		9,000 YARDS
1– 3" AA	85°		9,000 YARDS

PROTECTION—
CONNING TOWER—5.5"
BELT—   6" AMIDSHIPS; 4.5" ENDS
DECK—   1.5"
TURRETS—   6"

PROPULSION—
MACHINERY—   TWO TRIPLE EXPANSION RECIPROCATING
BOILERS—   TWELVE KAMPON
FUEL—   1,200 TONS, COAL
DESIGNED HP—   13,500
DESIGNED SPEED—20 KNOTS @ 105 R.P.M.

- -

HIRADO, YAHAGI (EX-OCL)—COMPLETED 1912

DIMENSIONS—475' OA x 46'6" x 17'8" (NORMAL)

DISPLACEMENT—4,400 TONS (STANDARD)—4,950 TONS (NORMAL)

ARMAMENT—	MAX. ELEV.	MAX. RANGE (HORIZONTAL)	MAX. RANGE (VERTICAL)
8–6"	20°	14,200 YARDS	
4 (?)–3" AA	85°		9,000 YARDS
2–AAMG			
3–18" TORPEDO TUBES			

PROTECTION—
CONNING TOWER—4"
BELT—   3" AMIDSHIPS, 2" ENDS

PROPULSION—
MACHINERY—   GEARED TURBINES
BOILERS—   16 KAMPON
FUEL—   COAL, 900 TONS—OIL, 300 TONS
DESIGNED HP—   29,500
MAXIMUM SPEED—26 KNOTS

THIS CLASS IS NO LONGER LISTED.

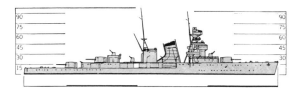

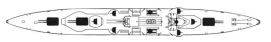

LENGTH—	360' 0" OA, 330' 0" PP	
BEAM—	39' 0"	
DRAFT—	13' 0" (MAXIMUM), 11' 5" (MEAN)	
DISPLACEMENT—	1900-1990 TONS (STANDARD)	

ARMAMENT (OLD)	MAX. ELEV.	MAX. RANGE
6–5.5" (50)	30°	20,000 YARDS
8(?)-2.4"		
6–3.1" (45) AA		
4-AAMG		4-21" TORPEDO TUBES
2-D.C. GUNS		9- DEPTH CHARGES
2-SCOUT OBSERVATION PLANES CARRIED		

PROTECTION— DECK—1"
GUNHOUSES, HULL SIDE AMIDSHIPS LIGHTLY ARMORED
MACHINERY—GEARED TURBINES
BOILERS—
FUEL—COAL, 645 TONS, OIL, 110 TONS
DESIGNED HP—   7100-9500
DESIGNED SPEED—22-23 KNOTS
ENDURANCE—   5000 MILES @ 12 KNOTS

	BEGUN	COMPLETED
NING HAI—PG 8—	2/22/31	8/19/32
PING HAI—PG 9—	6/28/31	1936

THESE VESSELS WERE CAPTURED FROM THE CHINESE IN 1937, AND ARE NOW BELIEVED TO HAVE BEEN RETURNED TO THE NANKING GOVERNMENT. NEW NAMES, ARMAMENT UNKNOWN. NOTE DIFFERENCES IN AFT DECKHOUSE ARRANGEMENT. PROFILE IS OF **NING HAI**

↑ PING HAI—1937 ↓   NING HAI—1937 →

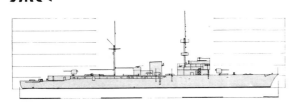

ERITREA—(ITALIAN PG-5)

LENGTH— 317'11" OA; 296'11" WL
BEAM— 48'8"
DRAFT— 12'2" (MEAN)
DISPLACEMENT—2,172 TONS (STANDARD)

ARMAMENT— 4-4ʺ7 (45)
6-AAMG
100-MINES

PROPULSION

MACHINERY— 2 FIAT DIESELS
FUEL— OIL, 320 TONS
DESIGNED HP— 8,000
DESIGNED SPEED—20 KNOTS

BEGUN—7/25/35; COMPLETED—6/37

STATIONED IN PACIFIC

THE STATUS OF THESE EX-CHINESE SHIPS IS DOUBTFUL, NEW ARMAMENT UNKNOWN

EX-CHAO HO 1912

DIMENSIONS— 320'0" OA x 30'0" x 14'9" (MAXIMUM)
DISPLACEMENT—2,600 TONS (NORMAL)
ARMAMENT— 2-6"
4-4"
2-3"
6-1ʺ85
2-1ʺ57 AA
2-1ʺ46
2-18" TORPEDO TUBES

PROPULSION

MACHINERY— PARSONS TURBINES
BOILERS— 6 YARROW
FUEL— OIL, 100 TONS
DESIGNED HP— 6,000
DESIGNED SPEED— 20 KNOTS

EX-HAI CHI 1898

DIMENSIONS— 424' (WL) x 46'10" x 19' (MAXIMUM)

DISPLACEMENT— 4,300 TONS

ARMAMENT— 2-8" (45)
10-4ʺ7 (45)
12-3 PDR
?-AAMG
5-18" TORPEDO TUBES

DESIGNED HP— 17,000

DESIGNED SPEED—24 KNOTS

EX-KIANG CHEN 1906

DIMENSIONS— 180' (WL) x 28' x 7'
DISPLACEMENT—550 TONS
ARMAMENT— 1-4ʺ7
1-3"
3-PDR
4-AAMG

PROPULSION

FUEL— COAL, 113 TONS
DESIGNED HP— 950
DESIGNED SPEED—13 KNOTS

EX-HAI CHEN 1898

DIMENSIONS— 314'0" (WL) x 40'10" x 19'0" (MAXIMUM)
DISPLACEMENT— 2,950 TONS (NORMAL)
ARMAMENT— 3-5ʺ9
8-4"
4-1ʺ85
1-1ʺ57 AA
4-1ʺ46

DESIGNED HP— 7,000
DESIGNED SPEED—19.5 KNOTS

ONI 41-42

FOR FURTHER INFORMATION SEE
ONI 225-J — JAPANESE LANDING
OPERATIONS AND EQUIPMENT

LANDING CRAFT

DIVISION OF NAVAL INTELLIGENCE—IDENTIFICATION AND CHARACTERISTICS SECTION —JUNE, 1943

TYPE A—DIMENSIONS—47' OA x 12' BEAM
(ARMY) ARMAMENT— BOW MACHINE GUNS
　　　　CAPACITY— 100-120 TROOPS
　　　　SPEED— 8-10 KNOTS
MAY CARRY 2 TANKETTES

TYPE A—SIMILAR WITH BOW AND STERN MACHINE GUNS
(NAVY) CAPACITY—80 TROOPS
SPLINTER SHIELD AFT
DECKHOUSE ADDITION

TYPE B—DIMENSIONS—30'4" OA x 7'6" BEAM
　　　　ARMAMENT— BOW MACHINE GUN (SHIELDED)
　　　　CAPACITY— 40 TROOPS
　　　　SPEED— 8-10 KNOTS

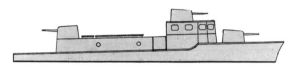

TYPE C—DIMENSIONS—49' OA x 13' BEAM
　　　　ARMAMENT— 1-.303" MG IN TURRET
　　　　　　　　2-MG
　　　　CAPACITY— 50 TROOPS
　　　　SPEED— 25 KNOTS
STEEL PLATE CONSTRUCTION THROUGHOUT

TYPE D—DIMENSIONS—38'6" OA x 11' BEAM
　　　　CAPACITY— 60 TROOPS
ARMAMENT, PROPULSION VARIABLE

TYPE E—DIMENSIONS—63'2" OA x 8'9" BEAM
　　　　ARMAMENT— 1-2 MG (BOW SHIELDED)
　　　　CAPACITY— 60 TROOPS
　　　　SPEED— 10 KNOTS (AIRSCREW
　　　　　　　　PROPELLED)

TYPE F—DIMENSIONS—21' OA x 7' BEAM
　　　　CAPACITY— 20 TROOPS
　　　　SPEED— 8-10 KNOTS
STEEL PLATE CONSTRUCTION

TYPE G—DIMENSIONS—52'1" OA x 13'3" BEAM
　　　　CAPACITY— 50 TROOPS
　　　　SPEED— 8 KNOTS
USED MAINLY AS EQUIPMENT LIGHTER

LANDING CRAFT MAY BE TRANSPORTED OR
TOWED BY MISCELLANEOUS
CARGO TYPES, AS SHOWN ABOVE

PTC—NAMES AND NUMBERS UNKNOWN

(A)—DIMENSIONS—200' x 24' x 9'

    ARMAMENT— 1-2"   3-AAMG
                  2-TORPEDO TUBES AFT

(B)—DIMENSIONS—120' x 24' x 7'

    ARMAMENT— 1-2"   2-AAMG
                  1-TORPEDO TUBE AFT

(C)—DIMENSIONS—80'-100" x 20' x 7'

    ARMAMENT— 1-2"   1-3 AAMG
                  2-TORPEDO TUBES AFT (VARIABLE)

PT—50 OR MORE—APPEARANCE UNKNOWN

(D)—DIMENSIONS—32'6" x 6'6"

    ARMAMENT— 1 AAMG
                  2-TORPEDO TUBES
                  1-D.C. GUN
                  4-DEPTH CHARGES

DESIGNED HP—   400

MAXIMUM SPEED— 45 KNOTS

ENGINE—RADIAL AIRCOOLED AIRCRAFT TYPE

(E)—DIMENSIONS—49' x 9'9"
    ARMAMENT— SAME AS (D)
    MAXIMUM SPEED—30 KNOTS

(F)—BUILDING
    DIMENSIONS—32'6" x 6'
    ARMAMENT— SAME AS (D)
    MAXIMUM SPEED—45 KNOTS
    STEEL FRAME, WOOD PLANK CONSTRUCTION,
    PROPELLED BY AIRCRAFT (RADIAL) ENGINES

2 THORNYCROFT 55' MTB—1923

1 EXPERIMENTAL—1925

IX—MIDGET SUBMARINES—NUMBERS UNKNOWN

CARRIED BY I-CLASS SS OR MOTHER SHIPS
DIMENSIONS—   80' OA x 6'
DISPLACEMENT— 40-50 TONS (STANDARD)
ARMAMENT—   2-18" TORPEDOES (BOW)
               300 LB. DEMOLITION CHARGE
MAXIMUM SPEED—24 KNOTS
ENDURANCE—   70 MILES @ 12 KNOTS
             170 MILES @ 6 KNOTS

ANOTHER TYPE— 41' OA x 5' BEAM

AT—TUGS
APPEARANCE, CHARACTERISTICS UNKNOWN
    YOKOSUKA—NOS. 1, 3-7
    KURE—   NOS. 1, 3-6
    SASEBO—   NOS. 2-5
    MAIZURU— NOS. 1-3—313 TONS
    RYOJUN—   NO. 1
    KAIYO—   NOS. 1-4

"MISCELLANEOUS DUTY" BOATS
COASTAL, HARBOR, RIVER EMPLOYMENT

EX-ODD—NIRE
          ASHI
          KAKI
          SUMIRE
          (SEE ODD—MOMO CLASS FOR DETAILS)
SOME OF THESE VESSELS ARE CONVERTED FOR DMS DUTY

EX-PR—KOTAKA—1930

DIMENSIONS— 98'5" PP x 16'1" x 2'2" (MEAN)
DISPLACEMENT—50 TONS (STANDARD)
ARMAMENT—   5 AAMG

CHIKUBU—1940
(SISTERSHIP TO PR—SUMIDA CLASS)

← CL—LAMOTTE-PICQUET (FRANCE) 1927

DIMENSIONS—   594' 10" OA x 57' 5" x 17' 3" (MEAN)

DISPLACEMENT—7,249 TONS (STANDARD)

ARMAMENT—   8-6.1" (50)
4-3" (60)
12-21.7" TORPEDO TUBES
1-AIRCRAFT CARRIED

DESIGNED HP—102,000   DESIGNED SPEED—33 KNOTS

DD—DESTROYERS
U. S.—STEWART—1919—FLUSH-DECKER TYPE

GB—THRACIAN   3/31/22

DIMENSIONS—   276' 2" OA x 26' 10" x 9' 2" (MEAN)

DISPLACEMENT—905 TONS (STANDARD)

ARMAMENT—   3-4"   1-12" PDR AA
4-21" TORPEDO TUBES   1-2 PDR

DESIGNED HP—   27,000

DESIGNED SPEED—36 KNOTS

GB—VOYAGER   5/8/18

DIMENSIONS—   312' OA x 29' 6" x 10' 10" (MEAN)

DISPLACEMENT—1100 TONS (STANDARD)

ARMAMENT—   4-4"
6-21" TORPEDO TUBES

SHAFT HP—27,000

DESIGNED SPEED 34 KNOTS

NETHERLANDS
BANCKERT, WITTE DE WITH   1928-29

DIMENSIONS—   322' OA x 31' 3" x 10' (MAXIMUM)

DISPLACEMENT—1316 TONS (STANDARD)

ARMAMENT—   4-4.7" (50)
1-3" AA PLUS 9 SMALLER   6-21" TORPEDO TUBES

SHAFT HP—31,000   DESIGNED SPEED—36 KNOTS

SS—SUBMARINES

US—S-36

NETHERLANDS—K-7—1920

K-10—1922

DIMENSIONS—   210' 3" OA x 17' 9" x 11' 8"

DISPLACEMENT—521/712 TONS

ARMAMENT—   1-3.5" AA   1-AAMG
4-17.7" TORPEDO TUBES

HORSEPOWER—1500/630   SPEED—16/9.5 KNOTS

K-13   12/24

DIMENSIONS—   218' 9" OA x 19' x 12' 6"

DISPLACEMENT—611/815 TONS

ARMAMENT   —1-3.5"   1-AAMG
2-21" TORPEDO TUBES
4-17.7" TORPEDO TUBES

HORSEPOWER—2400/   SPEED—17/8 KNOTS

K-18   9/32

DIMENSIONS   —242' 3" OA x 25' x 12' 8"

DISPLACEMENT—782/1024 TONS

ARMAMENT   —1-3.5"   2-AAMG
8-21" TORPEDO TUBES

HORSEPOWER—3200/1000

SPEED—17/9 KNOTS

SEIZURES

DIVISION OF NAVAL INTELLIGENCE—IDENTIFICATION AND CHARACTERISTICS SECTION — JUNE, 1943

ONI 41-42

CM—CMc—MINELAYERS

GB—REDSTART   5/3/38

DIMENSIONS— 163'9" OA x 27'2" x 8'
DISPLACEMENT—498 TONS
INDICATED HP— 400
SPEED— 10.5 KNOTS

NETHERLANDS

GOUDEN LEEUW   9/31

DIMENSIONS— 216' x 36' x 11'
DISPLACEMENT—1291 TONS
ARMAMENT— 2–3" AA   6-AAMG
HORSEPOWER— 1750   SPEED—15 KNOTS

KRAKATAU   1924

DIMENSIONS— 213' x 34'6" x 10'6"
DISPLACEMENT—982 TONS
ARMAMENT— 2–3" AA   4-MG
HORSEPOWER— 2500
SPEED— 15.5 KNOTS

NETHERLANDS

RIGEL   1929

DIMENSIONS— 242'9" OA x 36'3" x 10'
DISPLACEMENT—1631 TONS
ARMAMENT— 2–3"   2-AAMG
HORSEPOWER— 1400   SPEED—12.5 KNOTS

PRO PATRIA   1922

DIMENSIONS— 154' x 28'3" x 9'3"
DISPLACEMENT—537 TONS
ARMAMENT— 1–3" AA   2-MG
HORSEPOWER— 650   SPEED—10 KNOTS

PR—RIVER GUNBOATS

GB—MOTH— 625 TONS
ROBIN— 226 TONS
TERN— 262 TONS

PT—MOTOR TORPEDO BOATS

GB—8 IN NUMBER

AM—MINESWEEPERS

NETHERLANDS

PIETER DE BITTER, ELAND DUBOIS   10/36

DIMENSIONS— 183' x 25'6" x 7'
DISPLACEMENT—525 TONS
ARMAMENT— 1–3" (55)   5-AAMG
HORSEPOWER— 1690   SPEED—15 KNOTS

A, B, C, D   1929–30

DIMENSIONS— 140'6" x 19'9" x 5'
DISPLACEMENT—179 TONS
HORSEPOWER— 700
SPEED— 14 KNOTS

NAVAL AUXILIARIES

U. S.—AS—CANOPUS
AT—NAPA
GB—AO—EBONOL
WAR SIRDAR
AG—ALDGATE, BARLIGHT,
MAN YEUNG, WAI FOONG,
WATERGATE

DUGUAY-TROUIN—CL 6

DIVISION OF NAVAL INTELLIGENCE—IDENTIFICATION AND CHARACTERISTICS SECTION —OCTOBER, 1942

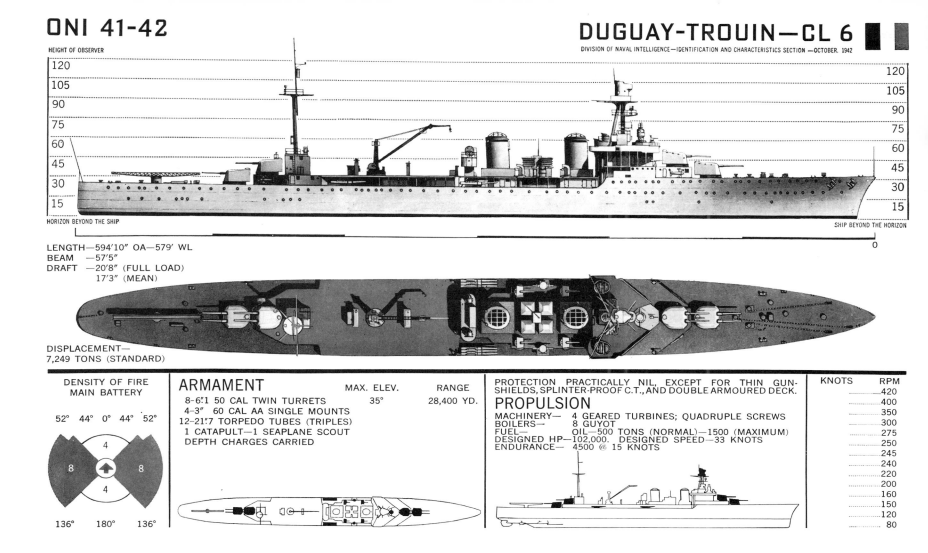

HEIGHT OF OBSERVER

120	120
105	105
90	90
75	75
60	60
45	45
30	30
15	15

HORIZON BEYOND THE SHIP

SHIP BEYOND THE HORIZON

0

LENGTH—594'10" OA—579' WL
BEAM —57'5"
DRAFT —20'8" (FULL LOAD)
          17'3" (MEAN)

DISPLACEMENT—
7,249 TONS (STANDARD)

DENSITY OF FIRE MAIN BATTERY

52° 44° 0° 44° 52°

4

8   8

4

136° 180° 136°

ARMAMENT

	MAX. ELEV.	RANGE
8-6".1 50 CAL TWIN TURRETS	35°	28,400 YD.
4-3" 60 CAL AA SINGLE MOUNTS		
12-21".7 TORPEDO TUBES (TRIPLES)		
1 CATAPULT—1 SEAPLANE SCOUT		
DEPTH CHARGES CARRIED		

PROTECTION PRACTICALLY NIL, EXCEPT FOR THIN GUN-SHIELDS, SPLINTER-PROOF C.T., AND DOUBLE ARMOURED DECK.

PROPULSION

MACHINERY— 4 GEARED TURBINES; QUADRUPLE SCREWS
BOILERS— 8 GUYOT
FUEL— OIL—500 TONS (NORMAL)—1500 (MAXIMUM)
DESIGNED HP—102,000. DESIGNED SPEED—33 KNOTS
ENDURANCE— 4500 @ 15 KNOTS

KNOTS	RPM
	420
	400
	350
	300
	275
	250
	245
	240
	220
	200
	160
	150
	120
	80

DUGUAY-TROUIN—CL 6

DIVISION OF NAVAL INTELLIGENCE—IDENTIFICATION AND CHARACTERISTICS SECTION—OCTOBER, 1942

DUGUAY-TROUIN—CL 6

BEGUN
8/4/22

COMPLETED
8/ /26

THIS UNIT WAS LAST REPORTED AT SAIGON, AND MAY BE
SEIZED BY THE JAPANESE

ONI 41-42

1937 ↑

1937 ↑

SIAMESE (THAILAND) NAVAL VESSELS—LIST BY DESIGN CLASSES
PRINCIPAL COMBATANT TYPES
LIGHT CRUISERS
"MODIFIED REGOLO" CLASS

CL1	NO. 1	—BUILDING IN ITALY
CL2	NO. 2	—BUILDING IN ITALY

DESTROYERS

DD1	PHRA RUANG	(EX-HMS RADIANT)

SUBMARINES
VIRUN CLASS

SS1	VIRUN
SS2	MACHANU
SS3	SINSAMUDAR
SS4	BLAI JUMBOL

FOUR SUBMARINES—PROJECTED

MINOR COMBATANT TYPES
COAST DEFENCE SHIPS
RATANAKOSINDRA CLASS

CD1	RATANAKOSINDRA
CD2	SUKHODAYA

DHAMBURI CLASS

CD3	DHAMBURI	—SUNK. SALVAGED & REFITTING
CD4	SRI AYUDHYA	—REFITTING

TORPEDO-BOATS
SUA-TAYANCHOL CLASS

TB1	SUA-TAYANCHOL	—STATUS DOUBTFUL
TB2	SUA-KHAMRONSINDHU	—STATUS DOUBTFUL

No. 1 CLASS

TB3	NO. 1	—STATUS DOUBTFUL
TB4	NO. 2	—STATUS DOUBTFUL
TB5	NO. 3	—STATUS DOUBTFUL
TB6	NO. 4	—STATUS DOUBTFUL

TRAD CLASS

TB7	TRAD	(NO. 11)	
TB8	PUKET	(NO. 12)	
TB9	PATTANI	(NO. 13)	
TB10	SURASDRA	(NO. 21)	
TB11	CHANDARABURI	(NO. 22)	
TB12	RAYONG	(NO. 23)	
TB13	JUMBARA	(NO. 31)	
TB14	CHOLBURI	(NO. 32)	—REPORTED WAR LOSS
TB15	SONGKLA	(NO. 33)	—REPORTED WAR LOSS

"MODIFIED SPICA" CLASS

TB16	NO. 1	—BUILDING IN ITALY
TB17	NO. 2	—BUILDING IN ITALY
TB18	NO. 3	—BUILDING IN ITALY

GUNBOATS
PG1 MONGKUT RAJAKUMARN (EX-SPANISH FILIPINAS)

BALI CLASS

PG2	BALI	—STATUS DOUBTFUL
PG3	SUGRIB	
PG4	SURIYA MONTHON	

TAHCHIN CLASS

PG5	TAHCHIN
PG6	MAEKLONG

TWO SLOOPS—PROJECTED

SUBMARINE CHASERS
KLONGYAI CLASS

PC1	KLONGYAI	
PC2	TAKUBAI	
PC3	KANTANG	
FIVE OF 100 TO 110 TONS		—REPORTED BUILDING
SEVEN PC'S		—PROJECTED

MOTOR TORPEDO-BOATS
THORNYCROFT 55-Ft. DESIGN

PT1	NO. 1	—STATUS DOUBTFUL
PT2	NO. 2	
PT3	NO. 3	
PT4	NO. 4	
PT5	NO. 5	

THORNYCROFT 16-TON DESIGN

PT6	NO. 6
PT7	NO. 7
PT8	NO. 8

FOUR UNITS BELIEVED COMPLETING
TWENTY UNITS—PROJECTED

NAVAL AUXILIARIES

AO1	SAMUI
AO2	NO. 2

AP1	CUONG
AP2	CHANG
AP3	ANGTHONG

PANGAN CLASS

AP4	PANGAN
AP5	SICHAUN

AT1	SAMET

HAN THALE CLASS

AGS1	HAN THALE
AGS2	LIEU THALE
AGS3	CHEN THALE

CHAO PHRA

AGS4		(EX-HMS HAVANT)

OIL TANKERS
—PROJECTED

TRANSPORTS
(EX-PRA YOM)
(EX-VIDES KICHKAR; EX-BUK; EX-LYCIDAS)
(EX-ROYAL YACHT-MAHA CHAKKRI)

TUG
(EX-PI-SUA-NAM)

SURVEYING SHIPS

DISTRICT CRAFT
BANGRADIAN CLASS

CMc1	BANGRADIAN	
CMc2	NONG SARAI	
CMc3	NO. 3	—PROJECTED

SARA SINDHU CLASS

YP1	SARA SINDHU	
YP2	THIEW UTHOK	
YP3	TRAVANE VARI	
YP4	NO. 4	—PROJECTED
YP5	NO. 5	—PROJECTED
YP6	NO. 6	—PROJECTED

COASTAL MINE LAYERS

PATROL VESSELS

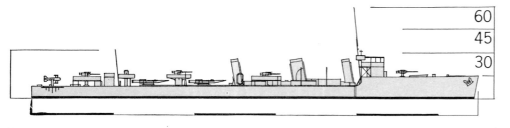

60
45
30

PHRA RUANG — DD-1 — (EX-HMS RADIANT) — COMPLETED — 1917
PURCHASED—1920

DIMENSIONS—	274'0" OA x 27'4" x 11'1" (MAXIMUM)
DISPLACEMENT—	718 TONS (STANDARD); 1037 TONS (NORMAL)

ARMAMENT—
  3—4"
  1—2 PDR MULTIPLE
  1—AAMG
  4—21" TORPEDO TUBES

FUEL—	OIL, 285 TONS
DESIGNED HP—	29,000
DESIGNED SPEED—	35 KNOTS

VIRUN CLASS—SS 1-4   COMPLETED—1938

DIMENSIONS—	164'1" x 13'5" x 11'10" (MAXIMUM)
DISPLACEMENT—	325 TONS (STANDARD) SURFACE

ARMAMENT—
  1—AAMG
  5—21" TORPEDO TUBES

DESIGNED HP—	1000/540
DESIGNED SPEED—	14½/8 KNOTS

↓ **SUKHODAYA—CD-2**—FOREMAST SINCE LOWERED, MAINMAST HEIGHTENED.

RATANAKOSINDRA CLASS—CD-1, 2

DIMENSIONS—	175'0" OA x 36'11" x 10'9" (MAXIMUM)	
DISPLACEMENT—	886 TONS (STANDARD), 918 TONS (NORMAL)	

ARMAMENT—	MAX. ELEV.	MAX. RANGE
2—6"	30°	20,430 YARDS
4—4" (50) AA	90°	11,160 YARDS

PROTECTION—
BELT—	2½" AMIDSHIPS; 1¼" ENDS
BARBETTES—	2½"
CONNING TOWER—	4¾"

PROPULSION—
MACHINERY—	TRIPLE EXPANSION
BOILERS—	2 WATER TUBE
FUEL—	OIL, 96-102 TONS
DESIGNED HP—	850
DESIGNED SPEED—	12-13 KNOTS

RATANAKOSINDRA—CD-1—COMPLETED: 8/25
SUKHODAYA—   CD-2—COMPLETED: 3/17/30

DHAMBURI CLASS—CD-3, 4

DIVISION OF NAVAL INTELLIGENCE—IDENTIFICATION AND CHARACTERISTICS SECTION —JUNE, 1943

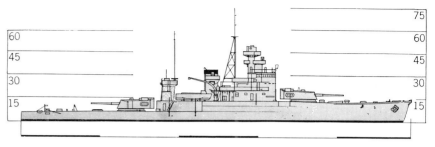

DHAMBURI CLASS—CD-3, 4 BUILT IN JAPAN

DIMENSIONS
    LENGTH—246' 1" OA
    BEAM— 42' 8"
    DRAFT— 13' 10" (MAXIMUM)

DISPLACEMENT—2,015 TONS (STANDARD)

ARMAMENT	MAX. ELEV.	MAX. RANGE
4—8"		
4—3"		
4—AAMG		

PROTECTION—LIGHT ARMOR BELT

PROPULSION
    MACHINERY—   2 SETS DIESELS
    FUEL—   OIL, 150 TONS
    DESIGNED HP—   5200
    DESIGNED SPEED—15.5 KNOTS

		BEGUN	COMPLETED
CD—3	DHAMBURI	7/6/37	8/5/38
CD—4	SRI AYUDHYA	1936	6/16/38

BOTH GROUNDED IN ACTION WITH FRENCH 1/16/41; NOW REFITTING

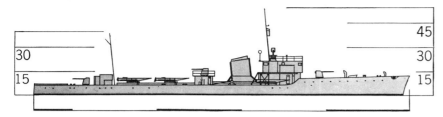

TRAD CLASS—TB 7-15

BUILT IN ITALY

LENGTH—223′ 1″ OA; 219′ 10″ WL

BEAM— 20′ 10″ — 21′ 2″

DRAFT— 6′ 4″ (MEAN); 7′ 0″ (MAXIMUM)

DISPLACEMENT—385—470 TONS (STANDARD)

ARMAMENT
    3—3″ DP
    4—.79″ TWINS
    6—18″ TORPEDO TUBES

PROPULSION

MACHINERY—	PARSONS GEARED TURBINES
BOILERS—	YARROW
FUEL—	OIL, 76–102 TONS
DESIGNED HP—	9,000–10,000
DESIGNED SPEED—	31 KNOTS
ENDURANCE—	3500 @ 12 KNOTS
	1700 @ 15 KNOTS

		BEGUN	COMPLETED
TB 7—TRAD	(NO. 11)	2/ 8/35	1/21/36
TB 8—PUKET	(NO. 12)	2/ 8/35	1/21/36
TB 9—PATTANI	(NO. 13)	3/26/36	3/37
TB 10—SURASDRA	(NO. 21)	3/26/36	3/37
TB 11—CHANDARABURI	(NO. 22)	3/26/36	3/37
TB 12—RAYONG	(NO. 23)	6/ 6/36	3/37
TB 13—JUMBARA	(NO. 31)	1/11/37	4/37
TB 14—CHOLBURI	(NO. 32)	SUNK BY FRENCH—1941	
TB 15—SONGKIA	(NO. 33)	SUNK BY FRENCH—1941	

SILHOUETTE APPLICABLE TO PG 1-4

MONGKUT RAJAKUMARN; PG-1—1887—NOW TRAINING VESSEL

DIMENSIONS—   175'0" OA x 23'6" x 11'0" (MEAN)
DISPLACEMENT—700 TONS (NORMAL)
ARMAMENT
    2—4.7"
    2—6 PDR
    3—3 PDR

BALI, SUGRIB—PG-2, 3—1901

DIMENSIONS—   162'0" OA x 23'0" x 10'0" (MEAN)
DISPLACEMENT—413 TONS (NORMAL)

SURIYA MONTHON—PG-4—1908

DIMENSIONS—   137'0" PP x 18'0" x 6'6" (MEAN)
DISPLACEMENT—225 TONS (NORMAL)
ARMAMENT
    1—6 PDR
    4—MG

---

2 SLOOPS—BEGUN 1937—TO BE USED FOR CADET TRAINING

DIMENSIONS—   280'0" OA x 34'6"
ARMAMENT—   4—4.7"; 4—?" TORPEDO TUBES
DESIGNED SPEED—18 KNOTS

TAHCHIN CLASS—PG-5, 6—BUILT AS CADET TRAINING SHIPS

DIMENSIONS—   269'3" WL x 34'5" x 10'3" (MEAN)
DISPLACEMENT—1400 TONS (STANDARD)
ARMAMENT
    4—4.7" (45)
    2—.5" AAMG
    4—12" TORPEDO TUBES
    20 MINES
    ? DEPTH CHARGES
    1 SCOUT OBSERVATION PLANE
FITTED FOR MINESWEEPING

PROPULSION
    MACHINERY—   TRIPLE EXPANSION
    BOILERS—   2 WATER TUBE
    FUEL—   OIL, 487 TONS
    DESIGNED HP—   2500
    DESIGNED SPEED—17 KNOTS
    ENDURANCE—   3000 @ 12 KNOTS

	BEGUN	COMPLETED
PG-5 TAHCHIN	3/12/36	6/37
PG-6 MAEKLONG	7/24/36	6/37

BANGRADIAN CLASS—CMC 1-2

DIMENSIONS— 160'9" WL x 26'1" x 6'6" (MAXIMUM)
DISPLACEMENT—368 TONS (STANDARD)
ARMAMENT— 2–3"   142 MINES
DES. HP— 540
DES. SPEED— 12 KNOTS

	BEGUN	COMPLETED	
CMC-1 (S-1)—BANGRADIAN	1/20/36	11/28/36	BUILT IN ITALY
CMC-2 (S-2)—NONG SARAI	1/20/36	11/28/36	BUILT IN ITALY

CHAO PHRA—(EX-HMS HAVANT)

COMPLETED 1918-19; PURCHASED 1923
DIMENSIONS— 231'0" OA x 28'7"x7'6" (MAXIMUM)
DISPLACEMENT—669 TONS (STANDARD)
                        840 TONS (NORMAL)
PROPULSION
    MACHINERY—TRIPLE EXPANSION
    BOILERS—   YARROW
    FUEL—   OIL, 160 TONS
    DES. HP—   2,200
    DES. SPEED—16 KNOTS

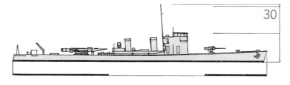

KLONGYAI CLASS—PC—1-3

DIMENSIONS— 131'5" WL x 15'5" x 4'1" (MAXIMUM)
DISPLACEMENT—110 TONS (STANDARD)
ARMAMENT— 1–3" 4–.79" AAMG
                  2–18" TORPEDO TUBES
DES. HP— 1000   DES. SPEED—18 KNOTS

	BEGUN	COMPLETED
PC-1—KLONGYAI	10/3/36	6/37
PC-2—TAKUBAI	10/3/36	6/37
PC-3—KANTANG	10/3/36	6/37

2 OF 110 TONS BEGUN—1938

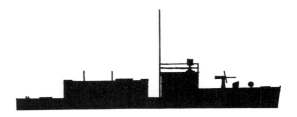

SARA SINOHU CLASS—YP—1-3

COMPLETED 11/36

DIMENSIONS— 72'2" OA x 13'1" x3'1" (MEAN)

DISPLACEMENT—50 TONS (STANDARD)

ARMAMENT— 1–1.46"

DES. HP— 150

DES. SPEED— 9.5 KNOTS

NOS. 1–5 PT 1–5—1922 (THORNYCROFT TYPE)

DIMENSIONS— 55'0" OA x 11'0" x 2'1" (MEAN)
DISPLACEMENT—11 TONS (STANDARD)
ARMAMENT—2 AAMG 2–18" TORPEDO TUBES 2 DEPTH CHARGES
DES. HP— 750
DES. SPEED—37 KNOTS

NOS. 6–9 PT 6–9—1935 (THORNYCROFT TYPE)

DIMENSIONS—53'9" WL x 11'0" x 2'1" (MEAN)
ARMAMENT— 2 AAMG 2–18" TORPEDO TUBES 2 DEPTH CHARGES
DES. HP— 950   DES. SPEED—42 KNOTS

4 UNITS BEGUN 1936—55'0", 11 TONS, 35 KNOTS

ANGTHONG—AP-3 COMPLETED 1918, REBUILT 1937

DIMENSIONS— 335'3" OA x 40'0" x ?

DISPLACEMENT—2716 TONS (NORMAL)

ARMAMENT—

    4-3"

PROPULSION—

MACHINERY—	2 SETS TRIPLE EXPANSION
BOILERS—	4 KAMPON
FUEL—	OIL, 200 TONS
DESIGNED HP—	2000
DESIGNED SPEED—15 KNOTS	

ALSO EMPLOYED AS SUBMARINE TENDER.

↑ SAMUI—AO-1 8/36

DIMENSIONS—249'4" OA x 42'8" x 13'11" (MEAN)

DISPLACEMENT— 1800 TONS (STANDARD)

DESIGNED HP— 2140

DESIGNED SPEED—12-13 KNOTS

ANOTHER OILER OF 150 TONS CAPACITY PROJECTED.

CUONG—AP-1—108 TONS (STANDARD)

CHANG—AP-2—443 TONS (STANDARD)
SIMILAR WITH MAINMAST ABAFT BRIDGE.

SAMET—AT-1

DIMENSIONS—100'0" OA x 20'0" x 8'6" (MAXIMUM)

DISPLACEMENT—89 TONS (STANDARD)

HAN THALE CLASS—AGS—1-3

DIMENSIONS—160'0" OA x 27'0"

DISPLACEMENT—443 TONS (STANDARD)

↓ PANGAN, SICHAUN—AP-4, 5—
    COMPLETED 1/38

DISPLACEMENT—650 TONS (STANDARD)

MACHINERY— DIESEL

HAI WEI—(EX-JAPANESE KASI, MOMO CLASS)—ACQUIRED 1937

DIMENSIONS—	275' PP x 25' x 7'9" (MEAN)
DISPLACEMENT—	835 TONS (NORMAL)
ARMAMENT—	3-4".7 (45), 6-18" TORPEDO TUBES
DES. HORSEPOWER—16,000	DESIGNED SPEED—31.5 KNOTS

PR—RIVER GUNBOATS

COMPLETED 1935

TINGPIEN, CHINGJEN—

DIMENSIONS—	191'11" OA x 28'10" x 3'6" (—5'?) (MAXIMUM)
DISPLACEMENT—	290 TONS (STANDARD)
ARMAMENT—	2-4.7" MAX. ELEV. 85°
	6-AAMG
DESIGNED HP—	680
MAXIMUM SPEED— 15 KNOTS	

COMPLETED 1934

YP—PATROL CRAFT—

1933

HAILUNG, HAIFENG—

DIMENSIONS—	148'6" OA 20'4" x 4'6" (MEAN)
DISPLACEMENT—	184 TONS (STANDARD)
ARMAMENT—	2—3.1" 2-AAMG ?-DEPTH CHARGES
MACHINERY—	2 SETS DIESEL
DESIGNED SPEED—14 KNOTS	SIMILAR TO JAP PC-3 CLASS

HAI KUANG, HAI JUI, HAI JUNG, HAI HUA,   1933—42 TONS

DAICHI, KAIHEN, KAINI KAIHEN.

4 OR MORE ARMED LAUNCHES—15-20 TONS

SHUN TIEN, YANG MIN—

DIMENSIONS—	180'5" OA x 28'10" x 2'10" (MAXIMUM)
DISPLACEMENT—265 TONS (STANDARD)	
ARMAMENT—	2-4.7" 3-AAMG
DESIGNED HP— 680	DESIGNED SPEED—12 KNOTS

LI SUI (1910), **LI CHI** (1904)—EX-GERMAN—266 TONS

KUANG NING (1903), **KUANG CHING, CHIANG TUNG** (1897-1900)]

EX-RUSSIAN—150-200 TONS

TA TUNG, LI MIN—COMPLETED 1933—56 TONS

ONI 220-J

JAPANESE SUBMARINES

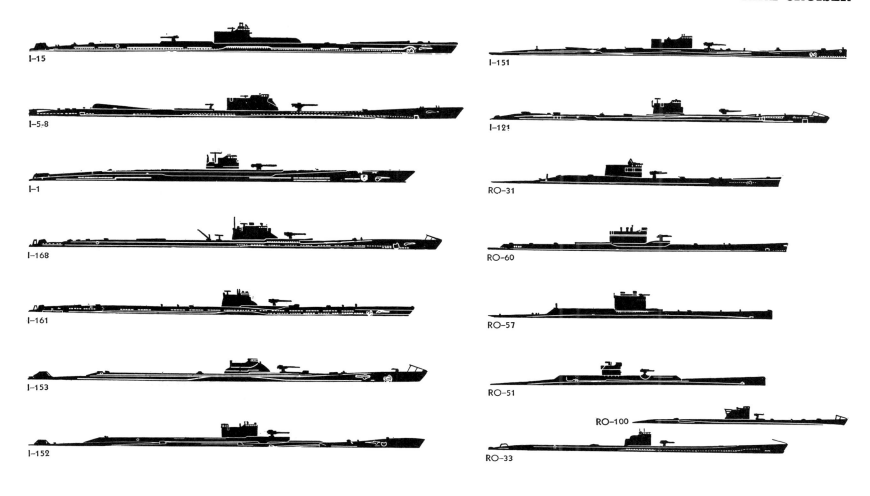

I-15

I-151

I-5-8

I-121

I-1

RO-31

I-168

RO-60

I-161

RO-57

I-153

RO-51

I-152

RO-100

RO-33

LIST OF JAPANESE SUBMARINES

(Classes are also shown by Japanese designations)

CRUISER TYPE (JUN)

I–1 Class (completed 1926–1928)

(I–2 Class)

I–1	I–3
I–2	I–4

I–5 Class (completed 1932–1938)

I–5	I–7
I–6	I–8

I–9 Class (completed 1943)

(I–10 Class)

I–9	I–12
I–10	I–13
I–11	

I–15 Class (completed 1938–1943)

(I–19 Class)

I–15	I–32
I–17	I–33 (salvaged)
I–18	I–34
I–19	I–35
I–20	I–36
I–21	I–37
I–22	I–38
I–23	I–39
I–24	I–40
I–25	I–41
I–26	I–42
I–27	I–43
I–28	I–44
I–29	I–45
I–30	I–46
I–31	I–47–49?

(I–16 Class)

I–16	I–22
I–18	I–24
I–20	

SUPPLY TYPE (YUSEN)

I–54 Class

I–54	I–56
I–55	I–57

FLEET TYPE (KAIDAI)

I–151 (completed 1924)
I–152 (salvaged) (completed 1925)

I–153 Class (some units used for training) (completed 1927–1930)

I–153	I–157
I–154	I–158
I–155	I–159
I–156	I–160

I–161 Class (completed 1928–1932)

(I–162 Class, I–165 Class)

I–161	I–165
I–162	I–166
I–163	I–167 (salvaged)
I–164	

I–168 Class (completed 1935–1938)

(I–169 Class)

I–168	I–172
I–169	I–173
I–170	I–174
I–171	I–175

I–176 Class (completed 1941–1944)

I–176	I–183
I–177	I–184
I–178	I–185
I–179	I–186
I–180	I–187
I–181	I–188
I–182	I–189

MINE LAYERS (KISEN)

I–121 Class (completed 1927–1938)

I–121	I–123
I–122	I–124 (salvaged)
I–125 (completed 1943)	

COASTAL DEFENSE TYPE (KAICHU)

RO–26 Class (completed 1923–1927)

(RO–31)

RO–26 (removed from list)
RO–27 (removed from list)
RO–28 (removed from list)
RO–29
RO–30
RO–31
RO–32

RO–33 Class (completed 1937)

(RO–34 Class)

RO–33
RO–34

RO–35 Class (completed 1943)

RO–35 (salvaged)
RO–36

RO–37	RO–43
RO–38	RO–44
RO–39	RO–45
RO–40	RO–46
RO–41	RO–47
RO–42	RO–48

RO–51 Class (removed from list) (completed 1920–1923)

RO–51	RO–54
RO–52	RO–55
RO–53	RO–56

RO–57 Class (completed 1922–1923)

RO–57	RO–59
RO–58	

RO–60 Class (completed 1923–1927)

(RO–62)

RO–60
RO–61
RO–62 (training)
RO–63
RO–64
RO–65 (salvaged)
RO–66
RO–67 (training)
RO–68

SMALL COASTAL TYPE (KAISHO)

RO–100 Class (completed 1942–1943)

RO–100
RO–101
RO–102–120

MIDGET SUBMARINES (number unknown)

The Japanese submarine fleet is made up of obsolete units which are still in service and of relatively modern units which reflect an intensive pre-war building program. This program has produced some of the largest submarines in the world which are, however, characterized by substandard design and performance qualities. Many units have hitherto been employed in supplying advanced bases and in reconnaissance activities. As allied forces advance upon the inner defense ring of the Japanese home islands and their supply lines become further extended, it is anticipated that the submarine will become one of Japan's most important defensive weapons.

Up to the present time, however, the Japanese submarine fleet has not been employed as a major tactical weapon. Their fleet consists of approximately 100 units which may be subdivided into five general groups, all of which are represented in the current building program.

Cruiser type—30 units. This is a large, long-range combatant boat which may also be used for transport and reconnaissance missions.

Fleet type—25 units. The Japanese equivalent of our own standard operational submarines, used mainly in conjunction with their surface fleet.

Coastal type—40 units. This group includes a miscellaneous assortment of medium-sized submarines, a great many of which are now obsolete.

Mine laying type—5 units. Most of these craft are now believed to be obsolescent.

Supply type—4 units. Very little is known at present of this newest group, since most of the units are still under construction.

A complete list of all Japanese submarines known to have been built follows.

RO-51 CLASS (REPORTED REMOVED FROM LIST)

Operational use	Coastal patrol and training duties.
Dimensions	Length 232' o. a. Beam 23'6". Draft 12'3" (mean).
Displacement	893 tons surface. 1,082 tons submerged.
Armament	One 3."15 DP. One .25" AAMG.
Torpedoes	Six 18" torpedo tubes (four 21" in RO-53). Twelve 18" torpedoes carried.
Speed (designed)	Surface 17 kts. Submerged 9 kts.
Endurance	7,500 miles, surface.
Machinery	Two 12–cylinder Vickers Diesels @ 2,400 HP. total.
Motors	4 electric @ 1,200 HP. total.
Fuel	65 tons oil.
Complement	48 officers and men.

	Begun	Completed
RO-51 (ex. 25)	——	Scrapped '32
52-56	1919-1922	1920-1923 at Kobe

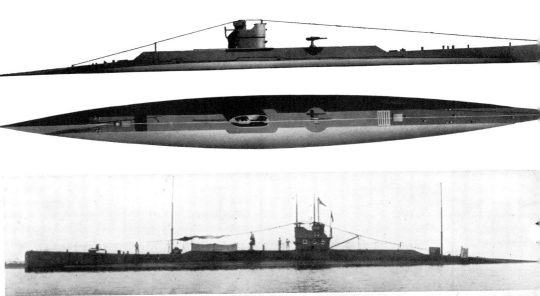

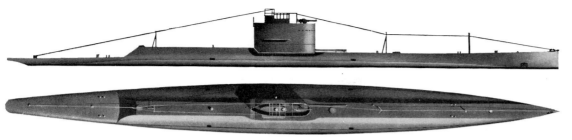

Operational use   Coastal patrol and training duties.

Dimensions   Length 238' o. a.   Beam 23'7''.   Draft 13' (mean).

Displacement   Surface 889 tons.   Submerged 1,082 tons.

Armament   One 3'' DP mounted in CT extension.
One .25'' AAMG.

Torpedoes   Four 21'' bow torpedo tubes.
Eight 21'' torpedoes carried.

Speed (designed)   Surface 17 kts.   Submerged 9 kts.

Endurance   7,500 miles, maximum.
4,500 miles @ 10 kts.
3,600 miles @ 14 kts.

Diving   197' safe depth (max.).

Machinery   Two BI 12-cylinder Diesels.

Horsepower   2,400 HP. total @ 380 RPM.

Motors   4 electric @ 1,200 HP. total.

Batteries

Fuel   67 tons oil.

Equipment   Radio—Transmitter—Special 4.
Receiver-2.
Hydrophones—K Type.

Complement   7 officers, 52 men.   (65 reported.)

	Begun	Completed
RO–57 (ex. 46)	11/20/20	7/30/22 at Kure
RO–58 (ex. 47)	2/15/21	11/25/22 at Yokosuka
RO–59 (ex. 57)	5/18/21	3/20/23 at Yokosuka

NOTES:

RO-60 Class   Built as an enlargement of the RO-57 design, and now considered obsolete for offensive operations.

Photo above shows old type conning tower.   Number on bow designates flotilla.   Number on conning tower is the ship's numeral.

	Begun	All were built at Kobe
RO–60 (ex 59)	12/21	Completed 10/23
RO–61 (ex 72)	5/22	Completed 2/24
RO–62 (ex 73)	9/22	Completed 6/24
RO–63 (ex 84)	4/23	Completed 12/24
RO–64	10/23	Completed 4/25
RO–65	11/24	Completed 6/26
RO–66	12/25	Launched 6/27
RO–67	3/25	Launched 12/26
RO–68	2/24	Completed 10/25

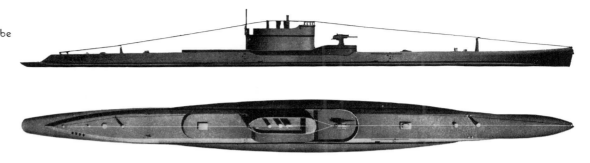

▲
▼ Note variation in 3'' gun position.

Operational use   Coastal patrol and short-range operations from advance bases.   May also be used as transports in emergencies.

Dimensions   Length, 250' o. a.   Beam, 24'3''.   Draft, 12'4''.   (Mean)

Displacement   Surface 988 tons.   Submerged 1,300 tons.

Armament   One 3''.15 DP. or 3'' AA.   Torpedoes   Six 21 ' (4 bow, 2 stern) tubes.
One .303'' AAMG.   Twelve 21'' torpedoes carried.

Speed   Surface 15.1 kts.   Submerged 7.8 kts.

Diving   197' safe depth (max.).

Endurance   6,000 miles @ 10 kts., 3,000 miles @ 14 kts.

Machinery   Two 8-cylinder Vickers BF Diesels.   Horsepower 2,400 HP. total @ 380 RPM.

Motors   2 electric @ 1,800 HP.   Fuel   75–96 tons oil.

Equipment   Radio: Transmitter—Special 4, Receiver–2, RDF–T.4.
Hydrophones: K Type (Echo-sounding vertically only).
Degaussing: Three ⅝'' coils looped directly below deck, 2 fitted on CT.
Periscopes: 2 with 60 mm. diameter head.

Complement   6 officers, 52 men (RO–61).

NOTES:

RO–26 Class   Photos illustrate minor superstructural differences within this group.   ▲ RO 29–32. ▼ RO 26–28.

NOTES:

Operational use	Short-range operations, patrol, and training duties. RO-29-32 are also adapted to minelaying operations.
Dimensions	Length 243'7" o. a. Beam 20'9". Draft 12'3" (mean).
Displacement	Surface 746 tons (655 tons RO-29). Submerged 1,000 tons.
Armament	One 4".7 DP or 3".15 DP (old armament). One .303 AAMG.
Torpedoes	(RO-26-28) 4 bow, 2 stern tubes. (RO-29-32) 4 bow tubes. Eight 21" torpedoes carried.
Mines	42, laid through stern chutes. (RO-29-32.)
Speed	Surface 12.5 kts. Submerged 7.3 kts.
Diving	148' safe depth (max.).
Endurance	6,600 miles @ 10 kts.
Machinery	2 Fiat Diesels—@ 2,600 HP. total (RO-26-28). 2 Sulzer Diesels—@ 1,200 HP. total (RO-29-32).
Motors	2 electric—@ 1,200 HP. total.
Fuel	114 tons oil (60 reported).
Equipment	Radio—Transmitter—M4. Hydrophone—K Type.
Complement	3-5 officers, 40 men.

	Begun	Completed at Kobe
RO-26 (ex 45)	1921	Reported removed from list
RO-27 (ex 58)	1922	Reported removed from list
RO-28 (ex 62)	1922	Reported removed from list
RO-29 (ex 68)		10/23
RO-30 (ex 69)		1924
RO-31 (ex 70)	12/20/24	5/10/27 at Kure
RO-32 (ex 71)		1924

RO-33 CLASS

Operational use	Experimental medium-range submarines for antishipping and coastal operations, mine laying, and transport duties.
Dimensions	Length 248' o. a. Beam 22'. Draft 10'9'' (mean).
Displacement	700 tons surface.
Armament	One 3'' DP, One .303'' or .50 cal. AA MG.
Torpedoes	Four 21'' bow tubes, 8 torpedoes carried.
Mines	Reported carried.
Speed	Surface 18.8 kts. Submerged 8.3 kts.
Diving	262' safe depth (max.), 72 seconds to periscope depth.
Endurance	11,000 miles @ 10 kts.
Machinery	Two 8-cylinder Mitsubishi Diesels, Mk 21, Type 8.
Horsepower	3,000 HP. total @ 450 RPM.
Motors	2 electric 1,500 HP. total @ 325 RPM.
Batteries	240 cells, Mk 1, Type 7.
Fuel	107 tons oil.
Equipment	Radio—Transmitter—Special 4, Receiver—2, RDF—Type 4, Telephone Type 90 Hydrophones—Type 93.
Complement	42-54 officers and men.

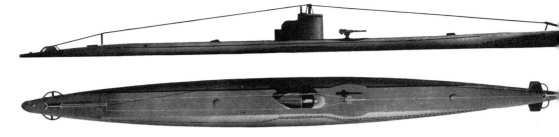

	Begun	Completed
RO-33	10/10/34	At Kure (photo)
RO-34	12/12/35	1937 at Mitsubishi

NOTES:

▼ RO 33

RO-35 CLASS

A development of the RO-33 design; this type is now the standard coastal submarine.   Units of this class have been reported used for supply operations.   The appearance of this type is unknown.

Dimensions	Length 255'. Beam 24'. Draft 12-13' (mean).
Displacement	950 tons surface.
Armament	25 mm. twin deck mount or 2—40 mm.
Torpedoes	Four 21'' bow tubes, ten 21'' torpedoes carried.
Speed	Surface 20 kts. Submerged 8 kts.
Diving	262' safe tested depth. 50 seconds time to periscope depth.
Endurance	Surface, 5,000 miles @ 16 kts. Submerged, 60 hours @ 3 kts.
RO-35-48	Begun, 1942. Completed, 1943.

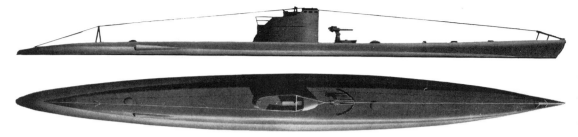

Operational use Short range coastal operations sometimes involving supply and evacuation of troops; also escort duties.

Dimensions Length 180′ o. a. (estimated). Beam 20′ Draft, ?.

Displacement 500 tons surface (estimated).

Armament 1 Twin .98″ (25 mm.) deck gun.

Torpedoes 4 bow tubes; eight 21″(?) torpedoes carried.

Mines Reported carried.

Speed Surface 14.2 kts. Submerged 8 kts.

Diving 246′ safe tested depth.
45 seconds time to periscope depth.

Endurance Surface, 2,500 miles @ 12 kts.
Submerged, 60 hours @ 3.5 kts.

Machinery Motors. Batteries. Fuel.

Equipment Hydrophones.

Cargo capacity 7 tons in hull, 4 tons on deck.
2 Landing Craft are carried (nested).

Complement
RO-100-107 Completed 1942.
RO-108-125 Completed 1943.

Others were building at a rate of 16 a year.

The two tubular projections aft may be deck torpedo tubes or mine chutes.

NOTES:

I-151

NOTES:

I-151 and I-152 were both experimental submarines which became the prototypes of the subsequent Fleet type standard designs. I-151 follows British designs, while German practices influenced the design of I-152.

Dimensions	300' o. a. Beam 28'11'' Draft 15'3''.
Displacement	Surface 1,390 tons. Submerged 2,000 tons.
Armament	One 4.7''; one AAMG (probably .303'').
Torpedoes	6 bow, 2 stern torpedo tubes; twenty 21'' torpedoes carried.
Speed	Surface 17 kts. Submerged 9 kts.
Diving	
Endurance	
Machinery	4 Sulzer Diesels—5,200 HP. total @ 340 RPM.
Motors	4 electric @ 1,800 HP. total.
Batteries	
Fuel	470 tons of oil.
Equipment	
Complement	60 officers and men.

I-151 (ex 44) completed at Kure 6/24.

Note: This and following submarines are oceangoing types called I-(eye) Classes.

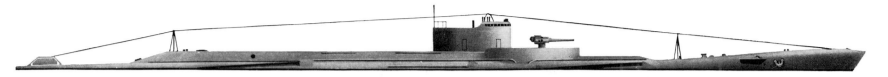

NOTES:

Dimensions	Length 330'11'' o. a. Beam 25'1'' Draft 16'10''.
Displacement	Surface 1,390 tons. Submerged 2,000 tons.
Armament	One 4.7''; one AAMG (probably .303'').
Torpedoes	6 bow, 2 stern torpedo tubes; twenty 21'' torpedoes carried.
Speed	Surface 20 kts. Submerged 9 kts.
Diving	
Endurance	
Machinery	2 Sulzer Diesels—6,000 HP. total
Motors	2 electric—1,800 HP. total.
Batteries	
Fuel	470 tons of oil.
Equipment	
Complement	60 officers and men.

I–152 (ex 51) completed at Kure 4/25.

I-153 CLASS—Characteristic Japanese conning tower and tail-fin design are clearly visible in the photographs.

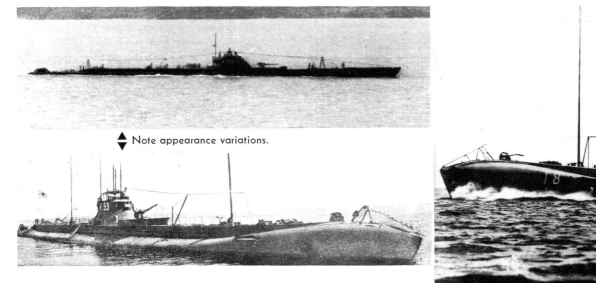

▲ Note appearance variations. ▼

There are two distinct appearance groups in this class. I-156, 159, and 160 are typified by the drawings. I-153, 155, and 158 vary slightly in conning tower and bow design, as illustrated by some of the photos. The appearance group to which I-154 and 157 correspond is undetermined.

	Begun	Completed		Begun	Completed
I-153	4/1/24	3/30/27 at Kure	I-157	7/8/27	12/24/29
154	11/15/24	12/15/27	158	12/3/27	3/15/28
155	3/1/24	9/5/27	159	3/25/27	3/31/30
156	11/3/26	3/31/29	160		12/26/29

NOTES:

Description   The oldest class of Fleet submarines now operational, developed from the experimental I-151, 152 designs. Slight variations among these standard submarines (I-153–175) constitute class differentiations.

Dimensions   Length 331' o. a. Beam 26' Draft 16'1'' (max.).

Displacement   Surface 1,635 tons. Submerged 2,100 tons.

Armament   One 4''.7, one .30 cal. MG (2 AAMG reported).

Torpedoes   6 bow, 2 stern tubes; sixteen 21'' torpedoes carried.

Aircraft   1 floatplane reported carried on I-154.

Speed   Surface 20 kts. Submerged 8.0 kts.

Endurance   6,970 @ 14 kts., 5,200 @ 16 kts.

Diving depth   176' safe, 200' tested. Time, 81 seconds to periscope depth. This class is the most maneuverable of Fleet type submarines.

Machinery   Two 8-cylinder Diesels (Zuruza Swiss model, Mk 3).—6800 hp. total—300 RPM.

Motors   Two electric—1,800 HP. total—190 RPM.

Batteries   240-cell Exide (Mk 1, Type 5). Fuel capacity, 255 tons oil.

Equipment   Periscopes, 3.
Radio, Transmitter—Special 3, Receiver—3, Telephone—90 Type, Direction finder—93 Type.
Sonic gear, Hydrophones—93 Type, Echo—ranging—93 Type.

Complement   9 officers, 73 men.

I-161 CLASS ⬍ Older units.

⬍ Newer units—note similarity to I-168 class.

Number of folding radio masts has probably been reduced to a single mast forward, or removed altogether.

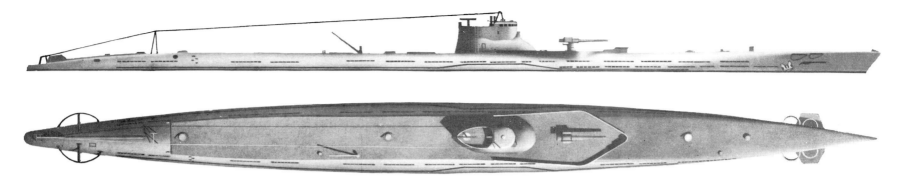

Two designs are included in this class. I-165-167 is illustrated by the drawing. I-161-164, shown by some of the photos, embodies much of the I-153 Class design in its conning tower and superstructure.

	Begun	Completed at Kobe, Sasebo, Kure
I-161	11/15/26	3/6/29
162	4/20/27	3/24/30
163		7/10/28
164	3/28/28	8/30
165	12/19/29	12/1/32
166	11/8/29	11/10/32
167	10/2/29	1932

NOTES:

Operational use	Standard Fleet submarines. Slight variations differentiate these from the I-153 Class.
Dimensions	Length 321' o. a. Beam 26-27' Draft 16' (max.).
Displacement	Surface 1,638 tons. Submerged 2,100 tons.
Armament	One 4''.7 (or one 4'' reported). One .30 cal. MG.
Torpedoes	4 bow, 2 stern tubes. Fourteen 21'' torpedoes carried.
Speed	Surface 20.2–21.6 knots. Submerged 8.3–8.5 knots.
Endurance	Surface: Submerged: 7,350–7,960 @ 14 knots. 10 hrs. @ 5 kts., 20 hrs. @ 4 kts. 6,200–6,500 @ 16 knots. 40 hrs. @ 3 kts., 80 hrs. @ 2 kts.
Diving	197' safe; 246' tested depth. Time, 81 seconds to periscope depth.
Machinery	2 Sulzer Diesels @ 6,000 HP. total.
Motors	2 electric—1,800 HP. total—190 RPM.
Batteries	
Fuel capacity	207–252 tons oil.
Equipment	Radio, Transmitter—Special 3, Receiver—3, Direction finder—Type 4, Telephone 90 Type. Sonic gear, Hydrophones—91 Type (I-165); 93 Type (I-161).
Complement	9 officers, 70–73 men.

I-168 Class—Two or more Type "A" or smaller landing craft can be nested and stowed on deck abaft the conning tower.

Photographs and drawing show original 4" armament.   Conning tower design may also be changed with increased AAMG armament.

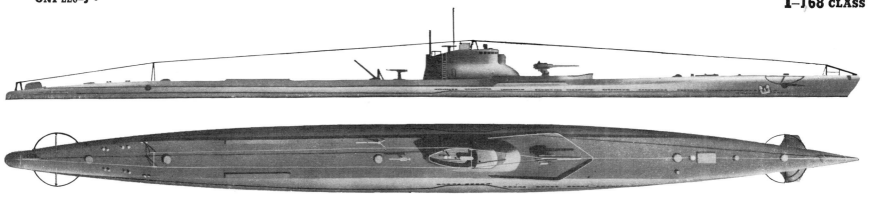

	Begun	Completed at Kure, Sasebo, Kobe
I–168	5/26/33	6 /26/35 Transport
169	1/25/33	
170	1/25/33	11/9/35
171	2/15/33	12/24/35
172	12/16/33	1/8/37
173	4/5/34	1/8/37
174	10/16/34	Transport
175	11/1/34	1938

NOTES:

Dimensions — Length 343' o. a.   Beam 26'11''   Draft 13' (mean).
Displacement — Surface 1,400 tons.   Submerged 2,100 tons (?).
Armament — One 4'' DP or one 4''.7 (I–171 on), four 13 mm. AAMG.
Torpedoes — 4 bow, 2 stern tubes, fourteen 21'' torpedoes carried.   Some units may be equipped to carry midget submarines.
Speed — Surface 23.9 kts. (des.).   Submerged 8.8 kts.
Endurance —
Surface:
10,500 nautical miles @ 14 kts.
8,170 nautical miles @ 16 kts.
Submerged:
10 hrs. @ 5 kts.
25 hrs. @ 4 kts.
40 hrs. @ 3 kts.

Tested depth — 229–278'   Horsepower, 6,000 total @ 350 RPM.
Machinery — Two 8-cylinder Diesels (Kampon Mk. 1, Model 8).
Motors — 2 electric—1,800 HP. total—190 RPM.
Batteries — 326 cells, Mk. 2, Type 3 (also Mk. 1, Type 9).
Fuel capacity — 342 tons oil.
Equipment — Some units fitted with lateral periscopes.
Radio, Transmitter—Special 3, Receiver—3, 4, Telephone—90 Type, Direction finder—T.4.
Sonic Gear, Hydrophones—93 Type, Echo—ranging—91 Type (I–168, 169), 93 Type (I–170–   ).
Complement — 9 officers, 75 men (84–95 reported).

I-121 CLASS—A new minelayer was reported completed in 1943. No characteristics are known. This single unit minelayer may be the I-125, on which all work was stopped in 1928.

These ships are easily recognized by their broad hulls and a deck gun, placed far forward.

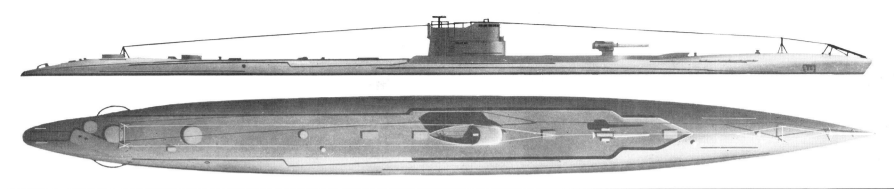

	Begun	Completed at Kobe
I-121 (ex 48)	10/20/24	3/31/27
122 (ex 49)	2/28/25	10/28/27
123 (ex 50)	5/12/25	4/28/28
124 (ex 24)	4/17/26	10/12/28
125(?)	—	1943

NOTES:

Operational use	Submarine mine layers for Fleet operations. Also used as transports for supplying and evacuating troops.
Dimensions	Length 279'6'' o. a. Beam 24'6''. Draft 14'1'' (mean).
Displacement	Surface 1,142 tons. Submerged 1,470 tons.
Armament	One 5''.5 deck gun, one .303 AAMG.
Torpedoes	4 bow tubes, twenty 21'' torpedoes carried in place of mines.
Mines	42 mines laid through 2 stern shafts; 6 mines can be loaded in 8 minutes; all mines can be laid in 4 hours @ 11 fathoms. Maximum depth of each mine—137 fathoms—effective for over a year.
Speed	Surface 14 kts. Submerged 6.5 kts.
Diving	246' safe depth (max.).
Endurance	12,000 miles @ 10 kts. 5,500 miles @ 14 kts.
Machinery	Two 8-cylinder Rozenblatz Swiss (RA) Mk. 1 Diesels.
Horsepower	2,400 HP. total @ 450 RPM.
Motors	Two—1,200 HP. total—450 RPM.
Batteries	240-cell type, Mk. 1, Type 10.
Fuel	218 tons oil.
Equipment	Radio, Transmitter—Special 3, Receiver—Type 2. Hydrophones—Type 93, Periscopes—3.
Complement	8 officers, 58 men.

I-1 CLASS—All photos show pre-war rig and armament.   Aircraft hangar is visible on port side of hull abaft the conning tower.

	Begun	Completed at Kobe
I–1	3/12/23	3/10/26
2	1923	6/26/26
3	6/8/25	12/1/26
4	4/26	Launched 5/22/28

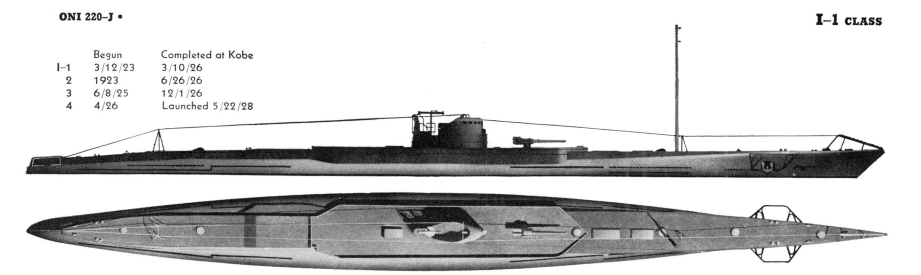

Operational use	This class represents the first long-range "cruiser" design; was a close copy of the World War I German prizes, U–183–190. In recent operations these ships have served as submarine transports in the support of landing operations.
Dimensions	Length 320' o. a. Beam 29'7'' (max.). Draft 15'9'' (mean).
Displacement	Surface 1,955 tons (standard). Submerged 2,480 tons (normal).
Armament	One 5''.5 (aft 5''.5 gun removed on all units). One .303'' AAMG (1-twin .50 cal. reported).
Torpedoes	4 bow, 2 stern tubes, twenty-two 21'' torpedoes carried.
Aircraft	1 collapsible floatplane formerly carried in hull compartment.
Speed	Surface 18.8 kts. @ 310 RPM. Submerged 8.1 kts.
Endurance	12,400 miles @ 14 kts.; 9,500 miles @ 16 kts.
Diving	197' safe, 245' tested, 50' periscope depth. Time—80–90 seconds to periscope depth.
Machinery	Two 10-cylinder MAN Diesels (RA model, Mk. 1).
Horsepower	6,000 HP. total @ 390 RPM. Motors—two electric.–1,800 HP. total.

Batteries	240 cells in 2 groups, Mark 1, Type 8.
Aux. Generator	6-cylinder, 450 HP. Diesel.
Fuel	43,000 gal. (normal). 170,000 gal. (max.).
Equipment	Periscopes—2 (not fitted with altiscope). Radio—Transmitter—Special type 3. Receiver—Type 3. Direction finder—Type 4. Telephone—Type 90. Sonic gear— Hydrophone—Type 93. Echo—ranging—Type 91.
Complement	7–8 officers and 85 men.

Capacity as submarine transport—50 troops and 20–40 tons cargo, landed by means of a barge carried on the deck abaft the conning tower.   Reports indicate that an additional 500 tons of aviation gasoline, 200–599 kg. bombs, and supplies enough for 200 men for 20 days were carried on different operations.

NOTES:

I-5-8 CLASS

NOTES:

Operational Use

Large, cruiser-type submarines for trans-Pacific patrols. In recent operations they have been employed as submarine transports in support of combined operations. Their fuel capacity also indicates use as supply submarines.

Although dimensions and statistics vary considerably, photographs show all units as similar to the I-7 type, illustrated by drawing and photographs.

	I-5, 6	I-7, 8
Dimensions	320'-323' o. a. x 29'5'' beam	359' o. a. x 30' beam
Displacement:		
Surface/Submerged	1,900-1,955/2,500 tons	2,230/2,600 tons
Draft	15'5''-15'9'' (mean)	14'5'' (mean)
Armament	One 5''.0, one .47 mm. and one 37 mm. or .303'' AA MG	1-(twin?) or two 5'' .5, 2 twin .50 cal. MG's (1 1-20 mm. quad reported on CT)
Torpedo tubes	4 bow, 2 stern	6 bow
Torpedoes	Twenty 21'' torpedoes carried	Twenty 21'' torpedoes carried
Aircraft	1 floatplane (on all types, this may be replaced by cargo)	
Speed		
Surface/Submerged	18.8/8 knots (I-5) 21.3/9 knots (I-6) Actual speed is probably 18-20 kts. (surface)	23/8 knots
Endurance		
Surface	11,150 (I-6)-12,700 mi. (I-5) @ 14 kts. 9,500 (I-6)-10,500 mi. (I-5) @ 16 kts.	15,130 mi. @ 14 kts. @ 14 kts. 14,000 mi. @ 16 kts.

	I-5,6	I-7,8
Endurance Submerged	8 hrs. @ 5 kts. 18 hrs. @ 4 kts. 70 hrs. @ 3 kts. 35 hrs. @ 3 kts. (I-6)	
Safe Diving Depth	246'-262' (I-6)	328'
Diving time to periscope depth	70 seconds (I-7)	
Machinery (I-6)	Two 7-cylinder Diesels (Kampon Mk 1, Model 7)	Two 10-cylinder Diesels (Kampon Mk 1, Model 10)
Horsepower	6,000 total	6,000 total @ 350 RPM.
Motors	Two electric—1,800 HP. total	Two electric 1,800 HP. total @ 200 RPM.
Batteries	240-cell Mk 2, Type 5	240-cell Mk 2, Type 6
Fuel capacity	589 tons	800 tons oil
Equipment: (I-5, 6) Radio	Transmitter: Special 3; Receiver: 3 or 4; Telephone: 90 Type; Direction finder: T-4	Transmitter: Special 3, 4; Receiver: 8; Telephone: 90 Type; Direction finder: T-4
Underwater Sounding Gear	Hydrophones: 93 Type; Echo ranging gear: 91 Type	Hydrophones: 93 Type; Echo ranging gear: 93 Type
Complement	88 men (I-5) 97 men (I-6)	12 officers, 88 men
Begun	10/30/29 (I-5) 10/14/32 (I-6)	9/12/34 (I-7) 10/1/34 (I-8)
Completed	7/31/32 at Kawasaki (I-5) 4/15/35 (I-6)	3/31/37 at Kure (SUNK) (I-7) 1938 at Kawasaki (I-8)

Note: One collapsible floatplane is carried in two 9' x 30' hull sections abaft the conning tower. The plane is assembled on deck and catapulted off on the 50' slanting runway. Handling is facilitated by a folding kingpost and boom, which are secured on deck when not in use.

I-15 Class	Completed	Equipment
I-15	1939	Plane
I-16	3/30/40	Midget SS
I-17	1940	Plane or barge
I-18	1939	Midget SS or plane
I-19	1940	Barge
I-20	1940	Midget SS or plane
I-21	1940	Barge
I-22	1940	Midget SS or plane
I-23	1938	Plane
I-24	1940	Midget SS or plane
I-25	1941	Barge
I-26	1941	Midget SS or plane
I-27	1941	Midget SS or plane
I-28		Plane
I-29	1941	Midget SS or plane
I-30	1941	
I-31	1941	
I-32	1941	
I-33	1941	
I-34	1941	Plane
I-35	1942	
I-36	1941	
I-37	1941	Plane
I-38	1942	Transport
I-39	1942	Plane
I-40	1942	
I-41	1942	Plane
I-42	1943	
I-43	1943	
I-44	1943	
I-45	1943	
I-46	1943	
I-47		Plane
I-48		
I-49		Plane

All units were built at Yokosuka, Kure, Sasebo, Kawasaki-Kobe, or Mitsubishi-Kobe.

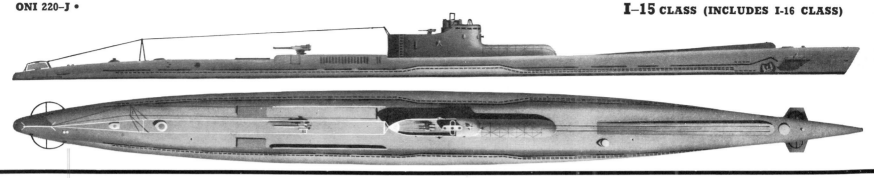

Drawing and photos are of the I–16 as it appeared at St. Nazaire in 1943. The hangar forward houses a collapsible floatplane. Photo on the left, showing one of this class submerging, illustrates the Rising-Sun recognition device sometimes painted on decks and conning towers.

NOTES:

Operational use	Long-range cruiser-type submarines for Fleet operations and patrol, also capable of refueling and supplying short-range submarines. Certain units carry aircraft, midget submarines, or landing craft, while others have been converted to minelayers and transports.
Dimensions	Length 357–359' o. a. Beam 30'6''. Draft 16'.
Displacement	Surface 1,950–2,190 tons. Submerged ?
Armament	One 5''.5 deck gun aft (removed when landing craft are carried), one 25 mm. twin AA mount.
Torpedoes	6 bow tubes (8 reported), twenty 21'' torpedoes carried.
Mines	3 units are known to be minelayers. Aircraft, 1 floatplane carried in hangar forward of CT, launched on elevatable bow catapult.
Midget SS	1 carried on deck in place of hangar (I–16 only).
Landing craft	1 or more Type A, B, or F carried on deck aft, depending on operational assignment.
Speed	Surface, 22 kts. (I–15–46); 23.6 kts. (I–16–24). Submerged, 7 kts. (I–15–46); 8 kts. (I–16–24). Actual speed is probably 20 kts. maximum (surface).
Diving	328' safe tested depth. Endurance, 14,000 miles @ 16 knots.
Machinery	Two 10-cylinder Diesels, Kampon Mk. 2, Model 10.
Horsepower	6,000 total. Motors, 2 electric @ 2,000 HP. total @ 169 RPM.
Batteries	240 cells—Mark 2, Type 5.
Fuel	816 tons oil, probably carried for refueling other submarines.
Equipment	Radio—Transmitter—Special 3, Mk. 4, Receiver—Type 4. Telephone—Super Mk. 3. RDF—T4. Sonic gear—Hydrophones—Type 93, Echo ranging gear—Type 93. Radar—Installed on all units.
Complement	101–115, depending upon duties.

Pearl Harbor type is shown on this page, Sydney Harbor type on opposite page.   Both types have been reported discontinued.

ONI 220-J •

Publications and Distribution Branch
Division of Naval Intelligence

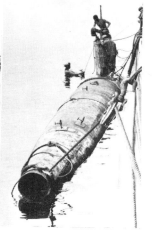

Photos show salvage operations in Sydney Harbor.

MIDGET SUBMARINES

	Pearl Harbor Type	Sydney Harbor Type (MATO)	Ko Hyoteki Type
Length	41'	80'6''	82'4''
Beam	5'	6'	6'
Conning tower	4'6''	4'6''	4'6''
Periscope height	5'	5'	
Torpedoes	two 18''	two 18''	two 18''
Speed			
Surface	24.3 kts. max.	24 kts. max.	
Sub-merged	4 kts.	12 kts.	
Endurance	175 mi. @ 5 kts.	180 mi. @ 6 kts.	
	18 mi. @ 20 kts.	70 mi. @ 12 kts.	
Diving		100' safe depth	
Motors		one 600 HP. electric	
Batteries		224 cells, Type D	
Equipment	1 Gyrocompass—Type 97	same	
	1 Magnetic compass	same	
	1 Radio transmitter	8,000–10,000 kc.	
	1 Radio receiver	same	
	Underwater listening gear	Automatic stabilizer; depth setter up to 30 fathoms	
Structure	1/4'' plate	1/4''–5/16'' plate	
	5 compartments	5 compartments plus	
	2 for batteries	2 torpedo compartments for'd	
		1 oil compartment aft	(The appearance of this type is unknown.)
Scuttling charge	300 lb.	same	
Complement	2	2	

Midget submarines are transported to their operational areas by large I-Class submarines or mother-ships. Only I-16 is believed left in operation as a submarine mother-ship.

When carried on a submarine, the midget SS is secured to the pressure hull with four heavy clamps and one auxiliary clamp. An access hatch, telephone and battery-charging leads connect the two submarines. The Midget is launched by releasing the four main clamps from the parent ship, and the auxiliary clamp from within the midget.

The Midget SS has also been carried in the holds of large CHITOSE and MIZUHO Class seaplane tenders and in whalers. Hoisted by the two port cranes, they were lowered into the hold and secured on tracked cradles or trucks.

NEW TYPES

I-9 CLASS A cruiser type, completed during 1940–1943. The appearance of this group is thought to be similar to the I-5–8 Class.

Operational use	For long-range patrol, supply, and operations. One aircraft is carried for spotting purposes.
Dimensions	Length 373′ Beam 31′ Draft 14′5″
Displacement	Surface, 2,400 tons (I-9-10) 2,200 tons (I-11-14) Submerged, 2,600 tons.
Armament	One 5″.5 deck gun for'd Two 25 mm. twin AAMG
Torpedoes	Six to eight 21″ bow tubes Twenty 21″ torpedoes carried.
Aircraft	One collapsible floatplane.
Speed	Surface 23 kts. Submerged 8 kts.
Diving	327′ safe tested depth.
Endurance	Surface, 16,000 miles @ 16 kts. Submerged, 60 hours @ 3 kts.
Machinery	Two 10-cylinder Diesels, Kampon Mk, Model 10.
Horsepower	6,000 HP. total
Motors	2 electric 1,800 HP total. @ 177 RPM.
Batteries	240 cells, Mk 2, Type 5.
Fuel	936 tons
Equipment	Radio: Transmitter—Special 4 Receiver —Type 8 Telephone—Super 3 RDF—T4 Sonic gear: Hydrophones—Type 93 Echo—ranging —Type 93

Complement 114–135, depending upon operations.

I-176 CLASS A continuation of the "Medium" or Fleet type submarine design. The appearance of this class is unknown.

Dimensions	Length 335′ Beam 27′ Draft 13′ (estimated)
Surface displacement	1,609 tons
Armament	One 5″.5 deck gun One 25 mm. twin AAMG. (Some units have two 25 mm. twins for total armament.)
Torpedoes	6 bow torpedo tubes Twelve 21″ torpedoes carried
Aircraft	1 floatplane may be carried
Speed	Surface 23.5 kts. Submerged 8 kts.
Diving	262′–275′ safe tested depth
Endurance	8,000 miles @ 16 kts.
Machinery	2 sets of Diesels @ 2,600 HP. total
Motors	
Batteries	
Fuel	352 tons oil
Equipment	Hydrophones—Type 93 Echo ranging gear—Type 93 Radar installed on all units
Complement	88 officers and men Some of these units have been employed as transports
I-176-180	Completed 1941
I-181-185	Completed 1942
I-186-189	Completed 1943

MISCELLANEOUS

SIAMESE Submarines

Dimensions	Length 164′1″ Beam 13′5″ Draft 11′10″ (maximum)
Displacement	325 tons, surface.
Armament	One AAMG Five 21″ torpedo tubes
Speed	Surface 14.5 kts. Submerged 8 kts.
Horsepower	Surface 1,000. Submerged 540
Fuel	27 tons oil.
Complement	24

MACHANU, VILUN, completed 12/36

BLAJUNBOL, SINSAMUDAR, completed 4/37

ITALIAN Submarines in the Far East

COMMANDANTE CAPPELINI

LUIGIR TOELLI

REGINALDO GUILIANI

Since these submarines have been reported as having been turned over to the Germans, they are illustrated with Italian Submarines shown in ONI 220–G

SEIZURES

ex-DUTCH Submarines

	K–10 (1920)	K–13 (1924)	K–18 (1932)
Dimensions	210'3'' x 17'9''	218'9''x19'	242'3'' x 25'
Displacement	521/712 tons	611/815 tons	782/1,024 tons
Armament	One 3''.5 AA, 1 or 2—AAMG for all		
Torpedoes	Four 17''.7 tubes	Four 17''.7 tubes	Eight 21'' tubes
Speed	16/9.5 kts.	17/8 kts.	17/9 kts.

Sisterships in these classes are illustrated in ONI 220–G, German Seizures.

ex–U. S. Submarine S–36

REPORTED TYPES

I–54 CLASS Large supply type (YUSEN) submarine
Two of four units are reported completed

Surface displacement	2,800 tons
Length	360' o. a. Beam 29'10'' Draft 14'5''
Armament	Two 25 mm. multiples Two 21'' torpedo tubes, 4 torpedoes carried
Speed	Surface 16 kts. Submerged 7.5 kts.
Endurance	Surface, 8,000 miles @ 16 kts. Submerged, 60 hours @ 3 kts.
Capacity	560 tons aviation gasoline 200–500 Kg. bombs or 200 aerial torpedoes Provisions for 200 men for 1 month.

CRUISER TYPE (OTSU)

12 units (similar to I–15 Class)

Surface displacement	2,100 tons
Speed	Surface 22 kts.: Submerged 8 kts.
Endurance	Surface, 16,000 miles @ 16 kts. Submerged, 60 hours @ 3 kts.

Aircraft to be carried by 6 units

Another type (KO) of 2,200 tons is reported building

FLEET TYPE (KAIDAI)

Surface displacement	1,600 tons Length, 346'
Armament	Four 25 mm. AAMG. Six bow torpedo tubes Twelve 21'' torpedoes carried
Speed	Surface 23.5 kts. Submerged 8 kts.
Endurance	Surface, 8,000 miles @ 16 kts.
Diving	262' safe tested depth
Complement	86 officers and men

SEAGOING TYPE (RO) (KAICHU)

18 units.

Surface displacement	950 tons
Armament	? 20 mm. twins Four 21'' torpedo tubes
Speed	Surface 20 kts.
Endurance	5,000 miles @ 16 kts.
Diving	262' safe tested depth 50 seconds crash diving time

KAISHO DESIGN

18 units.

Surface displacement	997 tons.
Armament	One 25 mm. AAMG. Four bow torpedo tubes Eight 21'' torpedoes carried
Speed	Surface, 14.2 kts.; Submerged, 8 kts.
Diving	246' safe tested depth 45 seconds crash diving time

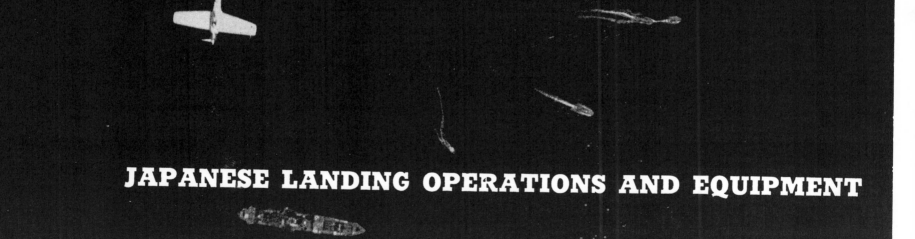

JAPANESE LANDING OPERATIONS AND EQUIPMENT

ONI 225 J—
Division of Naval Intelligence • Identification and Characteristics Section

CONTENTS

FOREWORD   2

ORGANIZATION OF JAPANESE LANDING OPERATIONS   3

NOTES ON LANDING OPERATIONS   4

LANDING CRAFT FORMATIONS   7

DIVISION FORCES   8

BRIGADE FORCES   10

SMALLER LANDING FORCES   12

LANDING CRAFT TYPES   14

LANDING CRAFT CARRIER   24

TRANSPORT TYPES   25

LANDING CRAFT STOWAGE   26

EQUIPMENT   28

AIRCRAFT   33

NAVY DEPARTMENT

Office of the Chief of Naval Operations
Washington
May 21, 1943

1. ONI 225-J is a compilation of data on Japanese landing craft, equipment and landing operation techniques. It became apparent, while collecting materiel data, that some discussion of methods employed by the enemy in the use of his equipment would render this publication of greater value to operating personnel. Tactical information on this subject has consequently been interpolated, along with drawings, photographs and diagrams.

2. The early phases of the Pacific War were highlighted by an almost unbroken series of successful Japanese landing assaults. Since that time counter measures by the United Nations have halted enemy conquests throughout the Pacific theater. Air power at Buna and in the Solomons has rolled back many a contemplated landing. Surface forces in the fourth Solomons battle repelled a major assault, destroying or scattering the Japanese naval forces, while Japanese transports succumbed to American bombers.

3. Although the tide of enemy conquest may have receded, a familiarity with the enemy's tactics and the ability to recognize his equipment will be of value to combat personnel in anticipating the enemy's future aero-amphibious operations.

H. C. TRAIN,
Rear Admiral, U. S. Navy,
Director of Naval Intelligence.

FOREWORD

No universal pattern can be developed from a study of Japanese landing operations. Conditions of warfare change so rapidly that reports which form the basis for these notes were "cold turkey" before they ever reached the Navy Department. The recent methods employed by Japanese landing forces can only be evaluated by the men who have set them back on their heels at Guadalcanal and in New Guinea. No statement that appears here should be taken as an estimate of what the Jap is going to do, but only as a statement of what he did in a number of instances, of what equipment he used and how he used it. No effort has been made to draw conclusions from these data, and the following notes and diagrams simply represent a compilation of facts from which operating personnel may conceivably draw a few useful bits of information.

In July 1937 along the beaches and in the river mouths of the Chinese coast, fleets of modified sampans, "ramp" fishing boats and other familiar small Japanese craft appeared under the protection of aircraft and naval vessels. These hitherto innocuous little ships were loaded with specially trained troops who proceeded to occupy their objectives with method and despatch. This was our introduction to the type of modern large-scale amphibious warfare that has formed the pattern for Japanese conquest.

Japan, as an isolated group of islands from which access to an objective can only be obtained over water, was the first power to develop fully the technique of ship-to-shore attack. Through carefully rehearsed operations she has been able to spread her tentacles throughout the western Pacific islands and down through Malaya. Since we are confronted with the problem of winning back these territories, the methods and equipment used in this maritime blitzkrieg may well be a subject for our study.

We may anticipate changes and developments in equipment and methods, but thus far the techniques of Japanese "aero-amphibious" warfare have remained fairly constant. In the following pages typical operations are discussed and shown diagrammatically, and the organization of task forces outlined. Information on the appearance of landing craft, ordnance and other equipment is also given, with a view to acquainting combat officers operating in the Pacific area with the materiél as well as the methods employed by the Japanese in the earlier phases of the Pacific war. These drawings and notes may suggest some of our opponent's weaknesses as well as the careful planning and bold execution that have characterized his operations.

Compared to our own landing equipment that of the Japanese task forces may appear flimsy and inadequate. It has, however, produced astonishing results. Always ready to take their losses in gaining an objective, the Japs have not permitted the vulnerability of their landing craft to limit their employment, and these little ships, although simple adaptations of non-military types, have proven highly effective. The pages that follow will serve to give the reader some idea of how they did it, and it is hoped that they may contribute to some degree in keeping them from doing it again!

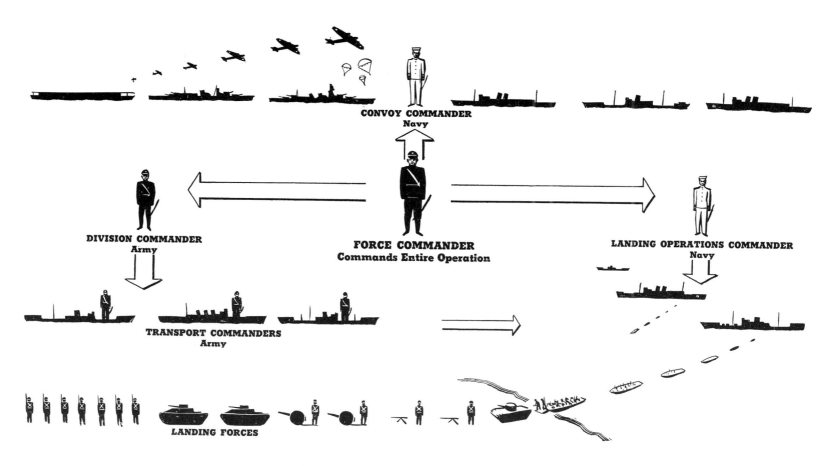

ORGANIZATION OF JAPANESE LANDING FORCES

CONVOY COMMANDER
Navy

DIVISION COMMANDER
Army

FORCE COMMANDER
Commands Entire Operation

LANDING OPERATIONS COMMANDER
Navy

TRANSPORT COMMANDERS
Army

LANDING FORCES

NOTES ON LANDING OPERATIONS

Japanese "aero-amphibious" operations reflect close cooperation among naval, air, and land forces. All services are organized into basic task forces. A usual organization for larger task forces appears on the preceding page. On later pages will be found statements of divisional and brigade organization and of the forces used in various individual operations.

Since the element of surprise is essential to any landing operation, approach to an objective is characterized by caution. Convoys are sometimes divided at sea and draw near their destinations from unexpected quarters. The Force Commander of a convoy may elect to return to his base if he suspects that his convoy has been observed at sea. Escorting naval vessels will often precede their convoy when the goal is near, as at the fourth Solomons Battle. Air blanketing is increased as the moment of landing approaches. In the several Java landings fleet units cruised up and down the coast to scatter and confuse the defenders.

AIR PREPARATION

Air power constitutes the most effective defense against landing operations where sea defense is lacking, and the Japanese have in these circumstances devoted their first efforts to neutralizing any air installations within range of their objective at the outset. Initial reconnaissance will, therefore, usually be followed by bombing attack on a defender's airfields. Through this method the landing at Appari, in the Phillipines, was effected without opposition.

In the opening phases of Japanese landings, aircraft are often employed to supplement naval bombardment by bombing and strafing a defender's batteries. Paratroops may also be dropped behind a beach head to deal with military units behind the actual line of battle and to seize airfields, as in the case of the Palembang attack.

LANDINGS

As surprise is an important factor in these operations, periods of rain or storm are preferred by the Japanese in attempting their landings. Simultaneous attacks are often made at several points to conceal the main effort.

Initial landings, necessarily the most highly organized, usually take place during the later hours of darkness. These are effected under heavy naval support where artillery defense is anticipated. Successive echelons, often in radio contact with supporting aircraft, are launched from troop transports, landing craft carriers or even from destroyers. Troops usually wear life jackets and when near shore can plunge into the water, allowing the waves to carry them in. Thus the first assault groups can be put ashore at points least expected and secure the intended beachhead for the main body by flanking movement. At Guam, each of eight AP's carried two large landing craft which made repeated trips to isolated points along the shore. At Bali one landing craft carrier launched several waves of assault boats which embarked one or two regiments from four transports. At Rossel Island in the Louisiades troops were put ashore directly from a destroyer.

Since it is equipped with a flap ramp and has considerable carrying capacity, use of the type "A" landing boat (see page 14) predominates in attacks on open beaches. Types "D" (Page 20) and "G" (Page 23), improved sampan types, are commonly used in later phases as lighters for ammunition, equipment and personnel.

On the beaches at Guadalcanal the marines discovered, buried in the beaches, small collapsible landing boats cached for a possible withdrawal.

Landing craft are operated by naval personnel or army engineers. Infantry, field artillery, and light V-front tanks are carried. Machine guns are frequently set up in the bow of each boat, while 75-mm. guns were mounted on landing craft in the attack on the east coast of

NOTES ON LANDING OPERATIONS

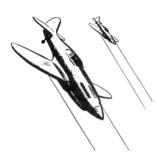

Bataan. Use of type "E" landing craft, driven by airplane motors, is to be guarded against in cases where conditions are favorable to their use. These shallow-draft units are especially designed to turn a defensive flank or penetrate within an opponent's lines by use of shallow bays, estuaries, and other means of access from the sea (it is noteworthy that concentrated strafing on the exposed engines of these craft by low-flying Allied aircraft proved most effective in breaking up the Milne Bay assault).

CONSOLIDATION

A beachhead having been gained, consolidation and penetration to the interior is rapidly effected, and accumulated supplies are distributed. An effort is promptly made to establish fighter squadrons on captured airfields and to make these ready for use by bombers. Landing forces may be augmented by paratroops. Through radio contact, landing parties are often able to direct their air support.

Light equipment and dress permit the Japanese maximum mobility. This, coupled with their ability to live off the land, accounts for their apparent

independence of supply lines. Under cover of darkness, Japanese patrols penetrate the defenders' lines to harass their positions from the rear, cut communications, and attempt to force withdrawals toward the beach.

Detachments from the landing group direct early attacks at industrial establishments, refineries, and power plants. At Palembang, as many as 400 of the initial paratroops force of 700 were assigned to the job of seizing the two oil refineries.

LANDING FORMATIONS

Several schemes of Japanese landing formations are illustrated on the opposite page.

Conditions of surf, beach, and defenses ashore are among factors involved in the choice of boat formations.

Command boats are usually in lead positions. An exception is noted in the cruciform-shaped formation some 800 yards in line and 700 yards in column. The command boat is in center position in this formation and maintains radio contact with point boat and base.

A low-powered light is used for signalling from the stern of the command boat. Lead boats approach at low or half speed until shore is visible, and then signal for normal speed is given.

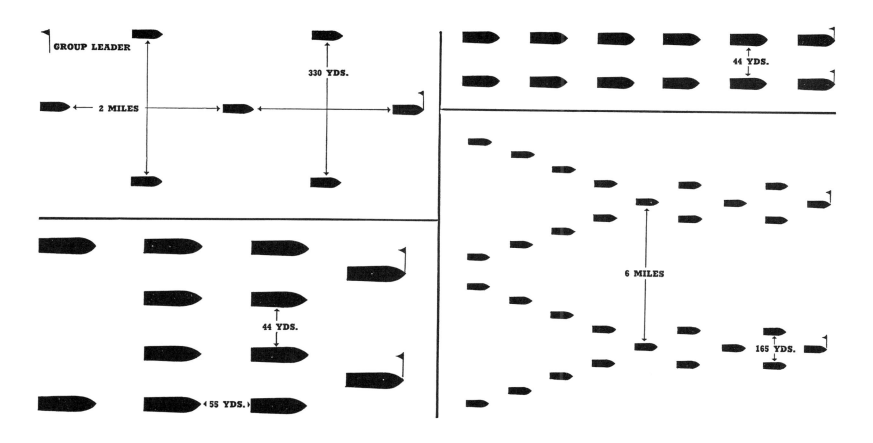

DIVISION FORCES

Strong naval forces supported the Japanese divisional occupation of Palembang. The gallant Dutch garrison of 1,500, forewarned one hour before the attack, dealt successfully with the greater part of the parachute battalion which landed astride the river on the first day. The Japanese, however, succeeded in holding one of the two oil refineries until the main body of the divisional force appeared on the second day. This force was brought up the Moesi River in air screw propelled boats (type E Landing Boats). The defense of Palembang disintegrated on the second day of the attack.

Note: Upon establishing a beachhead, additional transports and supply ships may be moved in. At Rabaul, the expeditionary force of 13 AP's was more than doubled four days after the initial attack.

It has been reported that in convoy, troops constituting two-thirds of a division have been carried in two or three transports. The remainder are divided among smaller vessels which may also function as supply ships.

NAVAL TASK FORCE	AT PALEMBANG	OTHER DIVISIONAL OPERATIONS
Aircraft Carriers	1	1–2
Battleships	1	0–2
Cruisers (CA–CL)	6	4–8
Destroyers	14	10–14
Submarines	?	2–4
Transports	23	12–20 See note.
Hospital Ships	. . . .	1

AIR TASK FORCE	AT PALEMBANG	OTHER DIVISIONAL OPERATIONS
Carrier Borne	80	40–80
Shore-based:		
Flying boats ⎱		
Bombers (Heavy) ⎰	6 Squadrons	5–10 Squadrons
Fighters–F ⎰		

GROUND TASK FORCE	AT PALEMBANG	OTHER DIVISIONAL OPERATIONS
Troops	1 Division	1–4 Divisions
Paratroops	1 Battalion	1 Battalion

THE ATTACK ON PALEMBANG

1. Paratroop battalion, 700–800 strong, was released from 70–80 transport planes.
2. Main Japanese force used the Moesi River to penetrate to Palembang.
3. Over a score of transports disembarked a division of troops.
4. Fourteen destroyers performed patrol duties inshore of the heavier ships.
5. Six cruisers, a battleship, and an aircraft carrier are also believed to have participated.

BRIGADE FORCES

A few miles of shore line of the Lingayen Gulf in the Philippines was the scene of this brigade landing operation, typical of the Japanese procedure in that theatre. (See illustration on opposite page.)

Two waves of landing craft at 15-minute intervals carried 7,500 men to the beach. Each of the 50 boats carried 2 or 3 machine guns and upwards of a hundred troops. Lack of substantial opposition on the beach or in the air afforded the Japanese easy entrance into the Philippines in several of their landings.

NAVAL TASK FORCE	AT PHILIPPINES	OTHER BRIGADE OPERATIONS
Aircraft Carriers	1	0–1
Cruisers (CA–CL)	3	1–6
Destroyers	6	3–11
Submarines		0–2
Transports	10	6–16
Hospital Ships		0–1

AIR TASK FORCE		
Carrier Borne		
Shore-based:		
Flying boats		
Bombers (Heavy)		3–7 Squadrons
Fighters–F		

GROUND TASK FORCE		
Troops	1 Brigade	1–2 Brigades

Landing force aboard transport

AN ATTACK IN THE PHILIPPINES

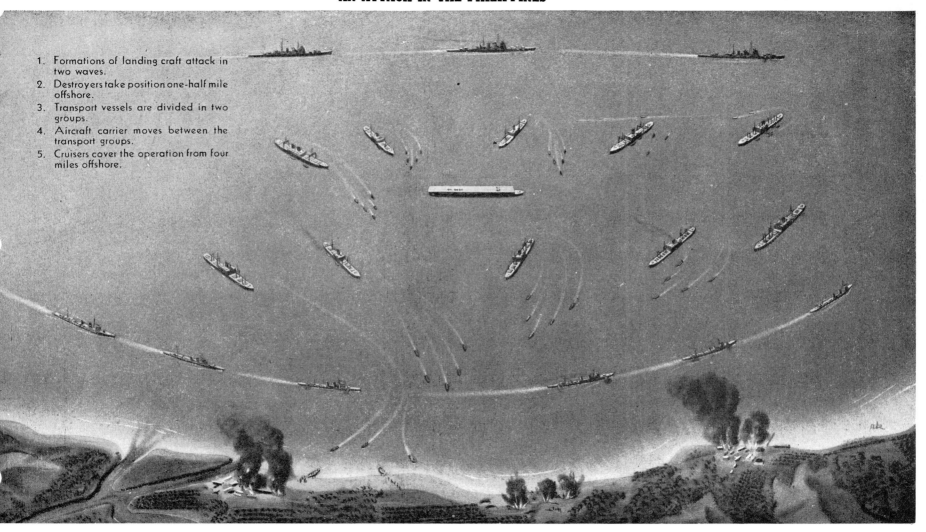

1. Formations of landing craft attack in two waves.
2. Destroyers take position one-half mile offshore.
3. Transport vessels are divided in two groups.
4. Aircraft carrier moves between the transport groups.
5. Cruisers cover the operation from four miles offshore.

SMALLER LANDING FORCES

Landing forces below brigade strength may be supported by large or small naval task forces depending upon the intensity of opposition expected.

A strong naval force was employed to put ashore fewer than 1,000 marines at Wake. Unfortified as the islands were, the Japanese nevertheless appear to have taken into account the character rather than the equipment of its defenders in providing so large a fleet for the operation. Our two 6-inch guns on the beach, boresighted and breech-operated, substantiated Japanese fears. A cruiser and destroyer are thought to have been sunk in the final assault and extensive damage inflicted.

The effects of concentrated fire from heavy calibre guns, in an area as small as Wake, finally made possible a landing. (See illustration of action on opposite page).

In contrast with such powerful support, small landing forces from one or two DD's or "I" type submarines have landed under cover of dense fog or on uninhabited islands where no opposition could have been encountered.

TABLE OF JAPANESE AERO-AMPHIBIOUS FORCES

LOCATION		TROOPS	AIR SQUAD-RONS	CV	BB	CA-CL	DD	AP	SS
GUAM				1		3	3	8	
MALAYA	Khota Baru	1 Div.	24 (?)	2	1	2	7		
WAKE		900		1		6	8	1	
BALI		½ Reg.				4		5	
ALASKA	Attu, Kiska			3		7	4	6	
CELEBES	Kema, Menado	1 Div., 1 Bn. Para.	5	1		8	18	16	3
	Macassar	1,000				2	16	6	
NEW GUINEA	Lae, Salamaua	1 Brig.				1	4	6	
	Buna, Gona	2,500				1	5	4	
NEW BRITAIN	Rabaul	1 Div.	7	2		4	6	13	
	Gasmata					2	6	4	
	Kendari	1 Brig.				?	?	30	
NEW IRELAND	Kavieng	900				2	3	3	
JAVA						9	21	40	
SUMATRA	Palembang	1 Div., 1 Bn. Para.	4	1	1	6	14	23	
TIMOR	Kupang	1 Brig.	4	1		3	8	6	2
GUADALCANAL	Faisi, Buka	1,000				4	1	1	
	Lunga	1,200				6	5	4	
PHILIPPINES	Davao	1 Div.			1	4	20	18	
	Cagayen	4,000		1			2	7	
	Legaspi	1 Brig.				5	11		
BORNEO	Ambon	1 Div.	5	2		6	10	10	2
	Balikpapan	1 Div		1		4	14	38	
	Miri	2,500	2	1	1	3	4	10	
	Tarakan	1 Brig.	2	1		6	6	16	2
	Kuching	1 Brig.	3			2	3	10	

THE ATTACK ON WAKE

1. Cruisers, in line of bearing, provide heavy fire from rear.
2. Column consisting of a transport, carrier, and light cruiser, illustrated in their relative positions.
3. Destroyers fan out, gaining wider front for the attack.
4. Planes from carrier seek island objectives prior to landing.
5. Landing craft from transport disembark Japanese Marines.

TYPE "A" LANDING CRAFT (ARMY)

Length: 49' 4" o. a., 41' w. l.

Beam: 11' 5".

Draft:

Propulsion: 2 cyl. gasoline engine (or 6 cylinder Diesels).

1 propeller.

Unbalanced rudder.

Speed: 8–10 knots.

Capacity: 100–120 men.

Anchor: Large stern anchor weighed by hand.

Armament: 1-2 25 calibre machine gun.

Armor: Engines and coxswain's position protected by light plate.

Notes: This boat is an adaptation of the Japanese "flap-ramp" fishing boat. It has a metal hull with wooden braces and guard rails. Twin keels provide stability after grounding. Two fins extending from keels support landing ramp when lowered from bow. Transverse bulkhead about ¾ of the length of the boat from bow. Gunwale has pronounced sheer.

TYPE "A" LANDING CRAFT (NAVY)

Length: 49' 4" o. a., 41' w. l.

Beam: 11' 5".

Propulsion: 2 cyl. gasoline or 6 cyl. Diesel.

Speed: 10 knots.

Capacity: Approx. 80 men.

Anchor: Large stern anchor weighed by hand.

Armament: Two OERLIKON type machine guns; one forward, one aft.

Armor: Metal shield ($\frac{3}{8}$"?) protects after-works from light fire.

Notes: This boat is similar in construction to type "A" Army. A deck house has been added in the Navy type. Other refinements are bulwarks forward and added shield protection for control personnel.

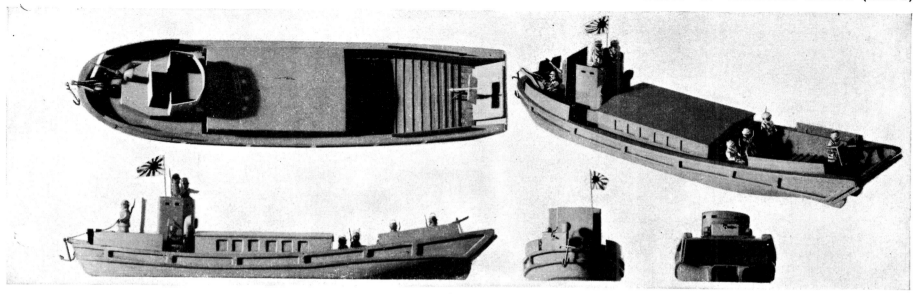

TYPE "B" LANDING CRAFT

Length: 30'4" o. a.
Beam: 7'6".
Propulsion: Gasoline engine.

Speed: 8–10 Knots.
Capacity: Approximately 40 men.

Anchor: Large stern anchor weighed by hand.

Armament: Machine gun in bow.
Armor: Some carry bullet-proof shields in bow.   Capable of stopping .50 calibre bullets.
Notes: Employed by initial covering parties.   Similar to merchant life boats in appearance. Successfully strafed by low flying fighters when fire was concentrated on power-plant in stern.

Length:	49'.	Armament:	1-.303 Machine Gun on forward turret, 360°–60° elevation—1 Machine Gun forward 1 Machine Gun aft.
Beam:	13'.		
Propulsion:	Diesel.		
Speed:	25 Knots.	Armor:	Steel plate construction.
Capacity:	Approximately 50 men.		
Anchor:	Large stern anchor weighed by hand.	Notes:	May be used to support landings with fire from its three guns, or may land personnel. Also used in reconnaissance and patrol duties.

TYPE "D" LANDING CRAFT

Length: 38'6".

Beam: 11'.

Propulsion: Some have gas engines; others not powered.

Capacity: Approximately 60 men.

Armament: None.

Armor: None.

Notes: Some have clipper bow, others sampan type. Stern is decked over. Resembles U. S. M. C. artillery lighter. Functions of this type parallel those of Type "A."

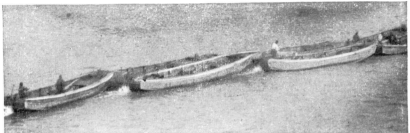

TYPE "E" LANDING CRAFT

Length:	63'2" o. a., 55'6" w. l.	Armor:	Shield protects machine gun in bow.
Beam:	8'9".	Notes:	Air screw propulsion affords advantages in navigation of shallow waters. Flat bottom construction enables Type "E" to penetrate waters inaccessible to ordinary craft.
Propulsion:	Air screw propellor.		
Speed:	10 Knots.		
Capacity:	Approximately 60 men.		
Armament:	1 or 2 machine guns.		

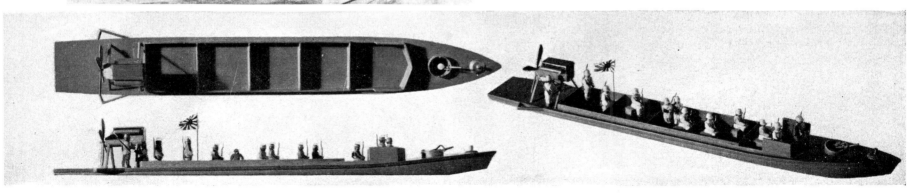

TYPE "F" LANDING CRAFT

Length: 21' o. a.
Beam: 7'.
Propulsion:
Speed: 8–10 Knots.
Capacity: Approximately 20
            men.
Armament: None.
Armor: Steel plate con-
            struction.

Notes: Movable crossbeam
provides convenient means of shift-
ing inboard compartment arrangement.

    A two-section col-
lapsible composition board boat
with rubber joints has been noted
at Guadalcanal. Approximately
15 feet long, 4 feet wide and fitted
with oars and outboard motor, this
boat is believed capable of carrying 20 men.

Length:	52'1" o. a., 43'9" w. l.	Armament:	
Beam:	13'3".	Armor:	None.
Propulsion:	Gasoline engine.	Notes:	The straight or jutting prow observed in earlier types appears to have been abandoned for a curved bow, better able to withstand impact.
Speed:	8 Knots.		
Capacity:	Approximately 50 men.		

LANDING CRAFT CARRIER

Length: 367'.
Beam: 50'–55'.
Draft:
Displace-   7,500 tons.
ment:
Propulsion:
Speed: 18 Knots.
Capacity: 24 large LC (1,920
             troops) 120 small
             LC (6,620 troops)
             "Type C" 14
             launches.

Armament:
Armor:

Notes: Beyond its function as a carrier this ship appears to have been designed as a floating supply base to support landing operations. It was used in the Chinese landings and possibly in Bismark Archipeligo, East Indies and New Guinea operations.

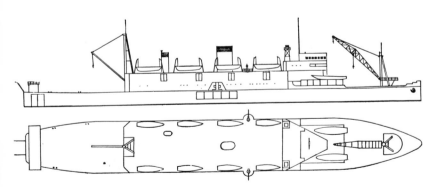

Goya Maru.

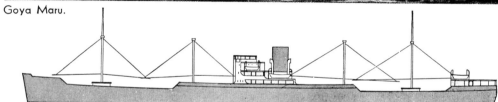

Azumasan Maru.

These are typical of merchantmen employed in amphibious convoys. Vessels with ample deck stowage space lend themselves to ready disembarkation. Cargo booms forward and aft in this type of transport provide rapid launching of a deck load of landing craft.

Azumasan (Overhead).

LANDING CRAFT STOWAGE

These photographs illustrate adaptation of Japanese merchant ships to landing operations. Transportation of landing craft seems to be undertaken with a minimum amount of conversion. The boats, lined up on deck, are nested in tiers two or three high.

Strafing a Deck Load of LC's.

Destroyer With Landing Craft In Davits.

Interrupted By Our Planes.

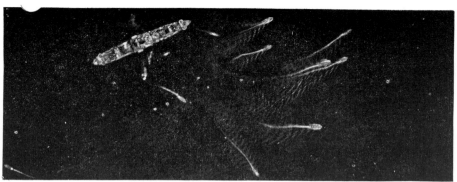

Landing Craft Scattering from Carrier Under Attack.

A Mast High View of Stowed Landing Craft.

A Nest of Type A's

Landing Craft Alongside Their Carrier.

Japanese Automatic Arms as employed in initial stages of landing operations have consisted wholly of these derivations of foreign designs. The infantry squad light machine guns (M2596 and Nambu) and the heavy Taisho 3 (or 1914 version of the Juki) fire 6.5-mm. ammunition. Deficient in stopping power this .256 cartridge is advantageous only in lightness of ammunition in mass, and in lack of recoil, permitting the M2596 to be fired from the hip as a makeshift submachine gun. As fired from the Arisaka long rifle, the 6.5 mm. is noteworthy in that almost complete combustion takes place, resulting in no flash at night. Newer 7.7 (cal. .303) rounds as employed in the Juki but not in the belts of the Vickers aircraft guns sometimes mounted on landing barges, are rimless, and are not to be confused with rimmed British .303 cartridges. The "tommy" guns are of European make.

Bergmann-Type Submachine Gun, Submachine Gun, Cal. 9 mm.

Solothurn-Type Submachine Gun, Cal. 7.63 mm.

Czech Praga—Z. B.—Type Light Machine Gun, M2596, Cal. 6.5 mm.

Hotchkiss Nambu Light Machine Gun, Taisho 11, 6.5 mm.

Japanese Weapons represent a mixture of the modern with the obsolete, the copy of foreign design—even the use of foreign made arms—with the originality of native products. Japanese adaptability and capacity to improvise are further indicated by their utilization of arms captured from United Nations forces. British and Netherlands automatic weapons have been found in Japanese hands on Guadalcanal and in New Guinea, along with some German antitank guns taken from the Chinese. The automatic weapons include British Lewis guns of .303 caliber (possibly favored because they fire the same cartridge as Japanese 7.7-mm. aircraft machine guns), Dutch 6.5-mm. Madsen short-barreled light machine guns, and Colt automatic rifles. Belgian made, these Colts are a version of the Browning auto-rifle.

Vickers Aircraft Machine Gun, 7.7 mm.

Combination Periscope-Telescopic Sight.

Solothurn-Type Antitank Rifle, Cal. 20 mm.

Hotchkiss-Type Juki Heavy Machine Gun, M2592, 7.7 mm.

Two-Man 3-Ton Tankette M2592.

Light 7-Ton M2595 Tanks With 37-mm. Guns.

Top View of M2595 Light. Armor Is .45-in.

Infantry Gun Squad With M2592 70-mm. Howitzer

Close-Support Artillery is a feature of Japanese organization closely copied from modern German doctrine. The specially designed 70-mm. howitzer is a battalion weapon; the old 1908 75-mm. gun is a regimental piece, was formerly a mountain gun.

M2592 70 mm. Howitzer With Shell.

Heavy 75-mm. Infantry Gun, Meiji 41.

Antitank Gun M2597, Damaged by Machine Guns.

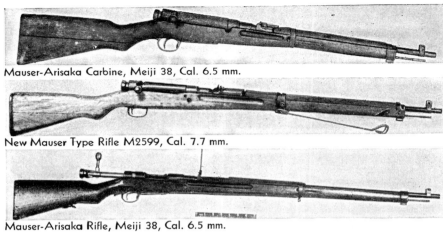

Mauser-Arisaka Carbine, Meiji 38, Cal. 6.5 mm.

New Mauser Type Rifle M2599, Cal. 7.7 mm.

Mauser-Arisaka Rifle, Meiji 38, Cal. 6.5 mm.

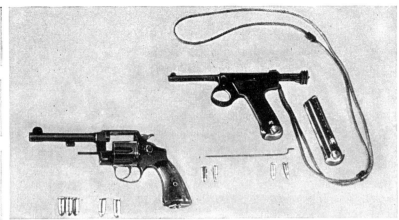

Officer's Revolver and Taisho 14 Luger-Type 8-mm. Automatic.

Taisho 10 Grenade.

M2589 50-mm. Grenade.   Light 50-mm. Trench Mortar on Base Plate.

M2589 "Knee Mortar" 50-mm. Grenade Dischargers: Taisho 10s Similar.

Lily—Army Twin Engine Medium Bomber.

Nell—Army and Navy Twin Engine Medium Bomber.

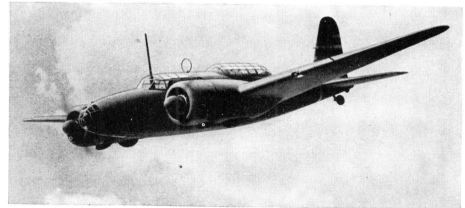

Sally—Army Twin Engine Medium Bomber.

Zeke—Army and Navy Single Engine Fighter.

Hap—Navy Single Engine Fighter.

Zeke	Carrier- or land-based Army and Navy fighter. Occasionally carries light bomb loads for antiaircraft or antipersonnel bombing. Used to "protect" Bismarck Sea convoy. Maximum speed 300 m. p. h.
Hap	Carrier- or land-based Army and Navy fighter. Square wing tips readily distinguish HAP from other types. Speed approximately 310 m. p. h.
Rufe	Catapult or water-based Navy float-plane fighter and reconnaissance often launched by seaplane tenders as at Attu and Kiska. A conversion of the Zero (ZEKE) but not equal to it in range, ceiling or speed.

Reference to ONI 232, Japanese Military Aircraft, is suggested for a more complete picture of Japanese aircraft.

Rufe—Navy Single Engine Seaplane Fighter.

Sonia — Land-based Army light bomber and reconnaissance plane. Maximum speed 250 m. p. h.

Nell — Carrier- or land-based Army and Navy medium bomber. Widely used in aero-amphibious operations in the Philippines and East Indies. Maximum speed 230 m. p. h. at 10,000 feet.

Lily — Land-based Army medium bomber and reconnaissance plane. Recently used in southwest Pacific operations. Lacks heavy armament and leak-proof tanks. Estimated maximum speed 240 m. p. h.

Sally — Land-based standard Army bomber. Operates largely from bomber strips within range of the Solomons. Maximum speed 230 m. p. h. at 10,000 feet.

Topsy — Land-based Army transport. Used in paratroop attack on Palembang. Maximum speed approximately 260 m. p. h.

Mavis — Water-based Navy long range reconnaissance plane. Usually used far in advance of main forces. Similar to our "Catalina." Maximum speed 160 m. p. h. at 13,000 feet.

Topsy—Army Twin Engine Transport.

Sonia—Army Single Engine Light Bomber.

Mavis—Navy Four Engine Flying Boat.

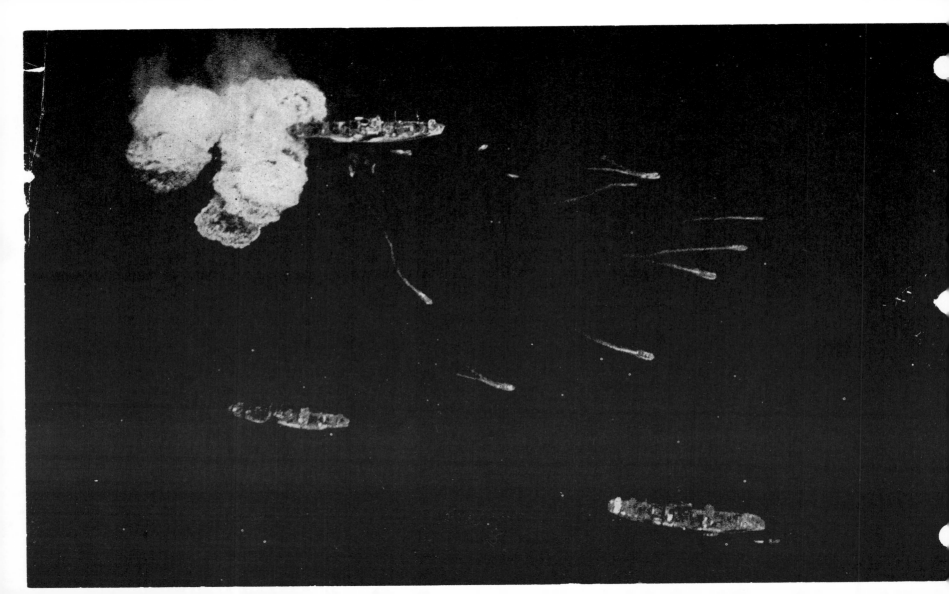